BRITISH ACADEMY CENTENARY
1902-2002

Laver

BIOGRAPHICAL MEMOIRS OF FELLOWS, I

PROCEEDINGS OF THE BRITISH ACADEMY · 115

BIOGRAPHICAL MEMOIRS OF FELLOWS
I

Published for THE BRITISH ACADEMY
by OXFORD UNIVERSITY PRESS

Oxford University Press, Great Clarendon Street, Oxford OX2 6DP

Oxford New York
Auckland Bangkok Buenos Aires Cape Town Chennai
Dar es Salaam Delhi Hong Kong Istanbul Karachi Kolkata
Kuala Lumpur Madrid Melbourne Mexico City Mumbai Nairobi
São Paulo Shanghai Singapore Taipei Tokyo Toronto

British Library Cataloguing in Publication Data
Data available

ISBN 0–19–726278–3
ISSN 0068–1202

Typeset in Times
by J&L Composition, Filey, North Yorkshire
Printed in Great Britain
on acid-free paper by
Bookcraft (Bath) Limited
Midsomer Norton, Avon

The Academy is grateful to Professor F. M. L. Thompson, CBE, FBA
for his editorial work on this volume

Contents

The Biographical Memoirs of Fellows of the British Academy have hitherto been published in the same *Proceedings* volume as the texts of the British Academy's Lectures.

Because of the increasing size of this annual volume it has become necessary to publish the Lectures and the Memoirs in separate volumes.

The *2001 Lectures* are published as *Proceedings of the British Academy*, Volume 117 (ISBN 0–19–726279–1).

For further information please see the British Academy website www.britac.ac.uk

JAMES BRYCE
Reproduced with the permission of the Provost and Fellows of
Oriel College, Oxford.

CENTENARY ESSAY

James Bryce and the Future[1]

WILLIAM RANULF BROCK
Fellow of the Academy

JAMES BRYCE (VISCOUNT BRYCE) was elected President of the British Academy in 1913 and delivered his last presidential address in July 1917. He was seventy-nine years old (age being then no bar to office), and the assembled Fellows probably expected reminiscence. What they got was 'The Next Thirty Years' with 'Thoughts on the work that awaits students of the human sciences' as its subtitle. Why 'thirty years'? Because this was 'the period of activity to which the younger members of our body may look forward'.[2]

He was at the end of a career distinguished in letters and public life. An outstanding intellect, phenomenal industry, and a likeable personality had brought deserved fame to this son of a Glasgow schoolmaster. His *Holy Roman Empire,* originally written as an Oxford prize essay, established

---

[1] This paper on James Bryce was not delivered as a lecture but is offered as a tribute, in the Academy's centenary year, to a distinguished founding Fellow and former President of the Academy. It is a commentary on his last presidential address rather than a précis. It does not take up points in their original sequence but examines themes developed in different parts of the address. Most space is devoted to ideas on methods and future developments in History and the Social Sciences. It examines the intellectual equipment of this eminent late-Victorian Liberal (in many ways typical of his time and politics but exceptional in his range and application). In retrospect the address also prompts reflection on changed interests and attitudes in learning and teaching since its delivery in 1917.
[2] 'The Next Thirty Years', *Proceedings of the British Academy 1917–1918*, pp. 3 31. Bryce's successor, Sir F. G. Kenyon, described this address as one that no Fellow would readily forget (ibid., p. 37). The subtitle is not in the *Proceedings* but in the address printed as a separate pamphlet. Page references are to the *Proceedings* and will be given as 'Next Thirty Years'.

Proceedings of the British Academy, **115**, 3–27. © The British Academy 2002.

his reputation as a historian. He qualified as a barrister, was appointed Professor of Civil Law at Oxford in 1870, revived the study of ancient law, and later published *Studies in Jurisprudence*. His lengthy *American Commonwealth*, published in December 1888, was welcomed as a masterpiece on both sides of the Atlantic (the fourth edition appeared in 1910). *Impressions of South Africa* followed in 1897 and the principal occupation of his later years was a pioneering venture in comparative politics to be published as *Modern Democracies*.

His career as a public man stretched back to 1867 (when his chapter in *Essays on Reform* demolished the historical arguments against democracy). Since then a long list of published addresses, articles, and pamphlets on contemporary political and social questions had won him recognition as a leading Liberal intellectual. In addition to domestic politics he wrote on justice for persecuted Armenians, race relations, and higher education. He was elected to Parliament in 1880, served for twenty-seven years, and though his ministerial experience was limited he was Chief Secretary for Ireland under Campbell-Bannerman. The crown of his public career was his time as a very popular Ambassador to the United States from 1907 to 1913. He held honorary degrees from thirty-one universities, was awarded the Order of Merit in 1907, and in 1902 had been named as a founding Fellow in the royal charter incorporating the British Academy.[3]

In those days the President could deal with formal Academy business in a few minutes and devote the rest of his time to any topic of general interest. Bryce introduced 'The Next Thirty Years' with a question. Scientists were inspired by 'the sense of a boundless vista down which they gaze into the unknown', did a 'like vista of endless progress' stretch before those who dealt with the thoughts and acts of human beings? In what followed he forecast probable lines of development but his emphasis was on opportunities to be taken up. Cautious prediction was combined with positive admonition.

His remarkable range recalled the nineteenth-century expectation that a well-educated man would keep abreast of everything that moved in the world of learning. One can imagine his hearers mesmerised as he travelled rapidly from spelling reform to biblical studies, from the emendation of ancient texts to problems of disputed authorship (with a quick look at Ossian), and on to contemporary literary criticism. Some specialists in his

---

[3] 'The Historical Aspects of Democracy' in *Essays on Reform* (1867). When he died in 1922 *The Times* printed messages of condolence and eulogy from a galaxy of notables on both sides of the Atlantic.

audience may have wished to qualify, correct, or expand particular observations but all were amazed by his omniscience and gratified by his conclusion that the possibilities were inexhaustible.[4]

Only when he came to philosophy did he seem to falter. An Oxford man could hardly deny its importance but he anticipated nothing new because 'the minds that have a real gift for high constructive thinking are extremely rare'. Nevertheless philosophers would be kept busy because every question had as many sides as there were men to discuss it and 'these metaphysical inquiries make a real appeal to the desire of man to understand himself and his relations to the universe'. On this uneasy note he descended from 'this high and difficult air to the solid ground of fact', from eternal verities to 'the sciences which deal with human relations in society'.[5]

These 'sciences' differed from those dealing with the natural world. In human society there were no fixed relationships or universal rules. 'History is being made faster than it can be written. We have to deal not with a lake that can be drained but with a river whose current swells daily.' Political systems did not stand still and even when institutions retained their original form the opinion that sustained them shifted. As he wrote on another occasion: 'Manners depend upon sentiment, and sentiment changes slowly. Still it changes. It has changed as regards torture. It has changed as regards slavery.'[6]

Before following Bryce into these domains a glance at his intellectual background is appropriate. As a very young man he had attended the University of Glasgow where the Scottish 'common sense' philosophy ruled unchallenged and the imprint remained. Basic moral sentiments were so uniformly found in human minds that they required no proof and must be treated as self-evident. When there was a simple choice there could be no dispute—what was wrong could never be right—but the choice was seldom simple. Varied concepts were embedded in the different traditions, conventions, laws and political institutions of races or societies so that actions approved in one might be condemned in another. In practice, when the verdict on private conduct or public policy was in doubt, he may well have settled it with one unspoken question: 'What would Mr Gladstone have done?'

[4] 'The conclusion of the whole matter . . . is that there is abundance of work to be done in the departments of learning wherewith this Academy is concerned, more work indeed than there are workers to do it.' ('Next Thirty Years', p. 30.)

[5] 'Next Thirty Years', p. 24.

[6] 'Next Thirty Years', p. 30; the second quotation is from *The Relations of the Advanced and Backward Races* (Romanes Lecture, 1902), p. 43.

Like others of his time Bryce frequently expected history to teach lessons. Writing in the *American Political Science Review* he argued that 'tendencies in human nature' were sufficiently uniform 'to lay down general propositions . . . and form them into a connected system of knowledge'. This was not the first step toward historical determinism. The response of a free and rational man, faced with straightforward alternatives, was predictable, but the choice was seldom simple, reason seldom ruled, and leading men went often astray.[7]

What was progress? He put the question to a Harvard audience in 1907. Rapid improvement in modern times had tempted men to treat progress as a law of nature but it was neither predetermined nor predictable. 'The bark that carries Man and his fortunes forward traverses an ocean where the winds are variable and the currents unknown. He can do little to direct its course, and the mists that shroud the horizon hang as thick and low as they did when the voyage began.' This analogy was too simple. Human beings could navigate, with steam they could sail against the wind, and in other writings he pressed for positive action to counter drift.[8]

Twelve years later he returned to the subject with a more satisfactory analysis. If progress meant material improvement and the advancement of knowledge in modern times the answer was clear and positive. If it meant greater intellectual capacity there was doubt. Men were as clever or as stupid as they had always been and great scientific discoveries, made by gifted individuals, provided no proof that the general level of intelligence had been raised. Great art and literature from the past had not been surpassed. Moral progress was the most difficult to assess. Had standards in justice, honour, good faith, truthfulness, kindliness, compassion, and sympathy risen? Before 1914 the confident answer would have been 'yes' but since then terrible lessons had been learned. 'The lava is still hot under the crust of our commonly accepted social and international morality . . . The fires beneath may again burst forth.'[9]

One thing was clear: improvements were made by human beings and there was no way to stand outside and view a master plan. All being due to individual effort it followed that one man's delight was often another's bitter fruit. Hence the paradox that 'an Age of progress might be an Age

---

[7] 'The Relations of Political Science to History and its Practice', *American Political Science Review*, 3. 2–4, 9. Reprinting his address to a joint meeting of the American Political Science and American Historical Associations in 1908.

[8] 'What is Progress?', *Harvard Graduates Magazine*, 16 (Sept 1907), 19. (Address to the Harvard Chapter of Phi Beta Kappa, June 27 1907—also published in *The Atlantic Monthly*.)

[9] 'World History', *Proceedings of the British Academy 1919–20*, pp. 208–10.

of Discontent'. Expectations rose, demands became strident, timid men took fright, and those in authority resisted all change. Obstinate conservatism proved to be a prescription for catastrophe as protest turned to revolution. Then a new heresy took hold as violence was justified by appealing to an apocalyptic vision of a promised land that never had and never would exist.[10]

In an emotive passage in the *American Commonwealth* Bryce dismissed utopian illusions. 'The vision of a golden age has often shimmered far off before the mind of men when they have passed through some great crisis, or climbed to some specular mount of faith.' This mirage of distant felicity was compared to a traveller's first sight of distant mountains from high pastures in the Jura. 'The line of Alpine snows stands up and glitters with celestial life.' Journeying on he would find no 'delectable Mountains' but an awesome region 'scarred by storms and seamed by torrents, with wastes of stone above, and marshes stagnating in the valleys'.[11]

'He had an aversion to political action directed by abstract principles, or founded on abstract considerations,' observed Charles W. Eliot, the celebrated president of Harvard and Bryce's lifelong friend, in a memorial address. Even in his admired America Bryce regretted 'the spirit of 1776' with its declaration of abstract rights, and praised 'the spirit of 1787' with its respect for past experience and practical solutions to perceived problems.[12]

False prophecy nourished illusion but so did tenacious loyalty to vanished ideals. In the introduction to his first published book Bryce wrote of continuity and decay.

> The Empire, which a note issued by a diplomatist on the banks of the Danube extinguished, was the same which the crafty nephew of Julius had won for himself against the powers of the East beneath the cliffs of Actium; and which had preserved almost unaltered, through eighteen centuries of time, and through the greatest changes in extent, in power, in character, a title and pretensions from which all meaning had long since disappeared.

Chance, duplicity, and force had created the Empire. Revived in a later age it had been kept alive by the ideal of a Europe in which diverse people shared a single faith and acknowledged, under God, one universal ruler. The vision was noble but never more than a dream. The Emperor might

---

[10] 'What is Progress?', p. 19. 'Timid' was a favourite word with Bryce—often used to describe men who meant no harm but could always find reasons for not doing what ought to be done.
[11] *American Commonwealth*, 3rd edn. (1893), vol. II, pp. 870–1.
[12] *Proceedings of the Massachusetts Historical Society*, 55 (Oct. 1921–June 1922), 204; *Commonwealth*, vol. I, pp. 30, 307.

be strong in his own kingdom but away from the centre was frequently harassed and weak. Ceremonies endured with little meaning, authority became shadowy, the final indignity was insignificance.[13]

This struck a pessimistic note, but Bryce was the most optimistic of men. An empire faded but the race endured. At the close of 'The Next Thirty Years' he declared that 'in the long run, those principles which the study of man in history has established as permanently true can no more be violated with impunity than can the laws of external nature be defied'. The assurance was welcome in the dark days of 1917, but was he restoring the idea of inevitable progress?

A horticultural analogy explains what he probably had in mind. Without light and rain plants perish; what people did with the plants was another matter. The basic requirements never varied, but knowledge or ignorance, skill or stupidity, determination or timidity decided the success or failure of a crop. The seed was good but might fall on stony ground or the shoots might be choked by weeds. Principles were immortal but people were tempted by the worshippers of false gods. A good system could be ruined by bad government.

All was not clear because the magic word 'principle' begged every kind of question. A critic might object that these 'permanently true principles' meant little to anyone outside the Anglo-American circle or a handful of other countries. To those who knew them not they were an abstraction and therefore unsuitable as a guide to political action. This would not have worried Bryce. Constitutional government was not a vision, present in some prophet's imagination, but an existing polity and the best yet devised to satisfy human aspirations. Regimes that refused to adopt its principles—the rule of law, limited government, and representation of the people—were doomed to decay and defeat; those that honoured them prospered. Nations would discover or restore these principles when they had paid the price for failure. Few of Bryce's older British and American contemporaries would have disagreed. He was an exceptional man but also a representative man. 'The Next Thirty Years' was a personal statement but can also be read as a testamentary disposition from high Victorian culture to the twentieth century.

Bryce made a clear distinction between prophetic utterance and theory required to explain existing phenomena. In 1904 he regretted that so little had been done in Britain for 'the development of the theoretical side of systematic inquiry into the sciences connected with human progress'.

---

[13] From the Introduction to *The Holy Roman Empire* (many editions).

More attention should be given in universities to 'the teaching of theory in all branches of social inquiry.'[14]

In 'The Next Thirty Years' he developed this theme only when dealing with economics, and then to insist that theory must explain real not imagined facts. Traditional political economy, originally designed to explain market behaviour, had become an abstraction because it no longer described the facts of life. Conservative economists still regarded the system loosely described as laissez-faire as coherent and comprehensive, but it was leading only to confusion. 'Everything is in disorder . . . Many of the propositions which forty years ago were thought most firmly established are now confidently assailed.' Thirty years before, in a brilliant but neglected chapter of the *American Commonwealth*, he had demonstrated that although eminent Americans believed that state governments interfered very little, laissez-faire had had its day in the freest states of a free nation. Confusion arose when some believed that an illusion was real and actuality an aberration—but confusion was not stagnation. 'So far from being exhausted economic science may be expected to make a fresh start, though it need not neglect either past facts or the wisdom of Adam Smith or his earlier successors.'[15]

In the study of politics there was already too much theory in the air. Bryce argued for systematic observation to expand knowledge but 'political science' was 'a slightly misleading phrase' because it implied precision. Physical scientists explored the unknown but knew that whatever frontiers were crossed the same fixed and universal laws would apply; political scientists had to allow for irrationality and realise that circumstances always changed.[16]

This did not clear the way for cloudy supposition. 'Keep close to the facts,' he told American political scientists in 1907. 'Never imagine that a general proposition means anything more than the facts which it sums up . . . The fact is the first thing. Make sure of it. Get it perfectly clear. Polish it till it shines and sparkles like a gem.' This reads like a parody of empiricism but the key phrase was 'first thing.' A fact alone was of little use and had no scientific value until its relationship with other verified facts had been established.[17]

---

[14] From his address to the newly formed Sociological Society (see below, n. 37).

[15] 'Next Thirty Years', p. 24; *Commonwealth*, vol. II, chap. xcv. Bryce may not have followed his own precepts—he generalised before studying the facts. Did he know what Alfred Marshall was doing? But his principal point was valid: laissez-faire no longer described the economic system.

[16] 'Next Thirty Years', p. 27.

[17] 'The Relations of Political Science to History and its Practice,' *American Political Science Review*, 3. 2–4, 9. Reprinting his address to a joint meeting of the American Political Science and American Historical Associations in 1908.

It was often assumed that finding the facts was easy. In 'The Next Thirty Years' Bryce made an excursion into the nature of historical evidence to demonstrate that it was difficult. Official records were usually incomplete, earlier investigators had asked the wrong questions, and conventional opinion was frequently wide of the mark. Work in the field was essential to penetrate the fog of ignorance or complacency but even then the whole truth might remain hidden.

He spoke from experience. As long ago as 1867 he had been an assistant commissioner for a royal commission on secondary education with Lancashire as his principal assignment. He circulated a list of questions—27 on general issues, 18 on boys' and 20 on girls' education—but not content with written replies he visited 62 endowed and 40 private schools, questioned teachers, and examined pupils. He had conversed with 'persons of intelligence or influence in the neighbourhood, with clergymen of all denominations, with employers of labour, with tradespeople, with working men who might be taken as fair exponents of the wishes and feelings of parents in their own rank of life.'[18]

The outcome was the longest report (over 400 folio pages) and most thorough submitted to the Commissioners. 'Having entered on the inquiry with no foregone conclusions,' he told them, 'I have endeavoured ... to represent to you impartially and with equal fullness the feelings, wishes, and arguments of every social class and every religious community with which I was brought in contact.' Apart from information the great value of his report was its demonstration that so much of the real truth was hidden until someone set out to discover it systematically.

Twenty-seven years later he again inquired into the state of education but this time as chairman of another royal commission. He would have been enormously gratified by the retrospective verdict pronounced by the historian, R. C. K. Ensor. 'If the test of a royal commission's success is that behind the evasions of government and parties it should discern the unescapable trends of high policy, the Bryce Commission was a singularly successful one.' By default or design some facts were normally concealed. They would never be found beside the highway; someone must go down the byways to find them.[19]

Even with diligent enquiry truth was elusive. Evidence for remote events had been thoroughly sifted but there was always the possibility that

---

[18] *Parliamentary Papers*, 1867–8, vol. XXVIII, Part 8, 426–840. He submitted shorter reports on Shropshire, Worcestershire, Monmouth, and North Wales.
[19] R. C. K. Ensor, *England 1870–1914* (Oxford, 1936), p. 320.

more would be found or that past conclusions would be questioned. In the contemporary world vanishing evidence—lost beyond recall before it had been recorded—was a perennial difficulty with far too little being done to overcome it. Vital evidence was lost while scholars stuck to their books. The study of primitive and formerly isolated people was an obvious example of evidence about to be lost. All learned bodies and societies had a duty 'to urge on the governments of civilized nations the need for collecting and recording those phenomena of a savage life which is rapidly vanishing under the contact of European nations'. A special responsibility rested upon Britain because the Empire included so many varied primitive or backward people. If the effort were made a rich harvest would be reaped with light thrown on the early history of religion and social organisation, contributions made to the unending argument on heredity versus environment, and vital information obtained on the effect of contact between different cultures.[20]

Bryce was particularly interested in the future of races and had included thoughts on their fusion by interbreeding in an important public lecture. In some circumstances it had produced a new strain equal or superior to either original stock, but in others the progeny were judged, rightly or wrongly, to be inferior. All the great peoples of the world were of mixed ancestry but when races were far apart (white and black) the outcome was doubtful. In 'The Next Thirty Years' he could only conclude that 'we seem to need a new science . . . of ethnology, and it must take a good while in the making'.[21]

Philologists should be particularly interested in the study of primitive people and of ethnic minorities in more advanced societies. Many languages were on the verge of extinction and it was imperative to 'obtain and record the words, and also (if possible) the pronunciation of words of these vanishing tongues'. This evidence would be of vital importance for future historians of language but without present effort it would be lost for ever. In this as in other fields there was a duty to serve posterity as well as the present.[22]

---

[20] When summarising the arguments of 'The Next Thirty Years' I have not presented them in the same order as the original but have identified leading themes and selected passages (see above, n. 1).

[21] 'Next Thirty Years', pp. 7–8; *The Relations of the Advanced and Backward Races of Mankind* (1902 Romanes Lecture at Oxford), pp. 15–16. See also (p. 27) 'Race antagonism, an evil more dangerous, because rooted in nature, than any political enmities, cannot but vanish when the races have been blended'. But white and black were best apart for the foreseeable future and American and Australian attempts to exclude the Chinese might be justified.

[22] 'Next Thirty Years', p. 19.

In a few fields the present had little worth recording but evidence from the past that should be rescued before it was lost. In the history of architecture a steady flow of new material could be anticipated but little that would be worth recording for future use. 'Posterity will not greatly care to investigate the ruins of our railway stations and town halls.' Meanwhile ancient and medieval buildings were crumbling away or threatened with wanton destruction.[23]

Gaps in the evidence were difficult to bridge, and the abundant data available for recent events did not necessarily make it easier. Historians of modern times had to select from a huge mass of data and though they chose honestly might still be mistaken. Recent German history provided a leading example. Long after the events of 1870 Bismarck described his use of the Ems telegram to provoke war. This revelation enabled historians to give a true account of events and without it they would have continued to repeat one that was factually incorrect. How often, in other crucial situations, had duplicity distorted the truth?[24]

In England there was an extraordinary cult of secrecy. Until recently no access to state papers later than 1780 had been permitted; As Irish Chief Secretary Bryce had read many state papers in Dublin Castle, and reflected that no scholars, except W. H. Lecky and possibly one other person, had been allowed to see them. 'Such caution, which amazed foreign, and especially American students, was surely over strained.' Since then the cut-off date had been raised to 1837 but the full history of the nineteenth century could not yet be written.[25]

The private letters by public men were an important source but in recent times their value had actually diminished. Formerly they had often contained confidential comments intended for the eye of the recipient alone, but now most letters were dictated to typists and contained no private thoughts. Bryce did not mention the telephone but might have noted that though confidential comments were once more uttered they left no trace for historians to unveil.

High politics presented problems but with social conditions or public opinion they multiplied—'unspeakably increased by the untrustworthiness of the sources and the lack of means for testing them critically'. Among them newspapers were the most readily accessible and recorded

---

[23] 'Next Thirty Years', p. 6. He did not foresee industrial archeology and would have been astounded to learn that before the close of the century some railway stations would be listed buildings.

[24] Ibid., pp. 16–17.

[25] Ibid., p. 11.

valuable detail, but a historian who tried to use one for information on major events or important policies would soon realise its limitations.

> He cannot learn from it, nor do its readers normally learn, the real qualities, perhaps not even the real aims, of the leading political figures. . . . Neither is it easy to gather from the daily or weekly press what is the general judgement and feeling of thoughtful and fair minded people at any particular moment.

Straightforward partisanship was easily discounted but deeply rooted assumptions and animosities were more difficult to handle. 'Long is the life of a controversy which engages religious or political or national passions.' The diagnosis of the effect of these ancient conflicts demanded much knowledge of distant times.[26]

The difficulties encountered when reconstructing the past strengthened the case for gathering evidence before it was lost. Bryce did not use the phrase 'contemporary history' but argued for it. The record of passing times must be not left to journalists and politicians but should be compiled by men trained to collect evidence systematically and evaluate it impartially. Oral history was not then a fashionable pursuit, but he pressed for its regular use. People who had played an important part in public life might be ready to talk and obscure men and women might provide invaluable information about the society in which they lived. He did not refer directly to the importance of local projects in oral history but a passing reference to the admirable work done by American state historical societies implied criticism of conditions at home. There were also mysterious ingredients in the character of every nation that only personal contacts could make clear. In the *American Commonwealth* Bryce wrote that 'America excites an admiration which must be felt on the spot to be understood'. The same would be true when trying to understand the pride of any nation.[27]

People of Bryce's generation did not appreciate the importance of the cinema as a historical source, but he might have mentioned photography then more than fifty years old. Photographs of eminent personalities or great historical events would probably be preserved but there was a wealth of evidence on social conditions from family or topographical photographs that were certain to be lost unless an effort was made to collect and

[26] Ibid., pp. 12–13.
[27] *Commonwealth*, vol. I, p. 10. It was natural for Bryce to stress the importance of direct contact because it was something that he did very well. To quote again from Charles W. Eliot's memorial address: 'He had a remarkable facility in getting into contact with the human beings that he wished to study. I never saw his match in that respect.' On the same occasion, A. Laurence Lowell described him as 'the readiest talker and readiest listener that I ever met'.

preserve them. Not everything could be covered in a single address and Bryce may have tacitly classed photography among other forms of contemporary evidence; but it would have been worth mentioning as an example of evidence that would vanish unless someone took it seriously.

Bryce made a strong plea for the study of non-European regions. Provision ought to be made 'for the systematic observation by trained students of such phenomena of special interest as may be visible at a given time in some other country'. From this clumsy phrase it might be inferred that 'special interest' would be defined with reference to issues at home, but the context made clear that he expected more than an occasional foray when British policy was affected. There was no satisfactory history of India. There was much commercial investment in the South American republics but little was known of their history. Who in Britain knew anything of the history of China? Conventional histories mentioned the self-governing dominions when some crisis drew attention to their affairs but where their full history ought to be written the pages were blank.[28]

Curiously he did not mention the history of the United States although he was keenly interested in its promotion. As he said four years later 'it was not that ancient history or modern European history had been studied too much but that American history had been studied too little'. In 1917 he may have been reluctant to advertise his own wares or have assumed that everyone was so familiar with his interest in the United States that it would be otiose to mention it. Nevertheless it is odd that he did not take this opportunity to hammer home the point.[29]

Political scientists as well as historians must leave their home terrain. All kinds of experiments were being tried in democratic countries and demanded investigation. There were some countries in which representative institutions were discredited; the causes must be ascertained. There were even countries in which the State had become 'a sort of deity, invested with a mystic sanctity . . . [with] incense burned on many an altar and prayer continually made'. The phrase 'totalitarian state' had yet to be coined but Bryce's guesses were good. British political scientists might be inclined to turn their eyes away from what they disliked, but their job was to diagnose political behaviour however repellent and not to avoid uncongenial tasks.[30]

There was an implied criticism of academic lawyers for preoccupation

---

[28] 'Next Thirty Years', p. 18.
[29] *The Study of American History*, 1921 (an inaugural lecture for the new Professorship of American History at University College London).
[30] 'Next Thirty Years', pp. 29–30.

with their own courts and law books. They could learn much from America about the law on corporations, monopoly, employer liability, public utilities, marriage, and divorce. These questions 'ought to be studied with constant reference to the experiments tried there and elsewhere'. It was equally important to study the mercantile law of other countries because standardisation was urgently needed to facilitate intercourse between trading nations. There would be a surge of interest in international law when peace returned, but Americans were well ahead and British legal theorists ill prepared to play their part. 'Thinkers must lead the march, examine the difficulties, suggest to governments methods for overcoming them.'[31]

Learning for its own sake satisfied some scholarly minds, but Bryce inherited the rationalist presumption that knowledge should be useful. History had many uses. Without it the other social sciences would lack essential data for performing their respective tasks. It recorded experience and 'experience must be our guide. What other guide have we?' The use of economics was also clear. Few policies proposed by government were without economic implications and economists must be ready with comment, advice, and assessment. Proposed laws should be subjected to minute scrutiny and the effects of past legislation carefully watched.

This forecast of public functions was ambitious but economists could not expect to move at one jump from their lecture rooms to the corridors of power. They must first win credibility by demonstrating their ability to handle issues of current concern. There was need for informed judgement on such problems as the disposal and ownership of land, capital and its relation to labour, emigration and immigration, taxation and tariffs, currency, wages, strikes and means of averting them, co-operation and profit sharing. Behind these and other economic issues lay a larger question: 'Is it expedient to extinguish private property, and substitute some kind of public ownership and enjoyment such as is vaguely described by the names of Socialism, Collectivism, or Communism?'[32]

Political scientists must also concern themselves with current questions and not stray into abstract realms.

> Our function is to gather and analyse and summarise, and set forth in a clear form, the data which history and the observation of present phenomena provide, stating facts, tracing out causes, describing actual results, estimating the good and the evil which have followed from various methods adopted and experiments tried.

[31] Ibid., pp. 25–7.
[32] Ibid., p. 24–5.

They should direct their attention to subjects that were 'practical, and belong to politics in the popular sense' and not waste time with the imagined response to hypothetical events.[33]

The priority for political scientists was to establish facts but they were not mere compilers. They shared with historians a duty 'to explain the Past by the Present, to illuminate the Present by the Past'. This sentence (more obscure in meaning than Bryce's usual pronouncements) might be read as an endorsement of the historical method conceived in Germany and adopted by some Americans, but Bryce had no time for attempts to endow the State with an existence of its own, separate from and superior to the people it governed. It was useful to study the history of institutions, discover their original purpose, and trace their subsequent evolution, but a political scientist was concerned with actual phenomena not with great abstractions that ignored real detail.[34]

Given this introduction the first question addressed to political scientists—'What is the State?'—may come as a surprise; but his intention was to get metaphysics out of the way before studying the actual functions of government. What limits were fixed to the control of individual freedom? Was the State bound to observe the normal moral code or was 'the preservation of its own existence a duty overriding honour, justice, and good faith?' What general principles could or should limit the interference of government with activities it deems to be pernicious (for instance, the consumption of alcohol)? How should the functions of government be divided between central and local authorities? These were the kind of practical questions to be asked when considering the fundamental character of a State.[35]

Having settled the nature and limits of State authority, political scientists should then seek to dispel the prejudice and misinformation that clouded rational discussion of many current issues. Where it had been tried what had been the practical consequences of giving the vote to women? A similar question could be asked of direct legislation by initiative, referendum, and recall. What factors affected the efficiency of a civil service? How were second chambers composed and what were their

---

[33] 'Next Thirty Years', p. 28.

[34] Ibid., p. 28. Bryce had been on friendly terms with John W. Burgess of Columbia, who adapted German theories of the State to American conditions, but found little to admire in his work or in that of Elisha Mulford whose *The Nation* (1872) was the first work in that genre.

[35] 'Next Thirty Years', p. 28. His language when describing moral limitations was coloured by his recent chairmanship of a committee considering alleged German authorities. And in the questions that followed his use of the word 'should' implied that a judgement ought to be made—not quite in accord with his insistence on facts first and judgement by results.

powers? In legislatures what was the consequence of strict party discipline? How were executive heads chosen in countries without hereditary rulers? Other contentious issues would arise in the next thirty years with more opportunities to shine light into dark corners.[36]

The number of channels proposed for history, economics, and politics was impressive but there were odd omissions. Bryce was well aware of the advance of sociology in Germany, France, and America but did not mention it in his review. This is difficult to explain. He had been president of the British Sociological Society and had opened its first meeting in 1904 with ambitious claims. The overall purpose of the new society was 'to survey with the eye of science the whole field of human activity'. It should bring all studies with a social content into 'systematic cooperation', promote the teaching of theory in 'all branches of social inquiry', and press for better library facilities for the social sciences. The nineteenth century had seen the transformation of physical and biological science but the social sciences lagged behind and the task of sociology was to bring them up to date. Nevertheless sociology was not mentioned in 'The Next Thirty Years'.[37]

There are possible reasons for the omission. Bryce was aware of hostility to the subject in British academic circles. Herbert Spencer, who had first introduced sociology to English readers, was admired as a pioneer in America but not in his own country. Except in the London School of Economics, Edinburgh, and perhaps two or three other places it was maintained that there was no need for a separate discipline when everything claimed for sociology was already covered by history, economics, and anthropology. It was frequently asserted that when tried the result had been needless complexity expressed in bizarre verbiage. Bryce may have reasoned that when dealing with opportunities for British scholars in the next thirty years it was unrealistic to include sociology.[38]

He may also have had doubts about sociology as a separate academic discipline. In 1904 his emphasis had been on communication and co-ordination. The Sociological Society was to provide a forum in which representatives of different disciplines could discuss and confer. Co-operation would help to promote scientific methods and encourage

---

[36] 'Next Thirty Years', p. 28. These questions, unlike those referred to in the preceding note, were neutral in terms; political scientists were to establish facts not deliver opinions.
[37] 'The Aims and Programmes of the Sociological Society', *Sociological Society. 1st Annual Report, 1905*, pp. xv–xvii.
[38] Bryce had a poor opinion of Herbert Spencer. As a sociological pioneer he had 'contributed little beyond formula', *Sociological Society. 1st Annual Report*, p. 223.

systematic teaching but sociology as an independent subject, with the right to exclude those not initiated into its mysteries, might have the opposite effect. Several of the questions presented to economists and political scientists were in the domain of sociology, as he had defined it in 1904, but the answers they gave would command more respect than those given by untried practitioners in an unpopular discipline.

More surprising was the omission of a direct reference to socialism as an intellectual influence in the coming years. Here was no shadowy abstraction but an established force. The Fabian Society had been founded in 1883 and won attention with the *Fabian Essays in Socialism* edited by Bernard Shaw. Several members had attended the first meeting of the Sociological Society and heard Bryce's inaugural address. It was twenty years since Sidney and Beatrice Webb had published *Industrial Democracy* and their relentless quest for facts in the history of local government should have commended them to Bryce. His personal hostility to socialism was no excuse when it was a safe prediction that every social scientist would have to reckon with socialism as a theory if not as a programme.

The omission of Marxism is easier to understand. The Bolshevik revolution was still to come and Bryce was not alone in expecting a version of constitutional government to emerge from the troubles. British socialists owed much to Marx but had rejected his revolutionary messianic message and it was impossible to anticipate the attraction that it would have for young intellectuals in the 1930s. In 1917 it was not perverse to play Marxism down; two years later he would be aware of its significance and tell a different story.

The opportunities were numerous but few would be taken up. The men who heard 'The Next Thirty Years' were in their prime with distinction in their chosen fields. They were unlikely to change direction during the remainder of their working lives and the majority of those they trained would continue to work on familiar lines. Some young men would question the wisdom of their elders but new ideas would normally flow in well-dug channels. Bryce was an old man ahead of his time.

With characteristic optimism he hoped too much from what had already been done and underplayed obstacles to be encountered. The London School of Economics was twenty years old. The School of Eastern European and Russian History had opened in 1915 and the School of Oriental and African Studies a year later. There were as yet no parallel developments in other fields but the precedent had been set for special institutes to promote advanced work on hitherto neglected regions. What Bryce did not take into account was the relationship between advanced research and university employment.

Most young scholars would have to earn a living. Posts in the institutes for advanced study were rare. Oxford and Cambridge had no organised programmes for graduate instruction. Professors could encourage and supervise research if they wished to do so, but there were no public and very few private awards for advanced study. 'Schools' were not wanted and the Ph.D. was regarded as an unwelcome transatlantic invention (all the worse on account of its German ancestry). Oxford and Cambridge colleges wanted men to teach their undergraduates not to spend time on subjects outside the honours curriculum. The majority of British universities followed suit.

The disciplines most likely to experiment in undergraduate instruction were new to the field and would not risk censure by offering 'soft' options. Despite the great contributions by British economists political economy had long enjoyed no more than minority status harnessed to philosophy or history and typically examined in one paper requiring no more than basic knowledge of the subject. The London School of Economics attracted good students but its reputation suffered from the belief that its leading men were more interested in the advancement of socialism than of learning. Even at Cambridge, where the great Alfred Marshall was Professor of Political Economy from 1885 to 1908, it was not until 1903 that he obtained a divorce from History and was allowed to offer an honours degree in economics. By 1917 independence had been won in most universities but students were few and vacant lectureships rare.

Political science was in a weaker position than economics. The name was long familiar but the substance normally dealt with the history of western political theory. Nowhere outside London did political science (as it was understood in American universities) have an independent place in university teaching or even play a minor part in work for an honours degree. Here Bryce could have declared a personal interest. The *American Commonwealth* had been the first major work in modern political science. It described, analysed, and applied standards that were utilitarian not ideological. In America the book (in the full or abridged version) was required reading in hundreds of university courses; in England the information was valued but the method regarded as pedestrian.[39]

History was in the strongest position among subjects dealing with

---

[39] It is misleading to say that Bryce studied America with no preconceived theory. He approached the subject with a full array of liberal ideas but did not see it in that light.

human society, but formidable difficulties prevented the development of non-European, contemporary, or oral history. Older professional historians could recall the fight for their subject as a separate discipline. At Cambridge it had been included in the Moral Science Tripos but then dropped on the ground that memorising dates and facts had no intellectual value. It was revived by J. R. Seeley but faced criticism as a soft option for idle men. Before 1890 several colleges appointed no Fellows in the subject and advised able undergraduates not to study it. History at Oxford had a longer history of independence but the Colleges, with an even greater influence on what was taught, resisted innovation.

Increased respect for History as an academic subject had been won by insisting that its study was as demanding as anything required in classics, philosophy, or mathematics. The close study of documents was never easy and students had also to master a hard core of historical knowledge. The typical honours syllabus, adopted in most British universities, required three papers on the history of the English constitution and two on European history. There was a choice of Special Subjects demanding intensive work on printed source material but the list was invariably limited to British and European topics. Two or three slots were left for optional subjects but the choice was normally limited to ancient or ecclesiastical history, western political theory, Scottish, Irish, or Welsh history (in those parts of the United Kingdom), and perhaps international law. There was no room for non-European history or demand for people to teach it.[40]

This rigid syllabus had many merits and was stoutly defended by the great majority of academic historians. At Oxford and Cambridge the assumed purpose of higher education was to train men for public life and study of the English constitution and European civilisation was an excellent preparation for it. Diversity could only weaken the central structure. Men with academic ambitions might expect scholarly fame and modest fortune for work in these familiar fields but for those who deviated the going would be rough.

Good writing was still praised but only when it built on the laborious study of original sources. Although some men of letters dabbled in history they were not taken seriously by professional historians. The scientific approach was carried to its limits at Manchester under T. F. Tout for whom the purpose of historical education was to train historians. There

[40] The statement that English history was taught in British universities is deliberate. It is a curious fact that outside Oxford by 1970 the only universities with three compulsory papers in English constitutional history were St Andrews, Glasgow, Aberdeen, Wales, and Queen's Belfast. Scottish history was not compulsory in Scottish universities.

was an even greater concentration on documents and a compulsory dissertation using source material. The majority of British historians were not going to abandon the broader purpose of higher education but the Manchester experiment was watched sympathetically by a growing number for whom history must be studied as a science.[41]

Perversely the belief that History must be studied scientifically worked against the exploration of new frontiers. Any suggestion that a new subject should be added to an honours curriculum met predictable opposition: it had no educational value, its source material was weak or inaccessible, its introduction would encourage the notion that anyone could 'get up' a historical subject, and there was no one to teach it. This last argument was often the most effective: a subject could not be studied at university level so long as it could not be taught and so long as it was not taught no one would be employed to teach it. This was stalemate.

Another way of looking at the typical History syllabus was to see it as the product of an era when European hegemony was unquestioned and there was no doubt that the British political system was the best model for emergent cultures. Bryce took a wider view. Believing as he did in the excellence of English traditions he nevertheless coupled 'American' with 'Anglo,' and argued that other countries, whose core values and institutions had originally been transmitted directly from England, had acquired distinctive national characteristics. Countries with different traditions must not be treated as inferior civilisations but studied sympathetically and given the respect that was their due. The world was one but nations varied and myopia was folly.

Some of Bryce's hearers may have been impressed by his plea for non-European history (though perhaps pursued in specialist institutions) but 'contemporary history' was a contradiction in terms. Oral evidence was welcome when a participant in great events was persuaded to talk, but most of the time it would do no more than record prejudice and misconception—precisely the obstacles to understanding that historians must surmount.

These factors help to explain why Bryce's score at the close of his thirty-year period was mixed with more low than high marks. Much had been put into cold storage during the Second World War, but before it there had been less movement than he would have liked to see. In

---

[41] For this and later comments on historical teaching and research see Peter R. H. Slee, *Learning and a Liberal Education: the study of Modern History in the Universities of Oxford, Cambridge, and Manchester, 1800–1914* (Manchester, 1986).

Economics (the social science in which he spoke with least authority) he scored well. As he foresaw, it had been a period of intense activity and J. M. Keynes had produced a theory that broke away from nineteenth-century concepts. It had yet to become a new orthodoxy but was likely to remain the centrepiece of economic debate for many years to come. Bryce had hoped that economists would win the right to advise governments and Keynes again filled the bill while others less in the public eye worked behind the scenes as consultants in the reforming Labour government. Less impressive was uncertainty and division in tackling practical issues. There was no agreement on the causes of depression or the remedies to adopt, and the chasm between those who wanted more or less state intervention had widened.

Other suggestions of 1917 still belonged to the land of dreams. Political scientists had not won credibility as practical experts or matched the academic success of their American colleagues. Some had concentrated on practical issues (as he had advised), others had become entangled in theoretical controversy, but in neither case was there much to show for their efforts. Apart from London and a few less prestigious universities political science had failed to win departmental autonomy. At Oxford political science still meant political theory to be studied in conjunction with philosophy or history; at Cambridge there was a Faculty of Economics and Politics but no doubt which was the senior partner. Harold Laski and G. D. H. Cole were the best known political scientists but Bryce would have deplored both their socialism and their polemical approach to teaching.

If Bryce's refusal to name sociology was intentional he was vindicated. Unmentionable in 1917 it was still a pariah subject in most British universities. The mildest response was sceptical; active hostility was common. The subject was taken seriously at the London School of Economics but its known or supposed leftward bias spread the illusion that sociology and socialism were two sides of the same coin.

The precept that every generation must write its own history had been proved true. A steady flow of academic monographs presented new views on old topics, successive volumes of *The Oxford History of England* were different in mood and emphasis from anything that nineteenth-century historians had produced, and a new Cambridge Modern History was planned with less attention than its predecessor to narrative detail and more to social and intellectual topics. Economic history had moved to the foreground with the realisation that political history without it was shallow. Bryce would have welcomed the histories of labouring people by the

Hammonds—questioning their political assumptions but approving their diligent quest for facts to illuminate the lives of inarticulate people.

The situation was very different for non-European history. *The Oxford History of India* had been published in 1919 with a second edition in 1923 but by 1950 it needed chronological extension and drastic revision. *The Cambridge History of the British Empire* in nine volumes had been launched in 1929 and continued publication after the war, but the editors had to rely on universities in the Dominions for many contributions. The School of Oriental and African Studies had not spawned a brood of similar institutions in other universities, and outside it encouragement for research in these fields was rare and little was undertaken. Chinese history was where Bryce had left it.

By 1950 the suggestions made in 1917 had had no effect on undergraduate teaching in most British universities. Compulsory papers in European and English constitutional history still dominated the curriculum and resistance to change was strong. American and Latin American history could be studied in London, and elsewhere Latin American history sometimes found a small niche in Departments of Spanish Language and Literature. Oxford had recognised the existence of the United States with a special subject on slavery and secession but there was no general course on American history. In 1944 Cambridge added a general paper on American history with lectures to be given by a visiting American professor but without provision for other lectures or tutorial teaching. An undergraduate who wished to spend less time on English and European history was best advised to enrol in an American university. Bryce's bid for territorial expansion had failed.[42]

The timing was wrong but not the foresight. Move on another forty years and unprofitable speculation becomes inspired prophecy. There were scientific and technological developments that had been beyond the furthest frontiers of imagination in 1917, and even the most pessimistic had not anticipated anything so awful as another world war and a cold war; but in his reflections on future work in the humanities and social sciences Bryce was proven true.

Economic departments were strong. Political science had won autonomy with professors and separate departments in nearly all British universities. The hopes expressed for sociology in 1904 though unvoiced in 1917 had been fulfilled, and a university with no professor in the subject

---

[42] At Cambridge in the 1930s one lecturer gave a short course on American history and two optional questions were appended to the paper on Modern Europe.

occasioned surprise and invited reproach. Two other major changes were marked by the first issue of *The Journal of Contemporary History* in 1966 and of *Oral History* in 1970.

Other British periodicals testified to a striking expansion in non-European history. In 1964 came *The Bulletin of the African Studies Association*, in 1967 *The Journal of American Studies*, in 1968 *Afrasia*, and in 1969 *The Journal of Latin American Studies*. The outdated *Oxford History of India* was extended, revised, and largely rewritten in 1958, and in 1978 came volume 10 (the first published) of the massive *Cambridge History of China* with volumes 3 and 11 following in 1978 and 1980.[43]

Developments in advanced study of non-European history were reflected in undergraduate study. Pressure from specialists (often reinforced by student demand) led first to some tinkering with the rigid syllabus but soon to its collapse. English constitutional history lost its dominant position. Compulsion survived only in an attenuated form (usually to provide protection for medieval history) and students were offered an expanding and sometimes bewildering choice. In some universities the introduction of 'studies'—interdisciplinary programmes combining literature, history, politics, economics, and popular culture—allowed students to do all their work for honours in one country or region.

Some historians (not all of the older generation) deplored fragmentation and the replacement of long general courses by closely cultivated patches; but most welcomed the introduction of compulsory or optional dissertations using original sources. Inevitably many of the subjects used source material locally available or collected evidence of recent events from people still living. Bryce would have been delighted by this incentive to capture and preserve evidence before it vanished. At a higher level of learning several universities and research institutes had programmes to collect and preserve contemporary data.[44]

Thus the title of Bryce's 1917 address might be amended. 'The Next Thirty Years' should be followed by an additional clause—'And Forty Years beyond that'. More seriously it prompts reflection on the great changes that have taken place in learning and instruction since he made

[43] A multivolume *Cambridge History of India* followed in the 1990s. In 1987 the Institute of Contemporary British History launched its own *Contemporary Record* and in 1989 the *Modern History Review*. Many other examples could be cited to demonstrate the vitality in fields that were uncultivated when Bryce gave his address.

[44] Medieval historians feared oblivion. In fact medieval history flourished when compulsion was removed; the students were fewer but their interest keen.

suggestions and sketched opportunities. For the social sciences and history the change has meant not merely the addition of subjects formerly
neglected but the semblance of an intellectual revolution. It need hardly
be added that it has signalled the retreat from empire and realisation that
west European civilisation was one among many.

Despite his advanced age 'The next Thirty Years' was not Bryce's last
thought about the future. In 1919 he was back at the Academy to deliver
a Raleigh lecture on 'World History', *Modern Democracies* was published
in 1921, and in the same year he welcomed the first professorship of
American History at University College London with an inaugural lecture. On the evening before he died in 1922 he was hard at work finishing
an obituary of Lord Reay (subsequently published) for the Academy.

In 1917 he had urged the Fellows to take up hitherto neglected opportunities in their respective fields; in the 1919 lecture he asked them to consider the place of their civilisation in space and time. Toward the close of
'The Next Thirty Years' he had stressed the fact that the war, hateful as it
was, made 'the whole earth one in a sense never seen before, every people
and State brought into direct political relations with every other'. This
was the leading theme in 'World History'. Mutual concern for peace and
international fair dealing was recognised in the proposed creation of a
League of Nations and there was hope that it would follow the precedent
set by the great American experiment of 1787 with every political unit
giving up a fragment of sovereignty to secure collective strength.[45]

Here on one side was a promised age of reason, but since 1914 deep
and impenetrable shadows had been cast. 'Who would have dreamt that
an international war would give birth to a class war?' Who would have
thought that cornerstones of the Liberal edifice would be so roughly
shaken? 'Was Liberty, in whose progress Acton saw the progress of
mankind, really advancing, and is it loved with the fervour of the last century. Liberty is the very thing that some among the latest prophets of a
new and better world seek to destroy.' An international war had ended
but new conflicts threatened to destroy what had been saved. Using his
favourite maritime metaphor he asked an unhappy question. 'Is the bark
to beat for ever along a rocky coast, where angry surging breakers
threaten shipwreck, or will it reach at last some quiet haven?'[46]

There were further disquieting thoughts. In the quiet haven, if ever

---

[45] 'Next Thirty Years', p. 29; 'World History', *Proceedings of the British Academy 1919–1920*,
pp. 187–211.
[46] 'World History', pp. 206, 208, 211.

reached, would it be found that all energy had been spent? A nation or even a race might suffer from intellectual exhaustion. Some ancient civilisations had been wonders of their times but of them nothing remained save ruined walls, broken statues, and a few inscriptions. For twenty-five centuries Europe had generated creative ideas but this era could draw to a close.

If the creative impulse passed to America the prospect need not cause alarm. In 1921 he repeated in substance the verdict delivered thirty-three years before in the final paragraph of the *American Commonwealth*. In long perspective a historian must marvel at 'America's achievement and deem it one of the longest steps in the march of social progress that mankind has yet taken'. This advance was not confined to political arrangements and material improvement. It was still the fashion in some English circles to disparage American higher education, but few knew it as Bryce knew it. He was full of praise for the best and warmly approved many less prestigious institutions for spreading the light of learning and opening their doors to so high a proportion of young men and women. When the *American Commonwealth* was published American universities commanded little respect in Europe but he had foreseen the excellence of the best and the potential of all.[47]

These glowing prospects had always been clouded by the unattractive politics. Bryce had not endorsed all complaints by the 'best men' but worried that American political management left no room at the top for an intellectual elite. He had spent his adult life defending democracy against its critics, but always with the reservation that it must be subject to constitutional restraints and depend on more than counting heads, but there were ominous signs that mass democracy threatened high standards. 'May the future lie not with the most gifted but with the most prolific?'[48]

These were possibilities that had to be confronted, but Bryce was the last man to suggest that any outcome was inevitable. He raised questions

---

[47] *The Study of American History*, 36. Compare the *American Commonwealth*, vol. II, p. 872. Bryce first visited Harvard in 1870 and corresponded regularly with Charles W. Eliot and O. W. Holmes jnr. and less frequently with J. B. Thayer and Gamaliel Bradford. He conducted a seminar at Johns Hopkins in 1881 and the intellectual vitality of the young graduates left a lasting impression. From 1887 friendship with Jesse Macy of Grinnell College, Iowa, introduced him to a different brand of higher education. He had a large number of other contacts, e.g. Universities of Michigan (J. B. Angell), California (Bernard Moses), Washington, St Louis (Marshall Snow), and Columbia (Frank Goodnow, E. A. R. Seligman, W. A Dunning, and others). He was President of the American Political Science Association in 1908 and gave an important address at a joint meeting with the American Historical Association (see above, n. 7).
[48] 'World History', p. 208.

but made no assertions. There was no reason why British scholars should accept a prospect of diminishing cultural returns provided that they could demonstrate their capacity for continued leadership—no longer alone but still among the best. In 'The Next Thirty Years' he had outlined a strategy for higher learning, in 'World History' he contemplated changes in the intellectual balance of power, but in both his advice can be briefly summarised. Progress is not made by unseen forces but by human beings. Civilisation is kept alive by curiosity. Nothing is gained by standing still. First find the facts and then be bold.

ELIZABETH ANSCOMBE

Gertrude Elizabeth Margaret Anscombe
1919–2001

ELIZABETH ANSCOMBE, who became a Fellow of the British Academy in 1967 and an Honorary Member of the American Academy of Arts and Sciences in 1989, was born in Ireland on 18 March 1919 and died in Cambridge on 5 January 2001. She is survived by her husband Peter Thomas Geach, formerly Professor of Logic in the University of Leeds, and their seven children. There are also several grandchildren.

Elizabeth Anscombe was the third child and only daughter of Allen Wells Anscombe who in 1919 was serving with a British regiment stationed in Ireland. Captain Anscombe and his wife Gertrude Elizabeth (née Thomas) were living in Limerick when their daughter was born. After the end of the First World War and the spell in Ireland Allen Anscombe returned to his civilian career as a schoolmaster, teaching physics at Dulwich College.

I. Academic life

Elizabeth Anscombe attended Sydenham School and then went up to St Hugh's College, Oxford with a scholarship. In 1939 she was awarded a Second Class in Honour Moderations and in 1941 a First in Literae Humaniores. The main elements in the courses for Hon. Mods. and Lit. Hum. are the philosophy, history and literature of ancient Greece and Rome.

Between 1941 and 1944 Anscombe was a research student first in St Hugh's College and then at Newnham College, Cambridge. In 1946

Proceedings of the British Academy, **115**, 31–50. © The British Academy 2001.

Somerville College, Oxford elected her to a Research Fellowship and in 1964 to an official (teaching) Fellowship. In 1970 she was appointed to the Chair of Philosophy in the University of Cambridge.

Anscombe received many academic honours. She was an Honorary Fellow of Somerville College (from 1970), of St Hugh's College (from 1972) and of New Hall, Cambridge (from 1986); an Honorary Doctor of Laws of Notre Dame University, Indiana (1986), Honorary Doctor of Philosophy and Letters, Navarra University, Spain (1989) and Honorary Doctor of Philosophy, University of Louvain-la-Neuve (1990). In 1978 Austria awarded her its Ehrenkreuz Pro Litteris et Artibus. In 1979 she received the Prize for Research from the Alexander von Humboldt Foundation.

In Oxford, Elizabeth Anscombe gave tutorials to Lit. Hum. undergraduates studying logic and/or the works of Plato and Aristotle and supervised graduate students enrolled for the degrees of Doctor of Philosophy and Bachelor of Philosophy. Her lectures and seminars, usually held in Somerville, were attended by visiting academics from Europe and America as well as students of the university. In 1971, shortly after her appointment to the Chair of Philosophy in Cambridge, she gave an Inaugural Lecture entitled 'Causality and determination' which is reprinted in the second volume of her *Collected Papers*. Some of her Cambridge lecture courses also dealt with causation, others with philosophical psychology and issues in ethics and political philosophy.

Those who have studied with Anscombe include Eric D'Arcy, Roman Catholic Archbishop of Hobart; Nicholas Denyer, of Trinity College, Cambridge; Michael Dummett, FBA; the photographer Flash Q. Fiasco; Rosalind Hursthouse, formerly of the Open University and now at Auckland; Hide Ishiguro, formerly at Columbia University and now at Kyoto; Anthony Kenny, FBA; Anne Lonsdale, President of New Hall, Cambridge; and Onora O'Neill, Principal of Newnham College.

One of Anscombe's duties as professor was to chair meetings of the Cambridge Moral Sciences Club. In this role she attempted, too often unsuccessfully, to enforce the club's Rule 5 which 'in the interests of discussion' asks that papers be kept short. Invited speakers were told of 'the 30-minute rule' but a surprising number chose to ignore it.

II. Personal life

There can be no doubt that the two most important events in Elizabeth's personal life were her marriage to Peter Geach and her conversion to

Roman Catholicism. It is not possible to fully understand her intellectual development without coming to know something about her religious faith and something, too, about her husband.

Peter Geach collaborated with Elizabeth Anscombe in three publications: an edition and translation of works by Descartes; the book *Three Philosophers;* and the editing and translating of Wittgenstein's *Zettel.*

On the other hand the philosophical trajectories of husband and wife turned out to differ in some respects. Geach is a distinguished logician, an authority on McTaggart and the author of four books on the philosophy of religion; Anscombe wrote about metaphysical questions, was an authority on Wittgenstein and published important papers on ethics.

Anscombe discovered Catholicism at the age of 12 when she read a book about the works and sufferings of recusant priests in Elizabethan England. (It was fitting, therefore, that her memorial service in Cambridge took place in the Church of Our Lady and the English Martyrs.) She began taking instruction, from a Dominican, during her first year in Oxford and became a Catholic in 1938. Meanwhile Geach too was taking instruction from the same Dominican. The two new converts met for the first time at a Corpus Christi procession in the summer of 1938. They were married in London, in the Brompton Oratory, on Boxing Day 1941.

Peter Geach is the only child of a Polish mother and a Cambridge-trained teacher of philosophy stationed in India. After the couple separated the wife left India and Peter was born in England. He lived in this country with his Polish mother and grandparents until he was four, after which the father was given custody. As a teenager the younger Geach was instructed in logic by Geach senior, using Neville Keynes' *Formal Logic* and Bertrand Russell's *Principia Mathematica* as textbooks. In later years when Peter decided to learn Polish he found that he had retained faint memories of the language from his infancy. He has published philosophical papers in Polish and has visited Poland on a number of occasions, sometimes accompanied by Elizabeth.

Geach had conscientious objections to the Second World War and was directed to forestry work. For six years following the end of the war he was engaged in private research, during which period he published 15 papers on logic. His occupations in those years included helping to care for his children and since he had no objections to the task he was angered when a headmistress tried to commiserate with him about his supposedly difficult home life.

Between 1941 and 1945 Elizabeth was carrying out philosophical

research in Oxford and Cambridge and Peter was working in a pine forest in the south of England. In 1946 Elizabeth moved into lodgings in
Oxford while Peter and the children, Barbara and John, remained in
Cambridge. When Elizabeth acquired the tenancy of 27 St John's Street,
Oxford, Peter and the children moved there too, though he soon afterwards accepted a lectureship in Birmingham. Because of these separ-
ations Anscombe and Geach liked to say they practised telegamy, marriage
at a distance—which was something of an exaggeration because they
were together at weekends and during university vacations.

In 1951 Elizabeth inherited a small rural property from her mother. It
was in Shropshire and consisted of two houses, some fields and a little
wood on the edge of a stream. One house was occupied by a tenant farmer
and the other is a primitive building in which Peter and Elizabeth and their
children spent the holidays. Its non-modern inconveniences included a
cooker fuelled with paraffin, a log fire for heating, and oil lamps for light.
When I saw the place in the 1970s the lavatory (outdoors) had no door and
no roof. One of the bedrooms doubled as a storeroom and contained a
lot of horsy gear, including a side-saddle that had belonged to Elizabeth's
mother. The family owned horses and everybody could ride though Peter
chose not to. The children rode rather badly, I thought, in that they were
often unable to make their ponies obey them. They assumed, I think, that
the human–horse relationship is necessarily a battle of wills. The animals
became confused and recalcitrant because of the shouting, the yanking at
the reins, the sawing at the bits and the rocking to and fro in the saddles.
Elizabeth was a better rider though somewhat too relaxed; she said that
she once fell off a horse when it was standing still.

A distinguished Oxford don has described the way in which the Geach
children exhibited their lack of horse sense, or perhaps their addiction to
practical jokes, on a day when they suggested they teach him to ride. The
young people put the poor man up on a mare and led him into a field
occupied by an amorous stallion whose attempts to make love to the mare
must have seriously inconvenienced her rider.

During the winter the tenant farmer kept an eye on the house and the
horses, in the spring he planted potatoes for the family to dig up and eat
in the summer, and each December his mother sent a Christmas goose
down to Oxford or Cambridge.

Elizabeth's world-wide circle of acquaintance consisted mainly of academic folk, including a sprinkle of learned priests. She was willing to discuss philosophy, or anything else, with people of different faiths or no

faith at all, but tended to avoid ex-Catholics who had openly disavowed their former beliefs.

Some of her admirers were clerical bigwigs. Pope John Paul II became a friend after meeting Peter and Elizabeth in Poland in the days before he was Pontiff. The Cardinal Archbishop of Amargh, Cahal Daly, who gave a moving homily at her memorial mass, wrote in 1994:

> I had both chastening experience of Elizabeth's frankness and encouraging experience of her generosity. Once she wrote to me in reference to something I had written about Wittgenstein's *Tractatus* and bluntly and rightly named it the nonsense that it was. Another time, in reference to something which I wrote about British moral philosophy, she was so kind as to say to a novice philosopher such as I was that she wished she had written a sentence she cited from my piece . . . I felt hugely flattered.

Another friend, Michael Dummett, wrote an account of what it was like to study philosophy with Elizabeth Anscombe:

> Tutorials with her, which I was lucky to have for a brief period, were more stimulating than with anyone else. They might last for three hours (one hour is the regulation time). If I wrote anything with which I thought she might agree she attacked me more vigorously than ever. I owe an immense amount to her.

An obituary notice by her Somerville colleague, Philippa Foot, included the following words:

> We were close friends in spite of my atheism and her intransigent Catholicism . . . she was an important philosopher and a great teacher. Many say 'I owe everything to her' and I say it too on my own account.

Nicholas Denyer, a former pupil, said:

> To me she was kindness itself.

Susan Haack wrote:

> My most vivid memory of Elizabeth is of New Hall lunches [in Cambridge], from the time when I was a very young Fellow, and she newly arrived to take up her chair. She would arrive at lunch, look around to see if I was there, and then say something provocative like 'nobody ever wrote anything interesting in the philosophy of science', knowing I'd rise to the bait . . . I got indigestion but also a valuable informal philosophical education.

Cora Diamond attended Elizabeth's Oxford lectures and later met Anscombe and Geach at conferences. She said:

> I have never seen anyone as visibly thinking as Elizabeth did. If you asked a question she would think for two or three minutes and then say something much deeper than you had thought the question implied.

Some of my own early experiences with Elizabeth Anscombe resembled Cardinal Daly's first encounter with her. For instance I once wrote an essay which I privately thought was pretty profound; after I had read this production to Elizabeth she rose from her chair, walked across the room, turned around and said, in a sepulchral voice: 'I'm afraid **That Kind of Stuff** is no good at all'. It was not my impression that she intended to cause pain. Anyway, tutors, like doctors, should tell the truth.

It has to be admitted, though, that Anscombe was not invariably benign. (Is anyone?) To one or two people she said things which she must have known were harsh and unkind.

Elizabeth was a fearless individual and cared little for public opinion. Moreover she had a knight, Peter, whose fury when she was attacked in print was something to behold.

The intellectual climate of the late twentieth century was such that Anscombe's views on sexual morality provoked more disagreement than her arguments about justice in war. Her paper 'Contraception and chastity', which appeared in *The Human World* in 1972, inspired two rejoinders: a polite one from Peter Winch and an unusually impolite one from two Cambridge dons, Michael Tanner and Bernard Williams.

In her essay Anscombe had said that societies which accept contraception will come to accept abortion and the downgrading of marriage; that Christian authors, both Catholic and Orthodox, have repeatedly condemned the practice; that the use of contraceptive barriers is akin to perversions such as sodomy; and that philosophical considerations about the nature of intention show that even oral contraceptives must be condemned.

Winch took up the last point, arguing that preventing conception by taking a pill which reduces fertility is no different from taking advantage of the naturally occurring infertile safe period. For the intention is the same in each case. Anscombe rejected his objection, though (strange to say) she once remarked to me that eating a natural food which temporarily reduced fertility might not be wrong, just as it is not wrong to prolong lactation.

Tanner and Williams accused Anscombe of happily accepting 'rotten thinking' when it comes from Pope and Church. They said her reasoning was 'offensive and absurd'. They accused her of sophistry and bluffness and shallowness and of being ridiculous. They stated that her essay included 'higher order absurdity, or even indecency'. They asked 'how dare she assert that some homosexual [acts] are "rewardless"?' They said 'it becomes increasingly difficult . . . to suppress feelings of outrage at some of her attacks on the spirit of the age'. Elizabeth addressed her response, rather wryly, to 'my friendly neighbourhood philosophers'.

A few years later, when Anscombe published a short paper on voting in *Analysis* (1976), someone wrote a response entitled 'Lies, damned lies and Miss Anscombe'. The editor quickly apologised for allowing the statement that Elizabeth Anscombe was a damned liar, and worse than a damned liar, to appear in his journal; the author, however, churlishly refused to apologise for the insult.

Many anecdotes have been told about Elizabeth Anscombe. A particularly silly story was perpetrated by a German author who stated, in print, that Elizabeth married Peter Geach 'in spite of her former relationship with Wittgenstein'. The implication seems to be that Anscombe had a romantic or sexual relationship with Ludwig Wittgenstein before her marriage. The suggestion is silly because she was already married to Peter Geach when she first met Wittgenstein; moreover it is widely believed, and is probably true, that Wittgenstein's romantic and sexual inclinations, if any, were not directed towards women. On the other hand it is clear that he admired Elizabeth's abilities and regarded her with affection. He once said to a friend, a sculptor, that she had 'ein schöner Kopf', a beautiful head.

An anecdote recorded by John Geach, who had it from his parents, concerns an occasion when Wittgenstein called on the Principal of Newnham College and tried to persuade her to extend Elizabeth's one-year research studentship. He disliked wearing ties but donned one for his visit to Newnham. On meeting Elizabeth and Peter a few hours later he pointed to the tie and said 'Look what I have done for you!' Newnham's archives confirm that Elizabeth spent more than one year in residence but not, it seems, because her studentship had been extended. It would appear that the Principal of Newnham, unlike many other people, felt able to ignore the demands of Professor Wittgenstein.

Another story was told by a Proctor's 'bulldog' (or whatever those officers are called in modern times). Bull-dogging for a Proctor is a part-time job and the man's main work was as a clerk in the university's administration building. In 1970 one of his duties was to make arrangements for the payment of salaries or wages to newly appointed people. The recently appointed Anscombe wandered into his office, no doubt wearing her usual slightly scruffy slacks and tabard, and was greeted with the query 'Are you one of our new cleaning ladies?' There was a slight pause before she replied ('quite softly', he reported) 'No, I am the

Professor of Philosophy.' 'She wasn't angry, she didn't go through the roof' (he said) 'but *I* wanted to sink through the floor.'

Elizabeth always wore trousers. She was once accosted by a university Jack-in-office who insisted that ladies must wear dresses when giving lectures. Thereafter, it is said, she carried a plastic bag containing a skirt to the lecture room, pausing outside the door in order to pull on the garment—*over* the trousers of course.

Finally there is the true story about Elizabeth's final *viva voce* examination. Because of her intense interest in philosophy she tended to neglect the rest of the syllabus and consequently flunked the Roman History paper. The philosophy examiners wanted to give her First Class Honours but the Roman History man objected, and objected even more, no doubt, when his questions in the *viva* met with a blank face. He eventually asked: 'Miss Anscombe, can you name a governor or procurator of a Roman province? *Any* Roman province?' to which she replied 'No', having forgotten all about Pontius Pilate. The historian, in despair, asked: 'Miss Anscombe, is there *any fact at all* about the history of Rome which you would like to comment on?' But again the answer was 'No' and a mournful shake of the head. However the other examiners insisted that Elizabeth deserved a First and a First was duly awarded. For that to have happened her philosophy papers must have been very very good indeed.

III. Philosophy: translations

Anscombe first became well known as a translator. Her work on Wittgenstein's *Philosophische Untersuchungen* was begun a year or two before he died (in 1951) and the English version of Part I was produced under his guidance. In 1949, as part of that project, he arranged for her to spend some time in Vienna so that she might become familar with the nuances of the German language as it is spoken in that city.

Wittgenstein's Will named three literary executors: Elizabeth Anscombe, G. H. von Wright, and Rush Rhees.

The Oxford publisher Basil Blackwell described receiving a visit in 1952 from 'a young woman' who offered him the opportunity to publish a work by Wittgenstein. He of course agreed and in 1953 the German text of *Philosophische Untersuchungen* (edited by von Wright) was published *en face* with G. E. M. Anscombe's translation into English. This edition of the *Philosophical Investigations* has been reprinted many times. There are also editions of the German original alone and the English version alone.

Anscombe's other Wittgenstein translations include *Remarks on the Foundations of Mathematics*; *Notebooks 1914–1916*; *Zettel*; *Philosophical Remarks*; *On Certainty* (with Denis Paul); and *Remarks on the Philosophy of Psychology I*.

Translators are easy targets and are not often praised. Yet some of their works have never been surpassed but have become classics in their own right. C. K. Scott Moncrieff's version of *À la Recherche du Temps Perdu* is one example and Constance Garnett's translations of Chekov's short stories are others. In my opinion Anscombe's version of the *Philosophical Investigations* is just such a classic. There will be new translations in the future but it is not likely that hers will be superseded.

IV. Philosophy: original books and essays

Anscombe's original works comprise two books, *Intention* (1957, 1963, 2000) and *An Introduction to Wittgenstein's Tractatus* (1959) and part of a third, *Three Philosophers* (1961, with Peter Geach). She also published approximately 70 papers, 48 of which were reprinted in 1981 in a three-volume collection. Essays written during the last two decades of her life appeared in journals and books published in England, the United States, Austria, Italy, Latin America, France, and Germany.

Elizabeth Anscombe gave an account of her earliest philosophical ideas in the 'Introduction' to *Collected Papers II*:

> My first strenuous interest in philosophy was in the topic of causality . . . As a result of my teen-age conversion to the Catholic Church . . . I read a work called *Natural Theology* by a nineteenth-century Jesuit. . . . I found it most convincing except for two things. One was the doctrine according to which God knew what anyone would have done if, e.g., he hadn't died when he did. . . . I found I could not believe this doctrine: it appeared to me that there was not, quite generally, any such thing as what would have happened if what did happen had not happened . . . But it was the other stumbling block that got me into philosophy. The book contained an argument for the existence of a First Cause, and as a preliminary it offered a proof of some principle of causality according to which anything that comes about must have a cause. The proof had the fault of proceeding from a barely concealed assumption of its own conclusion . . . I thought it just needed tidying up. So I started writing improved versions of it . . . each one of which I then found guilty of the same error.

These topics remained in her head all her life. Causality, the second 'stumbling block', is the subject of her inaugural lecture, it is mentioned in the book *Intention* and discussed in the essays on Hume in *Collected Papers I* and throughout Part 2 of *Collected Papers II*.

Elizabeth Anscombe spent the best part of seven years as Wittgenstein's friend and student and several decades soaking herself in his ideas. A different kind of pupil might have written nothing except commentaries on the ideas of the master but that was not the case with Elizabeth who published only a handful of items about the works of her Mentor. Moreover there are some notable differences between her writings and his. Wittgenstein hardly ever referred to the philosophers of the past but Anscombe, an Oxford-trained scholar, produced important essays on the Greeks (Parmenides, Plato, Aristotle), on mediaeval authors (Anselm, Aquinas) and on Hume and Brentano and Frank Ramsey. Secondly, Wittgenstein's general remarks on first-order moral questions were for the most part somewhat brief and cryptic; nothing could be less like them than Anscombe's essays about war and murder and sexual morality. As to ethical theory, Wittgenstein stated in the *Tractatus* that 'there can be no ethical propositions'. His insistence that the world can only be described by science now looks very vulnerable — partly because of Anscombe's papers 'Modern moral philosophy', 'On brute facts' and 'On promising and its justice'.

However she did follow Wittgenstein in certain other matters. She rejected the idea that the nature of mind can be discovered through introspection, a mode of enquiry which he had often denounced. She agreed with his view that in order to solve a philosophical problem it is useful to acquire an overview of ordinary concepts and to ask the questions 'How is such and such a concept learned? How do children acquire it?' and 'What concepts would we have if certain very general features of the world were radically different from what they are?'

It would be wrong to suggest that either the philosophy of Wittgenstein or the philosophy of Anscombe contains nothing except descriptions of language. It is true that some philosophers who came after Wittgenstein stopped short at the first question, that is, they asked only 'What do we say?' but not 'How did we acquire those concepts?' and certainly not 'What might we have said if . . . ?' Thus conceptual elucidation degenerated into linguistic analysis, a tedious enterprise.

The following sections will each describe one of Anscombe's books and some of her most characteristic papers.

Intention

The American philosopher Donald Davidson has described *Intention* as the most important contribution to the topic of practical deliberation since Aristotle.

The difference between intentions and predictions and motives and causes, Anscombe argues, can be best understood if one considers the several different ways in which actions are explained and justified.

She introduces the idea of non-observational knowledge, an example being knowledge of the causes of certain rather special movements of one's body: 'as when I say why I gave a start'. The cause in such cases is a mental cause and cannot be analysed as constant conjunction. Mental causation is not important in itself but needs to be distinguished from intention and also from motive. 'Motive' is a wider notion than 'intention' and can look to the past as well as to the future (as in the case of revenge). What would intention be like if there was no such thing as an expression of intention? In such case the answer to the question 'Why did you . . . ?' would always be: 'For no particular reason'. If there are intentional actions there must be chains of reasons.

Is there any such thing as *the* intention behind a particular action? Here Anscombe introduces the idea of 'under a description', which she wrote about again in 1979, in a paper with that title. Her imaginary example has become well known; it can be paraphrased as follows: Suppose a man is employed by a group of people to pump water from their well to their house. Suppose the well has been poisoned by someone else who seeks the deaths of the people in the house. Suppose the man at the pump knows nothing about the poison or the would-be poisoners. Is there one single correct description of his, the pumper's, action? Many things are going on: he is using his muscles, casting a shadow, pumping water, making a clicking noise with the machine, earning his wages, and causing the deaths of the people in the house. Anscombe says all these descriptions are correct if they are true. But we can only locate his *intention* by asking him the right kind of question, which is a why-question or a set of why-questions falling within a certain range. The range of questions must be such as to exclude answers which refer to mental causes such as for example 'I am marching (or pumping) to keep time to the music of the band'. As to 'how' questions, those will not locate his intention but might locate ordinary causal conditions.

In short, the man's action, in the case as described, will be intentional under some descriptions (pumping, earning) and not intentional under others (clicking, poisoning).

Collected Papers I: 'Parmenides, contradiction and mystery'

This essay dissects an argument formulated by Parmenides from which he thought to reach several conclusions, all of which are incredible. The argument runs:

> It is the same thing that can be thought and can be
> What is not cannot be
> Therefore what is not cannot be thought.

(In this inference the idea of being covers states of affairs, i.e., what is the case, as well as the existence of things.)

Anscombe was interested in the argument for its own sake. But it is reasonable to suppose that she was also aware of its bearing on the last sentence in Wittgenstein's *Tractatus Logico-Philosophicus:* 'That whereof one cannot speak thereof one must be silent.'

She remarks that the second premise of Parmenides' argument is incredible because it implies: If p is false it is *necessarily* false.

As to the first premise, she notes that it will be false either if that can be thought which cannot be or if that can be which cannot be thought. She is interested in the second alternative because mysteries seem to be states of affairs which can exist but which 'cannot be thought'. Mysteries 'cannot be thought' in so far as they cannot be described in sets of sentences which are demonstrably consistent.

If Parmenides' first premise is true then only what can exist can be thought of. But that seems to be refuted, she says, by the fact that it is possible to draw pictures of impossible states of affairs.

Can we ever say of a particular proposition 'this is true but what it states is irreducibly enigmatic'? Or should such an assertion be dismissed on the grounds that 'whatever can be said at all can be said clearly'? The second alternative implies the conclusion that all mysteries, including of course the central mysteries of Christianity, are mere illusions.

Anscombe does not deny that conclusion in so many words. She says, instead, that there doesn't appear to be any ground for the view that nothing can be the case which cannot be grasped in thought—'It is a sort of prejudice.'

Collected Papers I: 'The early theory of forms' and 'The new theory of forms'

Plato's early theory of forms is the version to be found in *Republic, Phaedrus,* and *Phaedo.* Anscombe in her discussion of the early theory compares forms and particulars first with types and tokens and then with classes and their members. According to the notion of class as it occurs in modern logic classes are not to be identified with their members: in modern logic a class is something besides the things of which a certain predicate holds—which is just how Plato thought of the forms.

In the second paper, which is largely exegetical, Anscombe argues that Plato revised the theory in his later works (*Parmenides, Sophist*) as the result of coming to consider the possibility of there being forms not only of the beautiful, the large, the tall and so on but also of being and not-being, oneness and number, sameness and difference.

Collected Papers II: the essay about C. S. Lewis

In 1946 Elizabeth Anscombe read a paper to the Oxford Socratic Club which was subsequently printed in *The Socratic Digest*. This paper, a discussion of chapter 3 of C. S. Lewis's book *Miracles,* was her first publication in a philosophical journal.

Lewis himself was present at the meeting of the Socratic Club.

In *Miracles* Lewis had attempted to prove that there is an inconsistency between the theory that human thought is always the product of natural ('irrational') causes and a belief in the validity of reason. Anscombe pointed out that the non-rational is not the same as the invalid or the irrational and that physical states such as delirium are not irrational causes but the causes of irrational thoughts. Lewis's idea that thoughts must be either caused by physical events or caused by reason is based on a confusion between the concepts of reason and cause which arises because the expressions 'because' and 'explanation' are both of them ambiguous. Lewis, she said, held that there is a single fixed place for '*the* explanation' so that when the place is filled the subject of explaining a thought has been closed.

The different descriptions of what went on at the meeting are incompatible with one another and show the dangers associated with anecdotal history. Lewis's biographers, Roger Lancelyn Green and Walter Hooper, were not present but described the events nevertheless:

> The meeting is said to have been the most exciting and dramatic the Socratic has ever seen. According to Derek Brewer, who dined with him two days later, Lewis was 'deeply disturbed' and described the meeting with real horror. His imagery was all of the 'fog of war, the retreat of infantry thrown back under heavy attack.' . . . Even the contestants said different things: Lewis told Walter Hooper that he was not defeated, and Miss Anscombe told Hooper that he was. One certain result of the disagreement was that Lewis revised chapter 3 of *Miracles* before it was published as a Fontana paperback in 1960.

Anscombe's own account is rather different:

> The meeting . . . has been described by several of his friends as a horrible and shocking experience which upset him very much. Neither Dr Havard (who had Lewis and me to dinner a few weeks later) nor Professor Jack Bennett remembered any such feelings on Lewis's part. My own recollection is that it was an occasion of sober discussion of certain quite definite criticisms . . . some of his friends seem not to have been interested in the actual arguments or the subject-matter . . .

She remarked, too, that the manner in which Lewis carried on his side of the discussion showed that he was open-minded and quite prepared to adapt his ideas. The revised version of chapter 3 of *Miracles*, she said, is more interesting and more profound than its original.

Collected Papers II: 'Causality and determination'

Is everything which is caused determined? Anscombe's replies to that question depend partly on examples, partly on a discussion of indeterminism in physics and partly on considerations resembling those of chaos theory.

She begins by asking: does 'cause' mean 'determine'? And answers No, because nothing is caused until it happens, whereas an event can be determined in advance. 'Determined' means 'pre-determined'.

Her other questions and answers are as follows:.

What does the word 'cause' mean? There are many different kinds of cause, hence 'cause' is highly general. It could be added to a language which already had a lot of special causal concepts (e.g. *make, burn, hurt, carry, push*) but not to one which had none.

Are causal connections necessary connections? No—there are necessitating causes like rabies (you can't survive if not treated) and also non-necessitating causes like the Geiger counter which detonates a bomb but only when the random action of radioactive molecules happen to affect it. Anscombe says that here *the causation itself* is 'mere hap', adding 'and it is difficult to explain this matter any further'.

Are effects always dependent on their causes? No. When two different causes are able to cause the same effect the effect is not dependent on either.

Are 'causal laws' exceptionless generalisations? No, because 'Always, given A, B follows' is never true. To make it true you would have to explicitly exclude an endless, i.e., an impossible, list of the circumstances in which A does not cause B. The most neglected topics in philosophical speculation about causality, she says, are *interference* and *prevention*. It is supposed that one can always give a finite list of exceptions to a generalisation, beginning with the word 'unless'—but that is a mistake.

Are laws of nature generalisations about what always happens? No. Such laws as, for example, 'The freezing point of mercury is . . .' never have the form 'Always when A occurs, B follows.'

The accuracy of measurement is not infinitely extendable. Classical Newtonian mechanics cannot be used to calculate real results such as the movements of balls in a pinball machine because in such cases the multiplicity of impacts leads to loss of information.

It is one thing to say that there are clear-cut situations (e.g., in astronomy) in which the outcome is determined and another to suppose that in the hurly-burly of many crossing contingencies whatever happens next must have been pre-determined.

Newton's system is deterministic but does not entail determinism. The paths of the planets are determined but the paths of animals are not.

To see choice—any choice—as a predetermining causal event now appears as a naive mistake in the philosophy of mind.

Either Kant's reconciliation of freedom and physical determinism is gobbledegook or its account of freedom is wholly inaccurate. For physical indeterminism is indispensable if we are to make anything of the claim to freedom.

Yet physical indeterminism, though indispensable, is not sufficient, because freedom is the power to act according to an idea. And what is the subject of un-pre-determinism in indeterministic physics? Not something moved by ideas.

The physical haphazard might be the only physical correlate of human free action and the voluntary actions of animals. But neither freedom nor voluntariness is the same thing as the physical correlate. And they are not effects of the correlate, they are not produced by it.

Collected Papers III: 'On brute facts'

This essay has an obvious bearing on the so-called is–ought problem, which indeed it might be said to have solved.

Anscombe argues that certain facts can be 'brute' relative to other facts and also less brute, or as it were non-brute, in relation to a third set. She illustrates her idea with examples.

Hume said that truth consists in agreement with matters of fact or agreement to relations between ideas. Now, the truth of the statement 'X owes the grocer £1 for potatoes' consists neither in relations between ideas (as that 100 pennies make one pound) nor with what Hume would have allowed to be facts (as that the buyer asked for potatoes and the grocer supplied them and sent a bill). So if Hume was right the statement 'X owes the grocer . . .' is neither true nor false. Nor does the statement 'X owes . . .' state an *extra* fact or an *extra* relation that can be deduced from the ones referred to (in brackets) above.

Yet is clear that 'X owes . . .' might be true or might be false. How so? Anscombe answers: Its being true consists in the 'brute facts' (about the movement of potatoes and so on) in the context of an institution—the institution of buying and selling. She points out that exactly the same thing is true of the facts themselves as they have been described. For events only count as ordering and supplying in the context of an institution, a piece of paper only counts as a bill in the context of an institution. And this means that we can't say that 'owes' refers to a special mysterious non-factual relation because then we'd have to say the same thing about 'supplies', which would be absurd.

'The grocer carried potatoes from A to B' is a brute fact in relation to 'The grocer supplied X with potatoes' which is brute in relation to 'X owes the grocer money for potatoes'. At the other end we can say that 'X owes . . .' is brute in relation to X's not being bankrupt.

The implied conclusion is that there is no simple distinction between the factual and the non-factual, no simple difference between facts and values.

Collected Papers III: 'Modern moral philosophy'

We might ask: what facts would Anscombe regard as 'brute' relative to 'X (morally) ought/ought not do such-and-such'? An answer can possibly be gleaned from the essay 'Modern moral philosophy': perhaps the injunction against murder is non-brute in relation to a brute fact about the will of God.

Anscombe makes four suggestions.

One is that the differences between modern moral philosophers, from Sidgwick to the present day, are quite unimportant. Presumably Wittgenstein's *Lecture on Ethics* (1929) is one of the works she intended to include among those described as modern.

Another suggestion is that philosophers should stop trying to do moral philosophy 'until we have an adequate philosophy of psychology . . .'.

Thirdly, the concepts of the morally right and wrong, and the moral sense of 'ought', should be jettisoned because they are hangovers from a lost view of ethics, the view that morality stems from a divine law-giver and His law.

Finally, we should look again at Aristotle because he studied the virtues rather than the moral sense of 'ought'.

That last suggestion has been taken up by Philippa Foot, Alasdair Macintyre, Rosalind Hursthouse and N. J. Dent, all of whom, in their various separate writings, have re-introduced the philosophical study of virtue after a considerable interregnum.

Collected Papers III: the two papers on promising.

In 'On promising and its justice' Anscombe says that it is *prima facie* difficult to give a non-paradoxical explanation of the need to keep promises. For if a promise is to be genuine the agent must know that he is making a promise and that seems to create a paradox like the following: if a certain type of bottle was only a genuine example of the type when it had a picture of itself on it then the picture would have to have a picture which would have to have a picture . . . ad. inf. Here Anscombe decides that . . . '[the bottle example] need not trouble us if we say that to think something is *also* to think that you think it' (my italics).

Promising and its justice, she argues, can be explained in terms of two kinds of necesssity. The first she calls 'Aristotelian necessity', the other is 'language game necessity'. Actions and institutions have 'Aristotelian necessity' when they are needed in order to produce human good. Human beings invented promises and contracts and testaments because it is necessary for human good that we should sometimes be able to bind another person's will without recourse to force or fear or love. There are for example many good states of affairs which cannot be gained by force; you cannot use simple physical force to make people look after your children for you when you are in prison or dying. The other kind of necessity appears when someone asks: 'But why should I keep promises?' The answer to that question can go no further than a description of the language game.

In 'Rules, rights and promises' (1978) Anscombe remarks that the expression 'you must not . . . because . . .' (and its translations) are accepted and understood by everyone who speaks a human language. She names such expressions 'stopping modals' and in another paper 'The source of the authority of the State' she uses the notion to explicate the concept of rights.

Collected Papers III: the essays on war

Anscombe's papers on warfare deal with the traditional Christian doctrine of justice in war, with the Catholic doctrine of double effect and with the nature of intention. Two of the three essays strongly condemn pacifism.

Towards the end of 1939, during the period of the so-called phoney war, Elizabeth Anscombe, then aged 20, and another student, Norman Daniels, published a pamphlet with the title *The Justice of the Present War Examined: a Catholic View*. Anscombe's section is called 'The war and the moral law'. She outlines seven conditions needed before a war can be just and insists that even if only one is absent then the war is morally forbidden.

Anscombe predicted, correctly, that the Allies would eventually use aerial bombardment to attack the civilian populations of Germany. She inferred this from the fact that the British government stated that it would adhere to international law, i.e., would not attack civilians, but 'reserved the right "to adopt appropriate measures" if the Germans should break it'. Attacking civilians, she argued, is a mortal sin, it is murder, and the fact that the enemy too is a murderer does not make it all right. Her other prediction, that the Allies would impose an unjust peace on Germany, turned out to be wrong. And she did not forsee the Holocaust.

The premises of her arguments come from Aquinas and, according to a footnote, from '. . . any textbook of moral theology'—implying, rather naively, that the authors of Catholic textbooks never disagree with one another about the topic of warfare. Another footnote refers to a papal encyclical which was translated first in the Vatican and then by Mgr Ronald Knox. Anscombe remarked 'comparing these with the Latin original we have often found cause to alter the translation ourselves'. One cannot but admire the insouciance of that word 'often'.

The subtitle of the pamphlet, 'A Catholic View', caused the Bishop of Birmingham to tell the young authors that only works carrying an *imprimatur* may rightly be called Catholic. He did not give it an *imprimatur*.

Another paper about war, 'Mr Truman's Degree', was published privately in 1957. Its origin was as follows: in 1956 the University of Oxford proposed that Harry S. Truman be given an honorary degree. Elizabeth held the view that President Truman's decision to drop atomic bombs on Japanese centres of civilian population was very wicked. She decided to make a formal protest at a meeting of Congregation. She asked the Senior Proctor how she might do that, and he referred her to the Registrar, who informed the Vice-Chancellor of her intentions, as was his duty. She says that 'cautious enquiries' were made as to whether she had 'got up a party', to which she said No. It seems that word got round, so that very many dons turned up to the meeting, some in order to support Mr Truman, others to foil what they suspected of being a mysterious plot concocted by mysterious females. When the proposal for the honorary degree was put to the meeting Elizabeth said *non placet* (it does not please), the formula used both for demanding a vote and for voting No. Alan Bullock, of St Catherine's College, had the task of defending Mr Truman in a speech at which Anscombe later poked some rather grim fun. When the matter was put to the vote a large majority were in favour of giving the President his degree. Four people voted against: Elizabeth herself, her colleagues Philippa Foot and Margaret Hubbard and a man with a fine war record, the historian M. R. D. Foot, *croix de guerre*. In 1957 Elizabeth published the pamphlet which explains the reasons behind her *non placet.*

A third paper, 'War and murder', first appeared in 1961 in R. J. Butler (ed.), *Nuclear Weapons; a Catholic Response.* Anscombe later wrote: It was written in a tone of righteous fury. . . . I don't much like it, not because I disagree with its sentiments but because, if I was torn by a *saeva indignatio*, I wish I had the talent of a Swift in expressing it.' Her tone of voice in this paper is more like the Prophet Jeremiah's than Jonathan Swift's.

Papers published after 1981

Papers published by Elizabeth Anscombe after 1981 include 'On private ostensive definitions' in the *Proceedings of the 6th International Wittgenstein Symposium*, Vienna, 1982; 'Experience and truth' in the *Proceedings of the Aristotelian Society*, 1988; 'Wittgenstein, whose philosopher?' in *Philosophy*, 1990; 'Why Anselm's proof in the Proslogion is not an ontological argument' in *The Thoreau Quarterly*, 1985; and 'Russellm or Anselm?' in *The Philosophical Quarterly*, 1993. There are also essays on first-order moral questions including 'Were you a zygote?' in *Philosophy* (supplementary volume), 1984 and 'Why have children?' in the *Proceedings of the American Catholic Philosophical Association*, 1990. Much of *Euthanasia and Clinical Practice* (Linacre Centre, London, 1982) was contributed anonymously by Anscombe. 'Making true' was published in the collection *Logic, Cause and Action* (Cambridge, 2000) and an essay on Proclus and Wittgenstein entitled 'Grammar, structure and essence' in *Arete* (Peru, 2000).

Manuscripts which have not yet appeared in print include her Stanton Lectures delivered in the Divinity School in Cambridge in the 1980s.

Elizabeth's last years were clouded by misfortune, first when her daughter Barbara suffered a dreadful illness, and then when she herself was involved in a terrible accident. In 1997 a car driven by her son More in which she was a front seat passenger collided head-on with an American vehicle travelling in the opposite direction and on the American side of the road. More's sternum was broken on the steering wheel and Elizabeth's skull was fractured on the windscreen. After an operation to remove clots of blood from her brain she appeared to be making a slow recovery and felt able to accept an invitation to give some lectures in Lichtenstein but after delivering only three of her prepared talks she fell ill again and had to return to Cambridge. From that time on her health gradually worsened, her memory grew erratic and she began to suffer from delusions.

Elizabeth Anscombe died peacefully in Addenbrooke's hospital in the presence of her husband and four of their children. Her funeral mass took place in the Dominican chapel in Buckingham Street, Cambridge, and her grave is close to Wittgenstein's in St Giles' cemetery in Huntingdon Road.

Note.   This memoir owes a great deal to the help given by Peter Geach, John Geach, and Luke Gormally. I also owe thanks to Nicholas Denyer, Cora Diamond, Philippa Foot, Susan Haack, Hugh Mellor (who tracked down some missing minutes of the Moral Sciences Club) and my son Roger; also to Onora O'Neill and Anne Thomson, Principal and Archivist respectively of Newnham College.

JENNY TEICHMAN
New Hall, Cambridge

TONY BAINES

Anthony Cuthbert Baines
1912–1997

'ANYONE WHO PURSUES AN ARTISTIC LIFE often comes in contact with enthusiasts, and I always enjoy this when it happens to me. There are, of course, enthusiasts of two kinds: those whose enthusiasm throws their general judgement somewhat out of gear, and those who can keep their sense of proportion with their enthusiasm. Anthony Baines is emphatically of the latter group.' So wrote Adrian Boult in his introduction to Baines's Book *Wind Instrument and their History*.[1]

Enthusiasm is the word most frequently used in the reminiscences of those who knew Anthony Baines, that and his restless energy. Because of his publications his lifelong enthusiasm for music and musical instruments will never be forgotten, but his work as a professional musician, conductor, and teacher were equally important expressions of that enthusiasm and it could be said through them he played a seminal role in the development of early music and even public musical education. His enthusiasms were not limited to music: they included bird watching, wildflowers, and in his later years, drawing with pastels. His enthusiasm enlivened everything that he did, and spilled over into a desire to ensure that others enjoyed them too so that teaching was, for him, a necessary part of his own enthusiasms.

Anthony Baines, known as Tony, born on the 6 October 1912 in Chepstow Villas, London, W. 11, was the oldest of four children. His father, Cuthbert Edward Baines, held a position in the India Office and was author of several detective novels. His mother, Margaret Clemency, was

---

[1] A. C. Baines, *Wind Instruments and their History* (1957), p. 7.

Proceedings of the British Academy, **115**, 53–71. © The British Academy 2002.

the second daughter of Reginald Lane Poole, Fellow of Magdalen College, Oxford. It was his maternal grandparents, and their home in Oxford, which were to be powerful influences on the young Tony. There was no tradition of music making in the Baines family but Reginald Lane Poole, the medieval historian and British Academician, and his wife Rachel Emily,[2] were keen musicians, both active in amateur music-making.

With school days spent in London and holidays in Oxford or at Kidlington with grandfather, Baines's life was never dull. The children not only enjoyed music together but they also went on family sketching trips and would sit in a line, parent at either end, each member with an easel. Through her training as a zoologist his mother must have encouraged their observation of the world around them as well as fostering any artistic skills. But as Christopher writes it was music, particularly Bach, which surrounded them: 'to us children, music meant Bach. An aunt dragged us to Bach concerts in Oxford . . . At home, mother, a member of the Bach choir, hummed bits of Bach while doing the housework.'

Tony did not set out on a musical career; first a King's Scholar at Westminster School, he then won a Scholarship to read Chemistry at Christ Church, Oxford. In spite of having piano lessons as a young child, it was not until his days at Westminster that Tony was first, to use his phrase, 'gripped' by music. It was his fourth term which was to decide the general course of his future. Charles Thornton Lofthouse (appointed Director of Music shortly before) put on a series of lecture-recitals by top London professionals on the main orchestral woodwind instruments. As a result of these Tony was inspired to take up the clarinet which he was soon playing in the school orchestra; he also learnt to read full scores so as to lead a band which he founded. Whereas this school band only flourished for eight days he was more successful in spreading his enthusiasm among his brothers and sisters. As children he formed them into 'The Unhappy Family band' much to the despair of the neighbours in the flat below. His brother Christopher describes the band which

> was his way of drawing the family into music-making. He found the instruments (priced 10 shillings to 30 shillings) in a junk shop in King Street, chose and arranged traditional airs ('The beer they brewed at Burton' was our favourite) and wrote out parts complete with valve fingerings. Anthony led on F-trumpet, I was on cornopean, Francis on tenor trombone, Eularia on horn ... and father on a hybrid euphonium/baritone with rotary valves: the E flat bass was reserved for guests (mother did not take part). These instruments

[2] Rachael Emily (Malleson) Poole was the author of the *Catalogue of portraits in the possession of the university, colleges, city, and county of Oxford*, 3 vols. (Oxford, 1912–26).

formed the beginning of Anthony's collection, though he was not then a serious collector. There were regular complaints from the flat below, and we were once nearly threatened with eviction.[3]

This introduction to the fun of music making bore fruit in that his brother Francis became well known as the founder and leader of the Jaye Consort of Viols.

His interests in wind instruments led Tony to begin to take note of his observations of the military bands he saw in London. It is hardly surprising that in such a family of academics and writers he should not only take notes but also write them out in 'best'. He began making his own collection of old wind instruments by combing London junk and pawn shops. In 1927 he began the meticulous notebooks he was to keep throughout his life by compiling lists of instruments he saw played, notes about their players as well as lists of the instruments he saw stocked in the junk shops, together with his own drawings and newspaper cuttings. The bassoon was to be Tony's main instrument as the result of the gift of one from a much-admired relative, Colonel Ralph Henvey, RA. Henvey not only inspired Tony to take up the bassoon, he also encouraged his enjoyment of playing. Tony's brother, Christopher, still remembers the Colonel's Sunday visits which began with lunch and ended when he took Tony away with him to play in one of the amateur orchestras which met in the afternoon to 'romp through Beethoven and Brahms symphonies'. Tony remained an enthusiastic participant in Mrs Crump's orchestra at Oaks Farm in Croydon for many years, and in later life he often acted as the orchestra's conductor, although he always tried to creep in unnoticed to have 'a good blow' on his bassoon.

Probably as a result of his mother's influence (she had worked as a zoologist in Oxford under J. B. Haldane) Tony went up to Oxford to read science and got an honours degree in chemistry. However, his real interests became quite clear during his university years. His afternoons were spent cycling (having sold his motorcycle to buy a saxophone) around Oxfordshire scouring junk shops for instruments. In the evenings he indulged his love of jazz by playing clarinet and sax in a jazz band as well as playing bassoon at every opportunity. Just as he had watched the bands in London he observed the playing skills and traditions of the musicians, amateur and professional, playing in Oxford. Reminiscing about the Oxford musicians later[4] he described a musical world in which the best

---

[3] J. Rimmer, 'Anthony Cuthbert Baines 1912–1997—A Biographical Memoir', *The Galpin Society Journal*, LII (April 1999), 12–13.
[4] *Early Music*, ix (July 1981), 292.

string players were among the don's wives but in which the town musicians dominated the 'wind department'. Among these players he heard the individual styles of playing from those 'who loved their instrument but never listened to them on records or radio'. At Oxford he became fascinated by instrument history, first inspired by the purchase of a copy of Mersenne's Harmonicorum libri xvii of 1648.

After Oxford, Tony went to the Royal College of Music where, in his second year, he was awarded an open scholarship on the bassoon and studied orchestration with Gordon Jacob. In 1935 he was heard by Sir Thomas Beecham, then searching for a player of both bassoon and double bassoon for the London Philharmonic Orchestra. At the time the double bassoon (or contra) was not so common and Tony, with the help of the loan, and later gift, of a contra bassoon from Henvey, joined Beecham's London Philharmonic as bassoon and contra bassoon player, playing with them until 1939. At the outbreak of war there were no commissions for men of his age so, using slightly unconventional means of producing the required papers, he went to Swansea where he found a place as an Ordinary Seaman in the Merchant Navy on a ship bound for Buenos Aires and spent the first winter of the war at sea.

On his return he joined the army and in 1941 he received a commission to the Tank Regiment and volunteered for the Middle East. At that time, as the Mediterranean was mainly under enemy control, the journey to the Middle East had to be made around the coast of Africa. Once in Cairo, while awaiting posting to a battalion in the field, he made good use of his time acquiring invaluable knowledge of non-European instruments and music from Egyptian musicians. The diary, illustrated with pencil sketches and music transcriptions, which he kept throughout the voyage and days in Cairo shows his interest in everything he saw, birds, topography, ships and, of course, the music.

In 1942 he was wounded, and captured. He remembered little of the voyage to Italy and, on recovering consciousness was convinced that he must be in heaven as his first sight was that of a nun bringing him a tray containing a plate of pasta and a glass of wine. Recovering, he was sent to the Italian camp Chieti PG 21.

At a later date he was sent on through Italy, by train, to Germany. This journey was not without incident; he escaped twice: first by jumping from the moving train. This was no small feat as the trains had armed guards and search lights positioned on the roofs of the carriages. He escaped detection by rolling into a ditch beside the track. When the train had passed and all was still he made his way towards the light of a house;

luckily the inhabitants proved friendly and provided him with a change of clothes and food. For several months he was on the run disguised as an Italian shepherd; he later described nights spent hiding in straw filled mangers being woken by the cows' licking of his feet. Once again he turned this experience to good account making observations of the musical traditions he heard. Family legend has it that his English identity was only betrayed by the tins of Gold Flake tobacco in his pocket. Recaptured he was once again sent to Germany, this time in an army truck with members of a Sikh regiment who, incredibly, were still in possession of their kirpans. Tony borrowed one and cut his way out of the truck's canvas sides. It remained a source of pride to Tony that after this there was a price on his head although it was this bounty which hastened his recapture.

Once more a prisoner Tony was sent to Eichstatt where he remained until March 1945. Fellow POWs from Chieti and Eischstatt remember him with affection for the way in which his knowledge of and enthusiasm for music did much for morale. A contemporary description of Chieti:

> At the end of the year, Chieti was more like a university than a prison camp. There were eight hours a day of classes on philosophy, languages, literature, engineering, science, art, and military studies. There were scores of clubs, such as the Sketching Club, the Motor Club, the Angling Society, and various 'Old Boys' organizations. Major Lett ran the Chieti News Agency, with his weekly analysis of the progress of the war. There were six orchestras, including the Symphony orchestra of twenty players under the maestro Tony Baines ... Tony Baines wrote and conducted his first symphony in Chieti.
>
> The educators, the artists and artistes, were the creative aristocracy of camp life. They made a narrow life full and rich for those chaps who were the victims of an education that taught them 'more and more about less and less'. His escape was legendary amongst his fellow prisoners as was his total dedication to music, a contemporary description of him:
>
> 'Tony Baines was an artist. He always looked as though he needed scrubbing—even when he had just bathed. His clothes were worse than disreputable, his hair long and unkempt, and his gaze either dreamily soulful, or violently fanatical. When he dropped his baton it was to take up his vino mug!'
>
> The maestro worked like a demon, writing or arranging the music he later conducted. After his escape from the train to Germany, he spent several months wandering from village to village, collecting folk music, and imbibing the local wine.[5]

Peter Wood, a fellow POW, wrote of Tony's effect on morale and 'what he achieved under trying and difficult, at times exceedingly depressing

[5] G. Horner, *For You The War is Over* (1958). Photocopy of the text kindly supplied by Peter Wood.

conditions. He and his orchestra, in spite of cold, poor rations, lack of space and suspicious camp commandants, did much to keep up morale, to relieve the boredom and, on occasions, to keep our minds off the latest dangers which surrounded us. To him, and to Tommy Sampson who ran the other band, many thousands of POWs owe a tremendous debt for their courage, tenacity and enthusiasm.'[6]

The symphony orchestra described at Chieti was, in its early days, unorthodox. The first instruments were acquired by purchase from the town's music shop. Later the Red Cross would provide both instruments, music and records. At the beginning, however, the unconventional band consisted of two violins, a double bass, two clarinets, a tenor Sax and two trumpets. The programme of their first concert, with music all arranged by Tony from memory was: Schubert's ballet music from Rosamunde, three numbers from Handel's Water Music, a selection from Tchaikovsky's Casse-noisette, Borodin's dances from Prince Igor and a selection of arias from the end of Act I of Puccini's Bohème arranged for tenor and orchestra.

Throughout the time spent in the two camps Tony and his orchestras were to give a total of fifty-five performances of thirty-nine programmes; as he proudly noted this came to an average of five performances per month. Once sheet music was sent it all still had to be rearranged for the available musicians and instruments. Also, with only a small number of pieces in sheet music there was the need for more pieces to provide a varied programme. This deficit was supplied by the arrangements Tony made from piano scores, and transcriptions from gramophone records also sent by the Red Cross.

The first concert at Eichstatt proved to be a special experience from which Tony learnt an important lesson which was to remain with him for the rest of his life. The programme which was to be repeated for five performances was: Freischutz overture, Beethoven's Pastoral Symphony, parts being available for both of these, Ravel's Pavane, orchestrated by Barrie Grayson (lecturer in Fine Arts at Birmingham University) the Overture in F composed by Dugald Stewart (a fellow POW), and Wagner's Liebestod transcribed by Tony from piano transcriptions. In an article written for the *Philharmonic Post* Tony described the support he received from the other departments of expertise in the camp and described how he had the programme written out and posted without giving the audience any preliminary instruction. This was contrary to the advice that any

[6] Personal communication. Photocopy of the text kindly supplied by Peter Wood.

concert would attract an audience made up of people, most of whom had never heard classical music. The audience, unaware that the Beethoven Symphony had three separate movements, passed off the second movement of the Beethoven as the Pavane, 'Lieut Stewart scored a hit with the Storm, etc.' the Pavane was presumed to be the Liebestod (charming illusion) and we were asked what the two extra numbers were'.

As a result Tony began a scheme to ensure that the audiences learnt about the music that was to be played, as he wrote later: 'After that I introduced each piece individually at concerts, with prepared illustrations by the players. In addition, mid-week lectures on the programme were given by Capt. Barrie Grayson and the Gramophone Society correlated some programmes with ours. This led to the triumphant spectacle of two musically illiterate persons following a Haydn symphony on the full score. They identified the subjects by their shape on paper, and so traced them through the movements, deriving from this not athletic but wholly aesthetic pleasure.'[7]

Tony was not the only accomplished musician to be held in this camp, in addition to Grayson and Stewart mentioned above, in Italy they were joined by Herbert Perry, one of Walt Disney's musical collaborators. This information was imparted to the men in the camp and Perry was to conduct a programme containing several numbers used in 'Fantasia' to a packed audience. 'Once in Italy when Mr. Herbert Perry, American Army Air Corps, one of Walt Disney's six musical collaborators and on "Igor" terms with Stravinsky, was launched into the camp out of the blue, we told the camp all that and more, so that when he conducted a programme containing several numbers used in "Fantasia" he had a terrific success.'[8] Experiences such as these led Tony to realise the need to inform his audience about the programme they were to hear, and it may well have been as a result of this that he was to be involved continuously with educating about, and popularising, music for the rest of his life.

By the December of 1945 after demob Tony was described by Philip Whitaker in an *Evening Standard* review on Monday, 24 December, in his role as conductor of the London District Orchestra of Servicemen. He became involved with this orchestra as soon as he returned to London: 'Captain Baines conducted with immense enthusiasm and dash ... and if his forces were somewhat rough, they played with a rigour and life rare in semi-amateur orchestras, in a well-mixed programme which included a rarely heard symphony by C. P. E. Bach.'

[7] 'Audiences in Captivity', *London Philharmonic Post*, vol. III, no. 4 (March 1946), p. 3.
[8] Ibid.

The years immediately following the war were years of immense activity and innovation for Tony. In 1945 he returned to the London Philharmonic Orchestra as third bassoon and contra bassoon player. During this year he became joint secretary of the London Philharmonic's Arts Club with Philip Tongue. The Arts Club had been founded as 'The Orpheum Music Club' in 1942 at the theatre in Golders Green to be a meeting place for the patrons of the LPO to introduce new programmes and play chamber music. Interviewed by Whitaker for an article about his new role (*Evening Standard*, 15 April, 1946) Tony described his experiences with the audiences in the POW Camps and explained how he hoped to use the Arts Club as a vehicle for the education of new audiences, or old audiences to new music. The first event of the new regime which was held on 16 April 1945 was of chamber music; the Beethoven Septet, the Saint-Saens Trumpet Septet, and a Sonata for trumpet, horn, and trombone by Poulenc.

The programmes for the Arts Club were supported by many of the leading contemporary composers of the day. Events, if not involving members of the orchestra, might include recitals of recordings not obtainable in England at the time, such as the meeting held on 18 June of Modern American Music. In this, works by Leonard Bernstein, Walter Piston, Aaron Copeland, and Bernard Hermann were introduced by Bernstein. The following week a performance of Tippett's first and second string quartets by the Vandyl String Quartet were introduced with a lecture by Tippett on the Concerto for Double String Orchestra which was to be performed by the LPO on 30 June. The Arts Club did not limit its activities to the highbrow of modern composition but, on 9 July, included a performance by the LPO's own unofficial 'Swing Section' whose performers were made up of Jock Sutcliffe (oboe), Malcolm Arnold (trumpet), Anthony Baines (bassoon), George French (piano), Francis Baines (bass), and Dennis Blyth (drums). Edgar Jackson, writing in a review in the *Melody Maker* of 20 July 1946, describes how his preconceptions of finding the music played by 'a group of elderly long-hairs to patronise' were overturned by 'a group of rather bohemian, but serious-looking young men, who earlier in the evening had treated us to brilliant performances of works written by themselves in most modern "classical" vein, giving a burlesque of jazz that was full of ingenuity, wit and understanding'.

As well as being secretary Tony wrote for the Arts Club magazine. Through his short articles we meet Tony the professional musician. Some of his writing reveals the struggling musician on his first gigs lacking the necessary wardrobe, on one occasion finding himself without the required white waistcoat: 'Luckily I had a smooth shirt front on which I drew a very nice white waistcoat in pencil, complete with half-moon shading under the buttons, so that even the strings didn't spot it.'[9] In the same article he sums up the comparative virtues of various concert halls and reveals himself to be as pragmatic about the other numbers in the concert as any of his fellow bandsmen: 'The only places really worth playing in are the Queen's Hall and the Garden, though the Albert Hall is alright if you can park yourself at one of those little tunnel mouths which open onto the platform. Then, while the lads are slogging through the Dream of Gerontius, you, with your entries timed, are unofficially reclining in the buffet having tea.'[10]

In other articles his analytical eye is brought to bear on the various national styles of orchestral playing. A visit to Amsterdam commissioned by the orchestra enabled him to observe the Concertgebouw in rehearsal and he draws on this experience to compare them to the English players in '*Some Aspects of English Orchestral Playing*'. Observing the rehearsal Tony noticed that members of the orchestra not playing were sent to the back of the auditorium to comment upon the balance and ensemble; expressing his initial astonishment at this practice he then observes 'naturally an orchestra composed of ninety excellent executants, each with a conductor's insight into the sound of a piece as a whole, would have the miraculous ensemble of the Concertgebouw Orchestra'.[11]

In 'Various Schools of Orchestral Wind-Playing' he makes a more detailed study of the wind 'or "the breeze" (in the words of a famous foreign conductor who had little English)' of various national orchestras. Here he describes winds sounds and timbres almost lost today: 'Debussy's colouristic or impressionist use of wind requires tone colours as piquant, strongly characterised, and as distinct from each other as possible. This is particularly noticeable in the lower wind. In French orchestras it is impossible to confuse the horns, with their bright globular sound, almost bell-like, with the bassoons, whose hoarse tones strangely resemble human speech, while their trombones make a thin shivering noise like a Wimshurst machine.'[12]

---

[9] 'An Apprenticeship in the Musical Profession', A. C. Baines Papers, Pitt Rivers Museum, VI, 6.
[10] Ibid.
[11] 'Some Aspects of English Orchestral Playing', *London Philharmonic Post*, vol. III, no. 10 (March 1947), p. 3.
[12] 'Various Schools of Orchestral Wind-Playing', *London Philharmonic Post*, vol. III, no. 5 (May 1946), p. 6.

Tony's own wide knowledge is shown by his reflections on the traditions of English players' styles such as in his reflections on the celebrated eighteenth-century oboist William Parkes's playing of a concerto between the opera acts at Covent Garden: 'Imagine relaxing between Cav. and Pag. to a new clarinet concerto played—and preferably composed, complete with variations on "Ilkley Moor"—by Mr. Kell. Alas we are too serious, and fireworks are only allowed when consecrated by a great composer.'[13]

This excess of seriousness is bemoaned by him in the article 'Middlebrow" which must have been written with his experiences of his fellow POWs in mind. This article was written as a result of seeing programme notes 'when a Tchaikovsky symphony was cunningly debunked in an actual programme!' He likens this to greengrocers 'living on the brink of rebellion through having to feast their eyes daily upon great heaps of potatoes and cabbages, in spite of their souls' craving for slender dishes with pomegranates, mangoes and watermelons. But they do not steal round the shop whispering into customers' ears: whatever you do, don't touch cabbages; it is *so* vulgar to eat cabbages.'[14] He then continues to describe the wisdom of the musical public who migrated from the bandstand to the concert hall.

> We are jolly lucky that the public's first act on taking control has shown such fine discrimination, particularly as they entrust us musicians with the job of selecting the poisons. With the latter we have to be very careful; an overdose of French music, of Bartok, or of our own moderns, sentences us to a fortnight of solid Beethoven and Tchaikovsky to restore the balance sheet to what orchestras bank managers generously concede as sound.[15]

In the November of 1946 a series of recitals were given of musical editions researched by Tony which went back to the original sources, or were given on historic instruments. These concerts started with a concert of music played on a piano of 1788, followed by a concert of seventeenth- and eighteenth-century wind music. To mark Handel's birthday in the February of 1947 a concert was planned of the Firework Music and Water Music from the original scores. These plans were reported in *The Star*, 20 September 1946, *Shocks by the Score* by Preston Benson,

[13] 'Various Schools of Orchestral Wind-Playing', *London Philharmonic Post*, vol. III, no. 5 (May 1946), p. 6.
[14] 'Middlebrow', *London Philharmonic Post*, vol. III, no. 10 (March 1947), p. 8.
[15] 'Various Schools of Orchestral Wind-Playing', *London Philharmonic Post*, vol. III, no. 5 (May 1946), p. 6.

The Philharmonic Arts Club is displaying a lot of enterprise. At a concert next month, music will be played on a grand piano of 1788, a harpsichord and a modern grand to display the subtleties of piano tone development.

There will also be a concert of 18th-century flutes, oboes, bassoons, hand-horn, trumpets, and strings. To be followed by a 17th-century one with black cornets, sackbuts, dulcians, and so on.

An orchestra to play these old-time instruments—all genuinely old and playable, though demanding their own technique—is being formed. On Handel's birthday next February, it is proposed to play his Firework Music and Water Music on the original instruments.

Professional orchestral musicians are the mainspring of this move, for what fun they can get out of it. Leading spirit is Anthony Baines, contra-bassoon player.

Tony's earlier inclusion when conducting the London District Orchestra of Servicemen of that 'rarely heard symphony by C. P. E. Bach' was an indication of his interests in early music and his inclusion of Arts Club concerts on instruments from his by then substantial collection was another way to give the public insights into the music they might hear on the concert platform.

Since the war his collection of instruments had grown by leaps and bounds, and he also had a growing circle of like-minded friends. Together, in 1946 they formed the Galpin Society named (at Tony's suggestion) after the foremost British authority and collector up to that time. The Inaugural Meeting of the Galpin Society was held in Trinity College of Music on Saturday, 17 May 1947. In contrast to the Arts Club, the Galpin Society was to concentrate its activities on the publication of a journal which would record the current contributions being made in the study of musical instruments. This journal, which Tony was to edit for twenty-one years, was the first ever dedicated to musical instruments. At its inaugural meeting a concert was held which included a selection of French Military Music, c.1670 and Ayres to the Lute and Viols performed by friends and colleagues who included Eric Halfpenny, Edgar Hunt, and Thurston Dart. The programme of the following year also made use of recordings used to demonstrate the effects of various tuning systems as well as a performance of late eighteenth-century marches 'performed according to the original published full scores and on instruments of the time.'[16]

In October 1948 Tony was appointed Assistant Conductor of the London Philharmonic Orchestra, the office to begin on 1 January 1949.

[16] 'Programme of Music—Saturday, 22nd May 1948', *The Galpin Society* (1948).

As well as conducting during the concert season, he was able to develop his passion for introducing music to new audiences as the programmes included concerts for children. Works he conducted included the performances, at the Theatre Royal, Brighton, of Benjamin Britten's *Let's Make an Opera* which he shared with Norman Del Mar. This was followed by a time in the International Ballet Company as Associate Conductor from February 1950 up to the disbandment of the company in 1953.

Throughout this period Tony continued his study of early music; during his visits to his parents, then living at Great Rissington, he began his research into the cornetts at Christ Church and their repertory as well as his work on his historic editions of the Handel Water Music and Fireworks Music. He also made many visits to the Pitt Rivers Museum to start planning of his first book, *Woodwind Instruments and Their History*, as well as beginning the work on the catalogue of the collection of bagpipes there, later published as '*Bagpipes*'. At that time his brother Francis was coach to the Oxford Music Club and Tony would occasionally deputise for him. While working and on tour with the International Ballet other members spent the afternoons visiting the cinema but Tony used the time to visit the local museums and study any of the instruments he found. It was through this company that Tony first met Patricia Stammers, who was later to become his wife, when she was appointed oboist in 1950. Patricia Baines describes these days:

> The Ballet toured all over the British Isles, including Dublin and Belfast, performing some of the classic ballets which required the large theatres of the bigger cities; much of the time was spent in the North and Midlands. Tony did much recopying of parts to make them more legible, as well as some re-arranging. He transposed the National Anthem into A major to get round the copyright fees; deputy players of the orchestra had to be told of this unusual key. In his time off, he made good use of local libraries and museums for his musical instrument research. The Ballet made two tours abroad without the British orchestra, one to Verona and the other to Barcelona. On these occasions, Tony went ahead of the company to rehearse the local orchestras in readiness for performing soon after the Company arrives. The fruits of his researches in Oxford (performing editions of *Music for Sagbutts and Cornets* and the *Water Music*) were published during this period and he also provided a number of entries on instruments for *Grove V* which was issued in 1954. At the end of 1953 the International Ballet had been disbanded and from then on Tony's main interest was in research and writing.[17]

---

[17] J. Rimmer, 'Anthony Cuthbert Baines 1912–1997—A Biographical Memoir', *The Galpin Society Journal*, LII (April 1999), p. 20.

Tony's arrangement of Handel's Water Music pioneered the new style of music which sought to inform the player of earlier performance practice. Up to this period the commonly performed score was that by Hamilton Harty. This popular arrangement used an anachronistic romantic orchestration. This was heard with appreciation by the critics and described as going 'with a wonderful swing and naturalness and seems preferable'.[18]

Other performing editions of early music followed, one such being Lawes' music for Milton's Masque of Comus which was first performed at Ludlow Castle in 1954.

After the disbandment of the International Ballet Company, work in the performing world was hard to find, and in 1955 Tony went to teach wind instruments and become bandmaster at Uppingham school followed by a spell at Dean Close, Cheltenham. An article written as a tribute after leaving Uppingham once again comments on his enthusiasm and gives an idea of his influence as a teacher:

> Perhaps his outstanding merit is his lively enthusiasm and his ability to inspire in others the feeling of being in contact with the life-blood of music itself, rather than with pageants or arid symbols. The benefits of his work with the Band must be obvious to all ... Like many greatly gifted people, Anthony Baines does not suffer fools gladly, but nevertheless he well lives up to the definition of woodwind players given in his book, which refers to them as 'some of the most kindly and understanding people in the world' ... The Uppingham community will be the less colourful for his absence.[19]

In the brief period before returning to Uppingham for a second period between 1961 and 1964 Tony returned to London where he concentrated on writing and giving visiting lectures. One of these, at Harrow, was written up in *The Harrovian*, 10 December 1959. Entitled 'The Pied Piper' Tony is compared to the Pied Piper:

> So the Pied Piper has come to Harrow, disguised by a moustache. During the long years since 1376 which he has spent hidden in the depths of Koppelberg Hill, he has learnt to play, in addition to 'his long pipe of smooth straight cane,' the cow horn, the post horn, the basset horn, the distant horn and the hand horn ... But he has also mastered the cornet and the trombone, the shawm and the Spanish bagpipes, the key bugle and the serpent; single reed, double reed and brass instruments from most countries in Europe and every century since the Renaissance. He casts his spell with his talk, before even he starts to blow ... At only one moment in Mr Baines' display did we suspect that we were being

---

[18] 'Concert Review', *Surrey Times*, 5 May 1951.
[19] 'A. C. Baines esq.', *Uppingham School Magazine* (1958).

addressed by an ordinary mortal, when he searched uneasily with his fingers along his tuba for keys which were not there, only to discover that he had put in the mouthpiece the wrong way round ... He made himself joyful, and by the infection of his joy betrayed his real identity.[20]

Although these years as a school teacher must have been a big contrast at first from his life as a performing artist, they did give him the time to write. Now his notebooks were the resources for a number of books on musical instruments. Each one was, in its own way, innovatory in its field. The first, *Woodwind Instruments and their History*, was published in 1957. A colleague once described these books as being standard works used as much for reference as dictionaries, but books that once opened are very difficult to put down. The clue to this is in his evocative writing style, a style inspired by the observation of that rare combination of professional musician and scholar. His description of the orchestral flautist is one example:

> A flute player in the orchestra, leaning back comfortably in his chair, often forcibly brings to mind the god Pan resting against his forest tree and fluting magic spells; and still more so when the image is confirmed in sound as in *L'Après* ... [21]

Again describing the reed instruments:

> Oboists, clarinettists and bassoonists are entirely dependent upon a short-lived vegetable matter of merciless capriciousness, with which, however, when it behaves, are wrought perhaps the most tender and expressive sounds in all wind music.[22]

No one but a bassoon player could surely have written:

> The bright reediness of the oboe is transformed into a dark mellowness—a strange, unique quality impossible to describe adequately in words, but something between a male voice and a horn, and in many ways sweeter and more pleasing than either.[23]

Woodwind instruments and their History was followed by his monograph *Bagpipes*, the catalogue of the Pitt Rivers Museum's collection in 1960. This is a remarkable catalogue in that it is rarely recognisd as such but is still lauded as the only book which describes bagpipes in all traditions, excepting those few not represented in the Museum's collections.

---

[20] 'The "Pied Piper"', *The Harrovian*, 10 December 1959.
[21] *Woodwind Instruments and their History* (1957), p. 52.
[22] Ibid., p. 76.
[23] Ibid., p. 149.

European and American Musical Instruments published in 1967 is a remarkable book in that in it Tony was to bring together photographs of instruments from both continents. It is remarkable not only because of this achievement but because of the light it sheds on the breadth of Tony's knowledge of collections worldwide. In the introduction Tony describes it as being 'intended primarily for collectors and curators who are not already specialists in musical instruments, as a help to identification of types and varieties of the non-keyboard instruments of Western Society from the Renaissance onwards'.[24] It is an invaluable book not only for these but also for students and has become known by some as the musical instrument Bible.

This was followed a year later in 1968 by the official catalogue of non-keyboard instruments in the collection of the Victorian and Albert Museum; Pope-Hennessy in his introduction describes how

> The introductory notes that he has provided for each section in this Catalogue are therefore no mere superficial essays on the groups of instruments concerned, but are the quintessence of his wide and deep knowledge of this subject, framed in such a way as to show how the particular instruments in the Collection fit into the history of musical instruments as a whole.[25]

It is in this catalogue that Tony demonstrated his balanced appreciation of instruments as objects which can have more than one purpose. Here he writes of the place of instruments among objects of the decorative arts, and as such objects to be kept and preserved as well as to be played. He counterbalances Hayes' belief that historic instruments should be played and not kept in locked cases by reminding the reader that in many cases the decoration was not necessary to the instrument's musical function and that instrument makers created beautiful instruments to be admired for their decoration alone:

> In every type of musical instrument this is evident, either in the calculated beauty of form alone or, more often, in conjunction with decoration that is not essential to the instrument's musical function. And conversely, therefore, musical instruments may be legitimately considered in the light of their contribution to the study and enjoyment of the decorative crafts as well as to the world of Music.[26]

Through the period he edited *The Galpin Society Journal* as well as the Society's first book *Musical Instruments through the Ages* (1961). In his

---

[24] *European and American Musical Instruments* (1966), p. v.
[25] Victoria and Albert Museum. Catalogue of musical instruments, vol. II (Her Majesty's Stationery Office, 1968), p. v.
[26] Ibid. p. xii.

introduction, after describing the Society and its aims, he outlined the
importance of the study of historic instruments:

> the true comparison of an instrument of (say) Bach's day with the modern form
> is similar to a comparison of the styles of musical composition across the same
> interval of time, the older bringing immense intensity and variety of expression
> within a field of techniques that today may appear a relatively narrow one.[27]

Over the years Tony made numerous contributions to the *Journal*:
articles, Notes and Queries and Reviews. His article, on the James Talbot
Manuscript at Christ Church appeared in the *Journal*'s first issue and
he was largely responsible for encouraging others to transcribe and
annotate the sections of which they were specialists. Together with Claus
Wachsmann he translated the Hornbostel–Sachs Classification of
Musical Instruments.[28] This is not merely a translation but a careful correlation of the English words used by Sachs in his *Reallexikon*.[29] It is
owing to this first publication of the system in English that it has become
the standard used by academics and curators the world over.

His book *Brass Instruments*, published in 1976, demonstrates the synthesis of a lifetime's observation of instruments and their use, together
with the scholar's knowledge and the professional's awareness of contemporary techniques such as the preference of natural trumpet players for
playing an instrument with fingerholes and a modern mouthpiece. He
writes with the gentlest of critical touches:

> It is a modern trumpeter's training and skill exactly to centre every note as he
> produces it, which must make it more difficult to 'uncentre' notes on a natural
> trumpet. Moreover, players are on the whole reluctant to commit themselves to
> prolonged study of this instrument using a mouthpiece which has genuinely
> baroque rim, internal gradients and backbore; for it may prove that with such
> a mouthpiece the problem of baroque trumpet intonation can best be
> conquered by the modern artist—and indeed its full musical quality revealed
> also.[30]

In this monograph he did not only describe the histories of brass
instruments but also broke new ground in stressing the importance of
contemporary attitudes to playing techniques, embouchures, and
mouthpieces.

---

[27] *Musical Instruments through the Ages* (1961), p. 17.
[28] A. C. Baines & K. P. Wachsmann, 'Erich M. Von Hornbostel and Curt Sachs: Classification
of Musical Instruments translated from the original German', *Galpin Society Journal*, XIV,
3–29.
[29] C. Sachs, *Reallexikon der Musikinstrumente* (Berlin, 1913).
[30] *Brass Instruments their History and Development* (1976), p. 136.

His last book *The Oxford Companion to Musical Instruments* (1992), was a compilation and editing of articles written for the *New Oxford Companion to Music* (1983). The style of his own articles is still unmistakable, for example the entry for the bassoon, betraying his love of the instrument:

> In the classical orchestra especially the bassoon holds a unique position, not only as the chief solo melodic voice in the tenor range (so notable, expressing every mood, in the works of Beethoven), but equally as the all-purpose melodic 'octave doubler', blending, without asserting its individuality, at the octave blow with any of the smaller woodwind or equally with the violins.[31]

In 1970 Tony was appointed first Lecturer/Curator of the Bate Collection, where he was until his retirement in 1982. He publshed a catalogue of the instruments in 1976, in which as well as a brief entry for each instrument there was also a list of measurements for those of greatest interest to makers. Those who attended his lectures will not forget them, not only because of the content of his teaching and the depth of his learning, but also because of his own inimitable lecturing style and his endearing battles with modern technology. From his army years he had used his collection of instruments to illustrate his lectures, about the time of his marriage he had sold most of his collection to Philip Bate. Now he had them to hand once more, together with the collection he had made since, he enjoyed the use of them both in lectures and, the Bate Collection being a playing collection, in the founding of the Bate Band which gave concerts of Haydn and Mozart on the Collection's instruments. These were among the earliest performances of music of this period on original instruments.

In Oxford he was elected a Supernumerary Fellow of University College in 1975, in 1977 he received the Degree of D.Litt., and in 1980 was elected an Ordinary Fellow of the British Academy for services to music. Other honours followed; in 1985 he received the Curt Sachs Award from the American Musical Instrument Society. On the occasion of his eightieth birthday the garden at the Balfour Gallery of the Pitt Rivers Museum was named the Baines Music Garden after him and was dedicated to the growth of plants associated with music. In 1994, he was given an Honorary Degree of Doctor of Music by the University of Edinburgh.

This review of his working musical life is only one side of the man, however. Much as he loved music this was not his only interest. The diary of his journey around Africa shows his love of bird spotting which was a

---

[31] *The Oxford Companion to Musical Instruments* (Oxford, 1992), pp. 28–9.

lifelong passion. Another interest was inspired as, recuperating after an accident, he noticed the 'weeds' in the garden; this grew into a passionate hobby and he produced beautiful botanical notebooks recording the wild-flowers he saw. In the last four years of his life he found another interest: drawing and pastel painting.

He was equally enthusiastic in his support of his wife's work and inter-ests. Some of the line drawings which illustrate her prize-winning book, *Spinning Wheels, Spinners and Spinning*[32] are his. The clear observation of the mechanics of the spinning process is the same with which he drew the complex key systems of wind instruments. The scientist's love of finding out exactly how something worked, combined with his interest in botany spurred him on in his support for growing the flax and woad which visi-tors to the garden at their Oxford home will remember. As part of this Tony helped to prepare flax for spinning and dyeing.[33]

A true scholar for whom the passion of research was all in all, through every encomium and honour received he remained characteristically unassuming. He could be very impatient; tussles with modern technology, modern record players, and worse, computers, were a waste of time, and people who wasted his time were also given short shrift. He was, however, the most inspiring of teachers for those who loved the subject. He could make a student feel that he was just as enthusiastic about a discovery as though he had made it himself, even though he had probably known about it for some time. His writings are not only academically erudite but always fresh and enjoyable to read, his books once opened for reference are difficult to put down. His notebooks showed how hard he worked at his writing, its seeming effortlessness being the result of years of observation as well as working and reworking translations.

Tony Baines had a great impact on the musical life of the twentieth century. His scholarly advocacy for research into performance practice and his understanding of the insights to be gained through performance on original instruments have both added much to the appreciation of early music. His support for what he called the 'middlebrow' and enthu-siasm for opening up music to a wider public popularised music just at the point at which radio and television were able to carry on from his lead. His books, still central to the study of instruments, continue to be unsur-passed as works of reference and they remain witness to his scholarship and enthusiasm. His joy for music enriched life for many; this is recalled

[32] P. M. Baines, *Spinning Wheels, Spinners and Spinning* (1977).
[33] P. Baines, *Linen, hand spinning and weaving* (1989).

most evocatively in his own words describing the Bate Band's music for 'summer garden parties, white wine under the chairs and our technical blemishes waft aside among the big trees and the mildly interested listeners across the lawn. Hooray for the antiques and non-captive audience.'[34]

HÉLÈNE LA RUE

The Bate Collection of Musical Instruments, Oxford

[34] Editorial, *Early Music*, ix (July 1981), 292.

CHARLES BOXER   *Walter Stoneman*

Charles Ralph Boxer
1904–2000

CHARLES BOXER died on 27 April 2000 at the age of 96.[1] He was the most
distinguished historian of seventeenth-century Portuguese and Dutch
colonial history of his generation, but he also wrote widely on the history
of Japan, China, Indonesia, India, Brazil, and Portugal itself. When he
died he had 333 academic publications to his name including over thirty
major books.[2] Boxer served in the army from 1924 to 1947 and was a prisoner of war in Hong Kong from 1941 until the end of the war. He held
the Camões Chair of Portuguese at King's College London from 1947 to
1967, with a short interlude in 1951–2 when he occupied the chair of Far
Eastern History at SOAS. He was elected Fellow of the British Academy
in 1957. After his retirement from King's he taught at Indiana University
and was appointed to the chair of the Expansion of Europe Overseas at
Yale which he held from 1969–72. In 1997, shortly before his death,

[1] Much of the information in this biographical note has already appeared in earlier pieces written by M. Newitt after Charles Boxer's death. *Charles Ralph Boxer 1904–2000* (2000); 'Charles
R. Boxer', a memorial address given at King's College, 11 July 2000; 'Professor C. R. Boxer
1904 2000' for the *Journal of Renaissance Studies* (forthcoming); a review of D. Alden, *Charles
R. Boxer: an Uncommon Life* for Bulletin of Spanish Studies (forthcoming).
[2] Compiling bibliographies of Boxer's writings has become a minor cottage industry. S. George
West produced *A List of the Writings of Charles Ralph Boxer published between 1926 and 1984*
(1984) to celebrate Boxer's eightieth birthday. In 1999 the Centro de Estudos do Mar and the
Associação Fernão Mendes Pinto published *Homenagem ao Professor Charles Ralph Boxer*
(Figueira do Foz, 1999); Alden, *Charles R. Boxer* added a bibliographical appendix 'The
Writings of Charles Boxer, 1985–1996' pp. 581–5; an attempt to publish a comprehensive
bibliography was made in 'The Charles Boxer Bibliography, *Portuguese Studies*, 17 (2001),
246–76.

Proceedings of the British Academy, **115**, 75–99. © The British Academy 2002.

King's College established a chair in history named after him. In 1947 he married the American author, Emily Hahn, and had two daughters, Carola and Amanda.

Boxer was a very public figure and at the same time a very private man. He left no memoirs or diaries and gave few interviews about his life, but his early life with Emily Hahn was the subject of two books written by her, one of which, *China to Me,* became something of a best seller. A lengthy and exhaustive biography was published by Dauril Alden in 2001 entitled *Charles R. Boxer: an Uncommon Life.*[3]

Family and upbringing

Charles Boxer's family can be traced back only to the eighteenth century and may have been of Huguenot origin.[4] Three Boxers served in the Royal Navy during the Napoleonic Wars, one rising to the rank of rear admiral. His grandfather was drowned when the experimental warship, *Captain,* on which he was an officer, capsized in a gale. His father, Hugh Boxer, was an officer in the Lincolnshire regiment. He served with his regiment in many imperial postings and took part in Kitchener's Sudan campaign of 1897–8 where he was wounded at the battle of Atbara. Although afflicted with a limp for the rest of his life, Hugh Boxer was able to return to regimental duties, and in 1892 married Jeannie Patterson who came from a family of wealthy Australian landowners. Their first son, Myles, was born in 1898 and, after a second son had died of meningitis, their third child, Charles Ralph, was born at Sandown in the Isle of Wight on 8 March 1904. Charles's sister Beryl, the last child of the family, was born in 1905.[5]

Charles's maternal grandmother owned a country estate in Dorset known as Conygar, and it is there that the Boxers spent much of their childhood, inevitably acquiring something of the tastes and values of the minor rural gentry of the period. Remarkably little is known about

---

[3] Emily Hahn's main autobiographical works which refer extensively to Charles Boxer are *China to Me* (New York, 1944); *England to Me* (1950); *Hong Kong Holiday* (New York, 1946); *Times and Places* (New York, 1970). A biography of Emily Hahn was written by Ken Cuthbertson, *No One Said Not to Go* (1998). See also Dauril Alden, *Charles R. Boxer: an Uncommon Life* (Lisbon, 2001).

[4] For information about Boxer's early life see Miles Clark, *High Endeavours. The Extraordinary Life and Adventures of Miles and Beryl Smeeton* (1991), chap. 1; Alden, *Charles R. Boxer*, chaps. 1 & 2.

[5] For the life of Beryl see Clark, *High Endeavours.*

Charles Boxer's formative early years. He attended a catholic day school in Gibraltar where his father was stationed for four years, before being sent to Wellington College in 1918 at the age of 13. Wellington was a public school which made special provision for the sons of officers and prepared its pupils for Sandhurst and a career in the army. Charles passed through the College leaving few traces in its records, playing rugby, joining the OTC and winning a prize for recitation—apparently a typical and wholly unexceptional school career. In 1922, having been rejected by the navy because of poor eyesight, he went to Sandhurst. From there he was commissioned into his father's regiment, the Lincolnshires, in January 1924.

Some time during this period, this rather ordinary and unobtrusive younger son of an army officer had begun the study of the languages which were later to give him the basis for his remarkable scholarly career. He also began to study the history of the Far East, approaching it through an interest in maritime history, possibly derived from the exploits of his naval ancestors. While still only a second lieutenant, he used the long periods of peacetime leave to visit archives and learned societies in Britain, the Netherlands and Portugal making contacts with leading scholars including Edgar Prestage and Georg Schurhammer. He also began to collect books, which became a life long passion and led to the formation of one of the twentieth century's greatest private libraries. In 1926, at the age of 22, he published his first academic article 'O 24 de junho 1622: uma façanha dos Portugueses' in the *Boletim da Agencia das Colónias.*[6] He was meanwhile working on what would be his first two major publications, the editions in translation of the *Commentaries of Ruy Freyre de Andrada* and the *Journals of Maarten Harpertszoon Tromp.*[7]

By 1930, although still only 26 years old, Boxer's ties to his family had been loosened if not entirely severed. In 1915 his father had been killed in action at Ypres—the story being told that he had led his men over the top leaning on the arm of his batman, and in 1929, after suffering depression for many years, his mother committed suicide.[8] Although Boxer never

[6] 'O 24 de junho 1622: Uma Façanha dos Portugueses', *Boletim da Agencia das Colónias*, 2 (1926), 117–28.
[7] C. R. Boxer, *Commentaries of Ruy Freyre de Andrada* (1930) and the *The Journal of Maarten Harpertszoon Tromp* (1930).
[8] The fullest account of Hugh Boxer's death is to be found in Clark, *High Endeavours*, pp. 13–14 where it is made clear he was the victim of 'friendly fire' from British artillery. Cuthbertson, *No One Said Not to Go*, pp. 198–9 gives the story of the batman; Alden, *Charles R. Boxer*, p. 33 studiously omits all detail about Hugh's death.

talked about these events, or the subsequent suicide of his mother's brother, their effect on a young man can be well imagined.

At this stage Charles showed no sign of wanting to depart from an orthodox military career and, as a second lieutenant, he served with his regiment in Northern Ireland and at Aldershot. In 1930, however, his career took a very distinctive turn when he was seconded as a language officer to the Far East to specialise in Japanese.

The Far East

Charles Boxer's career in the Far East was to last until 1946, with one interlude between 1933 and 1935, and was to be the most adventurous period of his life. It was a period when he demonstrated to the full his ability to follow two wholly separate careers while at the same time travelling, leading a hectic social life and pursuing his all absorbing hobby of book collecting.

In 1930 Boxer sailed for Japan where, after a stay in Tokyo, he was seconded first to the 38th Nara regiment and then to the NCO School at Nagoya on which he wrote a report for the War Office. Boxer travelled widely throughout Japan and became an enthusiastic admirer of Japanese culture, meeting scholars and collectors like George Sansom, Jean Charles Pabst, and Okamoto Yoshitomo, becoming an expert in the Japanese martial art of Kendo and learning to speak Japanese 'like a Geisha'. He also made important contacts among the Japanese military and formed a healthy respect for their ability.

In July 1933 he returned to Britain via the Dutch East Indies and resumed his regimental duties with the Lincolnshires, as well as his book collecting and other scholarly pursuits. In 1935 after the suicide of his uncle, Myles, Boxer inherited the Conygar estate in Dorset and briefly established himself there as a member of the fox-hunting landed gentry. However, at the end of the year, after a spell at the War Office, he was promoted to the rank of captain and sent to Hong Kong as an intelligence officer. As usual Boxer combined business with scholarship and pleasure. He travelled in the company of his sister Beryl via Portugal, the Siberian railway, Manchuria, and Japan.

In January 1937 Boxer took up his duties as an officer in the intelligence gathering unit known as the Far Eastern Combined Bureau. During the following years he used his position to make frequent visits to Macao. He wrote extensively on the history of that small Portuguese colony, and in 1937 published there *Biblioteca Boxeriana* the catalogue of his by now famous library.[9] However, scholarship was also a cover for intelligence activities and Macao provided him with some of his most important sources of information. In July 1939, after another visit to Japan, he sent a report to the War Office warning about the vulnerability of Hong Kong to a Japanese attack. He also made frequent visits to China and in August 1940 tried to establish an exchange of intelligence information between the Chinese and British. In May 1941 Boxer was promoted to the rank of major and became the senior intelligence officer in Hong Kong.

Military and intelligence responsibilities in no way interrupted Charles's scholarly work or his social life. In 1938 alone he published no fewer than eleven academic articles, while his personal life underwent radical changes. As he later admitted 'It always happens when one lives in Hong Kong, you know, more than four years, one either becomes a hopeless drunkard, or one marries. I did both'.[10] In June 1939 he had married a teacher, Ursula Tulloch, but the marriage was not a success and in April 1940 Ursula left for Australia and later settled in Sri Lanka. She eventually divorced Charles in July 1945. Boxer meanwhile had met and struck up a friendship with the American writer Emily Hahn (always known as Mickey) who was engaged in writing a book about the Soong sisters—the wives respectively of Sun Yat Sen and Chiang Kai Chek. In 1940 Mickey moved to Hong Kong and rented a flat next door to Charles. In February 1941 the couple announced that Mickey was expecting Charles's child. Their daughter, Carola, was born on 17 October 1941, just two months before the fall of Hong Kong to the Japanese. In 1944 Mickey was to publish an amusing, but probably highly fictionalised, account of her affair with Charles Boxer in a volume entitled *China to Me*.

This period of Charles's life was deeply significant in other ways. Academically it was highly productive and the publications of those years laid the foundations for the important books on Far Eastern history that he was to produce after the war. However, his intelligence activity, and his meeting with leading political figures in the Far East, deeply influenced his political and moral outlook. Although he came from a family with a strong tradition of military service and shared many of the tastes of the public school educated gentry who were the mainstay of the empire, he

---

[9] *Biblioteca Boxeriana: Being a Short Title Catalogue of the Books and Manuscripts in the Library of Captain C. R. Boxer (March 1937)* (Macau, Tipografia Mercantil, 1937).
[10] Quoted in Cuthbertson, *No One Said Not to Go*, p. 172.

had always stood somewhat apart from his contemporaries, not least in his taste for book collecting and scholarship. Now he witnessed the rapid dissolution of the imperial system in the Far East. Boxer saw the hollowness of the racial arrogance on which the empire was built and predicted the inevitable triumph of Asian nationalism. He saw the Japanese as the Asiatic power which would inevitably supplant the British and, although all the evidence suggests that he fulfilled his military and intelligence duties with efficiency, he was deeply sceptical about the cause for which he was supposed to be fighting. Mickey remembered him saying on one occasion 'the day of the white man is done out here . . . we're finished and we know it. All this is exactly like the merriment of Rome before the great fall'.[11]

War

Japan declared war on Britain on 7 December 1941.[12] When the attack on Hong Kong began a day later, Boxer was the British officer detailed to meet the Japanese and respond to their demands for surrender. On 20 December, while attempting to rally some troops who had lost their officers, he was hit in the back by a sniper. He lay for many hours, losing blood before being removed to the Queen Mary Hospital. As he later said to Mickey, 'I lay there wishing I would hurry up and die, because it was cold out there'.[13] He remained in hospital for nine months but in November 1942, having refused to sign a no escape pledge, he was sent to the Argyle Street Camp. There, as a senior intelligence officer, he was one of those who knew of the existence of various escape plans and of the secret radio receivers which provided the news which was disseminated through the camps. The Japanese began to discover the existence of a secret communications network in May 1943 and in September Boxer himself was arrested. When he was finally tried by a military court in December, a number of officers and men had already been executed and Charles believed that this was to be his fate also. In the event he received a five year sentence of imprisonment.

Until March 1944 Charles and his fellow prisoners were kept in severe

---

[11] Hahn, *China to Me*, p. 153.
[12] For Charles's role in war time Hong Kong see Alden, *Charles R. Boxer*, Hahn, *China to Me* and *Hong Kong Holiday*. Also Oliver Lindsay, *The Lasting Honour, the Fall of Hong Kong 1941* (1982).
[13] Hahn, *China to Me*, p. 274.

solitary confinement—much of the time being made to sit on the floor and being fed starvation rations. When this ended, prison conditions somewhat improved and in December the sentences were cut to three and a half years. In June 1945 the prisoners were moved to Canton for the last two months of the war. Japan surrendered on 15 August and four days later Charles and a fellow officer were treated to a ceremonial reconciliation meal, dressed bizarrely in white uniforms and shoes specially made for the occasion, before being sent back to Hong Kong. On the way his train had to survive an attack by Chinese guerrillas.

Once back in Hong Kong, apparently little the worse for his experiences in prison, Charles resumed his duties as an intelligence officer, one of the first tasks being the location and then identification of the bodies of the officers and men executed in 1943. He also began the search for his library which had been stolen by the Japanese and which was to be a major preoccupation for the next two years.

The war, which did so much to destroy the British Empire and which proved physically and psychologically devastating for so many of those who experienced it, helped to turn Charles Boxer from an army officer of a slightly cynical disposition, who enjoyed the social life of the colony and who had a reputation as a gifted amateur scholar, into one of the most powerful historians and writers of the post war era. A close friend, Frank Lequin, wrote after his death that 'perhaps his greatest talent, surpassing his many other talents, was his acceptance of the innate cruelty of man, his capacity to transform negative into positive energy without complaints and traumatic hatred'.[14] The need to survive starvation, solitary confinement, and the threat of imminent execution required great self-discipline and mental reserves. Boxer's close friend J. S. Cummins recalled that Charles often quoted the Japanese proverb 'Bees sting a crying face'.[15] Somehow Boxer obtained copies of Marcus Aurelius' *Meditations* and the poems of A. E. Housman. These works, together with the plays of Shakespeare, were the intellectual sustenance of these years. It is said that survival of solitary confinement requires the ability to inhabit a rich inner world of the mind and imagination, and this Boxer was able to do, with consequences that were to prove remarkably productive once he was released.

While enduring imprisonment Boxer continued to suffer from severe

[14] Frank Lequin, 'Memorial address to Charles Ralph Boxer', delivered at King's College, 11 July 2000.
[15] Professor J. S. Cummins, 'Professor Charles Boxer', *The Times*, 1 May 2000.

disability as his left arm remained semi-paralysed and he received no treatment for it for the best part of two years. He was never to recover the use of this arm and, although he remained very sensitive about the disability and tried his best to hide it, it helped to ensure that his future would be in the intellectual world rather than on active service.

There is no doubt that in some respects Boxer received favourable treatment from the Japanese. He was well looked after in hospital and was allowed to remain there for the first nine months of the occupation. Subsequently he escaped the full consequences of his involvement in the reception of broadcasts from the secret radios. He certainly benefited from his ability to speak Japanese and from his pre-war acquaintance with many of the Japanese officers who admired and liked him. In some cases this was reciprocated and after the war Boxer refused to pursue Japanese war criminals in the way that some former prisoners did and even sent food parcels to Japanese guards who fell on hard times. It is also clear that on a number of occasions Boxer used his good relations with the Japanese officers to obtain better treatment for all the inmates of the camps. However, some fellow prisoners became bitterly jealous and allegations of collaboration were subsequently made against both Charles himself and Mickey—allegations, however, which were never substantiated by a shred of evidence.[16]

Post War

Charles eventually left Hong Kong at the end of October 1945 having spent a month looking for his library. He arrived in the United States early in November and on 28 November he and Mickey, who until July had not even been sure that Charles was still alive, were married. The marriage attracted a lot of attention as Mickey was a well-known literary figure, and the pair of them featured with Carola in a full page photograph in *Life* on 5 December 1945.

At the end of December Charles returned to Japan as a member of the

---

[16] For a discussion of Mickey's relations with the Japanese see Cuthbertson, *No One Said Not to Go*, p. 96. A deliberately sensational accusation of collaboration was made against Charles Boxer in the *Guardian* by Hywel Williams on 24 Feb. 2001 but see the response by Dauril Alden in the *Guardian* on 10 Mar. 2001 and the article of Kenneth Maxwell, 'The C. R. Boxer *affaire*: Heroes, Traitors, and the *Manchester Guardian*', *Notícia e Opinião* www.no.com.br—March 2001. Williams's large and prominent article is chiefly remarkable for the complete absence of any evidence on which to base his allegations.

Far Eastern Commission. There he successfully traced his lost books to the imperial library in Tokyo and arranged for them to be transported to Britain. By February 1946 he was back in the US receiving medical treatment for his hand. It was only in July that he and Mickey sailed to Britain to reoccupy and restore the family house at Conygar.

Charles lived at his large country house until he persuaded himself he had to sell it in 1953. Mickey, who hoped their stay in Britain would be a brief one, described the opening up of Conygar, and the first cold and uninviting years they spent there, in a second volume of autobiography, *England to Me,* which was published in 1950. Like her earlier account of life in China and Hong Kong, this book is a lightly fictionalised work, but was far less likely to cause offence than *China to Me*. It provided an intimate, amusing and ultimately affectionate account of Charles Boxer who is referred to throughout as 'the Major'.

After his return to Britain, Charles's relations with the government as well as with the army began to become strained. In October 1946 he had been nominated for an MBE along with other former prisoners of the Japanese. Boxer refused to accept the honour, in spite of some pressure being put on him to do so, and in August 1947 the withdrawal of the award had to be officially announced. It appears that Boxer resented the fact that two Hong Kong Chinese, who he had recommended for a medal, were ignored, as he believed, solely on grounds of colour.

As a serving army officer Charles now had to wait for a new posting and in the mean time underwent fresh medical treatment. He was apparently still intent on pursuing a military career and hoped for some posting to the Far East. He even did his best to stop the publication of *China to Me* in Britain because he feared it would damage his career. Other options were beginning to present themselves. Even before he and Mickey had left the United States, he had been approached separately by King's College and the University of Hong Kong about the possibility of an academic appointment. However, it was the proposal by the army to make him commandant of a prisoner of war camp which finally persuaded him to resign his commission and take the chair that King's had offered him.

The King's years 1947–1967

The Camões Chair of Portuguese at King's College, London, had been established in 1919. It had been filled by George Young between 1919 and 1923 and then, with great distinction, by Edgar Prestage from 1923 to

1936. Since that date it had remained vacant for lack of any suitably qualified occupant. Boxer had known Prestage before the war and Prestage had become one of his great admirers, famously relinquishing his own intention to edit the *Commentaries of Ruy Freyre de Andrada* when he heard that Boxer, then only twenty-six years old, was preparing an edition.[17] It was Prestage who suggested that Boxer be approached to fill the Camões Chair—an original and daring gesture as Boxer had no university degree and had never courted the academic establishment. The chair was formally offered and accepted in April 1947 and Charles gave his inaugural lecture on 31 October 1947. It was not until December 1947 that he finally resigned his commission in the army.

Boxer held the Camões Chair until he retired in 1967—though with one interlude. In April 1951 he accepted the Chair of Far Eastern History at the School of Oriental and African Studies (SOAS). The only reason to take this new appointment was that the salary offered was much higher than his salary at King's—and Boxer, saddled with a white elephant of country house, a London flat, the expense of his fast growing family (his second daughter Amanda was born in 1948) and still faster growing library was always seriously short of money. The move to SOAS proved an unfortunate experience and in May 1952 Charles resigned the chair and returned to King's. The following year he finally sold Conygar and moved to a house in Hertfordshire called Ringshall End, where he was to live for the rest of his life.

The years which followed his return to King's were astonishingly productive. He branched out from his original area of expertise in the history of the Portuguese and Dutch in the Far East, publishing three important works on Brazil and ranging over the whole field of Portuguese, Spanish and Dutch imperial history. The scope and quality of his work brought him widespread academic recognition. He received his first honorary degree from the University of Leiden in 1950 and in 1956 was offered, but declined, the Chair of Dutch Institutions at University College London. In 1957 he was elected Fellow of the British Academy.

While at King's Boxer had no responsibility for undergraduate teaching and supervised only a handful of postgraduates. His chair was almost exclusively a research post and he spent much of each year travelling to archives and building his unique network of international academic contacts which made him one of the best-known of all British academics. Every year he spent months abroad, visiting the United

---

[17] Boxer, *Commentaries of Ruy Freyre de Andrada*, p. xvii.

States, Brazil, India, and Africa. He not only accepted the usual invitations to conferences, where he was always very welcome because of his ability punctually to produce meticulously researched papers, but he undertook regular engagements as a visiting lecturer at American and South African universities. These lectures were published in a series of volumes which contained some of his most influential work—none more so than the lectures on race relations that he delivered at the University of Virginia in 1962 and which, when published the following year under the title *Race Relations in the Portuguese Colonial Empire 1415–1825,* caused major political and academic controversy (see below).[18]

Retirement years

While the controversy over *Race Relations* continued unabated, Charles Boxer was contemplating another major decision. Less than a decade after his financial worries had forced him to sell his country house, he began to contemplate the sale of his library and his departure from King's. In 1963 he agreed to be nominated to a chair at Harvard but the university declined to confirm the appointment. Undeterred he pushed ahead with his search for a new appointment and a purchaser for his books. By 1964 two major libraries were in negotiation with him—the Australian National Library in Canberra and the Lilly Library in Bloomington, Indiana. The Australian offer seemed most attractive, but determined opposition from his family, who made it clear they would not relocate to Australia, and his realisation that it would be impossible to obtain domestic servants in Canberra, tipped the balance in favour of Indiana. The sale was finally agreed in October 1965. Charles resigned from King's and departed in June 1967, two years before he had reached the official retirement age.

During 1968 Charles took up residence at Bloomington and began his American academic career. No sooner was he there than he was approached by Yale to fill a newly created chair. The negotiations went on most of the year with Boxer reluctant to leave Indiana where he was well paid and, somewhat to his surprise, found himself very much at home. However in 1969, after Yale had also offered a position to

---

[18] C. R. Boxer, *Race Relations in the Portuguese Colonial Empire, 1415–1825* (Oxford, 1963).

Mickey, he finally accepted the Chair of the Expansion of Europe Overseas, while retaining his consultancy position at the Lilly Library. It was the fourth chair he had been offered in a fourth different subject, and the third he had accepted. Charles remained at Yale for three years, in 1970 serving as acting Master of Saybrook College at a time when the Yale campus was torn by student demonstrations and radical upheavals. He finally retired in May 1972 having reached the statutory retirement age of 68.

Still very active mentally and physically, Charles was determined to continue his academic career. During his twenty years at King's he had done no undergraduate teaching but in the United States he found that teaching undergraduates became a large part of his duties. Already a distinguished researcher and writer now, very late in life, he had to develop the skills of a teacher as well. He returned to teach at Indiana in 1973 and then went with Mickey to teach a semester in Charlottesville, Virginia. In 1975 he taught at the University of Missouri. Between 1976 and 1979 he taught three more semesters at Indiana and one at Ann Arbor, Michigan—the final term at Bloomington being the last teaching that he undertook.

Boxer's outstanding academic achievement had been recognised as early as 1950 when he was awarded an honorary doctorate by the University of Leiden. For many years this remained the only degree of any kind that he possessed. In 1959 he received an honorary degree from the University of Bahia (having been awarded the prestigious Southey Prize in 1956). In 1965 he was given an honorary doctorate by the University of Liverpool and in 1969 he was made a papal knight of the Order of St Gregory the Great. In 1971 he received an honorary doctorate from the Robinson University in Hong Kong and in 1974 he became an Honorary Fellow of the School of Oriental and African Studies. In 1980 he received a doctorate from Indiana University where he had taught, on and off, for ten years. In 1990 Portugal made peace with the great historian of its empire and awarded Boxer the Gold Cross of the Order of Santiago. He finally received appropriate recognition from King's College when that University established the Charles Boxer Chair in History in 1997.

However, while accepting and enjoying these and other tokens of recognition, he once again refused an honour from the British Government. In 1975 he declined to accept a CBE on the grounds that there was no longer an empire of which to be a commander. The British Government reciprocated by declining to recommend him for a knighthood.

Charles Boxer in the eyes of those who knew him

In many ways Boxer was and remained an old fashioned figure who was most at home in a world where servants rather than machines ensured the smooth running of daily life. The Boxers always depended on domestic service of one kind or another. Conygar was run by a housekeeper and gardener and up to four additional staff; the Boxer girls always had a nanny and, when the family moved to Ringshall, they were looked after by a Dorset couple who moved with them. Boxer himself shunned technology of all kinds. He never drove and did not own a car until late in life; he always wrote with a fountain pen, having allegedly thrown the only typewriter he ever owned overboard in frustration at not being able to use it. Mickey wrote of him, 'He never broods about not being able to fix things . . . he not only doesn't like fooling around with tools, but he is quite frankly and honestly afraid of them . . . "All that sort of thing," he says vaguely, waiting for me to light the gas, for he is afraid of gas, "is woman's work." '[19]

After his return to England he lived something of the life of a country squire, attending hunt balls dressed in hunting pink, allowing the local hounds to meet at Conygar, taking long country walks and hosting regular house parties. However, this life style jarred increasingly with his convictions. He returned from Hong Kong with a contempt for the pretences which supported the Empire and, in particular, for the ingrained racism which he found in upper-class English society. In spite of having to pay heavy taxes, he was sympathetic to the ideals of the post war Labour government. After he sold Conygar in 1953 his life style changed to one of constant travel and of urban, or at any rate suburban, living.

Both the Boxers were very sociable. All their lives Charles and Mickey had a love of parties and of the liberating influence of alcohol, and both maintained a wide circle of friends. Both liked to dominate social gatherings and Charles in particular took pleasure in bringing together people of widely different interests to watch the reactions that would ensue. Although he always showed an old fashioned courtesy to strangers and casual acquaintances, Charles also took pleasure in being outrageous once a party was in full swing, a habit which sometimes took the disconcerting form of being publicly rude and insulting to his wife.[20] As Mickey herself was an ostentatiously unconventional figure—smoking cigars and

---

[19] Hahn, *England to Me*, p. 76.
[20] For example see Cutherbertson, *No One Said Not to Go*, p. 336.

opium, keeping gibbons as pets and posing nude for photographers—this was probably a form of self-protection on Charles's part. When they were not partying, however, the Boxers could be aloof and even cold. Both Charles and Mickey were enormously hard-working writers and spent long hours in their libraries—a pre-war acquaintance who came to live at Conygar subsequently wrote 'they lived in their own worlds, locked away in their respective libraries, writing away, all day, every day, and seemingly oblivious to anything happening around them'.[21]

Like so many Englishmen of his class and background, Boxer was a very private man. Although he wrote numerous letters to friends, he left no memoirs or diaries and, after twenty years' service, King's College found they had no information filed about him. The British Academy also found an empty file. However, this private man was married to someone who was an obsessive autobiographer and who described their life together in intimate and often embarrassing detail. Charles and Mickey lived extravagant lives, book collecting, travel, servants and entertaining swallowing up both their incomes and leaving them heavily in debt. Nevertheless it was a marriage which endured to the end, although after the unhappy experiences of trying to collaborate over writing the biography of Raffles and of living the country life at Conygar, Mickey and Charles went very separate ways, usually travelling alone, being apart for months on end and maintaining wholly separate financial arrangements. In 1974 Mickey finally decided to become resident in New York and, although she visited Ringshall End regularly, the couple 'shared a preference for intimacy built around absence' and lived apart.[22]

In spite of receiving six honorary degrees and numerous other honours which confirmed his reputation as one of the leading historians of the century, Boxer remained very insecure and uncomfortable in the academic world. He was sensitive about not having had a university education and believed, possibly correctly, that some colleagues at King's felt that his appointment was somehow inappropriate. He famously quipped that at formal academic occasions when others paraded in their purple robes he had to wear a lounge suit and the audience probably thought he was the man who had come about the gas. He resigned his chair at SOAS confessing that he felt out of his depth in that academic environment and that he had nothing to contribute even to his own seminars, and he also resigned his chair at King's before he reached retirement age. When he

[21] Quoted in Alden, *Charles R. Boxer*, p. 299.
[22] The phrase is that of Roger Angell and is quoted in Cuthbertson, *No One Said Not to Go*, p. 317.

hesitated to accept the chair he had been offered at Yale, his wife wrote to a friend 'he has the wild idea that he is not good enough for Yale, and if he goes he is sure to be Found Out'.[23] However, perhaps the most significant sign of Charles' feeling of insecurity was that he never tried to publish in leading academic journals. He seems to have felt that he was never completely accepted by the academic establishment and preferred to rule in his own private academic empire.

Those who knew Charles Boxer agreed to a remarkable extent in their estimation of him: his wit, which often verged on the ribald, his sociability, his meticulous attention to his correspondence, the smart dress, upright bearing and old fashioned good manners, his remarkable capacity for concentrated work, his linguistic ability, and his passion for travel and for book collecting. Ian Thomson, a colleague at Indiana described him as an

> exceptionally smart man with an immense stock of wisdom based on experience of the world. He was not a closeted academician. Not everyone understood his wit, which could be a trifle mordant, and others were simply not capable of keeping up with him intellectually. If he sensed a fellow spirit, he was the soul of affability. If he sensed a phony, I'm afraid it showed [24]

The feelings of his many friends were well summed up after his death by Professor Russell-Wood, who wrote of him in *The Independent,* 'His curiosity was unfailing, his knowledge encyclopaedic, his memory infallible. The most generous of scholars, he shared his time and his knowledge unselfishly and with enthusiasm.'[25]

Critical Assessment

Charles Boxer began publishing academic articles in 1926 and his last publication appeared in 1996. In 70 years he published 335 books and academic articles with, in addition, numerous conference papers and reviews. His work covered almost all the genres of academic history— including biography, historical narrative, edited texts, bibliographical studies, textbooks, lecture series and monographs.

His major research based monographs include *Fidalgos in the Far East*[26]

---

[23] Quoted in Alden, *Charles R. Boxer*, p. 458.
[24] Quoted in Alden, *Charles R. Boxer*, p. 445.
[25] A. J. R. Russell-Wood, 'Professor Charles Boxer', *The Independent*, 29 April 2000.
[26] C. R. Boxer, *Fidalgos in the Far East* 1550–1770. *Fact and Fancy in the history of Macao* (Den Haag, 1948).

The Christian Century in Japan,[27] *Salvador da Sá,*[28] *The Dutch in Brazil,*[29] *The Great Ship from Amacon*[30] and *The Golden Age of Brazil.*[31] These works were all based on numerous specialist academic papers, some of them bearing titles that he subsequently reused. They form a substantial body of research and academic narrative which covers the activities of the Dutch and the Portuguese in the Far East and Brazil in the late sixteenth and early seventeenth centuries. Only the *Golden Age of Brazil* stands outside this period as it deals with the eighteenth century. In composing these largely narrative histories Boxer was probably the first historian to have been completely at ease with Dutch, Portuguese, Spanish, and Japanese sources, a scholarly equipment which few historians are ever likely to equal.

Boxer was always happy to acknowledge the work of those who had preceded him—for example the writings of Sir George Sansom on Japan—and often claimed that he was only making available to the English public work that already existed in Dutch or Portuguese. However, in all these books Boxer added significantly to the knowledge and understanding of the subject both through the application of fresh archival research and through his unrivalled knowledge of the published sources. Although most of the topics about which he wrote have been revisited subsequently by scholars with different perspectives, Boxer's monographs have stood the test of time and are still the essential point of departure for all serious scholars.

The first books that Boxer published in 1930, at the age of twenty-six, were translated editions of key Dutch and Portuguese texts. These set the precedent for a range of similar editions that he published while working on his monographs. Undoubtedly the most important of these translated editions were his Hakluyt Society publications, *South China in the Sixteenth Century,*[32] *The Tragic History of the Sea*[33] and *Further*

---

[27] C. R. Boxer, *The Christian Century in Japan* (1549–1650) (Berkeley, 1951).

[28] C. R. Boxer, *Salvador Correia de Sá and the Struggle for Brazil and Angola (1602–1686)* (1952).

[29] C. R. Boxer, *The Dutch in Brazil 1624–1654* (Oxford, 1957).

[30] C. R. Boxer, *The Great Ship from Amacon. Annals of Macao and the Old Japan Trade 1555–1640* (Lisbon, 1959).

[31] C. R. Boxer, *The Golden Age of Brazil (1695–1750)* (Berkeley, 1962).

[32] C. R. Boxer, *South China in the Sixteenth Century: being the Narratives of Galeote Pereira, Fr. Gaspar da Cruz, O.P., Fr. Martin Rada, O.E.S.A (1550–1575)* (Hakluyt Society, 1953).

[33] C. R. Boxer, *The Tragic History of the Sea, 1589–1622: Narratives of the Shipwrecks of the Portuguese East Indiamen São Thomé (1589), Santo Alberto (1593), São João Baptista (1622), and the Journeys of the Survivors in South East Africa* (Hakluyt Society, 1959).

Selections from the "Tragic History of the Sea", 1559–1565.[34] There were also minor examples of the genre, for example his discovery and publication of the very significant *Nova e Curiosa Relação.*[35] In these works Boxer always adopted the same format. The main part of the book consisted of his scholarly translation of some key text, usually of the sixteenth or seventeenth century. This would be supplemented by a lengthy introduction which sought to place the text in its historical context, and by an essay in which Boxer explored its bibliographical history. These essays were, of course, based on the research he had undertaken when building up his own library.

The third category of Boxer's published work were the textbooks. Between 1965 and 1969 he published two books in a series edited by J. H. Plumb—*The Dutch Seaborne Empire*[36] and the *The Portuguese Seaborne Empire.*[37] Although he himself was not happy with the first of these, both books have become classics and have been reprinted many times. These volumes are excellent textbooks. They are lucidly and attractively written, they have introductory narrative chapters which make them accessible to the non-specialist, and they deal in a thematic way with important issues of contemporary concern to historians. Boxer has often been described as essentially a narrative historian, but neither of these books has a strictly narrative format. They are constructed from a series of thematic essays in which the institutional and economic history of the two empires is given full attention. In these books Boxer explored a favourite theme—that the struggle of the Dutch with the Iberian powers was in effect the first 'world war'. Both books grew out of previous work that Boxer had already published—for example many of the themes of *The Portuguese Seaborne Empire* had already been explored in published series of lectures like *Four Centuries of Portuguese Expansion*[38] and *Race Relations in the Portuguese Colonial Empire.*

A number of Boxer's books had their origin in public lectures and throughout his life he was constantly invited by learned societies,

---

[34] C. R. Boxer, *Further Selections from "The Tragic History of the Sea, 1559–1565": Narratives of the Shipwrecks of the Portuguese East Indiamen "Aguia" and "Garça" (1559) "São Paulo" (1561) and the Misadventures of the Brazil-ship "Santo António"* (1565) (Hakluyt Society, 1968).

[35] C. R. Boxer, 'Negro Slavery in Brazil', *Race*, 3 (1964), 38–47.

[36] C. R. Boxer, *The Dutch Seaborne Empire* (1965).

[37] C. R. Boxer, *The Portuguese Seaborne Empire* (1969).

[38] C. R. Boxer, *Four Centuries of Portuguese Expansion, 1415–1825: a Succinct Survey* (Johannesburg, 1961).

conference organisers and universities to contribute to their programmes. The style of his lectures as well as their content account for
their popularity—they seldom involved long and complex argument,
jargon, or suffocating detail, and they were strewn with apt quotations,
epigrams, and amusing asides. With great skill Boxer was able to pitch his
lectures at a level which could be appreciated both by a specialist and a
non-specialist audience. Some of these lectures were published as one-off
articles (often in *History Today* where he published no less than twenty-
six articles) but others were collected together and separately published as
books, notably, *Four Centuries of Portuguese Expansion, Race Relations
in the Portuguese Colonial Empire, Portuguese Society in the Tropics,*[39]
Mary and Misogyny,[40] *The Church Militant*[41] and *Portuguese India in the
Mid-Seventeenth Century.*[42] These publications are among his most important because they address themes of topical importance to academic
historians, invariably in an original and stimulating way.

A further distinct category of Boxer's work might be described as bibliographical and archival studies. All his life Boxer was a great collector
of books and manuscripts—a practice that contributed in a major way to
his continuing financial problems. As early as 1937 he published in Macao
a catalogue of his library entitled *Biblioteca Boxeriana.* The collection
had by this time acquired a certain amount of fame and it was subsequently seized and sent to Tokyo by the Japanese after Boxer was taken
prisoner in 1941. Most of the books were recovered after the war and
formed the core of an ever growing library. The size and quality of this
collection allowed Boxer to do much of his work without leaving his own
study and a number of his books contain the note 'This book has been
written mainly from the resources of my own library.'[43] In 1963 he produced a short pamphlet on the Portuguese medical scientist Garcia
d'Orta. The pamphlet was designed to popularise the work of this great
sixteenth century Portuguese scientist but, at the back, was appended a
note on the original edition of Garcia d'Orta's *Colóquios.* In this Boxer
traced every single known copy of the book and listed their where-
abouts—not surprisingly one of the twenty-four copies known to survive

---

[39] C. R. Boxer, *Portuguese Society in the Tropics. The Municipal Councils of Goa, Macao, Bahia and Luanda, 1510–1800* (Madison, 1965).
[40] C. R. Boxer, *Mary and Misogyny. Women in Iberian Expansion Overseas (1415–1815). Some Facts, Fancies and Personalities* (1975).
[41] C. R. Boxer, *The Church Militant and Iberian Expansion, 1449–1770* (Baltimore, 1978).
[42] C. R. Boxer, *Portuguese India in the Mid-Seventeenth Century* (Bombay, 1980).
[43] For example, C. R. Boxer, *The Dutch Seaborne Empire* (1965), p. v.

was listed as being in the library of 'C. R. Boxer'.[44] In the course of forty years of systematic collecting Boxer acquired many rare and unique items. The most famous of these, perhaps, was the *Codex Boxer* which he bought in 1947. The rare items he had discovered or acquired were used to great effect in his writings which were always scrutinised by scholars interested in the latest bibliographical discovery.

Boxer was also a great traveller and made a point of visiting libraries and archives wherever he went. He provided advice to many libraries, including the Library of Congress, on their acquisition policy in areas where he had expertise. This passion for collecting and for visiting archives led to many publications of an almost exclusively bibliographical nature an example of which would be, 'A Glimpse of the Goa Archives'.[45]

Over an active career of sixty years Boxer's interests changed and widened. His early studies were in the maritime history of the Portuguese and Dutch in the Far East. This led on to the study of the history of Macao, China and Japan and to what turned out to be an unfortunate decision to take the chair of Far Eastern History at SOAS. From there his interests branched out to Brazil, another field of Iberian-Dutch conflict, which resulted in three important monographs. These studies then broadened to include the whole of Portuguese imperial history and the history of Portugal itself. He also wrote on British and Spanish history—though usually only where it intersected with the Dutch or the Portuguese. One subject which he largely avoided, however, was the early phase of the Discoveries. The chronological range of his work extended from the sixteenth to the eighteenth centuries, with the year 1825 (the independence of Brazil) being established as the boundary beyond which he virtually never strayed.

Most of those who knew Charles Boxer or were familiar with his writings would have no difficulty in agreeing that his linguistic skills made him uniquely fitted for the work he undertook; that he had an unsurpassed knowledge of the published material in his field; and that he had a publishing record without rival for its quantity but also for its quality and range. However, there might be less agreement over the significance of Boxer's work within the wider context of twentieth-century historical scholarship.

It has sometimes been alleged that, for all his massive scholarship and

---

[44] *Two Pioneers of Tropical Medicine: Garcia d'Orta and Nicolás Monardes*, Diamante XIV, Hispanic and Luso-Brazilian Councils (1963), p. 34.

[45] C. R. Boxer, 'A Glimpse of the Goa Archives', *Bulletin of the School of Oriental and African Studies*, 14 (1952), 299–324.

prolific record of publication, Boxer ultimately had little of importance to say. During the period that he was active, academic history was convulsed by a series of major debates and movements. There were the heated controversies between the various schools of Marxist history and their opponents; the rise to prominence of the *Annalistes*; the development of feminist historiography, black studies, oral history, cultural history, and the debate over counterfactuals. In his own chosen field of the seventeenth-century debates ranged over the General Crisis, the Military Revolution, religion and protestantism, slavery and the slave trade, witchcraft, world systems theory and the origins of modern capitalism, and many more. Boxer seldom addressed any of these issues directly nor contributed to the debates, and it is significant that he seldom published in any of the major academic journals. He appeared to stand aloof from the concerns of academic history. This point can be illustrated from two of his most important works, his extracts from the *História Tragico Marítima*. While his introduction looks in considerable detail at the bibliographical history of these shipwreck accounts and at the development of the *carreira da Índia* and of ship construction, he hardly refers at all to the literary, symbolic, or sociological importance of the texts.

Boxer was aware that his work might be thought to lack theoretical underpinning. In 1970 he published a series of lectures on the subject of women in the Iberian empires entitled, *Mary and Misogyny: Women in Iberian Expansion Overseas, 1415–1815, Some Facts, Fancies and Personalities*. In the introduction to this he wrote

> since the published documentation on women in the Iberian colonial world is sufficient neither in quantity nor in quality to provide adequate material for 'structures', 'models', and other fashionable inter-disciplinary paraphernalia, this tentative essay does not presume to be anything more than what is explicitly indicated in the subtitle.

Rather than indulge in arcane theoretical discussions, he preferred to amass illustrative quotations and to summarise his views in short and often pithy epigrams. His writings are full of ideas, judgements, and conclusions but not of detailed and sustained argument. It is difficult to tell whether this apparent shying away from controversy and debate arose from a conviction that he did not have the academic training to embark on theoretical discussions, or whether he thought this form of debate to be unproductive and ultimately pointless.

However, it can be argued that Boxer did fully engage in contemporary debate but on his own terms and in his own way. He was deeply suspicious of ideologies, whether these were the imperial ideologies of the seventeenth or the twentieth centuries, the religious ideologies of the churches or the academic ideologies of his colleagues. It was not that he discounted the power of ideas in human affairs, and he always accepted that even at their most violent and rapacious the Portuguese of the seventeenth century were deeply moved by their faith and the desire to spread it throughout the world, but he preferred to see human beings as motivated by a confused, complex mixture of high ideals and more mundane considerations—God and Mammon.

Boxer was well aware of the political agendas with which many historians in the 1950s and 1960s approached their work. He himself did address the great themes of his time but deftly and often with a light touch that left the reader almost unaware of what he was doing. Take for example a short article entitled '"Christians and Spices"; Portuguese Missionaries in Ceylon, 1515–1658' which he wrote for *History Today* in 1958. This article was in many ways typical of Boxer, a light weight piece skating briefly over the history of Portuguese missionary enterprise and quoting in passing four or five less well known Portuguese writers. However, it was also a piece with a serious purpose. At the head of the article an unattributed text reads 'The methods used, or alleged to have been used, by Portuguese proselytisers more than three hundred years ago, remain a living issue in Ceylon politics.' The article suggests that, contrary to the claims of some Sri Lankan politicians,

> the Portuguese did not seek to impose Christianity at the point of the sword . . . but they did seek to foster their religion through coercive and discriminatory legislation . . . since it is admittedly the evil rather than the good which men do that lives after them, this helps to account for the rather strident and nationalistic tone which is sometimes observable in the statements of contemporary Sinhalese Buddhists.[46]

Charles Boxer's career coincided with the period of the *Estado Novo* in Portugal when history was a highly politicised activity, frequently called in evidence to underwrite the ideologies and policies of the regime. The great discoverers were routinely invoked as forefathers of the modern colonial state and in 1960 the celebrations of the five hundredth anniversary of the death of Prince Henry the Navigator took the form of a massive act of state homage to the man whom the *Estado Novo* had made into its culture hero.

---

[46] C. R. Boxer, '"Christians and Spices"; Portuguese Missionaries in Ceylon, 1515–1658', *History Today* (May 1958), 346–54.

It is perhaps significant that the year 1960 came and went with deafening silence from Charles Boxer. There was no publication and no comment by him on the Prince—an extraordinary omission from the greatest living scholar of Portuguese colonial history. This can partly be explained by the fact that Boxer never wrote much about the fifteenth century, but it is difficult not to see this silence as a studied snub to the regime in Portugal. That year he did give a series of lectures at the University of Witwatersrand which, he wrote, 'would be appropriate in the year during which the Portuguese are commemorating the 500th anniversary of the death of the Infante Dom Henrique', and he went on 'I have dwelt less on the policies adumbrated at Lisbon than on what actually happened overseas'.[47]

However, less easy for him to ignore, and requiring a different type of response, were the writings of Gilberto Freyre with his widely propagated views about 'Lusotropicalism'. Famous for his massive study of plantation society in Brazil, Freyre had been adopted by the Salazar regime and had written a number of books expounding the idea that the Portuguese had a unique affinity for the tropics and that their colonial tradition had avoided the polarisations of race seen in the British and Dutch and French empires. In the late 1950s this interpretation of Portuguese colonialism was intensely controversial and both supporters of the *Estado Novo* and its opponents eagerly sought endorsement or rejection from scholars working in this field.

It is not an exaggeration to say that all eyes turned on Charles Boxer to see how he would react to Freyre's views on the topic of race. In 1962, when the dust had barely settled on the events commemorating Prince Henry the Navigator's death, he delivered a series of lectures at the University of Virginia which were published the following year under the title, *Race Relations in the Portuguese Colonial Empire*. These essays were stripped bare of any theorising and avoided the windy generalisations and rhetoric which marked Freyre's later work. Using only contemporary Portuguese sources Boxer set out to demonstrate that in every part of the world and at every period the Portuguese had been intensely conscious of racial distinctions and had frequently discriminated against people of colour. The evidence was massive, indisputable, and overwhelming and it struck at the heart of the political mythology being peddled by the Portuguese regime. In one lethal sentence Boxer delivered his political judgement.

---

[47] Boxer, *Four Centuries of Portuguese Expansion*, Introduction.

> There were, of course, exceptions, but the prevailing social pattern was (and is) one of conscious white superiority. Captain António de Oliveira Cadornega, who lived for over forty years in Angola, is a safer guide in this respect than Dr António de Oliveira Salazar who has never set foot in Africa.

This barbed epigram, typical of Boxer's wit and the cutting edge of his scholarship, probably accounts for the decades of distrust that ensued between Boxer and the Portuguese. The public controversy that followed spilled over from the Lisbon Press into diplomatic channels and was partly responsible for the end of the meetings of the Luso-British Mixed Commission. Although Boxer was surprised and hurt by the bitterness this book caused in Portuguese circles, it is impossible not to conclude that such a careful scholar had chosen his words deliberately and that he was fully aware of the significance that his words would have in the existing international situation.[48]

In subsequent lecture series Boxer turned his attention to other areas of contemporary interest to historians. His essays on the town councils, on women, and on the church in the Iberian empires did much to define the debates on these topics. His writings on slavery related that issue to the wider question of race relations and to the story of the catholic missions. His writings on slavery, race and the church were designed to strip away the confusion which was often made worse by the impassioned pleading of those on each side of the debate. As always Boxer wanted common sense and realism to prevail. His focus was not on ideological positions but on the realities of colonial life.

He was aware that contempt for the Portuguese was deeply embedded in the English mentality, but having lived through the collapse of Britain's empire in the East he was less judgemental of the decline of Portugal's Estado da Índia. Indeed he often reflected on the courage and endurance of the Portuguese in the face of great adversity. For him both the traditional contempt of the British for Portuguese colonising efforts and the uncritical glorification of their achievements by the Portuguese were alike misguided. 'The truth' he wrote, 'was and is more complex. . . . The Portuguese were neither angels nor devils they were human beings and they acted as such; their conduct varying greatly according to time, place and circumstances.' In more than one of his works he contemplated the

---

[48] These views were first published in M. Newitt, *Charles Ralph Boxer 1904–2000* (2000). The controversy surrounding the publication of *Race Relations* is fully explored in Alden, *Charles R. Boxer*, chap. 12 and in J. S. Cummins and L. de Sousa Rebello, 'The Controversy over Charles Boxer's *Race Relations in the Portuguese Colonial Empire, 1415–1825*', *Portuguese Studies*, 17 (2001), 233–46.

apparently unequal struggle of the Portuguese and the Dutch and reflected on how the Portuguese in Brazil, Angola and East Africa were able not only to resist but to emerge victorious. Boxer believed that the strength of the Portuguese lay in their strong institutions, in the Câmaras and Misericórdias, in their strong family loyalties and above all in the catholic religious culture which gave a common identity to 'Portuguese' communities around the world.

The style of Boxer's writing was not the least significant part of his achievement as a historian. He tried to be accessible to the non-specialist and he set out to be concise, clear, amusing, and above all readable. Boxer loved epigram and always sought out some concise and witty phrase or quotation to introduce his work or to summarise his conclusions. There are many memorable lines, for example his description of the Lisbon mob as 'fanatical, filthy and ferocious' or his description of the Portuguese in East Africa as 'alternately fighting, trading and fornicating with the local inhabitants'. Some of his epigrams came to acquire a definitive quality. Few historians of the Portuguese overseas, for example, would quarrel with his famous description of the Estado da Índia as 'a commercial and maritime empire cast in a military and ecclesiastical mould'. Frequently, however, his search for an epigram led him to resort to clichés. For example, 'If trade followed the flag in the development of the British Empire, the missionary was close behind the merchant in the expansion of the Portuguese Empire'[49] or 'the close connection between God and Mammon which characterised the trade of Macao and Japan from its romantic inception to its tragic end' or 'the search for 'Christians and Spices' rather than new worlds to conquer was what brought the Portuguese to India'.[50] However, clichéd writing of this kind was a stylistic device which served to link Boxer's more esoteric researches into a mainstream of popular historical knowledge and thought.

Conclusion

Charles Boxer remained an active scholar almost to the last when failing eyesight eventually put an end to his remarkable career. He faced the prospect of ending his life with characteristic stoicism. A passage he

[49] Introduction to *Portuguese Merchants and Missionaries in Feudal Japan* (1986).
[50] C. R. Boxer, 'The Portuguese in the East 1500–1800', in H. V. Livermore, ed., *Portugal and Brazil* (Oxford, 1953), p. 185.

marked in his personal copy of the *Meditations of Marcus Aurelius* reads 'It is the part of a man endowed with a good understanding faculty, to consider . . . what it is to die and how . . . he can conceive of it no otherwise, than as of a work of nature, and he that fears any work of nature, is a very child.' 'It is significant that, after contemplating for sixty years the desperate struggles of Iberians and Dutch in all parts of the world, his best remembered remark should be, "nothing matters much, most things don't matter at all".'[51]

M. D. D. NEWITT
King's College London

Note. I am most grateful for the help given to me by Charles Boxer's daughter, Amanda, including the loan of some of her precious family books.

---

[51] From Newitt, *Charles Ralph Boxer*, p. 14. See also Professor J. S. Cummins 'Professor Charles Boxer' *The Times*, 1 May 2000.

KENNETH CAMERON

Kenneth Cameron
1922–2001

To everyone who knew him Ken Cameron seemed quintessentially Lancashire, but the Scottish ancestry on his father's side, which is evidenced in the surname, was not very far distant, and the Scottish connection is seen also in his Christian name and in those of his son, Iain Stewart. His great grandfather, Angus Cameron, was a Gaelic speaker from the Fort William area. He was a builder of dry stone walls, and he came south, initially to Liverpool, to find work. His wife followed him with the children, and the next two generations of male Camerons became textile operatives in Lancashire. Ken's grandfather, Donald Cameron, also had an intriguing sideline. He was an entertainer in the Harry Lauder style, and was very successful at this: a prized family possession is a watch-chain hung with medals for his performances in northern towns. His wife would not countenance his making a full-time career of this, as she disapproved of the life-style which she thought might have resulted.

Ken's boyhood was closely linked to his maternal grandparents who ran a provisions shop in Padiham, near Burnley. When this grandfather died Ken's parents went to live there. Ken's mother, who had had to give up her career as a primary-school teacher when she married, eventually ran the shop. This corner shop in Byron Street is still vividly remembered in Padiham and Burnley. Ken helped in the running of it, and contemporaries remember him flying round on his bike making deliveries after school. He also had a reputation for being able to slice bacon to the exact required thickness. Ken's father, another Angus, had health problems believed to date from service in the 1914–18 war. He suffered a stroke in

1939 and died in 1948. Ken's mother lived into her nineties, latterly in Nottingham.

Ken was educated at the pre-war Burnley Grammar School, where he became head boy and captain of cricket for Ribblesdale House. The passionate interest in sport which began in his schooldays was an outstanding characteristic throughout his life. His love of soccer was particularly strong. Iain Cameron recalled in his funeral address that to his grandsons, Ross, Rory, and Jamie, their grandad's main claim to fame was that he once 'stood between the sticks at Brighton and Hove Albion'. This was during the war when FA clubs had an arrangement with military bases enabling them to recruit temporary replacements for players who were overseas. 'Sport (supporting)' is the first of the recreations which Ken listed in his *Who's Who* entry.

Ken's spell in the RAF, from 1941–5, came at the end of his second year of English studies at Leeds University. In the two years before call-up he was taught by Bruce Dickins, whose support was later crucial in the early stages of his career. During his war service he was a pilot in Coastal Command, flying a Wellington bomber, and attaining the rank of Acting Flight Lieutenant. Several friends who knew him immediately after the war have commented on how rarely he mentioned his experience as a pilot. It left him with an enduring fascination with aircraft, but without interest in other means of mechanical transport. He only acquired a driving licence and a car at the end of his life under persuasion from Jean, his second wife.

The final year of English studies at Leeds, after demobilisation, was not as happy as the earlier two years had been. Professor Dickins had moved to Cambridge, and Harold Orton had taken his place at Leeds. Ken did not get on with Professor Orton, and in later years he attributed his failure to obtain a first class in his finals to this disharmony. The setback did not, however, prevent entry into an academic career. Professor R. M. Wilson, who had known him at Leeds, had become head of the English Department at Sheffield, and relying on his own and Bruce Dickins's high opinion of Ken's abilities Professor Wilson appointed him to an assistant lectureship, which he held from 1947–50. In 1947 he married Kathleen Heap, who was then teaching geography at Burnley High School for Girls. They had known each other since schooldays. There is more to be said of Kath's input to Ken's work and of the tragedy of her death in 1977, but it is appropriate to mention the marriage here as an event of the years in Sheffield. Their daughter, Susan, was born while they were there.

The terms of appointment at Sheffield included the requirement to complete a Ph.D. thesis by the end of three years. This, combined with the rigours of a teaching programme for a newly-graduated scholar, must have needed all Ken's immense resources of energy and dedication for its fulfilment. Professor Dickins was then Director of the English Place-Name Survey, and at his suggestion Ken decided to make Derbyshire place-names the subject of his research. The preparation of the thesis was achieved between 1947 and 1950, and in 1950 Ken moved to a lectureship in English Language at Nottingham.

Some of Ken's students at Sheffield have sent accounts of his teaching there. In 1947 the student body included an ex-service element, some of its members older than he was. This might have led to a 'Lucky Jim' situation, but Dr Geoffrey Barnes tells me that the members of this ex-service group 'took Ken to their hearts as one of their own'. It is clear from these accounts that while Ken was not able in the circumstances to do much more than use the content of teaching he had himself received as an undergraduate, his friendly personality endeared him to those he taught, and the lively participation of students in discussions on set texts caused them to be memorable experiences.

Ken remained at Nottingham for the rest of his career, and as a resident for the rest of his life. His career at the university was summarised by Professor Thorlac Turville-Petre in the festschrift presented to him on the occasion of his retirement in 1987.[1]

In 1950 Old English and Middle English studies at Nottingham were in need of the strong support which Ken was able to give them. A new syllabus was being drawn up for English, and the head of department, Vivian de Sola Pinto, said in an essay published in 1951 'I decided, therefore, that the first consideration in planning my new school would be the liberation of English studies from the incubus of compulsory Anglo-Saxon with the accompanying apparatus of Germanic philology.'[2] As Professor Turville-Petre comments, this was not a warm welcome for the new lecturer in English language, but in spite of this the relationship between the two was cordial. In 1961, when James Kinsley took over as head of department, the unity of English studies was reasserted. Professor Kinsley said in 1963 'At Nottingham we have removed the barriers between medieval and modern literature . . . We take the view that

---

[1] T. Turville-Petre and M. Gelling (eds.), *Studies in Honour of Kenneth Cameron*, Leeds Studies in English, NS, XVIII (1987).

[2] Quoted in T. Turville-Petre, 'Kenneth Cameron and the English Department at Nottingham' in T. Turville-Petre and M. Gelling (eds.), p. 5.

the "modernist" who knows little or nothing about medieval literature *at
first hand* is not properly equipped for his own work.'[3]

In 1951 Ken was joined at Nottingham by Ray Page, who took
responsibility for Old Norse studies until he moved to Cambridge in
1961. Professor Page had been one of Ken's students at Sheffield. He
recalls that for both of them there was a very heavy teaching load, but
Ken was nevertheless able during that decade to expand his Ph.D. thesis
into the English Place-Name Society's survey of Derbyshire, a three-
volume work which was published in 1959, and to write his remarkably
successful Batsford book, *English Place-Names*, which appeared in 1961.
These publications established a high academic reputation, and he was
promoted to Reader in 1962, and to the first Chair of English Language
at Nottingham University in 1963. Of the years which followed, Professor
Turville-Petre wrote

> Under Ken's leadership and with his determined and unwavering support,
> 'English language' (in the extended sense of that term) has flourished at
> Nottingham. Over the years new teachers have been appointed to the
> Department, with the result that today Old and Middle English, Icelandic,
> Modern English Language and the teaching of English to overseas students are
> all firmly established, and the strength of Linguistic studies led to the develop-
> ment of a separate Department of Linguistics in 1979. At the same time the
> Department has become fully integrated, so that students whose principal inter-
> ests lie in one field of study are often attracted to topics from another range of
> the Department's activities. The variety of subjects covered by the contribu-
> tions to this collection of essays indicates the general appreciation of the vital
> part Kenneth has played in establishing a working team.
>   The stiffest challenge came in 1984 on the sad death of James Kinsley. Ken
> took over as head of Department pledging 'open government', a strategy that
> accorded well with his frank and spontaneous manner. He has always been firm
> in support of his colleagues, willing to listen and to give his own views plainly
> but always with kindness. He was determined that he would leave the
> Department a united one, with none of the traditional hostility between
> language and literature. This he has triumphantly achieved.[4]

Notwithstanding the demands of Ken's position as head of department, he was determined to continue with his research work which, after
the completion of the Derbyshire survey, consisted of the collection of
material for an even more detailed survey of Lincolnshire. On most
Wednesdays there was a notice on his door: 'Professor Cameron is in
Lincoln today.' From 1966 onwards his responsibilities were greatly

---

[3] Quoted in T. Turville-Petre, 'Kenneth Cameron', pp. 5–6.
[4] Ibid., p. 6.

increased by the key position he held in the functioning of the English Place-Name Society, an account of which is given in a later section of this memoir.

During his years as Professor of English Language Ken was a robust debater on the faculty board, and he also made a great contribution to the life of the university as a whole. He served on many committees and was chairman of the University Staff Club. He held this last position during the building of the extension to the Staff Club bar which is known as 'Cameron's Folly'. He was also chairman of the Disabled Students' Committee, in whose work he was deeply interested on account of the tragedy which had occurred in his domestic life when his wife was diagnosed as having multiple sclerosis, from which she died in 1977. His interest in the problems of disabled people was also manifested in the help he gave at the Holmes Lodge Cheshire Home after Kath's death; and he gave the oration when Leonard Cheshire was awarded an honorary degree at Nottingham.

As noted above, Ken married Kathleen Heap, a geography teacher, in 1947. They had a daughter, Susan, and a son, Iain, and were a close family. Kath was deeply involved in the place-name research, and her influence as a geographer is clearly seen in his ground-breaking work on the relationship between place-names and geology. The hospitality at their house in Beeston became legendary. Professor Page comments 'There was a close and friendly link between students and staff that I haven't experienced since, and Ken and Kath were to a great degree responsible for this.' Kath's condition deteriorated over a long period, and Ken cared for her most tenderly and attentively throughout. Inevitably the strain affected his performance of administrative tasks, and during Kath's final years and the period succeeding her death he was helped, probably more than he realised, by the staff of his department. The extent to which his colleagues supported him through these dreadful years bears witness to the affection and loyalty which he inspired.

Support during these difficult years came also from Jean Russell-Gebbert. She and Ken were married in 1998. Before and after this she shared, as Kath had done, in his place-name researches. They lived mainly in Nottingham, but their base for Lincolnshire field-work was Jean's cottage in Tealby, and it was there that he suffered a fatal heart attack on 10 March 2001.

Ken's career was liberally punctuated by honours, the most notable of which were his election to the British Academy in 1976 and his appointment as CBE in 1987. His work on Norse names in England aroused much interest in Scandinavia, and he received an honorary doctorate from Uppsala University in 1977. In 1990 he was awarded the Jöran Sahlgren Prize by the Royal Swedish Gustavus Adolphus Academy. He was a fellow of the Royal Historical Society and of the Society of Antiquaries of London. Other honours include a Litt.D. from Sheffield University in 1991. The lectures he gave as O'Donnell lecturer in 1979 and as winner of the Sir Israel Gollancz Memorial Prize in 1969 are discussed in a later section. He was president of the Viking Society 1972–4.

Aspects of Professor Cameron's life which remain to be discussed are his achievements as Hon. Secretary of the English Place-Name Society and Hon. Director of the English Place-Name Survey, and the influence of his publications on his chosen area of scholarship.

The English Place-Name Society had its headquarters at University College London, from 1953, with Professor A. H. Smith combining the offices of Hon. Secretary and Hon. Director of the Survey. On the death of Professor Smith in 1966, Sir Frank Stenton, the society's president, nominated Ken as his successor. The vice-chancellor of Nottingham, Lord Dainton, welcomed the transfer of the society's headquarters from London, and the hospitality of Nottingham University has enabled this to be the centre of English place-name studies since that date.

The offices of secretary and director were separated for some years, as John Dodgson, who had worked closely with Hugh Smith, expressed a wish to retain the administrative aspects of the society's work at University College. The administration was managed jointly by John Dodgson and David Mills until 1972. They resigned in that year and the administrative records then joined the library and the archives at Nottingham. Professor Dodgson also resigned the editorship of the annual *Journal*, which he had initiated in 1968, and this additional responsibility passed to Professor Cameron. Much editorial help, especially with the *Journal*, was supplied by John Field, who acted as assistant editor from 1980 to 1986; and the essential secretarial help was provided by Mrs Esmée Pattison, who became the society's full-time administrator in 1972, and who gave devoted service to Ken and the society until she retired in 1994. In 1993 Ken resigned as director and secretary, wishing at last to give his entire attention to the survey of Lincolnshire.

Since this is an account of Ken Cameron's life and work, not a history of the English Place-Name Society, it is not necessary to give details of the society's progress since 1993, but it is appropriate to note that Professor Christine Fell's assumption of the secretaryship, and her strong support for the society, ensured that Nottingham continued to be the headquarters. The directorship was assumed by Victor Watts, who still holds this very important post. Professor Turville-Petre took over the Hon. Secretaryship after Christine Fell's untimely death in 1998.

The directorship of the English Place-Name Survey involves the general editorship of each of the volumes in the series. During Ken Cameron's tenure of this post twenty-one volumes were issued. This number includes three parts of his own Lincolnshire survey together with volumes by scholars working on Berkshire, Dorset, Cheshire, Norfolk, Rutland, Staffordshire, and Shropshire. Ken's policy as general editor was to allow the scholars who were producing county surveys to present the material very much as they chose within the general framework of the whole series. He wisely made no attempt to impose absolute conformity, and his editing was mainly a matter of providing helpful comments and pointing to comparative material. He was also a constant source of encouragement, which was much appreciated by the people engaged in this very laborious branch of scholarship. The only spell of disharmony between the general editor and the editors of county surveys occurred during the painful transmission from publication by Cambridge University Press to desk-top production, which took place during the middle years of the 1980s.

Ken's many virtues did not include a strong aesthetic sensibility and his satisfaction with the first volume to be produced by the new method, Part 1 of Lincolnshire, and with issues of the *Journal* at this date, was not shared by his colleagues. The situation was delicate, as production was being undertaken by Mrs Pattison, on whose help and support Ken depended heavily. It was the eventual recognition by Mrs Pattison that the machinery she was using could not produce suitable type which persuaded Ken to listen to the critics, and this led, through various stages, to the adoption of more satisfactory techniques. This was the only time, in more than thirty years of friendship and cooperation, that I was not able to give Ken my total loyalty and support.

It remains to consider Ken's published works and the influence which these had on the development of English place-name studies. The two books which established his reputation, *The Place-Names of Derbyshire* and *English Place-Names*, were not ground-breaking in the manner of the work he produced from 1965 onwards. The Derbyshire survey was more detailed than previous ones. It included a more generous quantity of field-names, and it listed all names on 6-inch Ordnance Survey maps, whereas previous county surveys had noted only those which appeared in earlier records. Both these practices were followed in future volumes in the series, and they were useful innovations; but the attitude to the historical bearing of the material which Ken showed in the Introduction to the Derbyshire volumes was essentially that found in all such Introductions since the inauguration of the English Place-Name Survey in 1923. Similarly, the general account of the subject in *English Place-Names* gave an exceptionally clear picture of the doctrines which scholars of Ken's generation had inherited from illustrious predecessors such as Sir Allen Mawer and Sir Frank Stenton, whose attitudes were formed in the second and third decades of the twentieth century. Reviewing this book I remarked that the subject seemed surprisingly static. In fact it ceased to be static at about that time, and shortly afterwards Ken became a pivotal figure in a great rethinking. It is ironic that the phenomenal success of *English Place-Names* perpetuated the earlier attitudes in the perceptions of the reading public. The book was reprinted several times, and an edition of 1988 (the fourth) was provided with Addenda which briefly indicated the areas in which the 1961 original was seriously out of date. It was finally replaced by a new version in 1996. Ken's most famous book performed a great service in stimulating interest among non-academic readers, but it did not foreshadow the changes which were imminent.

Place-names have always been recognised as an important source of information about the events of the post-Roman period in Britain, and it is mainly this aspect which has gained the subject its niche in university teaching. The 1960s saw the publication of a number of articles criticising assumptions about the historical bearing of place-name evidence which had held the field since the early 1920s. It had been assumed, for instance, that names of the Reading/Hastings type, which were originally group-names meaning 'followers of Rēad/Hǣsta', marked the first landtakings of Anglo-Saxon settlers, and that names which referred to Germanic paganism were similarly early. These tenets were now shown to be seriously at odds with archaeological evidence for early Anglo-Saxon settlement, and a general reappraisal of the chronology of place-name types was seen to be necessary.[5] Although this reappraisal negated a good deal of what he had written in *English Place-Names*, Ken gave it his full encouragement and support, and together with other place-name scholars of his generation embarked enthusiastically on a process of rethinking which seemed to those engaged in it to be revitalising the study. Ken's

---

[5] An account of the relevant papers can be found in chap. 5 of M. Gelling, *Signposts to the Past: Place-Names and the History of England* (3rd edn., 1998). The main protagonists were J. McN. Dodgson, M. Gelling, B. Cox, and K. Cameron.

main contributions were a paper setting out the significance of *ecles* in English place-names and a ground-breaking study of Scandinavian names in the East Midlands, and more will be said about these when the corpus of his published works is considered as a whole.

The necessity for a reappraisal of the historical significance of English place-names was not immediately perceived by senior scholars, and this became embarrassingly apparent in 1973, when the English Place-Name Society celebrated the fiftieth anniversary of its foundation. A number of well-intentioned articles appeared in that year, outlining the history and achievements of the society, but it was clear that most of our well-wishers were totally unaware of all the articles published in specialist journals between 1965 and 1973 which we thought had brought about a fundamental revision. This was the background to Ken's Israel Gollancz Memorial Lecture in 1976.

Ken used the occasion of this prestigious lecture to explain and give authority to the revisionist writings of the preceding decade. It was a memorable event, and the older generation of scholars who had either failed to notice or chosen to ignore what was happening in place-name studies were obliged to take note. This led to a good deal of backlash, some of it surprisingly fierce. The *-ingas* theory, in particular, was indignantly defended for some time. Writing in 1986 Dr J. N. L. Myres spoke scornfully of John Dodgson's 'new notion' (actually promulgated twenty years earlier) that *-ingas* names were not likely to refer to the earliest English settlements.[6] But despite the difficulty of convincing the preceding generation of scholars of the necessity for fresh thinking about the historical significance of place-names, the new attitudes led to a period of fruitful cooperation with contemporary and younger scholars in the disciplines of history, geography, and archaeology. It was fortunate that Ken had become Director of the English Place-Name Survey in 1966, enabling him to confer irrefutable academic authority on work which might otherwise have continued to be regarded as heretical.

Ken's inaugural lecture of 1965 has the title *Scandinavian Settlement in the Territory of the Five Boroughs: The Place-Name Evidence*. In this he developed a method of study which (as he acknowledged) had been suggested in 1935 by L. W. H. Payling: that of relating village names to the type of soil on which the village stands. In areas where the siting of settlements is not constrained by dramatic topography there is a preference for light, well-drained soils; and by use of detailed maps showing

[6] J. N. L. Myres, *The English Settlements* (Oxford, 1986), p. 41, n. 1.

drift geology it was possible to demonstrate that settlements with Scandinavian names were frequently on less desirable sites than those with English names. One of his maps from this exercise was reproduced in The British Academy *Review*, January–July 2000, in an account by Professor R. Coates of the work of the English Place-Name Society.

From the results of this study Ken concluded that a great many Scandinavian place-names in eastern England resulted from a migration of farming people who came there during the two generations when the land was under the control of Danish governors; and that many of the settlements with Scandinavian names were likely to be new foundations of the late ninth and early tenth centuries established in peaceful conditions, rather than pre-existing settlements taken over by members of disbanded Viking armies.

This interpretation cut across the prevailing ethos in settlement studies. The 1960s saw a great swing from the 'clean sweep' theory, which held that continuous English settlement history mostly began with the Anglo-Saxon settlement, to the opposite view that most of the settlement pattern went back, through the Roman period, into prehistoric times. The suggestion that settlement expanded substantially at this late date opened a long and acrimonious debate. The initial study, which was mainly of names in -*bý*, was followed in 1970 and 1971 by others which considered names in *thorp* and those in which Old English *tūn* was combined with a Scandinavian personal name. The three studies were reprinted in 1975[7] in a form which made them accessible to a wider readership. In other papers on this theme Ken stressed the density in some parishes of medieval field-names which contained Scandinavian terms, and the presence of clear traces of Scandinavian grammar and pronunciation. Finally, in 1985, he published a paper which (in the note he sent with the offprint) he described as 'my last will and testament on Danish settlement'.[8] This paper gives a generous summary of the debate and a clear statement of his final position. Some paragraphs deserve quotation:

> In the end, one must reach a conclusion on the balance of probabilities . . . I, and others too, still think that a secondary migration is necessary to explain the evidence as we have it at present. (1) Given in the East Midlands that members of the victorious army settled in established villages without altering the names in

---

[7] *Place-Name Evidence for the Anglo-Saxon Invasion and Scandinavian Settlements* (English Place-Name Society, 1975), pp. 115–71.

[8] 'Viking Settlement in the East Midlands: The Place-Name Evidence', in R. Schützeichel ed., *Giessener Flurnamen-Kolloquium* (*Beiträge zur Namenforschung*, Neue Folge, 23) (Heidelberg, 1985), pp. 129–53.

any way; (II) given the number of hybrids, both personal name and of the *Carlton* type; (III) given the Scandinavianised names like Fiskerton, Melton and Stainton; (IV) given over 80 place-names of Scandinavian origin other than those in the groups I have discussed, like *Eakring* 'the ring of oaks', *Holme (Pierrepont)* 'the island of land' and *Leake* 'the brook'; (V) given the fact that there are 303 Domesday place-names in -*by* of which, according to me, 192 have Scandinavian personal names as first part; (VI) given, at least, the Viking influence which was responsible for over 100 Domesday-names in *thorpe* and (VII) for the vast number of field-names here derived from words of Scandinavian origin; (VIII) given the linguistic influence of Old Danish on the Old English vocabulary, syntax, grammar and sound-system; given all these, even a third division of an army numbered in a few thousands[9] hardly seems a sufficient explanation.

We have also to remember that many of the place-names are those of units of land, which appear to be the results of colonisation in the strict sense, and that additional corroborative evidence for the agricultural activities of the settlers is to be seen in the numerous Scandinavian words connected with farming and land-measurement found in field-names. Everything seems to point to the presence of farmers settling the land, in addition to the soldiers of the 'great Danish army'. There seems now to be reasonable agreement that the fact that place-names borne by settlements in less attractive sites are regularly Scandinavian in most of the East Midlands suggests that it cannot merely have been a Viking military aristocracy that settled these land-units.

In this paper Ken stressed, as he had done in the Inaugural Lecture of 1965, that villages with names in which *tūn* was combined with a Scandinavian personal name (e.g. *Rollaston, Goverton, Thurgarton*) may reasonably be supposed to be ancient settlements which came into the possession of men who had fought in the Viking army. In the East Midlands the sites of such villages are comparable in desirability to those with wholly English names. It is important to note, however (though, since it was not immediately relevant, Ken did not mention this), that in some parts of England outside the Danelaw there are names of this type in which the reference is to later Danish overlords who were associated with the government of King Cnut.

These influential studies of Danish place-names in eastern England were at odds with some 1960s thinking about settlement history, but they accorded well with the growing belief that it is necessary to consider the physical setting of names in addition to studying them as linguistic phenomena. Since 1965 there have been many studies of topographical aspects of the subject, and Ken used to refer to these as 'practical place-names'.

---

[9] This alludes to the *Anglo-Saxon Chronicle*'s note of three settlements by retired Vikings, in East Anglia, the East Midlands, and Northumbria.

In two important papers Ken contributed to the search for toponymic traces of the descendants of the people of Roman Britain which has been a major preoccupation of place-name scholarship in recent decades. The first of these was 'Eccles in English Place-Names'.[10] In this he provided a corpus and a distribution map for a term borrowed by Anglo-Saxons from Primitive Welsh (the Dark Age reflex of the British language of Roman times) which is believed to refer to a centre of Christian worship. The relevant names are concentrated in the West Midlands, and Ken's map showed that they have a relationship to major Roman roads which cannot be accidental. This paper, which appeared in 1968, shows a striking similarity of approach to my paper of 1967,[11] which demonstrated the close relationship of the place-name Wickham to Roman roads and remains of Romano-British habitation sites. We were not aware of each other's work while these papers were in preparation; the realisation that distribution maps were a vital tool in estimating the significance of place-names was part of the new approach now characterising the subject.

When Ken was invited to give the O'Donnell lecture he regarded this as a challenge to find further evidence in place-names of a non-Germanic element in the ethnic composition of the Anglo-Saxon kingdoms. The endowment of these lectures states that they should concern 'the British or Celtic element in the existing population of England'.[12] Ken's contribution, an exhaustive study of the Old English word *walh* as used in place-names, is arguably the most satisfying of all his papers. It was published in 1980.[13] His starting points for the study were a previous O'Donnell lecture by J. R. R. Tolkien[14] and a paper by Dr Margaret Faull.[15] Both these papers included brief discussions of place-names containing *walh*, suggesting that these might refer to Welsh people rather than (as was the view prevalent earlier) to serfs; and Dr Faull's paper provided substantial evidence that 'Briton' was the earlier and commoner meaning of the term. Ken's paper provides a complete corpus and a

[10] In M. W. Barley and R. P. C. Hanson (eds.), *Christianity in Britain, 300–700* (Leicester, 1968), pp. 87–92. Reprinted in collection of papers cited above in n. 7, pp. 1–7.
[11] Reprinted in *Place-Name Evidence for the Anglo-Saxon Invasion and Scandinavian Settlements*, pp. 8–26.
[12] 'Note' in *Angles and Britons: O'Donnell Lectures* (Cardiff, 1963).
[13] K. Cameron, 'The Meaning and Significance of Old English *walh* in English Place-Names', English Place-Name Society *Journal*, 12 (1979–80), pp. 1–53.
[14] J. R. R. Tolkien, 'English and Welsh', in *Angles and Britons*, pp. 1–41.
[15] M. Faull, 'The Semantic Development of Old English *wealh*', *Leeds Studies in English*, VIII (1975), pp. 20–44.

distribution map of place-names containing *walh*. The assembling of the corpus required great care in distinguishing names in which *Wal-* certainly derived from this source, rather than from *wall* 'wall', *wald* 'forest' or *wælle* 'spring'; Tolkien had given this as his reason for not pursuing the matter. From this exercise Ken concluded that when early spellings show them certainly to contain *walh*, names such as Walton, Walcot, and Walworth indicate the continuance of Welsh speech in some communities for several centuries after the immigration of Germanic-speaking people. This is a substantial contribution to the evidence for a British presence in Anglo-Saxon England, and it has been widely accepted as such.

The main focus of research for Ken, as for all English Place-Name Society editors, was the production of the county volumes of the English Place-Name Survey. At the time of his death he had just completed Part 6 of *The Place-Names of Lincolnshire*, so that, together with the three Derbyshire volumes, he contributed nine items to the Society's total score to date of 77. Compiling these volumes is slow, laborious work, involving the extraction of early spellings from a vast number of printed and manuscript sources, the often tricky process of identifying these spellings with surviving place-names, and finally the provision of sound etymologies for all items which have sufficient documentation. Ken delighted in the search for material in medieval manuscripts, and his weekly visits to the Record Office in Lincoln must have been oases in a working life beset with administrative chores. They were convivial occasions also; an archivist who worked there for a time has told me that Ken and the staff regularly had lunch together on the Wednesdays when he was there. His friends among Lincolnshire archivists and historians included Dr Kathleen Major, to whom he dedicated Part 4.

A bibliography of Ken's publications in the years 1956–85 was compiled for his festschrift.[16] After 1985, there were Parts 2–6 of *The Place-Names of Lincolnshire*, and *A Dictionary of Lincolnshire Place-Names* which covered what are loosely known as 'major names' in the county. This last, which is Vol. 1 in the English Place-Name Society's Popular Series, appeared in 1998; it is one of several books in which county editors have presented material for the major names in a whole county while their life-time's work on the detailed survey is in progress. The dates of the Lincolnshire volumes are: Part 2, 1991; 3, 1992; 4, 1996; 5, 1997; 6 (posthumously), 2001. In these works Ken acknowledges the help of his former research student and friend, Dr John Insley; and Part 6 of the

---

[16] See above, n. 1.

county survey is dedicated to 'the memory of John Field, who worked with me on all six volumes of *The Place-Names of Lincolnshire*'. As noted above, the new version of the Batsford book *English Place-Names* appeared in 1996, and this will be the standard introduction to the subject for many years to come. There were also some articles and reviews. The most important of the articles was the printed version of a lecture given at Reading University in 1995, 'Stenton and Place-Names'. The last of his reviews (and this is a source of great pleasure to the present writer) was of M. Gelling and A. Cole, *The Landscape of Place-Names*: this appeared in *Lincolnshire Past and Present*, no. 44, summer 2001.

The present high academic status of place-name studies in England and the widespread public interest in them owe much to Kenneth Cameron's devoted work. He was an inspiring, supportive, and extremely generous colleague. Dr Peter Brown, when asked to comment on his work for the British Academy, said '. . . he was a loyal and conscientious attender of Section meetings . . . he endeared himself greatly to members of staff . . . he was always ready for a drink or a pub lunch, and, of course, he was the keyest of key figures in the English Place-Name Survey/Society and drew us most welcomingly into its affairs'. He was Chairman of Section 6 from 1986 to 1991.

MARGARET GELLING
Fellow of the Academy

Note. I have to thank Jean Cameron and Susan Cole for information about Professor Cameron's family background and domestic life, also Eric Higham for finding informants who remember his boyhood in Padiham. Information about his teaching at Sheffield University was supplied by Dr Geoffrey Barnes and Professor Ray Page. For the outline of his career at Nottingham University I am mainly indebted to Professor Thorlac Turville-Petre. Some additional information about this has been provided by Professor Page and Professor James Boulton, who also taught with him in the English Department there. Dr Karl Inge Sandred sent details of the honours Professor Cameron received in Sweden.

Professor Boulton has done me the great service of reading a draft and suggesting a number of improvements.

FRANCIS CARSTEN

Francis Ludwig Carsten
1911–1998

DURING HIS LONG and productive life as an academic teacher and widely-read scholar Professor Francis Carsten occupied quite a unique position in his profession. He was, in the half century between the end of the Second World War and his death on 23 June 1998, probably the most important and most understanding as well as the most suitable mediator in establishing closer contacts between British and German historians after a political disaster of appalling dimensions. More than any other scholar in his generation of 'refugee historians' or 'continental Britons' Carsten resolutely concentrated his research, writing and teaching on the history of Prussia and Central Europe, mainly in the nineteenth and twentieth centuries, thus inspiring over the years an influential and continually growing number of younger British historians with a strong interest in the history of Germany.

Likewise, discreetly and tactfully, but with the same determination as in his scholarly work, he spared no effort to forge relations between historians in Britain and Germany which, in the years preceding 1939, had never been particularly close and had to start from scratch after the twin catastrophes of the Nazi dictatorship and Hitler's military aggressions. They had made him suffer personally and had a profound effect on his development as a scholar. He had to flee Nazi Germany in 1936 and pursue a career in a country he had not visited before his rather unplanned short stay in that year. It became his permanent home shortly before the outbreak of war in 1939. In later life Carsten never spoke of the various difficulties he had encountered during those dangerous and unsettling

Proceedings of the British Academy, **115**, 119–129. © The British Academy 2002.

years. Instead, he never tired of expressing his admiration for and loyalty to a country that had offered him generous hospitality in times of oppression and the chance of becoming a respected scholar in his chosen field. In spite of personal persecution and emigration he had turned into one of those broad-minded emigrants who helped, with his modest means, to bring back a democratic Germany into the fold of civilised nations and its scholars back into the international community of learning. In his house in Hampstead, filled to the brim with books and paintings, he and his wife Ruth, *née* Moses, played host to countless German academics and brought them into contact with their British colleagues. For many decades the Carstens provided the entrée and the welcoming intellectual atmosphere for two generations of German historians whose work or research interests had directed them to London. Francis' and Ruth's role as go-betweens vis-à-vis two scholarly cultures and two former enemy nations, basically people of very different backgrounds and equally different experiences, is fondly remembered by all who were privileged to enjoy their friendship, and lives on in their memories.

I

Francis (Franz) Ludwig Carsten was born in Berlin on 25 June 1911, the second son of the ophthalmic surgeon Paul Carsten and his wife Frida, *née* Born, in a prosperous Jewish upper middle-class family. Frida Born came from a wealthy banker's family of Austrian origin which allowed her widowed mother Jennie to live in grand style in a villa in the rather posh *Tiergartenstraße* with servants and stables. In her spacious house and garden her three grandchildren spent much time. Paul Carsten's parents ran a business. They owned a clothing-house in the centre of Berlin, called 'Die Goldene 110', in the busy *Leipzigerstraße*, which is mentioned in Theodor Fontane's novel *Die Poggenpuhls*.

   Carsten's father was a well-known specialist with a small private clinic in the bourgeois *Tiergarten* area. As was almost common among Berlin's secularised Jewry, Judaism was not prominent in Carsten's education which was essentially left in the hands of a governess. In later life he spoke of his parents as 'rather remote' and the children seeing them mainly at meal-times. They were, in short, archetypical Wilhelmine conservatives with strong monarchical convictions. Like their gentile neighbours, they put the flags out to celebrate Sedan Day, imperial Germany's national holiday, and the German victories in the First World War. In the harsh war years his father, Carsten later remembered with hardly concealed amusement, very often appeared in uniform with a spiked helmet and sabre to demonstrate his patriotism and support for 'the cause'. Even after the demise of the Hohenzollern monarchy his mother who was related to Berlin's 'Jewish aristocracy' would still refer to 'our Empress'. For young Franz Ludwig, as he later recalled, all this represented 'a stifling bourgeois atmosphere'[1] which he tried to escape while he was still a pupil at the *Mommsen Gymnasium* round the corner from his father's clinic.

Of his schooldays in Berlin Carsten had no happy memories. He remembered the *Gymnasium* in these early years of the Weimar Republic as 'cold, Prussian and strictly disciplinarian', with many unpleasant teachers. 'Some of the teachers had been officers and would talk about their war experiences at the front and make anti-French and anti-Polish speeches, in particular at the time of the fighting in Upper Silesia in the early 1920s. The Treaty of Versailles was contemptuously pronounced "Versalj". My form master was a choleric petty tyrant and everybody was afraid of him. The teaching of Latin and Greek was excellent but I hated the whole atmosphere and did the minimum of work.'[2] In other words, Carsten like almost all his contemporaries grew up in a country that had suddenly adopted democracy but whose elites in their majority still stuck to antiquated political ideals and tolerated the educational system of a bygone age.

Carsten's activities in those formative years were very much focused on the Socialist Pupils' League which he had joined at the age of fifteen, much to the understandable consternation of his parents and teachers. Sympathies for the Left, at first for the Communists and soon for the Social Democrats and the labour movement, were to accompany him all his life and made him again and again toy with the idea of becoming a politician. Whenever Carsten referred to the ambitious aspirations of his youth and early adulthood his friends and colleagues found it hard to imagine that this most scholarly and private man would have found pleasure in crude political rhetoric or delivering political speeches, or that agitated crowds would have bothered to listen to him. His forte was certainly not the charisma of a public orator or the opportunism of a shrewd parliamentarian. Was he only joking or simply testing their reactions to a

---

[1] Francis L. Carsten, 'From Berlin to London', *Year-Book of the Leo Baeck Institute*, 43 (1998), 341.
[2] Ibid., 340–1.

prospect which his friends and colleagues perceived as being rather far-fetched? However, as one of his early students has observed, Carsten 'rightly regarded himself as a refugee from Nazi Germany foremost on the grounds of his political activity, not his Jewish origins.'[3]

Despite his open sympathies for the political Left and his work as the co-editor of a short-lived magazine called *Der Schulkampf* which exposed the reactionary and nationalistic bias of his teachers, Carsten earned his *Abitur* in 1929. By then he had joined the *Kommunistischer Jugendverband Deutschlands* and, in his own words, 'without much knowledge of Marxist theory or of the reality of Soviet Russia' became an 'enthusiastic young Communist'.[4] Although history had been his favourite subject at school and his maternal grandfather's library his treasure-trove for historical literature Carsten decided to read law and economics, in his first semester in Geneva, then in Berlin and, during 1930–1, in Heidelberg. There he met Richard Löwenthal who had been expelled from the Communist Party for, as the jargon went in those days, 'right wing deviationism'. Under Löwenthal's forceful influence Carsten slowly became more critical of Communist policies and propaganda and increasingly interested in the history of the German labour movement. Löwenthal, who also emigrated to England in the 1930s and then played a highly influential role in the ideological re-shaping of the West German Social Democratic Party (SPD) after the war, was to become a life-long friend and mentor.

After his return to Berlin from Heidelberg, however, Carsten's political activities still mainly centred in Communist youth organisations. Clashes with the much more numerous Nazi students were frequent and Carsten liked to point proudly to the visible scars of a head wound he had received in one of these heroic street battles. He noticed then, and always remembered in years to come, that anti-Semitism was not a preserve of the political Right. On the contrary, the Communist attitude towards Jewish groups and organisations was decidedly hostile, whether these were pro-German or Zionist. Both varieties of Jewish political awareness were equally considered enemies. This experience contributed to Carsten's disillusionment with the official Party-line. Consequently, he read the pamphlets in which Leon Trotsky attacked the Party and blamed it for not working for an urgently needed united front with the Social Democrats against the Nazis. These years witnessed their rapid growth as a mass

---

[3] Henry J. Cohn, 'F. L. Carsten, 1911–1998', *German History. The Journal of the German History Society*, 17 (1999), 95.
[4] Carsten, 'From Berlin to London', 341.

movement which the split Socialist movement was so obviously unable to oppose effectively. For Carsten the bitter ideological conflicts of the time sharpened his understanding of politics and induced him to acquire a substantial collection of books and pamphlets which were published by the labour movement and the Socialist parties in their fight against Capitalism, Nazism, and each other. This truly unique collection, covering the years 1894 to 1947, has survived all the upheavals and U-turns of his life and represents a historical source of great importance. In his will, Carsten donated it to the German Historical Institute in London where it is now easily accessible for researchers.

Through Löwenthal, early in 1932, Carsten was persuaded to join a newly-formed secret organisation whose aim it was to reunite the feuding working-class parties. The so-called 'Org' whose impact, with hindsight, Carsten was prone to overestimate, was strictly conspiratorial; the members and leaders used cover names. The 'Org' formed study groups concentrating on ideological and historical issues. So when Hitler came to power in January 1933 Carsten 'ran a large group in a red working-class district of Berlin on Engels' *The Origin of the Family, Private Property and the State*—a topic far removed from the German reality. At the same time I was forbidden, under Party orders, to make any preparation for the Party to go underground; its normal activities were to continue as if nothing had happened. The illusion would not last many weeks.'[5] At this point his involvement in politics did not stop Carsten from pursuing his legal studies and, in May 1933, he passed the first state examination with satisfactory results. But Hitler was now consolidating his iron grip on Germany and this was the end of Carsten's legal career as 'non-Aryans' were not allowed to continue. So, in his remaining years in Berlin Carsten worked briefly in a bank, then opened a bookshop on the *Kurfürstendamm* which, after a few weeks, was closed down by the Gestapo for some arbitrary reasons. He was eventually arrested for a couple of days in 1934 because of his political activities in his student days. Meanwhile, the 'Org' had turned into a small underground group, acquiring the name 'Neu Beginnen' from the title of a pamphlet published in Czechoslovakia by its founder Walter Löwenheim. Carsten, known in the organisation under the code name 'Herbert' or 'Zeiss', recruited members, in particular from the former Socialist Youth, tried to raise funds and to find flats suitable for clandestine meetings, collected reports on local conditions, and established contacts with other underground groups.

---

[5] Carsten, 'From Berlin to London', 343.

II

However, the days of the 'Org' and with it Carsten's days in Berlin were numbered. Friends advised him, after a tip-off that the Gestapo was after him, to leave the country. This he duly did in 1936 via Basle and Paris to London. Carsten was now a political refugee with hardly any means of support, let alone a job. In conversations with the sociologist Norbert Elias Carsten chose, for the time being, to leave politics and practising law, and take on the study of history instead. 'A plan emerged that I should develop my interest in history and work on early Prussian history. I aimed to discover the factors which had caused the peculiar development of Prussia, especially of its nobility, the Junkers, and the secret of the latter's long-lasting power.'[6] Thus the momentous decision could hardly be interpreted as a sign of despair and succumbing to the inevitable. In exile, too, Carsten kept contacts with friends in the Socialist movement and even had the dubious opportunity of meeting the post-war East German Communist leader Walter Ulbricht. According to Carsten the brief meeting did not go very well.

Early in 1936 Carsten moved to Amsterdam and spent three years there, in close contact with the newly founded International Institute of Social History and some supportive Dutch historians. Carsten could now work fairly undisturbed and was able to publish a number of articles from his field of research in Dutch learned journals. He was also able to assemble the source material which was soon to form the basis of his Oxford thesis, for the worsening political situation forced Carsten to move on. In April 1939 he returned to England with the intention of trying to obtain a scholarship. Recommendations from his Dutch friends proved helpful, and so was Patrick Gordon Walker of Christ Church, Oxford, whom Carsten had met years before in Berlin. In the autumn of 1939 Carsten was in fact fortunate to go up to Oxford with a research scholarship at Wadham College where he was welcomed by the Warden, Maurice Bowra, and received much encouragement from the Regius Professor of Modern History, Maurice Powicke. Soon joining the local Labour Club the 28-year-old refugee from Berlin became friendly with some contemporary and future luminaries of the British labour movement such as G. D. H. Cole, Anthony Crosland, and Roy Jenkins.

The outbreak of war inevitably affected Carsten's life. As an 'enemy alien' he had to appear before a tribunal in March 1940 and was classified

[6] Carsten, 'From Berlin to London', 345.

A, on a scale from A ('proven anti-Nazi') to D ('pro-Nazi'). However, this did not make him immune to police action. 'In the summer vacation [of 1940]', Carsten recalled, 'I wanted to work for the war effort and volunteered for the Oxford University forestry camp in the Forest of Dean. But as soon as I got there I was arrested by the Newport police—they were pleased to have found a German spy—and interned with many thousands of refugees, following Churchill's dictum "Collar the lot!"'[7] Carsten was first interned at Warth Mill near Manchester and later, as almost all the 'enemy aliens', on the Isle of Man. But Carsten was lucky. After only three months of internment he was released and voluntarily joined the Army Pioneer Corps at Ilfracombe in Devon. Again, this proved to be a short spell. In the winter of 1940/1 Carsten caught severe pneumonia, was pronounced unfit for military service and discharged with a small weekly pension of ten shillings.

The remaining years of the war which Carsten spent in Oxford and Bedfordshire were notable in three respects. First, he finished his Ph.D. thesis on 'The Development of the Manorial System—*Grundherrschaft* and *Gutsherrschaft* in Northeastern Germany until the Seventeenth Century' early in 1942. Secondly, Carsten met his future wife Ruth 'on a rainy day in Cornmarket', as he liked to say, though not giving further details about the circumstances. They married in 1945. And, thirdly, he found a job with the Political Warfare Executive, housed at Woburn Abbey and the surrounding villages, in late 1942. Carsten's task there was to prepare a handbook on Germany to be used by the occupation army after the war had ended. The handbook contained chapters on German administration, local government, education, social services—and a chapter on German history to be written by A. J. P. Taylor. However, Carsten drily liked to reminisce, it 'was so anti-German that it was rejected at my suggestion'.[8]

III

The end of war found Carsten in London. He had time to work in the library of the British Museum and lectured in prisoner-of-war camps in various parts of England, especially at Wilton Park near London, and to British officers who were being trained for administrative duties in

---

[7] Carsten, 'From Berlin to London', 346.
[8] Ibid., 348.

Germany. Carsten had now set his sights on a life as an academic, and after several fruitless attempts he finally succeeded and was appointed, in 1947, to a lectureship in modern history at Westfield College, University of London. After years of wandering about and existential insecurity Carsten, who had become a British citizen in 1946, could at last settle down, concentrate on his academic interests as well as his growing family and enjoy a more tranquil life.

In his fourteen years at Westfield College as lecturer and reader Carsten reintroduced practically single-handedly German and, to a lesser extent, Austrian history as an academic subject in England. At first, though he continued his work on Prussian history, he published a number of articles in the *English Historical Review* and his first book, *The Origins of Prussia* (1954). The book was well received in Britain, but in Germany there was criticism from some conservative historians who disliked Carsten's stress on social and economic factors. A German translation of the book had to wait until 1968. In the meantime Carsten had gradually broadened his interests. In his *Princes and Parliaments in Germany: From the 15th to the 18th Century* (1959) he pointed out that in many parts of Germany the Estates and Diets survived the period of princely absolutism and sometimes even played an important part in the history of the principalities as, for example, in Wurttemberg, Bavaria or Saxony. The twentieth century, too, now came into his view, partly, as Carsten later wrote, 'because of my old political interests, partly because German documents from the Weimar and Nazi periods had become available for research'.[9] A first result of Carsten's involvement with contemporary history was his *The Reichswehr and Politics, 1918–1933* (1966, German edition 1964). Understandably, the book made a much greater impact in Western Germany than in Britain, but the echo was not always friendly, to say the least. Again, there was severe criticism from the conservative camp, from historians and former army officers alike. They disliked Carsten's assessment of the army's political role (and activities) in the Weimar years. But Carsten had the satisfaction that the *Bundeswehr* bought hundreds of copies for its libraries, in spite of all the criticism and bad-tempered objections from men of the past, and that it made him well known in post-war Germany.

Carsten's shift to dealing with relevant subjects of contemporary history also had something to do with his taking over the Masaryk Chair of

---

[9] Francis L. Carsten, 'From Revolutionary Socialism to German History', in Peter Alter (ed.), *Out of the Third Reich. Refugee Historians in Post-War Britain* (London and New York, 1998), p. 33.

Central European History at the School of Slavonic and East European Studies, University of London, in 1961. From then onwards Carsten produced, with astonishing regularity, a substantial book almost every four to five years, and after retirement in 1978 even every two to three years. All his publications in these highly productive years are solidly based on archival material. Perhaps for this very reason his books are slightly too factual and descriptive, occasionally lacking a bit of imagination and colourful narrative. Most popular among this string of publications which, as a rule, appeared in English and German, was *The Rise of Fascism* (1967). His aim in the book, which sold particularly well in the United States, was to show the similarities and the differences between the major fascist movements in the various European countries and, at the same time, to explain why certain regimes, such as that of General Franco in Spain, were in his view only related to fascism. In a similar way Carsten's *Fascist Movements in Austria: From Schönerer to Hitler* (1977) showed that the regime of Engelbert Dollfuss and Kurt Schuschnigg, although authoritarian beyond any doubt, was not fascist, but that certain political movements in the defunct Habsburg Empire and post-war Austria had inspired Hitler. Both studies were truly pioneering achievements which, in the following years, led to a whole series of more detailed and comparative investigations of the questions raised in them.

The crucial problem of Central European history in the twentieth century, why democracy had failed there and what had prepared the ground for fascism, was constantly on Carsten's agenda. It was, one might safely say, at the core of his research and prolific writing as an academic and lecturer in his middle and later years. It had profoundly affected his own life and that of his family and many friends. Against this background Carsten wrote *Revolution in Central Europe, 1918–1919* (1972) which explained why the revolutionary movement at the end of the Great War had not led, in Germany and Austria, to a true 'democratisation' of state and society although democratic institutions were adopted in both countries, why the old structures in the bureaucracy, the judiciary and the army were preserved to a large extent, and why the workers' and soldiers' councils had faded away so quickly. Carsten returned to these questions, applied to a slightly earlier time, in *War Against War: British and German Radical Movements in the First World War* (1982). This study was a comparison of anti-war movements in the two countries during the war. Both books, each in a different way, broaden our understanding of the course of German history in the fateful twentieth century. So does *Britain and the Weimar Republic* (1984), based on the mass of reports by British

diplomats in Berlin, now held in the Public Record Office in Kew
Gardens. This collection of documents makes it clear how well informed
the Foreign Office was about political developments in Germany and how
closely it monitored the rise of the Nazis. A complementary publication
was Carsten's *The First Austrian Republic, 1918–1938: A Study Based on
British and Austrian Documents* (1986). However, Carsten's interest in the
history of Prussia lingered on, and proof for this was his *A History of the
Prussian Junkers* (1989) which took up the theme of his Oxford Ph.D.
thesis and discussed it over a much longer period.

In his late seventies and early eighties Carsten still visited archives and
libraries in Britain and Germany although the illness of his wife Ruth
increasingly restricted his mobility. 'Pensioners have plenty of time', he
used to say laconically when asked how he combined running the house-
hold, entertaining guests, and tending the garden with writing reviews,
articles and books. In his scholarly work Carsten had, in a way, returned to
his roots in the German socialist movement before the war. He published
two biographies, one on *August Bebel und die Organisation der Massen*
(1991) and another on *Eduard Bernstein, 1850–1932: Eine politische
Biographie* (1993). Both works appeared in German only. Carsten's last
book *The German Workers and the Nazis* (1995), published when he was
84 years of age, is based on the voluminous published sources, mixed with
his memoirs of underground work against the Nazis and the history of
'Neu Beginnen'. It was a book, as Carsten freely admitted, 'which is
strongly influenced by my own observations'.[10]

Francis Carsten was certainly the last person to deny the fact that his
upbringing and early political experiences in Berlin before the Second
World War had an enormous and lasting influence on his life and his
work as an academic. But he would have determinedly rejected the label
'emigrant' for himself when it implied something like 'suffering in exile'
or feeling like a foreigner in the adopted country. Carsten felt completely
at home in England. 'I was always much attracted by academic life in
England, with its relaxed and friendly atmosphere,' he wrote in an autobiographical essay[11] a few years before his death. He very much appreciated the honour of being elected a Fellow of the British Academy in 1971.
On the other hand, Carsten bore no grudge against his country of origin.
He welcomed the birth of a democratic Germany after 1945 and took a
close interest in its political affairs. He enjoyed contacts with German

---

[10] Carsten, 'From Revolutionary Socialism to German History', p. 36.
[11] Ibid.

historians, provided they were not of the conservative, nationalistic and narrow-minded ilk. He was an unfailing supporter of the German Historical Institute in London which opened, very much due to his energetic lobbying, in 1976. Besides his valuable collection of pamphlets Carsten donated his whole library of more than 5000 volumes to the Institute where, particularly in his later years, he liked to work and listen to lectures.

To a younger generation of German historians who had the good fortune to meet him Carsten appeared as the epitome of an anglicised Prussian or, rather, as a Prussian Londoner (if that is, after all, imaginable). For them and many of his friends and colleagues all over the world Carsten incorporated, in a very touching way, something that is, to all intents and purposes, extinct in modern Germany: A 'Kantian' Prussian with a love of scholarship, literature, the arts and good conversation, with a barely concealed antipathy for militaristic and nationalist thinking, a hard-working man with an overwhelming sense of duty, modest and frugal in his personal life-style. Carsten, always politically alert, was a scholar who, in spite of all that he had witnessed in his life, had not lost his faith in a better world where reason, tolerance and humanity would reign. He was unwavering in trying to make his own small contribution to the realisation of this utopia.

PETER ALTER
University of Duisburg, Germany

Note. A list of Francis Carsten's books and articles up to 1980 can be found in Volker R. Berghahn and Martin Kitchen (eds.), *Germany in the Age of Total War* (1981), pp. 258–60.

JOHN CHADWICK

John Chadwick
1920–1998

IN THE 1970s A DISTINGUISHED British scholar was visiting one of the main museums in the United States. He could not find the object that he wanted to see, and giving his name as Professor Chadwick from England at the enquiry desk, he asked if he could be shown it. He was gratified, if a little surprised, at once to be given the red carpet treatment, in the form of a conducted tour of the entire museum by the Director himself. It was only when he was taking his leave, and the Director made a remark about the decipherment of Linear A, that he realised that an embarrassing mistake had been made. It was not him, the Revd Professor Henry Chadwick, FBA, at that time Dean of Christ Church, Oxford, that the museum thought they were welcoming, but a namesake (though not a relative) whom he knew and greatly admired: John Chadwick, also a Fellow of the Academy, and Perceval Maitland Laurence Reader in Classics at Cambridge University.

Even in the 1970s, John Chadwick's celebrity, not least abroad, was not a recent development. It had its origins in the 1950s and his association, when still in his early thirties, with one of the great intellectual achievements of the century: the decipherment by an even younger contemporary, Michael Ventris, of the Linear B script used in the late Second Millennium BC in Crete and the Greek mainland. It was a fame that did not fade: when Chadwick died on 24 November 1998, aged 78, obituaries appeared, not only in all the English broadsheets, but also in publications not normally given to noting the passing of Cambridge Classical philologists, among them the *New York Times* and *Der Spiegel*.

Proceedings of the British Academy, **115**, 133–165. © The British Academy 2002.

We shall discuss later the collaboration with Ventris, and the creation of the new discipline of Mycenology which followed the decipherment. But we must first describe Chadwick's background and early life, and the acquisition of the skills which made him Ventris's ideal collaborator.

* * *

John Chadwick was born in East Sheen, Surrey, on 21 May 1920, the younger son of Fred Chadwick and Margaret Pamela Bray. The family originally came from Southport in Lancashire, but John's grandmother, Ann Chadwick (*née* Ogden), moved to London with her three children Clara, Fred, and Thomas when her husband John died prematurely. Both Fred and Thomas started in very difficult circumstances and were obliged to leave school at a very early age to find work in the National Savings Bank (the Slavings Bank, as they called it). Their progress was, for the time, little short of miraculous; starting in the bottom division of the Civil Service, they ended at the top, Fred as Treasurer to the Forestry Commission, and Thomas as Sir Thomas Chadwick, KCVO, Chief Accountant to the Treasury.

Both John's father and uncle were members of the New Church, founded in 1788 by followers of Emanuel Swedenborg (1688–1772), the Swedish scientific and religious writer; and in the 1930s Fred ran a New Church Sunday school. Chadwick and his elder brother, Kenneth, who had a successful career with the merchant bankers Morgan Grenfell, also became members of the Church. In later life John attended Anglican services but he never lost his interest in Swedenborg. He served for more than fifty years as a member (and for some years Chairman) of the Swedenborg Society's Advisory and Revision Board, and spent much of the later part of this period preparing a lexicon of Swedenborg's neo-Latin. He also produced new translations of no fewer than eight of Swedenborg's books, six of them in his later years when retirement gave him time for it. He was President of the Swedenborg Society in 1987–8, and in recognition of his services to the Society was given the rare honour of Honorary Life Membership. It is perhaps typical of the man that what for others would have been a purely religious or spiritual involvement in him turned also into a scholarly endeavour. He was legitimately proud of his Swedenborg lexicon (1975–90), a unique example, as he rightly said, of a lexicon of eighteenth-century Latin.

Because of Fred's success in the Civil Service, John and his elder brother had the education which Fred had had to miss. They both started at Colet Court, the preparatory school for St Paul's, and continued at St Paul's itself, which John entered in 1934 with a scholarship. He began Latin and Greek at Colet Court (indeed, he had learnt the Greek alphabet as early as the English one from his brother); and from his third year at St Paul's onwards, in the Middle and Upper Eighths, he specialised in classics. The school had a high academic reputation and classics was a flourishing subject. Among John's exact or near contemporaries were A. Geoffrey Woodhead, who became a Fellow of Corpus Christi in Cambridge, and (Sir) Kenneth Dover, who was first a Fellow of Balliol College, Oxford and then Professor of Greek at St Andrews before becoming President of Corpus Christi College, Oxford and President of the British Academy. Another contemporary was L. J. Cohen, who later studied at Oxford and became a distinguished philosopher and a Fellow of the Academy. Donald Nicol, who was slightly younger, went from St Paul's to Cambridge and eventually became Koraës Professor of Modern Greek and Byzantine History, Language and Literature at King's College, London and also a Fellow of the Academy. The competition was strong but by his final year John had advanced to second in his class. Geoffrey Woodhead, who knew him well, and who remained a lifelong friend, remembers him at school as pale and not very robust, but already with the single-minded devotion to his work which he was never to lose. It is quite possible that he had inherited this work ethic from his family, even if his generation was the first to turn it in an academic direction. Even as an undergraduate at Cambridge, as Chadwick himself later recorded, he 'did not take much part in activities other than work', except for singing as a tenor in the College Chapel choir and with the Cambridge University Musical Society under its conductor Boris Ord. But (nearly) all work did not make him a dull schoolboy; and Woodhead also recalls some academic humour: 'Perhaps the best example of it, at this early stage of his career, was the fragment (in English) of a spoof Greek drama entitled *The Bênidai* ("Children of [G. E.] Bean [the Upper Eighth Greek master]") which he wrote and circulated in typescript, complete with learned *apparatus criticus*. My only memory of it now is that the Chorus was composed of Pauline Classics on a treadmill, like the Chorus of Allies in Aristophanes' *Babylonians*; but it was enjoyed by us all at the time.'

John had very high regard for George Bean, whom he afterwards described as 'our admirable Greek teacher'; he may have owed to him the breadth of his academic interests, because Bean, far from being content with straightforward classical literature, in later years learned Turkish and became professor of Greek at Istanbul; he was well known for his indefatigable travels through Turkey and his publications of late Greek and Roman inscriptions; indeed he shared some of this epigraphical work with another pupil, John's friend, Geoffrey Woodhead. It is difficult now to imagine the thoroughness of the classical teaching imparted at St Paul's. There was of course serious analysis of texts and historical events, but there was also the laying of sound linguistic foundations. Not only were pupils required to learn by heart selected passages of Greek and Latin poetry and were regularly tested on this, but they also had to pass exams in Greek and Latin grammar, which were certainly far more advanced than those taken nowadays at university. For one subject at least, the study of Latin cases, the boys produced their own handbook, going back to the texts to find the best examples of usage. John Chadwick had a leading role in this enterprise; it was work which, as Woodhead noted, foreshadowed that of the later lexicographer. John's interest in language more generally also dates from his school days: he tried to teach himself Tibetan, but eventually decided that he needed the help of a native speaker, and none was available.

Later it was Bean who steered the young Chadwick in the direction of Cambridge, his own old university. In the autumn of 1939 John entered Corpus Christi College with a Major Scholarship, a closed Exhibition and a St Paul's leaving award. At the end of his first year, during which his studies were directed by H. D. P. (later Sir Desmond) Lee, he was awarded a First in the Classical Preliminary examination. But after the fall of France in 1940 he felt he could no longer remain a student and volunteered for the Royal Navy. He began as an Ordinary and later Able Seaman, and saw service in the Eastern Mediterranean on HMS *Coventry*. In 1942, however, somewhat to his surprise he was transferred to intelligence duties in Egypt, and in September of that year was promoted to Temporary Sub-Lieutenant (Special Branch), RNVSR. Most of his work initially consisted in deciphering Italian naval signals. He had been selected largely because of his knowledge of Latin which was deemed to be adequate preparation for dealing with Italian. Linguistic expertise was certainly needed: initially the group did not even have an Italian dictionary. The low-grade naval ciphers John was working on were mostly in a code named *Cifrario per Uso di Mare*, referred to affectionately by John and his colleagues as *Ouzo*. But transcripts of traffic in another code were also available in the office in Alexandria where he worked. These messages were prefixed by the one or other of the words GIOVE and DELFO. Strictly speaking, John ought not to have investigated this material, since instructions had been received from headquarters at Bletchley that it should be left to them to deal with. John, however, persuaded his local superior that it could be useful, for purposes of comparison with the Ouzo material, if he did take an interest in it. Much of the material in GIOVE/DELFO was routine, and could readily be deciphered. But John also noticed a much longer and clearly more important message containing many more groups than the routine traffic. Working on this with the head of his section, he was able to translate enough of it to establish that the message concerned a British submarine which had been sunk near Taranto, and attempts being made by the Italians to salvage it. This was of major importance, since if successful the enemy might well recover a copy of the British submarine code. The facts were immediately reported to the Admiralty in London, which prompted an inquiry of Bletchley why the news had come from Alexandria and not the Home Station. As John learnt much later, there were some red faces in the naval section; and Bletchley came to know the name of John Chadwick long before they saw him in person. When he was back in Cambridge after the end of the war he was sent for a supervision to L. P(atrick) Wilkinson, the Latinist at King's College who had held an important post at Bletchley: to his amazement he was greeted with the words GIOVE, DELFO.

In John's life code-breaking was important for what followed, but another event also had consequences. When he was at Suez in 1942 as an ordinary seaman he met a somewhat older cousin, W. N(eville) Mann, who was an officer in the Army and later became a well-known physician. There was a further encounter in Bombay but meetings were difficult because officers 'were forbidden to associate off duty with "ratings" (Navy) and "other ranks" (Army) by "King's Regulations"'. Nevertheless the two, who previously had hardly known each other (there was a nine year age difference), found a number of things in common and in the middle of the war in the Mediterranean kept up a correspondence, although it was slow and desultory. It was at one of their meetings that the project was formulated to translate the non-surgical works of Hippocrates, the Greek medical writer. The editor of the Loeb (Greek and English) text, W. H. S. Jones, was a distinguished Hellenist, but he was not medically trained and, as Neville told his cousin, doctors found his translation unsatisfactory. John had acquired a Teubner text in Alexandria and that was their starting point: John brought to the task his knowledge of Greek and his cousin his medical expertise. In the end the work was mostly done in calmer times between 1947 and 1950, but D. Mervyn Jones remembers being shown at Bletchley a tentative emendation in Hippocrates' text proposed by Chadwick. It impressed him as certainly right and made him aware that after the war he was likely to meet very strong competition in his project of an academic career as a classicist. *The Medical Works of Hippocrates*, by Chadwick and Mann, appeared in 1950 and was John's first publication. It was later adopted by the Penguin Classics series as their text; and it still remains in print, more than half a century later.

After the Italian surrender in September 1943 and after a short period of general duties John was sent back to England at the beginning of 1944 and began a Japanese language course at Bletchley Park. He completed it with distinction (he was one of two classical scholars who came top in the course) and was set to work with two Japanese experts at the translation of messages sent to Tokyo by the Japanese naval representatives in Stockholm and Berlin. Some of the most important of these were from the Naval Attaché in Berlin, who had access to secret reports prepared by the German navy. From his despatches Chadwick and his colleagues were able to obtain invaluable information about such matters as the new generation of U-boats that the Germans were building in 1945. The task was complicated not so much because of the difficulties of Japanese as such, but because of the subject matter: radar, night vision of pilots, espionage, railways, etc. required a knowledge of technical terms and realia which none of the group possessed; the fact that the texts were supplied in an inadequate transliteration in Latin letters made things worse. It was nevertheless a task which was successfully accomplished. To judge from his accounts of it, the young recruit never had any doubt of the importance of the work or of the fact that it was a privilege to be involved in it together with people far more expert than he was. It was impressed on him and his colleagues that the work had to be kept strictly confidential; the embargo on disclosure remained in place for many years. Until it was lifted, John never mentioned the obvious links between his war activities and his interest in decipherment, even if a number of people must have guessed it.

After the end of the war in 1945 Chadwick immediately returned to Cambridge to complete his degree. He was allowed to count his five years of war service as one academic year, and so was able to proceed at once to the second part of the course. This meant that after five years away, he, like the other returning ex-servicemen, had eight months from October to the end of May to get over the shock of his re-entry into civilian life, to relearn all that he had known before the war and to complete a new course in the same time as candidates who had not been away in the armed forces. John had to prepare for exams in Classical Literature, History, and Philosophy as well as his chosen specialisation, Classical Linguistics. This latter he found particularly enjoyable; he had decided that that was what he wanted to do even before coming up in 1939 and in preparation had tried to learn some Sanskrit. He had carried a Sanskrit grammar with him all through the war years and acquired in India a copy of the Bhagavad-Gītā, parts of which he memorised and still remembered in the last years of his life. He was taught by the Professor of Comparative Philology, N. B. Jopson (1890–1969), an extraordinary polymath who could speak every European language and a few further east, including Arabic. Jopson was less interested in research, however, and his lectures on Indo-European linguistics, though certainly lively, were not strong on developments after 1911, when he had himself taken his BA. The discovery of Hittite and Tocharian, which had revolutionised Indo-European studies, had not impinged on him. These deficiencies, however, were amply compensated for by the other lecturer, the Professor of Sanskrit, Harold (later Sir Harold) Bailey (1899–1996). Chadwick afterwards described Bailey as in many ways his ideal of a scholar. He was deeply impressed by Bailey's immense learning, devotion to his subject and modesty, and wrote that 'while it was often difficult to follow (his lectures) because of our ignorance . . . they gave us a taste of what real scholarship meant'.

It is difficult to imagine what those eight months of frantic learning must have been like, but we gain some insights from the recollections of a contemporary (A. G. Woodhead). After the week's hard work, he recalls, everyone needed some relaxation, and many of the ex-servicemen occasionally patronised the local pubs. For John Chadwick, however, relaxation appeared to consist of the occasional bicycle ride and the odd chat over tea or cocoa. In order to save coal in a bitterly cold winter Woodhead and he worked in the same room and at tea time had short breaks. The chats were largely about classics. One small group met once a week in the evening in D. Mervyn Jones's room in Trinity to read classical poetry and then listen to music. The end of this period of hard work was predictable: in June 1946 Chadwick obtained a First in Part II, with distinction in his special subject. Indeed, there were many First Class performances in that year, and several other ex-servicemen also obtained distinctions.

After the examinations all candidates had to take decisions about their future careers, but for John Chadwick, now 26, finding a job was even more urgent (we are talking of course of a period when post-graduate studies were not a normal option, even for future academics). In the summer of 1940 he had met Joan Hill, the daughter of a bank official and his wife who had given temporary lodging to his father when he was evacuated to Clevedon near Bristol in 1939. She was then a schoolgirl and they had become friends. Joan and he had kept in touch by letter during the war, but when they met again in 1945 she had grown up and the relationship deepened. They decided that they would marry when John finished his degree and got a regular job; in the event they waited until July 1947. It was a marriage between two very private persons who did not speak much about it or about personal matters in general, but it lasted 51 years, as John noted with pride; even the outsider could recognise the strong devotion that they felt for each other and for their son, Anthony, born in 1954.

The job which made the marriage possible had been offered to John even before he returned to Cambridge, because at Bletchley he had met one of the editors of the *Oxford Latin Dictionary*, Captain James M. Wyllie. In August 1946, two months after the end of his BA course, he joined the Clarendon Press, as Assistant to the Editor of the *OLD*. Training in lexicography was of course needed. It happened in a somewhat unconventional manner not at Oxford but in Scotland, where Wyllie had a house and did much of his work. After six weeks' instruction from Wyllie, John returned to Oxford, where he worked by himself, communicating as necessary with Wyllie, who would make periodic visits to Oxford to superintend operations there. The unofficial reason for this curious arrangement was to ensure that John did not fall under the control, and become part of the staff, of the other editor, Cyril Bailey, with whom Wyllie had extremely bad relations, and whom he was hoping to dislodge from his position, as he eventually succeeded in doing.

In spite of his increasing eccentricity and even bitterness (which eventually led to his resignation in 1954) Wyllie had a deep influence on John, to whom he transmitted the professional skills which he had learnt at the feet of Sir William Craigie, one of the editors of the *Oxford English Dictionary*. In later years John was a severe critic of those who attempted to discuss lexicographical matters without any training or actual experience. His own experience on the Latin dictionary had led him to the belief that a new dictionary had to start directly from the texts and not from previous dictionaries, as was normally done. As Wyllie used to say 'the new dictionary will contain errors, but they will be our own, not other people's'. Among Wyllie's maxims which John was fond of quoting were: 'always ask yourself what will be useful to the user of the dictionary' and 'the *hapax eiremenon* does exist, but it is much rarer than you think'. It followed from the second precept that the lexicographer should start by assuming that any example of a word which is the lone representative of a special sense is probably wrongly interpreted; only when all other possible interpretations have been considered and rejected should an isolated example be allowed to prove a new sense. In fact lexicography remained one of the dominant passions in John's life. An early paper analysed the problems encountered by the regular user of Liddell–Scott–Jones, the Greek Lexicon. Later followed the Swedenborg lexicon and very extensive work for the Supplement to LSJ produced by P. G. W. Glare on behalf of a British Academy committee of which Chadwick was part from the beginning. The one of us who was on the same committee remembers him as certainly the most active of its members, always ready to check successive drafts, make corrections, etc.; it is largely due to him that the Supplement, published in 1996, includes up-to-date reference to Mycenaean and Cypriot vocabulary. Chadwick was still demonstrating the validity of Wyllie's advice at the end of his life, in *Lexicographica Graeca* (1996), his last book, which arose from his work for the Supplement to LSJ. Here, after a trenchant introduction setting out his views on lexicography, he discusses the meanings of a number of Greek words which he believed to have been wrongly interpreted, in some cases, because of a failure to see that an allegedly unique sense for the term is nothing of the kind. Though some of his revised definitions can be criticised, the book is full of good sense, and contains an immense amount that will be of lasting value. Yet *Lexicographica Graeca* is not the only evidence for Chadwick's continuing interest in lexicography in later life. He lectured on lexicography at Cambridge, and shortly before his death led a successful campaign to raise funds for the compilation of a new Intermediate Greek Lexicon, a project of which he himself had been the prime mover, and which is now progressing.

By 1951 Chadwick was becoming dissatisfied with his position as an employee of the Clarendon Press. He still was greatly interested in his work which, as he put it, was the opposite of drudgery, since 'every word presents its own problems and there is a succession of difficult choices to be made'. However, his salary was low, there were few prospects of advancement and the advantages of being in a university town were limited since there were few connections between OUP employees and the University. Wyllie, too, was becoming more and more obsessive and was increasingly difficult to work with. The arrival of a new assistant, Peter Glare, was welcome, but John had to do most of the training, since Wyllie was too involved in his quarrels with the senior members of OUP and of the University on the one hand and in his own production of a series of pamphlets on subjects like 'God and Sex' on the other. Towards the end of the year John was interested to receive a letter from Professor Jopson which enclosed an advertisement for a post in Classical Philology at Cambridge and encouraged him to apply. He did not think that he stood much chance, but he applied all the same. As he wrote later, 'I had published nothing but my translation of Hippocrates, and my work on Latin was of course entirely unknown'. There followed a long silence but eventually he was astonished to receive the news that he had been appointed to a University Assistant Lectureship. There had been no interview (a practice which continued well into the 1960s), nor any chance to ask questions about the job; Chadwick assumed that Jopson had told the Appointments Committee that he was the best candidate and they had been content to take his word for it.

The appointment in Cambridge was from 1 October 1952 and its notification had arrived at the beginning of the year. Among the things John was due to lecture on was Greek dialects, and that worried him. He had heard a few lectures about the subject by A. J. Beattie, Jopson's assistant, whose appointment to the chair of Greek in Edinburgh had freed the Cambridge post, but that was six years earlier; in recent years he had concentrated on Latin. In his spare time therefore he started reading more about Greek dialects and taking notes. This meant that his mind was very much on the history of Greek when he saw in the *Radio Times* an announcement of a talk to be given on 1 July by a man called Michael Ventris about the Linear B script, then commonly referred to as Minoan Linear B. Even without his new appointment John would have certainly wanted to listen. The first clay tablets with a peculiar non-Greek script of the second millennium BC had been discovered by Sir Arthur Evans at Knossos in Crete in 1900, but though Sir Arthur had been able to distinguish the more frequent Linear B from the earlier Linear A, both scripts were thus far undeciphered. As undergraduates at Cambridge Chadwick and two friends (one was D. Mervyn Jones) had investigated the possibility of using their war-time code-breaking skills to decipher the script, but had rapidly concluded that the amount of material which had so far been published was totally inadequate for proper cryptographic analysis. In the 1940s only fifty or so Knossos tablets had been published together with a further four from Pylos on the Greek mainland, where they had first been discovered in 1939. Things changed with the publication in 1951 of E. L. Bennett's preliminary transcription of the Pylos tablets; moreover, in 1952 Sir John Myres, then 83, succeeded in completing Evans's *Scripta*

Minoa II, which made available a much larger corpus from Knossos. During his time at Oxford Chadwick had had several meetings with Myres to discuss Linear B, though he did not succeed in seeing any of the unpublished material. His normal dictionary work and his application to Cambridge had also prevented him from catching up with Bennett's 1951 publication and with *Scripta Minoa II* which had appeared in the spring. Even so, the broadcast was bound to be of interest and Chadwick listened carefully. Ventris claimed that it was possible to assign phonetic values to most of the signs of the Linear B tablets and that these were written in a form of Greek; if so, Greek would have been spoken in Crete and in the Peloponnese in the second millennium BC. It was a short broadcast and too little was said to enable the listener to make a judgement on it. If it was Greek, however, John needed to know about it for his forthcoming lectures. He went to see Sir John Myres to ask if he knew anything more about Ventris's work. Myres revealed that he was in touch with Ventris, and had received the regular bulletins, called *Work Notes*, which he had been circulating since 1950 to all those he knew were interested in the Minoan script problem. Chadwick was allowed to copy the provisional table of syllabic signs and to see some of the apparent Greek words, he went away to test the theory 'in the firm expectation' as he wrote later, 'that it would prove, like so many other abortive attempts, a mirage'.

To his astonishment, however, he found fragments of sense emerging from the tablets. There was much that was unintelligible, but, as his wartime experience had shown him, that was normal in the early stages of a decipherment. Yet in several cases the Greek words yielded by Ventris's sound values gave the meaning which could be deduced simply from the arrangement of the text. Totals were often preceded by a word read as *to-so* or *to-sa*, which could readily be interpreted as /to(s)soi, to(s)sai/, 'so much, so many'. Groups of women, recognisable from the pictorial sign for woman, were regularly accompanied by two words, *ko-wa* and *ko-wo*, followed by numerals. The context clearly suggested that these were references to children; and *ko-wa* and *ko-wo* could immediately be interpreted as /korwai/ and /korwoi/, 'girls' and 'boys': not the form of the word in any normal Greek dialect of the Classical period, but exactly what one could reconstruct for the form of the term used in the second millennium BC.

This was something no previous attempt at decipherment had produced: the right sort of Greek for a period 500 years before Homer. But there were few people equipped to approach it. Chadwick, however, with his philological training, was; and after some days spent finding Greek words on the tablets as transcribed with Ventris's values, he wrote to him on 13 July congratulating him on his 'magnificent achievement' and offering any help he needed to exploit his discovery. ('If there is anything a mere philologist can do please let me know'.) Ventris wrote back at once saying he was much in need of technical help with the Greek he had found. Thus began the legendary collaboration which was only to end with Ventris's tragically early death four years later.

As this account indicates, and as Chadwick himself always insisted, the decipherment of Linear B was Ventris's achievement, and his alone. (So modest, indeed, was Chadwick about his part in the collaboration that, as the obituarist in the *New York Times* noted, he made no mention of himself in an American encylopedia article he once wrote on Linear B.) But his role in helping to extend and exploit Ventris's breakthrough was nonetheless an absolutely crucial one. His first letter to Ventris contains several examples of the ways in which he was able to contribute. At this stage, all the signs, even some frequent ones, had not yet been assigned values; and Chadwick correctly suggested that an unidentified member of the *p-* series was *pu*, since this would give not only *pu-ro* = Pylos, but also the preposition *a-pu*: not *apo*, the Attic form of the word, but the form in the Arcado-Cypriot and Aeolic dialects. (Later, he was able to establish the value of another sign not yet transliterated, *nu*.) He also made a number of proposals about the interpretation of sign groups. Not all of these have stood the test of time, but his suggestions that *pa-ka-na* is /*phasgana*/, 'swords' and that *pi-ri-je-te* 'sounds as if it should mean "sawyer"' have. The main point, however, is that he could provide Ventris with information about the forms which one expected for Greek in the second millennium. This required the sort of technical expertise which Ventris did not have and few other people could have helped him with. And not only was Chadwick's help indispensable: we should note that to provide that help required a great deal of courage. Chadwick was a young man who needed to make his way and had no reputation in Greek studies. The tendency to assume that all decipherments are the work of obsessive madmen was and is strong. In siding with Ventris John was risking his future career and in a sense his livelihood. There was more; the decisions he had to take about the etymology of individual words, about the possibility or otherwise of certain forms in the second millennium BC, were often unprecedented. Given his current lack of experience it was more than likely that he would make bad blunders, and this too was dangerous in career terms. Yet, in the young Chadwick's mind, intuition and excitement prevailed over his natural caution.

The first fruits of the collaboration with Ventris appeared the following year: the cautiously titled paper 'Evidence for Greek Dialect in the Mycenaean Archives' in the *Journal of Hellenic Studies* for 1953. This was the first description of the decipherment in a scholarly journal; and Ventris insisted that it should appear under their joint names. The article, if reread to-day, almost fifty years after its publication, is as striking as it must have been at the time. Not a word is wasted nor is there any sign of complacency, but what is remarkable apart from the style of argumentation is how much is still valid both in the values given to the signs and in the interpretation of forms, words, and texts in general. In the final part, which summarizes the phonological and morphological characteristics of the Greek of the Linear B tablets, there is again a sureness of touch which is almost uncanny. When the article was finished in November 1952 Ventris was 30 and Chadwick 32; neither of them had ever published anything about Greek dialects or even Greek linguistics. The notes thank a number of people for their help, only one of whom (G. Björck) was a classical linguist. It seems likely that the observations on the archaic features of the texts, on the dialect features, etc. are all due to Chadwick, and they must have been written at the time when he was preparing or delivering his first lectures ever on Greek dialects. The sharpness and (with hindsight) the obvious correctness of his explanations are remarkable, but even more exceptional is the clarity and simplicity of the exposition in what is after all a set of very technical statements.

Following this, in the summer of 1954, Ventris and Chadwick began their next project. This was the massive *Documents in Mycenaean Greek*, which they completed in a remarkably short time—just under a year—and which was published by Cambridge University Press in 1956. The core of the book is an extended commentary on 300 representative tablets; but it also contains a lengthy introduction, with chapters on the decipherment, the Linear B writing system, the Mycenaean language and the evidence of the tablets for life in the Greek Bronze Age, as well as a vocabulary, a list of personal names and a bibliography. *Documents*—often referred to as the Bible of Mycenaean studies—is an astonishing achievement. Though developments in a rapidly-moving subject over the fifty years since it was written have rendered many of the details obsolete, it is remarkable how much of it still remains valid: a tribute to the breadth and solidity of Ventris's and Chadwick's learning, the excellence of their judgement and above all their caution. As the authors explain in the introduction, and as their correspondence of the time confirms, this was a genuinely joint enterprise, with each submitting his work to the other for criticism and revision. In 1973, Chadwick produced a second edition of *Documents*. Here, out of respect for Ventris, he preserved everything in the first edition except for the vocabularies and the bibliography, but added an Additional Commentary of some 140 pages, a fresh bibliography and an admirable new glossary. *Documents*[2] has all the same qualities of learning and sound judgement as its predecessor; and we shall have occasion to refer to it again later.

Documents was published in the autumn of 1956. By then, however, Michael Ventris was dead. On 6 September, as he drove home alone at night on the Great North Road, his car ran into a stationary lorry on the Barnet by-pass, and he was killed instantly. He was only 34. His death was a savage personal blow for Chadwick: he and Ventris had worked intensely together for four years and in the process had become friends. On rare occasions (such as that of the Gif conference) they had been able to relax with each other talking of other things than Linear B (*Stowe* 1984, p. 43). Joan Chadwick remembers all too clearly the blackness that descended on John when he heard of his friend's death. And he was soon to feel the loss of Ventris in another way, for Ventris's death left John to face alone the critics of their joint work. As he put it later, 'The storm didn't really break until after his [scil. Ventris's] death. Up to the publication of "Documents" we were fighting a battle, obviously, and he was very good at presenting, modestly, his achievements, but he was leaving it to other people to evaluate by saying: "Well this is what I think. I have people who support me, but you must make up your own mind." The real attack on the decipherment followed in the years after 1956 and for something like ten years I was involved with various kinds of running battles with critics of one kind or another, and it was a relief when these things gradually started to fade away and the critics bowed out' (quoted in *Stowe*, 1984, p. 44).

The idea that there could be Greek spoken in Crete in the second millennium had been strongly rejected by Evans, who indeed believed in a Minoan colonisation of the Mainland. Another leading archaeologist, Alan Wace, had advocated the idea of Greek take-over of the island, but this was far from generally accepted. Yet for a time after it was announced the decipherment encountered few objections, from non-archaeologists at least. Significantly, most of the leading experts in Greek historical linguistics gave their assent, and began themselves to work on the subject: Björck in Sweden, Chantraine and Lejeune in France, Risch in Switzerland, Ruipérez in Spain, and Palmer in England. In Britain, of course, the press made much of the coincidence in the *annus mirabilis* 1953 of a series of events: the Coronation, the success of a British-led expedition in making the first ascent of Everest, England's recapture of the Ashes for the first time after the war, and the British decipherment of Linear B. In 1953 a new discovery convinced many of the remaining sceptics: a tablet at Pylos showing pictorial ideograms of tripod cauldrons with varying numbers of handles, and with terms standing before them which if transcribed using the Ventris values could readily be interpreted as describing the objects: *ti-ri-po-de* as /*tripodes*/, 'tripods', *qe-to-ro-we* as /*kʷetrōwes*/, 'having four ears or handles', etc. Chadwick described how Ventris, who had received a letter from C. W. Blegen, the excavator of Pylos, informing him of the discovery, broke the news: 'Michael Ventris had called me from London in a state of great excitement—he rarely showed signs of emotion but for him this was a dramatic moment' (*Stowe*, 1984, p. 40). And he concluded his account with the comment '. . . this was a proof of the decipherment which was undeniable'.

In 1956, however, a major attack on Ventris's solution was launched; and it was followed by others over the next few years. Some of the criticisms, like those of the Germans Grumach and Eilers, could be answered relatively easily. A potentially much more dangerous opponent, however, was A. J. Beattie; for he, unlike many of the other critics, was a historical linguist and a philologist. He had, as we have seen, been one of Chadwick's own teachers at Cambridge before leaving for a chair at Edinburgh in 1952. His first assault on the decipherment appeared in the *Journal of Hellenic Studies* for 1956. He began with a criticism of the way the decipherment had been arrived at, and then levelled three further charges: (i) that the graphic system was inadequate to represent Greek, (ii) that the forms of certain words were unacceptable in the language; (iii) that there were large areas of text which yielded no sense. As the surviving member of the Ventris–Chadwick partnership, Chadwick had clearly to respond to this broadside; and in the following year's *JHS* he published a brief but effective reply. Beattie's account of the decipherment was 'tendentious and distorted', and what mattered in any event was not so much how the decipherment was arrived at, but the results it yielded. (As he put it, 'the cross-check provided by syllabic values which repeat in different words is itself sufficient guarantee of a correct solution; add to this the fact that the words identified are repeatedly—not on one tablet only—confirmed by self-evident ideograms, and the conclusion is beyond any doubt whatsoever'.) Nor were any of Beattie's other criticisms valid. Though the number of possible interpretations of any Mycenaean word was theoretically very large, it was much smaller in practice, given the possibilities of the Greek language and the requirements of the context; a number of the terms criticised by Beattie, such as *wanakteros*, were in fact perfectly acceptable as Greek; and the relative rarity of vocabulary words in the material was simply a reflexion of the high proportion of personal names it contained.

The debate then entered a much more unpleasant phase. In his 1956 paper, Beattie had devoted a lengthy appendix to an attempt to undermine the support for the decipherment provided by the Pylos tripod cauldron tablet. Clearly, however, this continued to trouble him; for in 1958 he made a second attempt to dispose of it. The tablet was found in 1952; Ventris, he suggested, must have seen it or a copy or a photograph, and then used the words in it to assign appropriate values to the signs. He would then have tried to give the impression that these values were confirmed by a new piece of evidence. These extraordinary assertions were quickly disproved by Blegen. The tripod tablet was found in two pieces, one on 4 June, the other on 10 June 1952. They were coated with lime and unreadable; and they were stored in a locked box, from which they were not removed until taken to Athens for cleaning and mending late in July. Thus, even if he had been in Greece, which he was not, Ventris could not possibly have seen the tripod tablet until long after his correspondents had received the twentieth *Work Note*, dated 1 June, in which he proposed for the first time his theory that the language of the tablets was Greek. Nor, as Blegen confirmed, had any photographs or copies of the tablet been made before 1953.

Faced with this impossibility in his reconstructed chronology, Beattie then resorted to an even more outrageous assertion, published in the *Glasgow Herald* in May 1959. Ventris might not have seen the tripod tablet in 1952; but he had seen a very similar document, which he had then destroyed, hoping that a similar one would be discovered later, thus giving support to his decipherment.

These attacks on Ventris's integrity were deeply upsetting. Those of us who saw John Chadwick, many decades later, violently reacting to unjustified assertions which unfairly 'did down' an individual, can easily guess how he must have reacted to something which was so close to his heart. As we have noted already, this was a very difficult time for him, and, in addition to dealing with the public assaults, he had to endure a difficult private correspondence with Beattie, with whom he had tried to maintain friendly relations until the nature of the later accusations made this impossible. He had some powerful support however, including that of Denys (later Sir Denys) Page, the Regius Professor of Greek at

Cambridge, who gave him invaluable advice on how to deal with Beattie, and Professors (Sir) Eric Turner and T. B. L. Webster in London, who wrote excellent letters to the press at various stages in the controversy. And he also had the satisfaction of seeing that Beattie attracted no significant support, particularly for his later assertions. Indeed, serious opposition to the decipherment ended after 1960, except perhaps for Scotland. Both of us remember Scottish graduates in the mid sixties turning up at Oxford and Cambridge classes and protesting not all that mildly that there was no reason to believe in the decipherment. However, in the 1980s John could say truthfully that 'the situation at the moment is that there is next to nobody left who does not believe in the decipherment' (*Stowe*, 1984, p. 40). At the time, in spite of the strain he was under, he managed to keep some sense of humour. About Beattie he commented: 'alas, I must see him as one of my failures'.

Whilst the Beattie controversy was raging, John Chadwick was at work on his next book, *The Decipherment of Linear B* (CUP, 1958). This is intended for a wider audience than *Documents*, and contains a lucid, if inevitably less than exhaustive description of the process of decipherment, an account of the new light it cast on Bronze Age Greece and a moving description of his collaboration with Ventris. Chadwick was exceptionally good as a populariser of his subject; and *Decipherment* was a huge success, not least because the genuine affection for Ventris and the emotional circumstances of his death come through in a restrained but highly effective fashion. The book has been translated into thirteen languages, and continues to sell well in English-speaking countries. It does not waste words, it is factual and not sentimental, but the reader finds it deeply touching.

Ventris was the decipherer, but credit for the establishment of Mycenaean studies must go to John Chadwick, not only because fate prevented Ventris from continuing his work but mainly because the two collaborators had different aims and interests. For Ventris the decipherment was the end of a long journey whose aim was to solve a tantalising problem; Chadwick, too, trained as he was in code-breaking, found the puzzle aspect of the problem irresistible, but he was also a classicist and a philologist who wanted to use the results of the decipherment to increase our knowledge of early Greek culture and language. It is doubtful that Ventris would have been equally interested in the Linear B texts if someone else had deciphered the script, but it is clear that John Chadwick would have found them just as compelling even if he had come to them not at the start of the inquiry but when some of the spadework had already been done. But it was the great fortune of the subject that John was there at the beginning and had sufficient authority to impose some order on what happened later and to define methods and standards. For the next forty years he continued to work on Linear B, and played a central and shaping role in the development of the new subject. As early as 1955, he and Ventris had attended the first international Colloquium on Mycenaean, held at Gif-sur-Yvette near Paris. Thirty years later Michel Lejeune, the organiser, described the event: 'Y arrivent de Grande-Bretagne, Michael Ventris et John Chadwick, les déchiffreurs du linéaire B. Le CNRS leur offre, après le *Journal of Hellenic Studies*, leur première grande tribune'. There followed at regular intervals nine more Colloquia, with the eleventh Colloquium taking place in 2000 after John's death. At Paris Ventris was the star of the occasion: as Chadwick recorded later, 'his fluency in French made a great impression, but he was equally at home chatting to the Swiss in Schwyzerdeutsch, or to the Greek delegate in Greek'. But Chadwick too made his mark and gained a respect from his French and other international colleagues that he was never to lose. He organised one of the later Colloquia and attended all the others held during his life-time. He was a central figure at them, giving admirably presented and often ground-breaking papers and contributing wisely—and never excessively—to discussions. His obvious enjoyment of the meetings, of the scholarly discussions and of the friendly encounters that the Colloquia allowed and encouraged was part of the role which largely unconsciously he came to play, that of moderator and guarantor of the propriety and integrity of Mycenaean studies. The Colloquia, which one attended strictly by invitation, encouraged young scholars by recognising their work and allowing them to find a forum for it, while excluding cranks and madmen. They also defined a working scenario. With one or two recent exceptions, it has always been the tradition in Mycenaean studies to share knowledge and information, and not only with the most senior scholars. This exemplary tradition had started at Gif, which was an exceptionally harmonious meeting, and 'l'esprit de Gif' continued to be invoked and maintained at all later Colloquia, with Chadwick himself acting as both its promoter and its guardian. The friendliness and the sharing of information was not limited to the Colloquia; in the early 1960s one of us, then aged 24 and a foreigner, was privileged to receive from John a number of newly edited texts in advance of publication with the permission and indeed encouragement to use them in her forthcoming lexicon; not much later the other, also in his early twenties, was chosen as John's coeditor for the important third edition of *The Knossos Tablets in Transliteration* which appeared in 1964.

In Britain, too, Chadwick played a leading part in the development of the new subject. He was a key participant in the Mycenaean seminars which met regularly in the 1950s and 1960s in the Institute of Classical Studies in London to discuss the texts; and even in later years, when the focus of the seminar had become much more archaeological, he continued to be a regular attender and contributor to discussions. He was very much involved in the yearly bibliographical survey of Mycenaean work (*Studies in Mycenaean Inscriptions and Dialect*) which began under the auspices of the ICS in 1956. At the same time, to again quote Lejeune, 'autour de Chadwick, Cambridge devient un des foyers de la mycénologie militante'. Such was his standing in the subject, and so well known had *Documents* and *Decipherment* made him, that from the late 1950s onwards a whole host of younger scholars from abroad made the pilgrimage to Cambridge to work with him on Mycenaean. Of the scholars who are now the leading experts in the field, a remarkably large number studied with Chadwick at some point in their early careers, and fondly remember his Mycenaean Epigraphy Room in Cambridge, particularly in its first manifestation, from the early 1960s to the mid 1980s, in the Laundress Lane Faculty Rooms off Mill Lane, with its marvellous view over the Mill Pond. Many of these visitors remained in touch with Chadwick, and he with them, for the rest of his life. In that sense he founded a school; in another sense he did not nor did he try. He never tried to impose on students or colleagues his view of what one should believe or how one should proceed.

Fame and what we could call his facilitator role in Mycenaean studies did not prevent John Chadwick from continuing with his own original work: some 140 articles and reviews in addition to his numerous books easily demonstrate that. His writings on Mycenaean from the late 1950s onwards covered an extremely wide range of topics. Not surprisingly, given his linguistic inclinations and training, many of his contributions focused on the language of the documents and other philological questions. The identification of sign values was of course part of the decipherment, but it was not always possible to assign a value to the least frequent signs and this remained a continuing subject of discussion. Chadwick wrote on the possible values of the rare signs nos *34/35, *64, and *82, the last of which he ingeniously suggested might be *swa*, since this would enable an equation to be made between the place-name *pi*-*82 at Pylos and the Classical toponym Pīsa. His paper at Gif concerned the phonetics of the series of signs transcribed by Ventris as *za*, *ze*, &c., and he returned to this problem on a number of occasions. His eventual conclusion, that the first element in these syllables was probably some kind of affricate, has found more support than the alternative view, that it is a palatalized velar. His lexicographical interests naturally led him to the study of the Mycenaean vocabulary; the glossary of *Documents*[2] has probably been more used than any of the other, more extensive, Mycenaean lexica, and he performed a great service for classicists by compiling a list of Greek words which are attested in Mycenaean (the second edition in collaboration with a South African colleague Lydia Baumbach). Finally, a number of his papers dealt with dialect, including the dialect relations of Mycenaean, and the early development of Greek. In 1956, he wrote a classic paper in *Greece & Rome* summarising for English-speaking readers the recently published theories of E. Risch and W. Porzig about the relations of the dialects in the Bronze Age, and in particular Risch's revolutionary suggestion that Ionic was a relatively recent creation which had developed as a result of contact between speakers of a Mycenaean-type dialect and West Greek (Doric) speakers in the period 1200–1000 BC. It was in this article that Chadwick first advanced the hypothesis, which he later developed further, that the Greek language, rather than having developed outside Greece and been brought into the area by three successive waves of invaders, as P. Kretschmer had argued, had originated within the peninsula itself, as a result of contact between incoming speakers of an Indo-European language and the indigenous population(s) of the area. His chapter in the *Cambridge Ancient History* on the *Pre-History of the Greek Language* (1963) which incorporates some of his earlier work on the topic has also been very influential. Starting in the mid 1970s he developed even further his attack on the view that the dialects arose as the result of different migratory waves, and argued that the Dorians were in fact not newcomers in the Peloponnese and in Crete but survivals of the lower classes which during the Mycenaean period had spoken a more conservative form of dialect than that which appears in the tablets. It was a daring view which remained controversial and may eventually be abandoned, but it led to a great deal of discussion and very useful rethinking.

Chadwick's training was indeed that of a philologist (in the English sense of the word) and this is how he introduced himself to Ventris in his first letter. His Greek research, as contrasted with the more specifically Mycenaean work, fits within this paradigm: on the one hand his lexicographical contributions, on the other his analysis of dialect texts and dialect features. In an important article (1992) he advanced a new theory about the accent of Thessalian; if his view that Thessalian had an initial stress is correct, this may explain a series of oddities in the Thessalian treatment of vowels and may also fit with the well-known accentual recessivity found in Lesbian, a closely related dialect. There are other contributions, etymological or epigraphic, which have lasting value and which in themselves would be more than enough to justify an academic career. By contrast, it would be difficult to speak of Chadwick's work on Mycenaean as only, or even mainly, philological. He started by applying philological techniques, but soon the data dictated the approach. If the Mycenaean documents were to be fully understood and exploited, skills other than purely linguistic ones were required. First, there was need for epigraphical work. While the Pylos tablets had been expertly edited by E. L. Bennett, and the meticulous records kept by the excavators of their find-places had enabled a great many joins between broken pieces to be made, the Knossos tablets were in a much less happy state. Many fragments, stored in the Iraklion museum, still remained unpublished; many joins between tablets had not yet been made (and the records of their find-spots were much less complete than those at Pylos); and much also remained to be done on the readings of the tablets. Bennett had done some admirable work to repair some of these deficiencies in the early 1950s; but Ventris and Chadwick also turned their attention to these epigraphical problems. Both worked in Iraklion in the mid 1950s; and both became expert epigraphists. During a stay in Iraklion in 1955 Chadwick made a celebrated join between fragments which yielded another striking proof of the correctness of the decipherment: a record of what the pictorial ideograms clearly showed were horses or donkeys, with the words *i-qo*, *po-ro*, and *o-no* standing before these signs. It was difficult not to accept that these were the Greek words /hiqq^{u}oi/, 'horses', /pōloi/, 'colts' and /onoi/, 'asses'; on seeing the join the Director of the museum, Nicholaos Platon, who had previously expressed some doubts about the decipherment, immediately began to reconsider his views.

Bennett, Chadwick, and Ventris published the results of their work in Iraklion in a new transcription of the Knossos tablets (KT^2) in 1956. After Ventris's death, Chadwick produced further editions of *KT* with other collaborators (J. T. Killen and J.-P. Olivier); and from the 1980s onwards he led an international team of scholars working to produce a major edition of the Knossos material, to include a text with critical apparatus, a drawing and a photograph for each of the three-thousand-plus documents. Happily, he lived long enough to see the virtual completion of this vast project. By the time of his death, three of the four volumes of the *Corpus of Mycenaean Inscriptions from Knossos* were in print; and he was able to see and correct the penultimate proofs of the fourth volume, which appeared at the end of 1998.

But his epigraphical work was not confined to Knossos tablets. He published, always with commendable promptness, new finds from Mycenae and Thebes; he wrote on the reading of the inscription on a Thebes transport jar; and he helped improve the readings of new fragments from Pylos. In later years, he did rather less epigraphy, particularly in museums; but he did not lose his skill in the art. When two of his younger colleagues, who thought of themselves as rather proficient epigraphists, were finding it difficult to read a newly discovered tablet from Tiryns which they had been asked to publish, and showed him a photograph of it, he quietly suggested that they might find their task a little easier if they looked at the document the other way up.

Though Chadwick's work on editing the Knossos tablets was solely concerned with the texts of these documents, his editions of the new Mycenae and Thebes material went beyond the actual reading of the tablets and discussed their interpretation. Here too his touch was masterly. One of his great contributions to Mycenology was his pioneering approach to the interpretation of tablets that involved looking at the documents, not in isolation, but in what he termed 'sets': groups of tablets written by the same scribe on the same subject and filed together in the same part of the palace archives. Because the tablets are so laconic it is often only the comparison of other records in the same 'file' that reveals what the scribe was doing and consequently what the tablets are about. The approach led to major advances in interpretation. A clear example is that of the *Na-* tablets of Pylos. The earlier hypothesis that they dealt with rations of linseed issued to the troops guarding the coast could be dismissed simply because in the parallel texts the same words had to be differently interpreted. The final interpretation is that at some places liable to contributions of flax to the palace part of the land was occupied by groups which provided the manpower to guard the coast.

Interpretation of texts is in the last resort what the work was all about: philology, epigraphy, etc. were all ancillary to this aim. But there was an even wider goal. From the texts one can get back to the realia or indeed to the culture of the place and the period. It is striking that while Chadwick the Hellenist was fundamentally a philologist interested in language who left historical and literary pursuits to others, Chadwick the Mycenologist was always on the lookout for the practical realities that lay behind the bureaucratic records. Many of his writings dealt with such subjects as the workings of Mycenaean administration, the nature of land-holding and taxation, and the minutiae of ration scales. He did more than anyone to reconstruct the geography of Mycenaean Pylos; and he also wrote on Cretan geography, again on the basis of the tablets. His book *The Mycenaean World* (1976), still in print after twenty-five years and available in six different languages, remains the most comprehensive and reliable account for the general reader of life in the Late Bronze Age as it is reflected in the tablets.

What is the explanation of the contrast between the Hellenist and the Mycenologist? Any answer must be speculative, and in all likelihood more than one answer is needed. But it is probable that consciously or subconsciously John came to realise that if anything of real value was to be derived from Mycenaean it was in fact necessary to pool all one's resources and look at the data from all angles. He was there at the start, he was one of the select few who could actually do it—and he did it. With Greek of the later period much more is known. If the quantity of evidence is overwhelming, as it is in the case of Greek, more than one specialist is needed. But in the case of Greek the specialist, i.e. the philologist or the historian or the textual critic, has more solid ground on which to build. We can discuss the forms of the genitive in classical Greek without agonising over whether we have identified the genitive correctly in one or the other text. The same is not true for Mycenaean, where all too often we can identify a genitive only if we are certain about the interpretation of the text where it is found. But the interpretation of the text will depend on the correct reading of the tablet, and this in its turn will depend on the identification of the scribal hands, etc. For Mycenaean Chadwick simply did what was needed—and that was everything. For Greek too, however, though his work was essentially linguistic, he did not think of himself as a linguist. He once said as much to one of us, and when asked what he meant by 'linguist', he illustrated it with examples of scholars he thought deserved the description. Once again the difference may have been that between application and theory. In lexicography John was interested in the user of the dictionary and the best way to find and communicate information about words and their meaning; he was not interested in modern semantic theory. Similarly for language in general he was more interested in how language or rather a particular language was used than in Universal Grammar. From this point of view the divergence between his work on Mycenaean and his work on alphabetic Greek was less substantial than might appear at first sight.

The impression we have so far given is of a full-time researcher who in addition to Mycenaean and Greek philology also found some time for his work on Swedenborg. But John Chadwick's life was not exclusively or even mainly one of research. He had a teaching position which he took very seriously. He had regular courses of lectures to give (mainly, but by no means exclusively, on Greek philology); and as a non-Professor in what was effectively a three-man sub-department of his Faculty he also had responsibilities for individual tuition (supervision in Cambridge terms), which took up a number of hours each week. After 1960, more-over, he had college duties to contend with. For the first eight years of his lectureship he did not hold a college fellowship. In 1960, however, he was elected Collins Fellow of Downing College, where his Faculty colleague W. K(eith) C. Guthrie, the Laurence Professor of Ancient Philosophy, was Master. Chadwick enormously valued his association with Downing (which made him an Honorary Fellow on his retirement and in whose gardens his ashes are buried); but the Fellowship involved him in yet more teaching, this time not necessarily in philology but in straight classics; he was also appointed Director of Studies in Classics, a post which he con-tinued to hold until 1983 and which obliged him to organise the studies and tuition of the college undergraduates even when he did not teach them personally. Some of his charges as Director of Studies found his dealings with them a little impersonal, but they appreciated the care and efficiency with which he performed his duties, and the promptness with which he took action if they complained that a teacher was not giving them what they needed. He was also active in other aspects of college life, and took his turn on a number of committees—though he did draw the line at undertaking the Vice-Mastership when this was suggested to him on one occasion. On top of this there were of course faculty administra-tive tasks. He was an efficient Chairman of the Faculty Board for the standard two years; he was a member of the committee that established the Intensive Greek programme for beginners in the language in the 1960s; and he was Chairman of the Management Committee for the Museum of Classical Archaeology for ten years from 1980. In short, he had a time-consuming set of duties all through his career which made his level of productivity even more remarkable.

He was a good teacher. He lectured mainly from a full script; eye-contact with the audience was not a frequent occurrence; and he did not waste words. One of his students talks of pens exploding as his charges struggled to get everything down. But his audiences quickly appreciated both the value of what they were hearing and the care that had clearly gone in to the preparation of his lectures; he was always ready to answer questions afterwards and he would take endless pains to explain anything which his listeners had found difficult. His real forte, though, was as a supervisor of research students. He had many Ph.D. students, by no means all working on Mycenaean. To mention only two: G. C. Horrocks, now Professor of Comparative Philology at Cambridge, worked with him on prepositional usage in Homer, and R. Janko, now Professor of Greek at UCL, worked on a statistical and linguistic approach to the dating of Homer, Hesiod, and the Homeric Hymns. He was excellent at suggesting subjects for his students to work on, and he took trouble: drafts were always returned promptly, with incisive comment attached. Praise from Chadwick gave his students confidence in their abilities as researchers; and many feel that they owe their careers to him. Nearly all his research students became his friends for life, and continued to benefit from his advice and support long after they had gained their doctorates.

Distinguished academic careers are marked by honours. From this angle Chadwick's career was both typical and eccentric. While still in his thirties he was made a Corresponding Member of the Deutsches Archaeologisches Institut (1957) and received an honorary degree from the University of Athens (1958). In the 1960s he was appointed to a readership in Cambridge (1966) and was elected a Fellow of the British Academy at the relatively young age of 47. After that, honour followed honour—internationally at least. He received honorary degrees from Brussels, Trinity College, Dublin, Vitoria, and Salzburg, as well as the medal of the J. E. Purkyně University of Brno, the Austrian Republic's *Ehrenzeichen für Wissenschaft und Kunst* (he was one of only sixteen holders of the award outside Austria) and the Greek Republic's Order of the Phoenix. He became corresponding member of the Austrian Academy, Honorary Councillor of the Athens Archaeological Society, Associé Etranger of the Académie des Inscriptions et Belles-Lettres (Institut de France), and Foreign Member of the Accademia dei Lincei, which in 1997 gave him its premier award, the Feltrinelli Prize for Linguistics. A Festschrift containing contributions by forty-three colleagues and former pupils was published in Salamanca in 1987 and a further volume, with papers by twenty-six contributors, mostly from Greece, was published in Thessaloniki in the same year. And yet in Britain he received no honorary degrees and no civil honour; foreigners never understood why they should not call him professor, but Cambridge never gave him the personal chair which he so richly deserved. Why this was so it is difficult to fathom. He was a modest man and did not court honours; if he had wanted a professorship he could have left Cambridge, but he loved that university more than any other. Obviously his subjects—Greek philology and

Mycenaean—were known only to a very few. There may have been other reasons, and at the start he may not have been helped by the somewhat cool relationship which existed between him and the other main Mycenologist in Britain, Leonard Palmer (1906–84), Professor of Comparative Philology at Oxford from 1952 to 1971. Both Palmer and Chadwick offered indispensable contributions to the early development of Mycenaean studies but they had different styles; the more passionate, enthusiastic and indeed overheated Palmer became, the colder and calmer Chadwick appeared to be. The outsider's impression was that one was intent on being brilliant, the other on being reliable. The older man found it difficult to yield to the younger one in anything, and at the start Chadwick certainly missed the support that he should have received from the more established scholar.

John retired from his university post in 1984, three years earlier than the absolute deadline. Predictably he continued to work and to write and most days went to the Mycenaean Epigraphy Room, often to type up work he had done the previous evening at home. He published two more classical books in retirement: *Lexicographica Graeca* (1996) and a volume, *Linear B and Related Scripts*, in the British Museum 'Reading the Past' Series (1987). Like all his books for a general audience, this was extremely successful, and it has been translated into Dutch, Greek, and Polish. Articles too appeared on various subjects, including the Thessalian accent article mentioned above. And, as he had always done, he kept up a large correspondence: on Linear B, of course, but also on a number of other interests: Swedenborg, New Testament Greek, Classical Greek inscriptions (with his friends Joyce Reynolds and John Graham), the Supplement, and his new Intermediate Greek Lexicon project. He was always punctilious about replying to letters, even from strangers asking for information or his comments on their 'decipherments', often of undecipherable material like the Phaistos Disc. 'Decipherments' arrived with remarkable frequency; and while many could be dealt with relatively simply—for instance, by pointing out to some of the Phaistos Disc experts that they had read the inscription starting from the wrong end—others required longer and more considered replies. Even schoolchildren got replies: John Ray, now Reader in Egyptology at Cambridge, wrote to Chadwick as a schoolboy—not about the Phaistos Disc—and received a prompt and courteous answer to his letter.

Travel is the only hobby John ever listed in *Who's Who*, and he continued to make expeditions, mostly with Joan to their country cottage in Norfolk or to Kent to visit their son, but also overseas to collect his numerous honours. In 1990 he attended the Ninth Mycenaean Colloquium in Athens; he was his usual self but he found it exhausting. Five years later he was somewhat reluctant to go to the Tenth Colloquium in Salzburg but was persuaded to do so by the organisers and enjoyed it. Nobody of those present will ever forget his touching address where he reminisced about the past of Mycenaean studies and expressed his wishes for the future; he received a standing ovation which never seemed to end.

In 1987 John had had a bad heart attack. He recovered and for the next eleven years remained in reasonably good health. He still did some teaching and only a month before he died had finished a short introductory course on Linear B for students taking Greek from Mycenae to Homer as one of their final year options. On 24 November 1998, however, he set out to travel to London for a meeting, and drove as usual to Royston to park his car before taking the King's Cross train. He never reached his destination. As he waited at the station, he suffered a major heart attack; and was dead on arrival in hospital in Stevenage.

* * *

The role that John Chadwick, Perceval Maitland Laurence Reader in Classics at Cambridge, performed in the history of scholarship is clear, and much of what he discovered has now become part of the basic knowledge which we impart to first-year undergraduates. There is something mythical about the events of his professional life. Once again Michel Lejeune knew how to describe it: 'Ainsi le sort avait-il un jour donné un royaume à John Chadwick. Il a su le mettre en valeur et lui imprimer sa marque; avec son autorité tempérée de modestie et de courtoisie; avec sa rigoureuse méthode, qui n'est pas exclusive d'intuitions fulgurantes. Il est un maître.'

It is more difficult to write about the man. In the brief account of his life between 1945 and 1952 which he left unfinished John Chadwick wrote 'I have no intention of disclosing details of my personal life which can be of no general interest'. The sentence is significant. Neither John nor Joan were likely to discuss their emotions or the private events of their life. Their mutual devotion was obvious, as was the harmony which surrounded their small family of three plus the siamese cat which was an integral part of it. In the early days one could feel a sort of stiffness round John, perhaps prompted, but this is guesswork, by a desire not to be found wanting, to do things correctly both from a scholarly and from a personal point of view. There was a reluctance to let himself go. But in time, as success and experience grew, the atmosphere round him became more relaxed. People said that John had mellowed, and even beyond the circle of his immediate friends it became possible to see how keen a sense of humour he had. And yet in some ways he remained a complex personality differently interpreted by different people. A friend spoke of him as an exceptionally calm person who never raised his voice and gave as an example the way in which he kept his head when he was on Wyllie's staff working at the *Oxford Latin Dictionary*. That is so, but perhaps it was a question not so much of calm as of stiff upper lip or maintaining control. The latter he could do and almost always did: it was the result of strict, often self imposed, training, but the calm was not always there. If John saw some injustice being done or even some instance of incorrect or unfair behaviour his reactions were strong. In those cases he did not hesitate to put pen to paper and write the strongest possible letter without calculating the consequences. He did not do that on his own behalf but he did it for others; for younger people who had not been made enough of, for colleagues who were not sufficiently appreciated, for decisions which had been improperly reached, for institutions which were underrated and should not have been. His own personal problems he kept at bay, and it was only in very exceptional circumstances that he allowed others to get a glimpse of them. Occasionally, very occasionally, if he acted with even more than the necessary emphasis in favour of a pupil or a younger person, one felt prompted to wonder whether he was in fact compensating for an injustice which he had endured himself.

John's word could be trusted. He had total integrity, no ulterior motives in his actions and no malice in his speech; not for him that type of destructive vanity which cannot bear to see anyone being more successful than oneself. Some teachers like to be surrounded by less brilliant students, but for John the opposite was true. He was proud of the achievements of his students and eager to tell others of them, just as he was eager to report about new discoveries or findings: 'You will know', he started, 'that a new tablet has been found in . . .'; 'you will know that X has now convincingly demonstrated that . . .'; 'you will know that it is now clear that the old interpretation of y was wrong'. These sentences, so frequently heard, said it all: there was the desire to inform but also the satisfaction of the man who now knows what the truth is. *Magna est veritas et praevalebit* was the natural gloss which came to mind. He was more hesitant when reporting his own results: 'I have a new idea, but I do not want to talk about it; it is too early'; perhaps the fear of making blunders was still there. In addition there was obvious generosity and less obvious, because often concealed, but very real warmth. A number of younger Mycenologists from abroad (one of the writers included) owe to him their first contact with the wider world of Mycenology and their chance to find their niche in it; in the bad period of the cold war more mature scholars from East Europe were helped to keep contact with the West and offered books and invitations. He was generous in his personal relationships and generous in more conventional senses too: a large part of the Feltrinelli Prize was given to the University of Cambridge to set up a fund for Classical Philology, though this was certainly not broadcast. The generosity could take the form of tolerance; this most punctilious of men who never missed a deadline and organised his time and his work to perfection knew how to smile indulgently when others did not answer his letters or did not meet their commitments; very occasionally he complained but with sympathetic understanding. The scholarly work will survive, but those who knew John Chadwick will miss him in his role as friend, adviser, and touchstone of decent behaviour. Decency may seem a dull word, but in this case at least it is not a dull concept.

J. T. KILLEN
Fellow of the Academy

A. MORPURGO DAVIES
Fellow of the Academy

Note. John Chadwick published little about his life. The Accademia Nazionale dei Lincei printed an autobiographical sketch (3 pages), written at their request, in a booklet recording the winners of the Antonio Feltrinelli prizes for 1997; and there is a little personal information, besides the extensive description of the collaboration with Ventris, in *The Decipherment of Linear B.* There are also some brief recollections of his war-time code-breaking experiences and of his career as a lexicographer in the introduction to *Lexicographica Graeca.* He left, however, three unpublished accounts of parts of his life, now held in the Mycenaean Epigraphy Room of the Faculty of Classics, Cambridge. The longest (82 pages of typescript) is an account of his wartime experiences. There is also a shorter version (10 pages of typescript) of the section of this document dealing with the period 1942–5, when he was engaged in intelligence work. This has now been published in *Action this day: Bletchley Park from the breaking of the Enigma code to the birth of the modern computer,* edited by Michael Smith and Ralph Erskine, London, Bantam Press, 2001, pages 110–26. Finally, there is an 18-page manuscript account, written shortly before his death and left unfinished, of his life between 1945 and 1952. We have drawn heavily on all three accounts, as well as on Chadwick's (and Ventris's) extensive correspondence files, also held in the Mycenaean Epigraphy Room, Cambridge. A small booklet *Michael Ventris Remembered* published by Stowe School in 1984 and compiled by Simon Tetlow, Ben

Harris, David Roques, and A. G. Meredith has a short preface by John Chadwick but also reports odd sentences and pieces of information which the authors had from him in 1983; here it is quoted as Stowe, 1984. We have not listed the numerous obituary articles which appeared but we have made use of a brief commemoration by J. T. Killen published in *Minos*, 31–2 (1996–7), 449–51 and of Anna Morpurgo Davies' address at John Chadwick's memorial service (February 1999) which was printed in the *Association Newsletter and College Record of Downing College*, Cambridge for 1999 (pages 50–5). We occasionally refer to the late Michel Lejeune's preface to the Chadwick *Festschrift* (p. 9 f.) mentioned below.

We are very much indebted to Mrs Joan Chadwick and Mr Anthony Chadwick for their help in compiling this memoir. We are also most grateful to the following for reminiscences and information: Revd Professor H. Chadwick, the late Professor R. G. G. Coleman, Professor Sir Kenneth Dover, Revd J. H. Elliott, Professor A. J. Graham, Professor G. C. Horrocks, Professor R. Janko, Mr. D. Mervyn Jones, Mr D. Mann, the late Dr W. N. Mann, Dr P. Millett, Mr J. D. Ray, Dr J. M. Reynolds, Dr A. A. Thompson, Mr C. R. Whittaker. Professor A. G. Woodhead has, inter alia, provided invaluable information about John Chadwick's years at St Paul's and about his final undergraduate year at Cambridge.

A bibliography of John Chadwick, covering the period 1950–87, is published in J. T. Killen, J. L. Melena, and J.-P. Olivier (eds), *Studies in Mycenaean and Classical Greek Presented to John Chadwick* (Salamanca, 1987). We append below a supplementary list compiled by J. T. Killen which covers the later work, together with a list of John Chadwick's writings on Swedenborg.

Bibliography of
John Chadwick

[Continuation of list in *Studies in Mycenaean and Classical Greek presented to John Chadwick* [= *Minos*, 20–2] (1987), pp. 11–19].
1986:
(With L. Godart, J. T. Killen, J.-P. Olivier, A. Sacconi, & I. A. Sakellarakis) *Corpus of Mycenaean Inscriptions from Knossos I (1–1063)*. Cambridge, Cambridge University Press; Rome, Edizioni dell'Ateneo, pp. xv + 433.
1987:
Linear B and related Scripts. Reading the Past, British Museum Publications, London, pp. 64.
L'économie palatiale dans la Grèce mycénienne. *Le système palatial en Orient, en Grèce et à Rome. Actes du Colloque de Strasbourg*, Amsterdam, pp. 283–90.
Some observations on two new inscriptions from Lyktos. Εἰλαπίνη. Τόμος τιμη-τικὸς γιὰ τὸν Καθηγητὴ Νικόλαο Πλάτωνα, Heraklion, pp. 329–34.
1988:
The women of Pylos. Texts, tablets and scribes. Studies in Mycenaean epigraphy and economy offered to Emmett L. Bennett, Jr. Suplementos a Minos núm. 10, Salamanca, pp. 43–95.

Differences and similarities between Cypriot and the other Greek dialects. *The History of the Greek Language in Cyprus. Proceedings of an International Symposium sponsored by the Pierides Foundation*, Nicosia, pp. 55–66.

1989:

Miḳenuli samq̇alo (Georgian translation of *The Mycenaean World* by T. Buachidze). Tblisi, Metsniereba, pp. 128.

Ζητήματα λεξικογραφίας. *Studies in Greek Linguistics. Proceedings of the 9th Annual Meeting of the Department of Linguistics, Faculty of Philosophy, Aristotelian University of Thessaloniki*, Thessaloniki, pp. 1–18.

Rev: J. Best & F. Woudhuizen (eds.), *Ancient Scripts from Crete and Cyprus. Publications of the Henri Frankfort Foundation 9. Antiquity*, 63, p. 181.

1990:

(With L. Godart, J. T. Killen, J.-P. Olivier, A. Sacconi, & I. A. Sakellarakis) *Corpus of Mycenaean Inscriptions from Knossos II (1064–4495)*. Cambridge, Cambridge University Press, Rome, Edizioni dell'Ateneo, pp. viii + 243.

Lineair B en verwante schriften (Dutch translation of *Linear B and related scripts* by Yolande Michon). Houten, Fibula.

The Pech-Maho lead. *ZPE*, 82, pp. 161–6.

The descent of the Greek epic. *JHS*, 110, pp. 174–7.

Reconstrucción de un sistema social prehistórico. *De la Grecia arcaica a la Roma imperial. Cursos de verano, el Escorial, 1989*, Madrid, pp. 11–24.

Rev: M. S. Ruipérez (ed. J. L. García-Ramón), *Opuscula selecta. Ausgewählte Arbeiten zur griechischen und indo-germanischen Sprachwissenschaft. CR*, 40:2, p. 303.

1991:

The origin of the Hellenistic κοινή. *Palaeograeca et mycenaea Antonino Bartoněk quinque et sexagenario oblata*, Brno, pp. 13–16.

Lydia Baumbach 1924–1991. A personal reflection. *Acta Classica*, 34, pp. 1–5.

1992:

Γραμμική Β και συγγενικές γραφές (Greek translation of *Linear B and related scripts* by N. Konomi). Athens, Papadimas.

Pylos Va 15. *Mykenaïka; Actes du IXe Colloque international sur les textes mycéniens et égéens*, Paris, pp. 167–72.

The Thessalian accent. *Glotta* 70: 1–2, pp. 2–14.

Semantic history and Greek lexicography. *La langue et les textes en grec ancien. Actes du colloque Pierre Chantraine*, Amsterdam, pp. 281–8.

ἥρυς—a Greek ghost-word. *Historical philology: Greek, Latin, and Romance. Papers in honor of Oswald Szemerényi II. Current Issues in Linguistic Theory 87*, Amsterdam/ Philadelphia, pp. 99–102.

1994:

The case for replacing Liddell and Scott. *BICS*, 39, pp. 1–11.

Cicero, *Ad Fam*. 9.22. *Živa Antika*, 44, pp. 123–4.

1995:

Løsningen av Linear B (Norwegian translation of JC 13 by Kåre A. Lie). Oslo, Pax.

Rev: F. R. Adrados *et al.*, *Diccionario Griego-Español, IV. CR*, 45:2, pp. 307–8.

1996:

Lexicographica Graeca: Contributions to the Lexicography of Ancient Greek. Oxford, Clarendon Press, pp. vi + 343.

A decifração do linear B (Portuguese translation of JC 13 by Maria do Céu Fialho). Lisbon, Cotovia.

Mycenaean language, pre-alphabetic scripts (Greece), pre-Greek languages. *The Oxford Classical Dictionary*. (Third edn., ed. Simon Hornblower and Anthony Spawforth), Oxford, New York, Oxford University Press, pp. 1015, 1243, 1243–1244.

1997:

(With L. Godart, J. T. Killen, J.-P. Olivier, A. Sacconi, & I. A. Sakellarakis) *Corpus of Mycenaean Inscriptions from Knossos III (5000–7999)*. Cambridge, Cambridge University Press, Pisa, Istituti Editoriali e Poligrafici Internazionali, pp. 328.

Ο Μυκεναϊκός κόσμος (Greek translation of *The Mycenaean World* by K. N. Petropoulos). Athens, Gutenberg.

L'utilità della linguistica storica. *Adunanze straordinarie per il conferimento dei premi A. Feltrinelli* (Accademia Nazionale dei Lincei), vol. III, fasc. 11. Roma, pp. 313–18.

1998:

(With L. Godart, J. T. Killen, J.-P. Olivier, A. Sacconi, & I. A. Sakellarakis) *Corpus of Mycenaean Inscriptions from Knossos IV (8000–9947) and index to vols. I–IV*. Cambridge, Cambridge University Press, Pisa, Istituti Editoriali e Poligrafici Internazionali, pp. 295.

Pismo linearne B i pisma pokrewne (Polish translation of *Linear B and related scripts* by Piotr Taracha). Warsaw, Wydawnictwo.

Θέσθαι τά ὅπλα. *Faventia*, 20:1, pp. 19–23.

The Greekness of Mycenaean. *Aevum*, 72, pp. 25–8.

Three temporal clauses. *Minos*, 31–2 (1996–7) [1998], pp. 293–301.

Rev: G. C. Papanastassiou, Compléments au Dictionnaire étymologique du grec ancien de Pierre Chantraine (Λ–Ω). *CR*, 48:1, pp. 216–17.

Rev: *Atti e Memorie del Secondo Congresso Internazionale di Micenologia. RFIC*, 126:2, pp. 219–43.

1999:

Linear B: Past, Present and Future. S. Deger-Jalkotzy, S. Hiller, O. Panagl (eds.), *Floreant Studia Mycenaea. Akten des X. Internationalen Mykenologischen Colloquiums in Salzburg von 1–5 Mai 1995*, Wien, vol. I, pp. 29–38.

2001:

Articles Γραμμική Β and Μυκηναϊκή ελληνική. Α.-Φ. Χριστίδης (ed.), Ιστορία της ελληνικής γλώσσας, Κέντρο Ελληνικής Γλώσσας, Ινστιτούτο Νεοελληνικών [Ίδρυμα Μανόλη Τριανταφυλλίδη], pp. 200–3, 291–8 (and Bibliography pp. 273, 372).

A biographical fragment: 1942–5. *Action this day: Bletchley Park from the breaking of the Enigma code to the birth of the modern computer*. Edited by Michael Smith and Ralph Erskine, London, Bantam Press, pp. 110–26.

Pylian gold and local administration: PY Jo 438. Forthcoming in *Minos* 33–4 (1998–1999) [2001].

Publications on Swedenborg

1961:

Religion and Life. A translation of the section on good works and the Ten Commandments included in the exposition of the fifteenth and sixteenth chapters of the Book of Revelation in the work entitled The Apocalypse Explained by Emanuel Swedenborg; translated by John Chadwick. London, The Swedenborg Society, pp. 92.

1975–1990:

A lexicon to the Latin text of the theological writings of Emanuel Swedenborg (1688–1772). Edited by John Chadwick; 6 fascicules and supplement. London, The Swedenborg Society, pp. x + 813.

1981:

Life in Animals and Plants. A translation of extracts from chapter nineteen of The Apocalypse Explained by Emanuel Swedenborg; translation and introductory essay by John Chadwick. London, The Swedenborg Society, pp. 35.

1988:

Emanuel Swedenborg, *The True Christian Religion.* Translated from the original Latin by John Chadwick; 2 vols. London, The Swedenborg Society, pp. xix + 920.

1990:

Emanuel Swedenborg, *The New Jerusalem.* Translated from the original Latin by John Chadwick. London, The Swedenborg Society, pp. 106.

1992:

Emanuel Swedenborg, *The Last Judgement.* A translation from the Latin by John Chadwick. London, The Swedenborg Society, pp. 173.

1994:

The translator and Swedenborg's Latin text. *Studia Swedenborgiana,* 9:1, pp. 59–70.

1996:

Emanuel Swedenborg, *Conjugial Love.* English translation by John Chadwick. London, The Swedenborg Society, pp. xxxvii + 507.

1997:

Emanuel Swedenborg, *The Worlds in Space.* English translation by John Chadwick. London, The Swedenborg Society, pp. xv + 150.

Emanuel Swedenborg, *On the Sacred Scripture.* English translation by John Chadwick. London, the Swedenborg Society, pp. v + 65.

DONALD COLEMAN

Donald Cuthbert Coleman
1920–1995

DONALD COLEMAN was perhaps the outstanding economic historian of the remarkable group of ex-servicemen who came to the London School of Economics in 1946, dubbed 'the liveliest intellectual cohort of our time',[1] which formed a band of economic historians that fanned out across the country to colonise the newly founded Economic History Departments which were a feature of the discipline's ascendancy in the 1950s, although he himself stayed put in London for the next two decades. As the separate Economic History Departments began to vanish in the 1980s, casualties of cuts in university finances and changes in academic fashions, Donald Coleman, by this time in Cambridge, remained the outstanding, outspoken, exponent and articulate defender of the 'real economic history' he had absorbed at the LSE and helped to shape and develop subsequently. He was a central, highly influential, figure in the narrative of what he felt had been the rise and decline of economic history; and in reality left behind a following of former students, and colleagues, who will undoubtedly ensure that the decline is only apparent and that the subject, adapting to trends in methodological fashion and successfully digesting what is useful from new approaches, will survive and flourish.

This economic history that he stood for, practised so productively and incisively, and defended so robustly, was transmitted by his teachers,

[1] Neil McKendrick and R. B. Outhwaite, eds., *Business Life and Public Policy: Essays in honour of D. C. Coleman* (Cambridge, 1986), Preface, p. vii. The cohort included Sidney Pollard: see *ante*, vol. 105, pp. 513–34; and also Ralph Davis, later Professor of Economic History at Leicester University, Walter Minchinton, later Professor of Economic History at Exeter University.

Proceedings of the British Academy, **115**, 169–191. © The British Academy 2002.

above all by Jack Fisher, and was drawn straight from the founding texts of the Economic History Society. These were the guiding principles of Coleman's scholarship: no history without theory; no simply descriptive writing, which was mere antiquarianism; and also, no ideological manipulation of the evidence. On occasion, when being dismissive of both mindless story-telling and arid number-crunching, he referred to his style as being 'analytical narrative'.

I

There was, indeed, no early indication that Donald was to become an academic of any kind, let alone an economic historian. Born in January 1920, he seldom talked in later life about his father, Hugh, an income tax inspector, or his mother who was in his eyes an obstinate and irrational Christian Scientist. He spent his childhood in Walthamstow, where he learnt to despise suburbia and to defy his parents' wish to send him to boarding school, instead attending Haberdashers' Aske's School, then in Hampstead, as a dayboy, and leaving when he was 17. He then worked as an insurance clerk in the City from 1937 to 1939, and had been accepted to enrol as an evening student at LSE in October 1939, presumably to take an accountancy course, when the war swept him into the forces instead. He tried to volunteer for the RAF but was rejected because he was mildly colour-blind, and so ended up in the army, at first commissioned into the Royal Warwickshire Regiment but quite soon transferring into the Royal Artillery, serving in a Medium Regiment, where as he said he acquired a great deal of useless knowledge about 5.5-inch guns. He went to North Africa in 1943, when the 17th Medium Regiment, RA, was formed, which went with the 8th Army to Italy in early 1944, where he was an OP [observation post] officer, at times observing the fall of shot from a spotter plane. Later in 1944 his northward move in Italy was interrupted for a while when he was seconded to a unit which monitored elections in Greece. He returned to Italy in time to end the war at Vercelli, midway between Milan and Turin, where the regiment was quartered in a barracks boasting a theatre. There the first recorded instance of Donald's musical and managerial talents took place, when along with his fellow-officer David Watson he organised a revue to entertain the troops. Shortly afterwards the regiment was moved to Pesaro on the Adriatic coast, where they occupied the opera house and with Donald as director staged a bigger and better revue, which went on tour to Cattolica, Rimini, and

Milan, until demobilisation began to decimate the cast. In early 1946 they moved to the south of Naples, and Donald was appointed to manage the Hotel Tramontano in Sorrento, which was an officers' rest camp, and he went straight from there to LSE in the autumn of 1946.

II

It was with this last experience fresh in his mind that the first-year undergraduate informed his tutor, Nicky Kaldor, that he no longer needed to learn economics, having done that while running a chain of requisitioned hotels in Italy at the end of the war—that at least was what Donald the raconteur liked to tell his own students in later years, conjuring up a vision of a self-taught military Forte rapidly reviving the run-down Italian hotel industry. He later described his decision to go to university after six and a half years in the army as a 'gamble' which he took, without giving much thought to what kind of career it might lead to, because of the pure chance that he had been left a small legacy by a 'romantic great-uncle whom I had never met' and the offer of sharing a flat in Baker Street with a friend [2] The B.Sc. Econ. degree, for which Coleman had enrolled, motivated as he put it by an earnest but unfocused concern with the economic and social issues of the 1930s, at that time had a compulsory first-year course including economics, international history, and economic history, with choices for specialisation to be made for the final couple of years. It seems that it was at the time of this decision that Donald, along with the rest of 'the liveliest intellectual cohort of our time', was drawn to economic history, in his case partly through the influence of the towering figures of the School's recent past, R. H. Tawney (by 1946 retired but still frequenting the Senior Common Room), and Eileen Power (who had died in 1940), and partly through the presence of the distinguished and very varied talents of the active panel of LSE economic historians of the time, T. S. Ashton, H. L. Beales, Eleanora Carus-Wilson, and A. V. Judges—who was succeeded as Reader in Economic History by F. J. Fisher in 1948. Jack Fisher, an outstanding teacher, supervisor, friend, raconteur, and critic, was to be the paramount influence on Donald's academic life, an intellectual father figure who excited the characteristic paternal effects of almost simultaneous admiration, imitation, resentment, and opposition. Donald's

[2] D. C. Coleman, *Dons: A Memoir of L.S.E. and Cambridge* (unpublished typescript, 1994, deposited in Cambridge University Library), chap. 2, pp. 1–2.

portrayal of Jack Fisher as 'sardonic, witty, convivial and with a remarkable capacity for bursting pretentious bubbles' could well have been
applied to himself too.[3] Thus Donald increased the stakes in his 'gamble'
by turning his back on the more vocational alternatives of specialising in
theoretical economics, applied economics, government, or accountancy,
all of which, contrary to the popular image of the School at the time, were
rather conventional and conservative subjects, while economic history was
if not an invariably left-wing subject one which was excitingly radical and
nonconformist.

So, in 1949, Donald took a brilliant first, at which point 'no course of
action other than to go on to do research seemed remotely worthwhile'[4]—
although it also seemed like another reckless gamble, since research and a
doctorate were not a job ticket—and no supervisor seemed possible except
Jack Fisher, who steered him towards the 1660–1760 period as being
untrodden territory for economic historians, and towards the economy of
Kent in particular because local history furnished readily manageable
Ph.D. topics and anyway 'it had never been tackled before; the source
materials were near at hand; and Kentish beer was good'.[5] He completed
his Ph.D. thesis on 'The Economy of Kent under the Later Stuarts' in the
remarkably short time of two years, an achievement which earned him
appointment to a lectureship in 'industrial history' at LSE in 1951. He
never saw fit to publish his thesis, regarding it as an apprentice's exercise in
the techniques of historical research, but its subject matter was an important contribution to the fulfilment of Ashley's enthusiasm for local history
as the most rewarding field for the future of economic history on the
grounds that 'local history, from its very nature, is bound to be largely
economic', a line of advance being pursued in the early postwar years
through several other regional studies which sought to enlist the specificity
of local evidence to illuminate the more general processes of economic
development.[6] Research, in diligent transcription of seventeenth-century
tax returns and port books in Chancery Lane and in 'a succession of lucky
dips into the documentary bran tub' in the Kent County Record Office in

---

[3] D. C. Coleman, *Dons: A Memoir of L.S.E. and Cambridge*.
[4] Ibid., chap. 2, p. 8.
[5] Ibid., chap. 2, p. 9.
[6] W. Ashley, 'The Place of Economic History in University Studies', *Economic History Review*,
I (1927), 5. One thinks of the work of W. H. B. Court, A. H. John, W. E. Minchinton, Edward
Hughes, T. C. Barker, J. R. Harris, W. H. Chaloner, J. D. Chambers and others as setting the
1950s context of a local and regional focus for economic and industrial histories.

Maidstone, was not an unrelentingly high-minded pursuit. From time to time he would be joined by Ann Childs 'and week-end country walks were taken in alleged pursuit of the long-vanished Wealden iron industry: an agreeable exercise later to be dignified with the name of industrial archaeology'.[7]

Coleman was appointed as a lecturer in 'industrial history' as part of a scheme to inject some civilising influences from the humanities into the curriculum of engineering students from Imperial College, a tall order made somewhat more attainable by his witty and racy lecturing style. The requirement to teach industrial history, as a distinct sub-branch of economic history, was the incentive to turn away from the Kentish material of his Ph.D., which in that essentially agricultural county was largely about brewing, charcoal iron, gunpowder, some textiles, and some paper, to tackle an entire manufacturing industry. The result was *The British Paper Industry, 1495–1860* (Oxford, 1958), a book which deliberately challenged the conventional idea of the industrial revolution by adopting its own technology-driven periodisation, with the adoption of the steam-driven Foudrinier paper-making machine after 1800 making virtually no impression on an output curve that moved gently but steadily upward from the adoption of water-powered rag-shredding mills at some indeterminate point in the later middle ages, but rather disappointingly with an administrative rather than an economic ending, the abolition of the paper duties in 1860, well before the wood-pulp revolution. A sceptical, irreverent, attitude to established orthodoxies was to be a hallmark of Donald's scholarship, but at the time this book was received by some with marked lack of enthusiasm or appreciation of its implications for a general re-interpretation of Britain's industrial history, Minchinton remarking rather oddly that 'the total picture produced is deficient in the attention devoted to the part played by the businessman in the evolution of the industry . . . [it is] a landscape largely without figures'.[8] Others somewhat condescendingly recognised it as 'an excellent book of its kind', and it was left to David Eversley in *Business History* to see the penetrating and highly original nature of 'Mr Coleman's discussion of the nature of industrial change and the validity of the concept of an industrial revolution' as the wider and intellectually important implications of the study of what on the surface was a small and relatively insignificant industry

[7] Coleman, *Dons*, chap. 2, p. 12.
[8] W. E. Minchinton, review of *The British Paper Industry*, in the *Journal of Economic History*, 19 (1959), 432–4.

when set alongside the economic historians' staples of cotton, woollens, iron and steel, and coal.[9]

Looking back in the 1980s, Jack Fisher claimed that 'Donald became the obvious candidate for appointment to a new lectureship in industrial history that had been established at the L.S.E.', while Donald himself recalled that it was Lance Beales, in the course of one of his informal seminars in the White Horse, who suggested he should apply for the post, and that Ashton, who was on the appointing committee, had not thought of him for the job but saw no harm in his applying. In the 1950s, Fisher continued, 'when students were less cosseted than they are now [1986], teaching duties at the School were light and, in any case, the demand for industrial history was small. Donald was able therefore to concentrate on writing and editorial work and he rapidly established his reputation through his books on Banks and on the paper industry, through a stream of important articles and book reviews, [and] through his activities from 1952 to 1961 as English editor of the *Scandinavian Economic History Review*'.[10] His first article, 'London Scriveners and the Estate Market in the later Seventeenth Century', had indeed been accepted by the *Economic History Review* before his appointment as a lecturer, and was published in December 1951.[11] The first scholarly account of the mechanisms of the early modern land market and its professional structure, this linked into H. J. Habakkuk's classic article 'English Landownership, 1680–1740',[12] and was an offshoot of Donald's work on Kent, where the financier Sir John Banks had been busily purchasing land. A full-scale book on Banks was to follow in 1963, foreshadowed by his chapter on 'Sir John Banks, Financier' in the volume of *Essays in the Economic and Social History of Tudor and Stuart England* edited by F. J. Fisher (Cambridge, 1961). The 'stream of articles' in the 1950s was developed out of the Kent thesis, with considerable further research, and featured contributions on the naval dockyards and the paper industry, with an emphasis on his interest in questions of the paramount importance of labour supply in the early modern economy in the absence of technologies or technological changes requiring appreciable amounts of fixed capital. The early culmination of this interest was his celebrated article on

[9] D. E. C. Eversley, review in *Business History*, 1 (1958–9), 106–8.

[10] F. J. Fisher in the Preface to Neil McKendrick and R. B. Outhwaite, eds., *Business Life and Public Policy* (Cambridge, 1986), pp. viii–ix. Coleman, *Dons*, chap. 2, pp. 16–17.

[11] D. C. Coleman, 'London Scriveners and the Estate Market in the Later Seventeenth Century', *Econ. Hist. Rev.*, 2nd ser. IV (1951), 221–30.

[12] H. J. Habakkuk, 'English Landownership, 1680–1740', *Econ. Hist. Rev.*, 1st ser. X (1940), 2–17.

'Labour in the English Economy of the Seventeenth Century', which succinctly outlined a labour-centred model of the pre-industrial economy, with a trenchant side-swipe at 'that misleading and cumbersome portmanteau, that unnecessary piece of historical baggage—the idea of "mercantilism"'.[13] His analysis of the views of contemporary writers and of the content and purposes of contemporary laws and regulations on labour and wages in terms of the character of the labour-intensive, 'backward', economy of the seventeenth century—which he compared to the third-world economies of the twentieth century, a trick no doubt derived from talk with Jack Fisher—has stood the test of time and subsequent research—perhaps most notably the massive work of historical demography of the Cambridge Population Group, which confirmed Donald's speculations about sixteenth- and seventeenth-century population trends. The economy which he described, with its necessarily considerable dependence on child labour because of the demographic structure, its inherent features of irregularity and seasonality of employment with long intervals of idleness, and strong leisure preferences induced by the extremely limited array of consumer goods, except for beer, on which any increased money income might be spent, was in marked contrast to the received wisdom of an economy shaped by laws and regulations which reflected adherence to some nebulous concept of a 'mercantilist system'.

Coleman's abrupt and provocative dismissal of 'mercantilism' was later somewhat softened in a more moderate and extensive statement of the case against the concept, in 'Eli Heckscher and the Idea of Mercantilism' in 1957, which gracefully acknowledged Heckscher's scholarship and the great contribution his research had made to the history of economic thought, while firmly adhering to the arguments refuting the existence of any such 'mercantilist system'. In his much-used 1977 textbook, *The Economy of England, 1450–1750*, Donald told students not to bother with mercantilism which, he explained, had

> given rise to debates about its existence, nature or value as a conceptual tool. That this should have happened is not a little due to its origins in the mind of the first great systematizer of economic ideas, Adam Smith. Most of Book IV of his *Wealth of Nations* of 1776 is concerned with what he saw as the principles and practice of something which he called the 'mercantile system'. He regarded it, in part at least, as a creation of merchants and manufacturers shaping the course of State economic action to their own ends, to the advantage of

---

[13] D. C. Coleman, 'Labour in the English Economy of the Seventeenth Century', *Econ. Hist. Rev.*, 2nd ser. VIII (1956), 280–95, esp. p. 295; reprinted in E. M. Carus-Wilson, ed., *Essays in Economic History* (3 vols. 1954, 1962), 2, 291–308.

producers and the detriment of consumers. Thus born as the brain-child of an economist, the concept in its life has been abused by historians, mishandled by economists, transmuted into *Merkantilismus*, and variously paraded for praise or blame, by anyone seeking historical illustrations for the latest nostrum in political economy. Guides to the debate exist. It may now therefore be sensible to move on to consider the topic of [the State and its Impact] without further reference to mercantilism as such.'[14]

This, only slightly modified in his 1980 article 'Mercantilism Revisited', remained his position, and although it has proved hard to wean undergraduates from a tendency to fall back on 'the mercantilist system' in their essays as a substitute for thought, the concept has irretrievably lost its intellectual respectability.[15] Meanwhile in the 1950s and 1960s Coleman extended his enquiries into many aspects of sixteenth- and seventeenth-century industry, and built up an impressive expertise in the history of the early modern textile industry in particular, with a whole sequence of articles: *The Domestic System in Industry* (Historical Association, 1960); 'Economic Problems and Policy' (F. L. Carsten, ed., *New Cambridge Modern History*, vol. V, 1961); 'Countryside and Industry' (A. Cobban, ed., *The Eighteenth Century: Europe in the Age of Enlightenment*, 1969); 'Politics and Economics in the Age of Anne' (D. C. Coleman and A. H. John, eds., *Trade, Government and Economy in Pre-Industrial England*, 1976); *Industry in Tudor and Stuart England* (Economic History Society, 1975); 'Growth and Decay during the Industrial Revolution: the Case of East Anglia', *Scandinavian Economic History Review*, 1967; 'An Innovation and its Diffusion: the New Draperies', *Economic History Review*, 1969; 'Textile Growth' (N. B. Harte and K. G. Ponting, eds., *Textile History and Economic History*, 1973).

The indiscriminate proliferation of 'industrial revolutions' in the academic literature, a label attached to thirteenth-century fulling mills, to the 1540–1640 century by Nef, to post-1868 Japan or post-1870 Germany, had also received a civilised reproof in another much reprinted article, 'Industrial Growth and Industrial Revolutions', an article which urged economic historians to confine the term to the classic Industrial Revolution—although Donald prudently omitted to attach any precise dates to that, since the advent of Rostow's 1780 take-off had just taken

---

[14] D. C. Coleman, 'Eli Heckscher and the Idea of Mercantilism', *Scandinavian Economic History Review*, V (1957), reprinted in James A. Gherty, ed., *Economic Thought: An Historical Anthology* (New York, 1965), and in D. C. Coleman, ed., *Revisions in Mercantilism* (1969). D. C. Coleman, *The Economy of England, 1450–1750* (Oxford, 1977), p. 173.

[15] D. C. Coleman, 'Mercantilism Revisited', *Historical Journal*, 23 (1980), 773–91.

the edge off the conventional 1760–1860 dates—which had seen the transformation not of one industry but of an entire economy and society. Presciently, he observed that diligent number-crunching might produce an 'index in which even the classical industrial revolution can be made if not quite to disappear at least to appear as no more than a small change in the industrial growth rate'.[16] In similar vein, years later and after he had retired, Coleman rather more pointedly deflated a new concept 'rattling around in the corridors of economic history' in his trenchant article on 'Proto-industrialization: A Concept Too Many', in which this new-fangled and half-baked theory that domestic, putting-out, industry flourished in harsh mountainous regions and paved the way for the transition from feudalism to capitalism by stimulating real mechanised industrialisation was dismissed as an exercise in which 'the familiar findings of various scholars [are] dressed up in long words and sociological finery'.[17] Subjected to empirical testing the concept simply disintegrated: many industries never had a 'putting-out' phase; some were capitalistic from the start; many regions once prominent in 'proto-industrial development' never moved on, but subsequently de-industrialised and reverted to agricultural economies. It was a devastating critique, although a few proto-industrial believers refused to renounce their faith. Never one to tolerate sloppy thinking or pretentious theorising and model-building that ignored or swept aside inconvenient evidence, or overlooked the work of earlier scholars, Coleman's critical pieces, while decisive, were always constructive and instructive, witty and readable, so that he contrived to praise the proto-industrialisers for stimulating much thought and research on early modern economies, just as he had admired Heckscher while thinking mercantilism misguided.

III

By 1958, when the arrangement with Imperial College for teaching industrial history to engineers was terminated, Donald Coleman had established a national and international reputation as a leading historian of the early modern English economy, a reputation which carried him to Yale for the

---

[16] D. C. Coleman, 'Industrial Growth and Industrial Revolutions', *Economica* (1956), reprinted in Carus-Wilson, *Essays in Economic History*, 3; D. S. Landes, ed., *The Rise of Capitalism* (New York, 1965); and A. Maczak, ed., *Genoza nowozytnej Angli* (Warsaw, 1968).
[17] D. C. Coleman, 'Proto-industrialization: A Concept Too Many', *Econ. Hist. Rev.*, 2nd ser. XXXVI (1983), 435–48, esp. p. 446.

1957–8 session and to a Readership in Economic History at LSE in October 1958. This had been achieved by hard work and light teaching duties, but the seven years as a lecturer had not been all research and writing. In 1950, before landing a job, he had acquired from a commercial artist friend a large third-floor flat, 90 Charing Cross Road, just north of Cambridge Circus, five minutes walk from the British Museum, ten from LSE, and twenty from Chancery Lane, with a brothel opposite which later had a fire when, Donald fondly related to students he entertained in the flat, you could smell the burning tarts. Ann Child, whose 1936 marriage had never been happy, finally separated from her husband in 1948 and married Donald in 1954. Ann carried on working for a West End solicitor for some time, and their two salaries meant that they enjoyed a life style of theatres, ballets, operas, and Soho restaurants somewhat superior to that of most university lecturers in the 1950s. The flat was remembered by generations of economic history undergraduates and graduates from LSE as a place of good talk and gossip, good wine, and bacon and eggs (sometimes more elaborate meals) always cooked by Donald. It was also, roughly between 1955 and 1959, something of an academic salon where an informal group, with a fluctuating membership that included Jack Fisher, Ralph Davis (1915–78, FBA 1973), George Holmes (1927– , FBA 1985), David Joslin (1925–70), Peter Mathias (1928– , FBA 1977), and Lawrence Stone (1919–98, FBA, Corresponding, 1983), 'used to meet for lunch and thereafter read papers and discussed the topics in an uninhibited fashion. The meetings . . . testified to the current zeal for a subject which seemed then to have endless promise.'[18] The idyll of Charing Cross Road began to fade when smitten by their American experiences Donald and Ann first of all bought a car in 1958, then a cottage at Dedham in 1959, and finally Over Hall, Cavendish, in Suffolk in 1961—using it for weekends and vacations until Soho in the 1960s lost its village atmosphere and became a sleazy tourist trap, the enthusiasm not for burning tarts but for sweeping them off the streets bringing with it 'a dreary rash of strip joints', so that disenchantment led Donald to quit Charing Cross Road in 1970 for a flat in Woodford, in the once-despised suburbia, conveniently en route for Cavendish. This, as he said, shifted his centre of gravity from London to Suffolk, although he resolutely claimed that it 'in no way represented a pursuit of rural bliss'.[19] Over Hall was, however, destined to become one of his absorbing occupations in later life.

[18] Coleman, *Dons*, chap. 3, p. 15.
[19] Coleman, *Dons*, chap. 5, p. 9.

Donald spent another thirteen years at LSE after 1958, eleven as Reader and the last two holding a personal chair as Professor of Economic History, and they were as productive, although he did not find them as enjoyable, as the previous twelve. The book on Sir John Banks came out in 1963, preceded by a chapter in Jack Fisher's collection of *Essays in the Economic and Social History of Tudor and Stuart England* in 1961; there was an unexpected article on eighteenth-century museums in 1959, and the major article on the New Draperies in 1969. This displayed his command of the technical details of the manufacturing processes and product differentiation and nomenclature of the whole range of 'old' and 'new' draperies of sixteenth- and seventeenth-century western Europe and Italy, and their adoption in some but not all of the English cloth-making regions, perhaps in such great detail that his general message about the enormous difficulties of defining and identifying 'new products' and the economic contexts that give rise to their 'invention' and conjured up consumer demand for them, necessary but commonly ignored ingredients of credible models of economic growth, was not widely noticed.[20] By 1969 Donald and Michael Thompson were the joint Editors of the *Economic History Review*, in which this article appeared—and he left the editorial pruning and polishing strictly to his fellow editor alone. His earlier editorial experience had been as joint English editor, with Jim Potter, an LSE friend and colleague, of the *Scandinavian Economic History Review*, the result of a chance meeting with some Swedish academics when as an undergraduate he spent a couple of months in the summer of 1952 doing some English language teaching in Sweden to earn a bit of pocket money:[21] So when Professor Söderlund started that journal in 1953 and wished to make sure that its English was idiomatic he turned to Donald and Jim, and they acted together for the next ten years, during which Donald had occasion to make many trips to Sweden, Denmark, and Finland, and acquired a reasonable reading knowledge of Swedish. His appointment as an Editor of the *Economic History Review* in 1967 was an altogether less casual affair, and followed a period when he had served the *Review* for three years as the author of the early modern section of its annual review of periodical literature, becoming a well-known figure in the Economic History Society. He worked with Max Hartwell (Editor, 1960–8) for a year, and then Michael

[20] D. C. Coleman, 'An Innovation and its Diffusion: the "New Draperies" ', *Econ. Hist. Rev.*, 2nd ser. XXII (1969), 417–29.
[21] The date is that given in Coleman, *Dons*, chap. 3, p. 16, but he was mistaken in believing that he was still an undergraduate in 1952. David Watson's recollection is that he and Donald spent two months in 1951 teaching English to some Swedish schoolteachers at Falsterbo, near Malmö.

Thompson joined him in 1968, performing as the second or 'junior' editor until he retired from the editorship in 1973. In 1968, during the 'troubles' in LSE the editors operated as the '*Review* in exile' as Donald was pleased to call it, from the History Department of Bedford College in St John's Lodge, Regent's Park. In those wonderful surroundings they hatched the new policies which converted the *Review* into a quarterly (previously it had three issues a year), and abolished the Editorial Board, a group of five elder statesmen which never met and whose advice was never sought—all articles which fell outside the editors' own fields of expertise were independently refereed, the referees being chosen ad hoc and not from the Editorial Board panel. Donald was a model editor. The reputation of the *Economic History Review* had never stood higher, and it could claim to be the leading journal in the field in which not only all aspiring economic and social historians in Britain were eager to be published, but also many from elsewhere in the English-speaking world, and many of the more ambitious European scholars as well. Jack Fisher, in a wonderfully barbed remark, said that 'There are those who believe that, under his rigorous and even autocratic editorship, the *Review* reached a level from which it has since declined.'[22]

While Donald enjoyed his editorial years and was not averse to being the centre of attention at Economic History Society conferences he otherwise consistently avoided involvement in administration or in institutionalised gatherings of societies or associations, sticking firmly to the informal socialising of the pub. At the same time he was increasingly disenchanted with LSE, which for him had ceased to be an almost magical place of exciting ideas, intellectual leadership, good talk, and good companionship, and had degenerated into a place of incompetent administration, conflict between academics and bureaucrats, disruptive students, and lazy colleagues. There were student riots in the School in 1968, ostensibly over the iron security gates which radical students claimed were turning the building into a prison or a fortress, confrontations which Donald put down to poor management. He had detected increasing alienation of staff from students in the 1960s, for which he blamed the administration's policy of allowing lecturers to opt out of first-year teaching and making promotion entirely dependent on publications, sending off a blistering letter in 1965 denouncing the School's rulers for deliberately disparaging the prime purpose of university teaching.[23] In turn, he alienated the School's Director by daring to write to *The Times*

---

[22] Fisher in Preface to McKendrick and Outhwaite, eds., *Business Life and Public Policy*, p. ix.
[23] Coleman, *Dons*, chap. 4, p. 6.

without seeking permission;[24] he quarrelled rather publicly with the School's Librarian; and he became disillusioned with the lack of leadership and downright incompetence of his mentor, Jack Fisher, as nominal convenor of the Economic History Department. It was therefore without regrets that he took the chance of quitting LSE in 1971 for Cambridge, having twice before turned down attempts to lure him there, in 1956 and 1962—the second attempt underwrote his threat to resign his Readership at LSE over the Library issue—by accepting the offer of the Chair in Economic History at Cambridge, unexpectedly vacated by the sudden death of the forty-five year old David Joslin in October 1970.

The following year, 1972, he was elected to the British Academy, and although he characteristically mocked himself for consenting to join the great and the good of the academic establishment he actually greatly appreciated this recognition, and he rapidly became a warm supporter of the Academy. He served as Chairman of Section 9, as it then was (the Economists and Economic Historians), from 1982 to 1986, and as Chairman of the Records of Social and Economic History Committee, 1977–90, having joined that committee in 1975. This project, for publishing expertly edited editions of original sources, fitted neatly with his methodological empiricism and emphasis on the historian's commitment to documentary evidence, and it was especially appropriate that he was instrumental in securing the Josselin Diary (ed. Alan Macfarlane) for the New Series, a volume which has been the best-seller of the whole series. In all a dozen volumes were published under his chairmanship.

IV

The University of London, and LSE, had already recognised Donald Coleman's increasing stature by conferring on him the personal title of Professor of Economic History in 1969. In spite of his strained relations with the School's authorities, and his consistent refusal to join either academic cabals or committees, this recognition could hardly have been denied, because the 1960s had seen his 'spectacular rise to eminence as a business historian'.[25] The rise was, in fact, less unexpected than this remark implied, since it was based on the twin foundations of Donald's

---

[24] *The Times*, 4 Feb. 1959. The letter was about a tendentious opinion poll on the nationalisation of the steel industry; see Coleman, *Dons*, chap. 4, p. 10.
[25] Fisher in Preface to McKendrick and Outhwaite, *Business Life and Public Policy*, p. ix.

expertise in textile history, and his interest in the long-term processes of industrialisation, which dated back to the early years of his career. His first stab at questioning the orthodox version of the 'classic' Industrial Revolution had been in his history of the paper industry, and concern with the Industrial Revolution provided one of the organising themes of his text-book *The Economy of England, 1450–1750* (Oxford, 1977), which was to see in what ways political, social and intellectual, agrarian, commercial and industrial change in England produced a 'divergence' from the experience of other European countries which led to industrialisation beginning in England in the eighteenth century rather than elsewhere in Europe. He found it mainly in the build-up of disposable income, rising agricultural productivity, the growth of extra-European trade, increasing levels of economic activity in the Midlands and North of England—'a moving frontier of the internal economy'[26]—with more buoyant levels of demand, a greater urban and non-agricultural population, and more diverse manufacturing industry. In short the book explored the apprenticeship to the Industrial Revolution.

Although a declared empiricist and dedicated to empirical research in documentary sources he had deep knowledge of the conceptual debates which had encompassed all discussions of industrialisation as an historical phenomenon and was widely read in the relevant continental scholarship. All the items in his principal collection of articles, published in 1992 under the title *Myth, History and the Industrial Revolution* (Hambledon Press) . . . 'hinged upon "one historical phenomenon"'.[27] The first eponymous essay is the most perceptive study in English of the historiography of the Industrial Revolution.[28] He used historiographical analysis as a means of explaining the ways in which different interpretations, embodying widely different concepts—some explicit others much less articulated—lay hidden behind the same terminology, inviting confusion when their implications were revealed. One of his principal objections to 'proto-industrialisation' theory was that it brought such conceptual confusion, as he saw it, to the pre-eighteenth century debate ('industrialisation before industrialisation'), while so much use of the same term had added to terminological and conceptual confusion both chronologically and in different contexts—the industrial revolution 'of the late bronze age', that of the thirteenth century, of the period 1540–1640, the second,

---

[26] D. C. Coleman, *The Economy of England, 1450–1750* (Oxford, 1977), p. 199.
[27] D. C. Coleman, *Myth, History and the Industrial Revolution* (1992), p. xi. [hereafter *MHIR*]
[28] First published, in briefer format, by the University of London in 1989 as the Creighton Trust Lecture of 1989.

and subsequent industrial revolutions *et al.*—their profusion flourishing in inverse proportion to their conceptual specification. Popularising the term spelled 'dangerous multiplicity'. This was, at heart, a vigorous defence of the empirical and historiographical identity of the English Industrial Revolution.

The depth of reading into these debates brought home many ironies. Continental romanticist thought and nineteenth-century Marxist scholarship had embodied the notion whilst it remained 'obstinately absent in the country which experienced the phenomenon' until the 1880s. This stubborn English refusal to hitch the reality of what was happening in Britain to any scheme of teleological historicism—least of all German— was then overborne by the sensitivities of social conscience and the eventual absorption of continental Marxist thought when legitimised through Fabian socialism and the Labour Party. This was the Industrial Revolution as social disaster. But irony piled on irony; paradox on paradox. Only when the industries upon which the Industrial Revolution had been based were collapsing did the interpretation swing from catastrophe to achievement. And the final irony—which Donald Coleman took grim satisfaction in stressing—was that the Industrial Revolution became an icon of 'collective, organised, commercialised nostalgia for the imagined past'. In the ultimate humiliating takeover it passed into the hands of the heritage business—its obsequies attended by 'cohorts of steam-railway buffs, canal restorers, cotton-mill conservers, industrial archaeologists and tourists galore . . .'[29] Here is Donald Coleman in his most stringent and trenchant mode, enjoying the demythologising of false gods and uncritical beliefs which had entered the pantheon of popular belief with historical fashion. He also had withering scorn for more recent attempts to promote an enterprise culture by invoking the 'values' of the Industrial Revolution and the myth of Adam Smith's supposedly unequivocal support of the free-market.[30]

Donald Coleman's own beliefs were sometimes less prominent than his castigations of false nostrums offered by others. But the essence was clear, both in his general statements and writ large in his monographs in industrial history. 'On its technical side', he wrote, 'the industrial revolution was the first major and large-scale success in man's efforts to apply his growing mastery of natural forces to economic production. It

---

[29] *MHIR*, p. 32.
[30] D. C. Coleman, 'Adam Smith, Businessman and the Mercantile System in England', *History of European Ideas*, IX (1988), 161–70; *MHIR*, chap. 7, esp. pp. 162–3.

transformed this country in a way in which no country had ever before been transformed . . .'[31] Much of the historiographical confusion lay in the fact that the concept of the Industrial Revolution was strictly speaking a metaphor for a complexity not otherwise describable. While sectors of the whole could be measured the totality had 'unmeasurable qualities' far beyond the component parts.[32]

Despite an inescapable degree of subjectivity involved in interpreting the past in our own way—hence the attention he always paid to historiography—solid foundations were possible. The nature and extent of the subjectivity had to be contained within the bounds of '. . . an accepted scholarly discipline, controlling accuracy and consistency, the critical use of research and the presentation of results'.[33] Beyond exposing absurdities, pretensions, and uncritical single-cause assertions historical research pursued the 'far more important goal of incorporating contemporary perceptions into the framework of retrospective analysis'.[34] And there were objective, testable conclusions to be drawn from the English 'classical' Industrial Revolution. Here, Donald Coleman affirmed the positive case: he was in the canon of T. S. Ashton at the LSE rather than the more sceptical F. J. Fisher (whose student he was). 'In a context of unprecedented population growth', he wrote, '. . . in spite of the dislocation of labour which it involved, in spite of the hardship to many, a vast amount of far more regular employment came into being in the course of the nineteenth century than had ever been known amongst the unemployed masses of the pre-industrial world. New jobs came into being, new categories of employment opened up, new skills replaced old skills. The skilled mechanic did not "survive" the industrial revolution, he was created by it.'[35]

In his view social and intellectual changes were integral to the transformation—a 'vital conjunction of changes in which population growth, large-scale and extensive industrial investment and the remarkably pervasive effects of the application of science to industry'.[36] With his work on the paper industry and Courtaulds over the very long term he was in a strategic position to make these judgements. To this was added a

---

[31] D. C. Coleman, 'Industrial Growth and Industrial Revolutions', *Economica*, NS XXIII (1956), 1–22; reprinted in *MHIR*, p. 61.
[32] *MHIR*, p. 42.
[33] *MHIR*, p. 40.
[34] *MHIR*, p. 41.
[35] *MHIR*, p. 60.
[36] *MHIR*, p. 61.

particular interest in the role of government and war in stimulating 'new' industries, which he explored in a detailed case-history of the development of nitro-cellulose and cellulose acetate for aircraft 'dope' at the time of the First World War. ('War Demand and Industrial Supply' in J. M. Winter (ed.) *War and Economic Development*, Cambridge, 1975).

V

Donald Coleman's expertise in textile history led to an invitation from Frank Kearton, Chairman of Courtaulds, to write the history of the business, envisaged on a large scale with all the expectations of professional research—for publication, 'warts and all'. Commissioned publications in business history, a large genre, fall into two sharply polarised groups: the very large number of glossy centenary volumes (excoriated by Donald Coleman himself at his most virulent—as being read only by other business historians and the occasional executive of the firm looking to see if there were any possible grounds for a libel action.) Too many were useful to scholars only for some piece-meal data or picturesque detail, being devoid of analytical context. On the other side stood a small group of serious works of scholarship by historians worthy of their profession. Fortunately their number has grown since the Courtauld history. This began in 1961/2, two volumes (to 1941) being published in 1969 and the third (1941–65) in 1980. They at once put Donald Coleman at the head of this select band for a feat of scholarship as impressive in its own field as the business which it recorded. Only Charles Wilson's *History of Unilever* (2 vols. 1954) was a comparable predecessor—and this was less documented and analytical—with a comparable immediate successor, W. J. Reader's *History* of ICI (2 volumes, 1970, 1975). Courtauld's history stood out, and still does. Courtaulds offered splendid opportunities to the historian because it embodied in microcosm the wider evolution of industry and business world-wide: from local family firm to the professionally managed multinational company; from London silversmiths to East Anglian silk-makers and then from silk to rayon and a succession of new artificial fibres. Courtaulds were typical entrepreneurs of the Industrial Revolution in a non-typical English industry—the protected, undercut, always import-threatened silk industry challenged by cotton, languishing in East Anglia but with Courtaulds prospering against the wind of the time by concentrating on the safest and most uniform mass upper-class market in silk—mourning crapes. When the firm took the English rights for viscose in 1904 the basis was laid for its transformation into an international giant. This was the crucial move to the unlimited horizons of low-cost artificial silk as the luxury of the rich became the necessity of the poor. A traditional textile firm was transformed into an international manufacturing chemical business, conjured into existence on the basis of a modern technology remote from any conscious search for a substitute fibre. From this point Courtaulds entered a world of international consortia in viscose and cellulose acetate, leading patent negotiations in the world market, forging international market-sharing agreements as the concomitant of marketing international patent rights, and setting up manufacturing plants in France, Germany, Italy, and the United States (from 1909).

All this was delineated with magisterial authority in the three large volumes. It was, indeed, an objective, quantified, and critical history. As a condition of accepting the invitation Donald Coleman had access to all the internal and surviving family documentation and exercised his freedom vigorously—setting out clearly, for example, the inter-war international cartel arrangements and the monopoly profits in the great rayon boom of the 1920s. He 'commented and quoted . . . with perfect freedom . . . in so far as the laws of libel permitted and with an unwillingness to cause gratuitous offence . . .'. This assertion was made of the final volume (for 1941–65) where many executives in the bruising battle of the ICI takeover were still very much alive. 'Some of my judgements', was the mild comment, 'may not be very agreeable to some people.' The point went to the heart of the issue: 'If business history is to lay claim to serious regard it must include analysis of loss as well as gain, of mistakes as well as victories.'[37]

At the root of long-term business success, he saw human effort. It was fashionable at the time the book was being written to decry 'entrepreneurship', excluded almost by definition from a perfectly competitive economy (as current neo-classical theory assumed), but to those seeking to understand enterprise in the real world it was different. 'The entrepreneur', concluded Donald Coleman, 'having been exorcised by abstractions, has reappeared through the back door. He insists upon intruding into the model.'[38]

In the long-running debate over the failings in the British economy after 1850, especially over the issue of 'entrepreneurship', Donald

---

[37] D. C. Coleman, *Courtaulds*, vol. 3 (Oxford, 1980), pp. v–vii.
[38] Ibid., p. 322.

Coleman's principal contribution was his seminal article 'Gentlemen and Players', *Economic History Review*, 2nd ser. XXVI (1973), pp. 92–112. This brought social and cultural influences, discounted by many relative to 'real' economic variables, back to centre stage as one cause of weak management in British business. Social advancement, he argued, had always been a driving motive in society (before, during, and subsequent to the Industrial Revolution) and the oldest social division was that which distinguished gentility from the common people. The Industrial Revolution had been driven by 'those who were not gentlemen' but subsequently business and industrial leaders succumbed to the values of the surviving elite and 'too many of the revolutionaries became too busy becoming gentlemen'. The rehabilitated public-school ethos (confirmed for those who went on to the ancient universities) produced a 'gentlemanly club' style in many boardrooms—illustrated by an analysis of the Courtauld directorate. Not the least weakness of this sectional English (and only English, he emphasised, not British) culture was the absence of a scientific tradition, expressed in the absence of science in the education received by the English elite. This was a recurrent theme for Donald Coleman. Thus a fatal link was forged between the 'educated amateur' and the 'practical man' which excluded professionalisation for the elite, with dire consequences. Of its nature this thesis is difficult to quantify, but the case was argued critically, yet strongly, with a long historiographical excursus into the concept of the gentleman. With the subsequent growth of interest in 'business culture' the issues put forward in 'Gentlemen and Players' remain on the agenda.

Donald Coleman's wide interface with business and businessmen—as author, adviser, assessor, and arbitrator—brought potential conflicts of loyalties. Much of his personal character is revealed in the respect (if not always the affection) he won from all parties. An adviser or arbitrator has to make judgements between or against fellow academics yet maintain their confidence. This is a common predicament, or course, for senior academics but the interface between academe and business has its special sensitivities. As an author he maintained academic independence and professional objectivity against company opinion but yet kept the goodwill of those in charge of the business. This was particularly the case with volume three of Courtaulds but the same principles governed his work as adviser to British Petroleum, British Rail, the Brewers Society, Schroders and other firms who had commissioned histories from academic historians. The respect of businessmen was won in the first instance by their awareness of his high status in his own world but then confirmed by their direct experience of his professional judgement and personal style. It was a matter of their perception of him and his of them. He was intensely interested in the practical and financial world of his day and sympathetic in principle to all manner of those who made it work. This was an important basis of his own perception: he had respect for achievement and admired success attained through hard work, commitment, intelligence, and insight—meritocratic success. He appreciated and was appreciated by the more reflective leading businessmen he encountered—such as Arthur Knight, Frank Kearton, David Steel, and Peter Walters. Perhaps he felt that his own talents might have won him advancement in the business world and that he might have enjoyed success there—as he had done in the army.

VI

The qualities he respected in others Donald exemplified himself. He was against privilege (unless privilege had been won by effort and merit); he was against posturing and pomposity in whatever manifestations: social, aesthetic or political, and in matters academic, intellectual or method-ological. He was his own master when identifying what he thought was flummery or pretentiousness and without reticence in saying so. Up to the limit of what *he* decided was an objective judgement he was outspoken in his views. He did not pull punches, whether for reasons of sentiment, a misguided (in his view) sense of obligation or loyalty or historical con-tinuity or personal friendship: he gave his views and explained them with-out fear or favour. Given this lack of reticence personal friendships were often conditional upon his opinions. He was an implacable opponent of any lack of professional standards, casualness or mystification which obscured objective judgement. He treated his colleagues (and superiors) on a par with others. He had a long memory, he was not particularly for-giving and hence created a reputation as a strong—if not a hard—man of astringent, acerbic views, forthright, sometimes over-resonant, and on occasion pompous in style but never in content. He was always willing to have these exacting standards applied to his own work and actions. Yet there was also personal sensitivity and sentiment present, if seldom revealed in a public stance. He earned the unremitting loyalty and the affection of his research students. Those able to earn his respect, even if not matching his standards, were fortunate in the warmth of his response.

With both work at LSE and life in London losing their attractions Donald Coleman's move to the chair in Cambridge and to a Professorial

Fellowship at Pembroke College brought greater professional and personal satisfaction. Life in Cavendish, at his spacious old vicarage and handsome garden became increasingly congenial—'Cavendish-les-deux églises' as Negley Harte dubbed it. Here was the right ambience for entertaining friends and colleagues (Donald, as in London, always cooking the meals). The cellar remained ample; his large collection of records, tapes and discs produced at will the music he loved. He worked enthusiastically until almost the end in the garden bringing nature to heel. Rufus, the inscrutable large ginger cat of immense age, known to so many economic historians, needed solace. Donald mellowed in this context, becoming more relaxed, showing kindness and generosity to all his visitors, devoted in his caring for Ann as she became more frail, and more generous even in his judgements of the failings of others. Being a Fellow of Pembroke he found more congenial than being a professor in the university and, until his final illness, he was increasingly drawn into the life of the college, particularly drawn to groups of the younger fellows, as they were to him.

He took early retirement from the Chair in 1981 (but not from his fellowship). Undergraduate teaching was becoming more tedious and lecturing a painful duty which he saw no reason to endure further. By contrast, Cavendish offered greater delights, the greatest of which professionally was the opportunity of working uninterruptedly in his upstairs study encompassed by his library. Ann, as always, undertook his secretarial work. He was not to be tempted into becoming chairman of the History Faculty Board, as he had previously declined the nomination of the Presidency of the Economic History Society—some disenchantment had spread there also. Nor did he agree to become a candidate for the headship of a Cambridge college.

Already in his inaugural lecture at Cambridge in 1972 he showed his disquiet over 'What has happened to Economic History?' (the title of the lecture), giving a statistical demonstration of the rise and fall of its popularity as a school and undergraduate subject since 1945, and attributing its declining appeal to the then recent fashion for reducing all economic history to the sophisticated number-crunching of the econometric historians and their mathematical models borrowed from economics.[39] In 1987 he elaborated on this theme with his history of economic history, *History and the Economic Past. An account of the Rise and Decline of Economic History in Britain*. A dispassionate analytical narrative of the founding fathers of economic history as a distinct discipline, this progressed into a

---

[39] D. C. Coleman, *What has happened to Economic History?* (Cambridge, 1972), esp. p. 27.

passionate exposure of what Donald saw as its decline from the point at which Lawrence Stone had announced a return to narrative history in 1970, the econometricians attempted a quantitative take-over of the subject, and the craze for social history captured many journals and university departments, a subject which had become 'a meaningless catch-all term' embracing labour history, demographic history, psycho-history, family history, women's history, magic history, mentalités, crowds, sports, crime, literacy, and children, and offering exciting and seductive articles on witchcraft, musical taste, menstruation, and rituals, in contrast to the 'unexciting offerings typically to be found in the pages of the *Economic History Review*'. Disillusionment with the Economic History Society, whose 'annual conferences long resembled little more than festive gatherings of the clan' and whose 'aura of Pangloss' had stifled intellectual thrust and innovation, was coupled with disillusion with his own achievement in business history, which had come to seem pointless because economists took no interest in business history and business schools largely ignored the growing body of scholarly histories of individual businesses.[40] Maybe this pessimistic assessment was no more than a case of old men remembering a golden past and regretting the shortcomings of the present, but it was a sad set of reflections on which to sign off. The sense of gloom may have passed, for in 1992 Coleman concluded a long review article on 'New Business History for Old' by claiming that 'there is hope for a more promising future in Britain for this very important subject, building upon a combination of conceptual analysis and archival research', a confident restatement of his abiding definition of serious historical work.[41]

His firm academic priority was to write, while responding to invitations to help and advise. He remained always accessible to his research students and kept their unswerving loyalty. His own commitment to the Pasold Fund for textile history continued until two years before his death, being Governor from 1977 and Chairman from 1985 to 1993. He spent some of his final year in reading Gibbon's *Decline and Fall of the Roman Empire*, his choice of the Pasold Fund's presentation to him in thanks for his services to the Fund. 'I can enjoy to the full', he wrote of Gibbon, 'its remarkable mixture of wit, irony, clarity and percipience which regularly brings pretentious humbug tumbling to the ground. It is not too difficult

---

[40] D. C. Coleman, *History and the Economic Past. An account of the Rise and Decline of Economic History in Britain* (Oxford, 1987), esp. pp. 110, 114, 117, 140, 145.

[41] D. C. Coleman, 'New Business History for Old?' *Historical Journal*, 35 (1992), pp. 239–44.

to think of some suitable cases for the Gibbonian treatment today.'[42] In Donald's time he had himself been a fine dispenser of the Gibbonian treatment. His productivity was remarkable. Apart from the many books and shorter pieces cited in this memoir he had published 8 detailed survey articles and 61 book reviews by 1984. Twenty of these reviews, 13 of the 27 articles, and 4 of the surveys appeared in the *Economic History Review*. There is a full bibliography of his publications before 1986 in *Business Life and Public Policy* (Cambridge, 1986). He died from cancer after a long painful illness on 3 September 1995.

PETER MATHIAS
Fellow of the Academy

F. M. L. THOMPSON
Fellow of the Academy

Note. This text incorporates many comments and written observations about Donald Coleman by himself, and by his friends and colleagues. Coleman wrote a book-length autobiographical piece, *Dons: A Memoir of L.S.E. and Cambridge* in 1991, now deposited in Cambridge University Library. His fellow-gunner, David Watson (who by chance later came to live near him in Glemsford) provided information on the war years, 1943–5. Amongst his academic friends and colleagues who have provided material are: Negley Harte obituary in the *Independent*, 9 September 1995 and in *Textile History*, 27(2), 1996, pp. 127–31; entry in *Who's Who*; contributions read at the memorial service in the chapel of Pembroke College, Cambridge on 3 February 1996 by Julian Hoppit, Peter Mathias, Clive Trebilcock, Daniel Waley, Oliver Westall, Richard Wilson; N. McKendrick, and R. B. Outhwaite, editorial preface in *Business Life and Public Policy: Essays in Honour of D. C. Coleman* (Cambridge, 1986).

---

[42] Quoted in Negley Harte, 'Professor Donald Coleman: An Appreciation', *Textile History*, 27 (1996), 131.

ROBERT COOK   *Eaden Lilly*

Robert Manuel Cook
1909–2000

ROBERT MANUEL COOK was born on 4 July 1909 in Sheffield, the son of the Reverend Charles Robert and Mary Manuel Cook. His younger brother, John Manuel Cook FBA, was destined for a somewhat different career in classical archaeology (see these *Proceedings*, 87 (1995), 265–73, also for the family). The young Cooks were educated at home until they were nine, then in a boarding school (Aysgarth School, Newton-le-Willows). Robert went to Marlborough College (1923–9), thence to Clare College, Cambridge, where he read Classics, achieving a Double First and a Distinction in Classical Archaeology. In 1932 he was awarded a Walston Studentship and went to the British School at Athens for two years' research. The Director at the School was Humfry Payne, who had learned skills in the classification of Greek pottery from Beazley in Oxford, and was applying them to the non-Athenian wares. His magisterial *Necrocorinthia* had appeared in 1931 (Oxford) and pointed the way for further work. Robert was one of the first recruits to the new discipline, along with his brother and Arthur Lane, and the results of his and Lane's research filled the volume of the *Annual of the British School at Athens* which appeared in 1936.[1] The contrast in styles is illuminating. Lane, working with Laconian pottery (which had at first been designated as Robert Cook's subject), presented his results in a somewhat more discursive manner, with greater emphasis on iconography and painters' styles; he went on to become an expert on Islamic pottery. Cook was doggedly scientific in his analysis of every single aspect of his vases, both shape and

---

[1] *BSA*, 34 (1933/4), 1–98.

Proceedings of the British Academy, **115**, 195–203. © The British Academy 2002.

decoration, and was no less thorough in treatment of issues of distribution, imitations, origins, and source; yet all presented economically and with a light touch. In those days his subject, 'Fikellura pottery', was generally agreed to be Rhodian in origin. Cook weighed the possibilities, admitted Rhodes' claim, but also speculated about a *koine*. He thought of Samos, but his scepticism has been rewarded by the results of clay analysis which seem to declare for Miletus, although for some scholars Samos remains in the picture.

In 1934 he returned to Britain to become Assistant Lecturer, then Lecturer in Manchester University, and Sub-warden of St Anselm's Hall (1936–8). In 1945 he was appointed Laurence Reader in Classical Archaeology in Cambridge, then Professor in 1962 until retirement in 1976. During the Second World War he joined the Civil Service. He continued an active scholar for many years after retirement; I revert to his tenure of the posts in Cambridge below.

The classification of Greek pottery, and thereby the revelation of its archaeological, art-historical and historical significance, remained his major, but not exclusive, interest. He published a study of Clazomenian pottery[2] where there was more definition by painter than by the broader groups which had seemed suitable for the Fikellura, and although he did not deal with Chian pottery in the same way he explored the evidence of its distribution and inscriptions (with A. G. Woodhead).[3] He remained devoted to the pottery of the east Greek world, which was certainly more difficult to control than mainland Greek wares. In a volume of the *Corpus Vasorum Antiquorum* he published the late archaic East Greek pottery in the British Museum, mainly from sites dug by the British in Egypt (Naucratis, Tell Defenneh) or acquired from Rhodes, an ideal opportunity for closer study of major sources for these wares.[4] He had published the Clazomenian painted sarcophagi found in his brother's excavations at Old Smyrna,[5] and was persuaded to put his comprehensive knowledge of the class into a magisterial book in the *Kerameus* series.[6] His interest in the pottery of the area culminated in the publication of *East Greek Pottery* which he wrote with Pierre Dupont, who dealt with the plain wares and analyses.[7] His determination to bring order into the subject,

[2] *BSA*, 47 (1952), 123–52.
[3] *BSA*, 44 (1949), 154–6; 47 (1952), 159–70.
[4] Volume Great Britain 13, British Museum 8 (1954).
[5] *BSA*, 69 (1974), 55–60.
[6] *Clazomenian Sarcophagi* (Mainz, von Zabern, 1981).
[7] R. M. Cook and Pierre Dupont, *East Greek Pottery* (1998).

but never at the expense of the evidence, by proposing convenient answers and classifications, led to several smaller publications dealing with problems of terminology and the questions posed by imitations of the Greek wares in other parts of Anatolia, such as Caria.[8]

These studies might be regarded as mainly art-historical, though they were certainly more than that in his mind, and were treated in the manner of an archaeologist rather than an art-historian; they have contributed to our ability to deal with the evidence of the pottery of the region on a more reliable basis than that of most parts of Greece, outside Athens and Corinth. They depended on scrupulous attention to detail and his main legacy to his pupils, apart from a wary scepticism, was to insist on the importance of looking at things properly and comprehensively. The merits of this may seem self-apparent, but they have been increasingly overlooked in modern studies which have other aims beside, a fact that he deplored since they then seem to be built on unreliable foundations.

Other areas of pottery study attracted him, notably the construction of ancient kilns, a subject into which the truly art-historical connoisseurs rarely ventured.[9] It led to consideration of purely scientific analysis, and especially the archaeomagnetic study of fired clays.[10] This depended on them being examined *in situ* at the time of firing, whether deliberately in a kiln or accidentally in a conflagration. This was worth investigation even though its useful application was bound to be limited. He also welcomed the opportunities offered by analyses of clays, though only once the study was properly established and with adequate comparanda available. These have done much to confirm or adjust his conclusions about provenance.

To avoid, he alleged, having to go on lecturing on Greek pottery in the same old way, he wrote *Greek Painted Pottery* which was published in 1960 (Methuen), with a third edition in 1992 (Routledge). This was the first comprehensive account of the subject since Ernst Pfuhl's *Malerei und Zeichnung der Griechen* of 1923, though there had been shorter studies, by Ernst Buschor and Andreas Rumpf (whom Cook admired). The book properly demoted Athenian vases to their just proportion of the whole, in terms of history if not numbers, and was generous in giving due value to many other aspects of the subject—technical and practical, but was

[8] *Oxford Journal of Archaeology*, 12 (1993), 109–16; 18 (1999), 79–93.
[9] *BSA*, 56 (1961), 64 7.
[10] *Antiquity*, 32 (1958), 167–78; *Archaeology*, 12 (1959), 158–62; *BSA*, 58 (1963), 8–13.

dismissive of the value of the subject for what it can tell of Greek trade, and regarded iconographic studies, beyond simple identification, as purely speculative. (Perversely, his inaugural lecture in Cambridge was iconographical.[11]) A splendid chapter on the history of the subject to the mid-twentieth century reveals many of the reasons for his sceptical approach to the possibility of knowing much more about it than it physically presents, and which can be analysed in the manner he and others had demonstrated in their work: 'Although there are rare students of genius, most are clever only in detail, normally uncritical of their methods or presumptions and blind to the further consequences of their arguments . . . We may laugh at these past follies, but they are also a warning to look for equal follies of our own.' His book will long be read with profit and pleasure by students who will judge for themselves what more the subject might offer.

Cook was not totally obsessed by pottery studies. Short essays on architecture demonstrate an unexpected interest,[12] which probably led to the appointment of a classical architectural scholar to a post in Cambridge (Hugh Plommer). He had toyed with the idea of teaching the principles of Greek construction with the help of toy blocks, like Lego. He enjoyed subjecting new theories to the closest scrutiny, even those of his pupils, dissecting them scrupulously yet with the clear presumption that there must be something either wrong or quite unprovable.[13] His reviewing was caustic and always to the point. The rather negative approach in much of his writing is belied by his obvious enjoyment in exercising his subject and in teaching it to the young.

He was ready to apply his archaeology to broader cultural and historical issues, with characteristic caution. His manner in such studies has been influential though seldom acknowledged, and he anticipated many of the more sceptical attitudes of scholarship of the last twenty years. There are few if any major issues of early Greek archaeology/history which he did not touch, taking major problems and dissecting them neatly and briefly, with cautious but acceptable conclusions, or none at all if the evidence would not bear it. These are mainly short essays, economical in wordage but packed with data and thought. In other hands they would have been major articles or books, though not the better for it, but his reticence means that they have been overlooked by all but those who read them as they appeared. In three pages he demonstrated

---

[11] *Niobe and her children* (1964).
[12] *BSA*, 46 (1951), 50–2; 65 (1970), 17–18.
[13] *Journal of Hellenic Studies*, 107 (1987), 167–71; 109 (1989), 164–70.

to prehistorians what they might learn from classical archaeology—that changes in burial custom need mean no change in population, that in religious matters archaeology and literature often conflict, that material remains may be no guide to true prosperity, that trade in pottery is not an index for trade in other things: 'It is a valuable corrective to consider the material remains of historical peoples and to test archaeological methods of deduction in problems where the answer is already known.'[14]

While still in Manchester he brought archaeological expertise to the problem of the date of the *Aspis* poem of Hesiod.[15] A long essay on Ionia and Greece in the early archaic period reduced the residual 'ionicism' of earlier scholarship to proper proportions,[16] though he did not suspect that Ionia's poor showing in early pottery was answered by precocity in decorated metalwork which was very influential in the homeland. The origins of coinage he ascribed to the need for large payments, probably for mercenaries.[17] There is a salutary essay on the origins of Greek sculpture, giving proper value to Syria and demoting Egypt.[18] The importance of painted pottery for studies in trade he judged slight;[19] and other studies in trade involve the Corinth *diolkos*, the Vix crater, and the non-relevance of the distribution of Laconian pottery to Laconian trade.[20] The diffusion of the Greek alphabet and its variety is explained by different and personal choices.[21] Having looked at the evidence for the Dorian invasion he decided that it is 'not a subject that is worth much study'.[22] Ischia and Cumae were founded for subsistence not trade, and Spartan 'austerity' is much exaggerated.[23] He coldly demolished the easy assumption that early artists were inspired or even influenced by epic poetry.[24] The pitfalls of absolute chronology were a recurrent interest.[25] Sculpture is not neglected.[26] Here and there in his work there is a residual antiquarian

---

[14] *Antiquity*, 34 (1960), 177–9.
[15] *Classical Quarterly*, 31 (1937), 204–14.
[16] *JHS*, 66 (1946), 67–98.
[17] *Historia*, 7 (1958), 257–62.
[18] *JHS*, 87 (1967), 24–32.
[19] *Jahrbuch des Deutschen Archäologischen Instituts*, 74 (1959), 114–23.
[20] *JHS*, 99 (1979), 152–5.
[21] *American Journal of Archaeology*, 63 (1959), 175–8.
[22] *Proceedings of the Cambridge Philological Society*, 8 (1962), 16–22.
[23] *Historia*, 11 (1962), 113–14; *Classical Quarterly*, 12 (1962), 156–8.
[24] *Bulletin antieke Beschaving*, 58 (1983), 1–10.
[25] *BSA*, 64 (1969), 13–15; *JHS*, 109 (1989), 164–70.
[26] *JHS*, 96 (1976), 153–4 (*meniskoi*); in *Festschrift F. Brommer* (Mainz, 1977), 77 (Praxitelean heads); *Journal of the Walters Art Gallery*, 37 (1978), 85–7 (the Peplos kore not a copy of a *xoanon*); *Archäologischer Anzeiger* (1989), 525–8 (composition of the Apollo Sosianus pediment).

chauvinism, reluctant to attribute too much to the foreigner. And he introduced a distinguished elderly lecturer at a Classical Triennial Conference in Oxford as 'Professor Luisa Banti, although a woman, . . .'.

Some of his writing for a wider public is as sceptical as anything he wrote for the professional, yet manages to be inspiring. This appeared especially in *The Greeks till Alexander* and his paperback *Greek Art* which is still in print.[27] The former carries comment on history and society as well as archaeology and art. 'The greatest service of the Greeks of the Classical period was that they created the first modern civilisation.' The Greeks were for Cook well worth studying, and in detail, but honestly: to mention the Parthenon only once, in passing, yet devote two pages to pottery in his Classical Period chapter, should satisfy even the most iconoclastic.

In *Greek Art* he concentrated on what could be known and was most plenteously preserved. Pottery was for the first chapter, therefore; the best chapter, and the longest, was on architecture. In some respects the work seems diminished by an unwillingness to explore beyond the immediate purpose and appearance of what he described, dismissing some possibilities rather unjustly; at the same time it makes the main narrative almost faultless since all possibly unjustified speculation is avoided.

The witty cynicism which is characteristic of much that he wrote, especially for a wider audience, is a welcome antidote to the romantic or hyper-imaginative which is still found in much literature on classical antiquity. It is sincere and provokes thought but at times may seem to have become almost wilful. The hard-headed approach excluded much that even the more conservative scholars of today would regard as essential elements in the study—notably iconography and the willingness to look beyond the image and object to the intentions of its creator and response of the ancient viewer: 'the metopes [of the Parthenon] had no particular relevance and . . . were chosen from the stock artistic repertory'; 'Not much [of the sculpture in Athens museum] of the Hellenistic and Roman periods is or deserves to be on view.' His final attack was timely and biting, on the antiques trade, on excavators who do not publish, and on museums that hoard: '"Cultural heritage" is a fine-sounding slogan, of which an ad-man would be proud; but if it means that every object above a certain age must remain for ever in the country in which it was found, it is hardly more reasonable than necrophilia.'[28]

---

[27] *The Greeks Till Alexander* (1961); *Greek Art* (1972), Penguin/Pelican reprint (1976). There is also a lengthy essay in *Masterpieces of Western and Near Eastern Ceramics* (Tokyo, 1979).
[28] In *Periplous* (eds. G. R. Tsetskhladze *et al.*, 2000), 68–9.

His remarks and attitude make the reader stop and think, and smile, and yet may leave a regretful if not even sometimes a sour flavour; but the sceptical heritage is a necessary ingredient in all honest scholarship, no less important today than it has ever been. It was as though he had decided at an early stage what scholarship was about and the attitudes to adopt, and found no reason to adapt or alter his views in the light of experience. He can never be accused of having been narrow but he was perhaps less critical of some of his own views than of those of others. But there will never be a time when Robert Cook will not be read by students and scholars with profit and pleasure.

In Cambridge after the Second World War the Professor was A. W. Lawrence, with whom the Cooks for a while shared a house, and the other classical archaeological luminaries were Jocelyn Toynbee, Frank Stubbings, and Charles Seltman. Classical archaeology figured optionally in the Tripos and was reasonably well attended, the teaching being done for undergraduates wholly by lecture, in the Museum of Classical Archaeology in Little St Mary's Lane, which housed the library and a substantial Cast Collection. Robert would arrive briskly and noisily in the lecture room and start speaking immediately. He was slim, with a shock of wiry red hair which flew off at a tangent to his left, and continued to throughout his life. He had a wary but ready and often mischievous smile, and his delivery was only occasionally impeded by a pipe-smoker's dry cough and mumble. He was not an impressive lecturer yet more than one of his audience can still trace their attitudes to archaeology back to what they heard in 'the Ark'. He was a major influence on the attitudes and work of more British classical archaeologists of the generation after the Second World War than is generally realised.

Towards the end of his tenure he had to fight attempts to replace the chair with two junior posts and to change the syllabus, largely promoted by Moses Finley, who never quite understood what Greek archaeology and art were about but was supported by others. The Museum of Classical Archaeology fell uneasily between the Fitzwilliam Museum and the Faculty of Classics, and Cook championed its independence. In Oxford the museums were more closely linked and Faculty role rather ill-defined; this seems a common problem with the subject, and 'Oxford' supported Cook's stand. Oxford's then Reader commented through him and with his approval to the Faculty that 'it is not easy to explain to those who profess literature and history that it is pointless to expect archaeologists to provide predigested information for their use without teaching the basic principles and background, which is what most of the art, as taught here and in Cambridge, is about'. Cook was successful. He drew comparisons with the teaching in other universities and judged that Cambridge had got the emphases about right, he also defended the broader syllabus of the Diploma in Classical Archaeology, noting that Oxford's more specialised course provided an alternative for those who wished it. He effectively saved the status of the subject in Cambridge for his successor, Anthony Snodgrass, to build on.

He devoted much thought and care to the Cast Collection. Experiment with cleaning and painting of the cast surfaces which lent them an appearance more of stone than plaster ('a slight crystalline sheen') led to the treatment of the whole collection, though it can be faulted by some as disguising the nature of the casts themselves. This is a case where Cook valued appearance, for teaching and display, over strict honesty, possibly because many casts were copies of copies anyway. He carefully prepared his successor for the fight which was to develop over the Ark when Peterhouse College thought to reclaim the territory, but he approved its new installation in Sidgwick Avenue, and wrote a brief Guide to the collection which was published in 1986. His views about casts have proved pessimistic, given the revived interest in them in recent years: 'Casts are now [1977] out of favour with most people who consider themselves civilised and even with some archaeologists. This is partly because they have been brought up on photographs and are not used to viewing objects in three dimensions, and partly because the surface of untreated plaster is dead and easily becomes dirty.' Besides the casts he built up the department's collection of sherds and pottery as aids for teaching; the resources of the Fitzwilliam Museum were rather neglected for this purpose.

He was a highly effective academic chairman, both of the Cambridge Faculty of Classics and, for 1983 to 1987, of the Managing Committee of the British School at Athens. He had no truck with members who had not read their papers or who seemed unable to come to a decision or even say anything at all, and was fierce with time-wasters, whatever their seniority. He was never a 'college man' and rather despised the pretensions of Oxbridge society.

He was elected a Fellow of the British Academy in 1974, but never attended its meetings, and had been made a Fellow of the German Archaeological Institute in 1953. In 1991 he was presented with a Festschrift volume of essays by pupils and friends, though its purpose was unnecessarily disguised by the Cambridge University Press. He naturally disapproved of Festschrifts as such, but he made an exception for *Looking at Greek Vases* which was a tribute he much appreciated.

To his family Robert was 'Freddie', probably for his red hair and early political views. His brother John, who was a year younger but began his career in parallel with Robert's and with similar interests, turned more to the field and excavation, in Greece and Turkey, so their academic paths seldom crossed thereafter, except where Robert helped publish John's finds, but they remained close. In 1938 Robert married Kathleen, daughter of James Frank and Eileen Hardman Porter. She supported Robert in many ways, with wit and excellent cooking, and as a critical companion on travels in south Greece which resulted in their joint *Southern Greece: An Archaeological Guide* (Faber, 1968). This typifies much of Robert's attitudes to his chosen subject, from the opening 'Most visitors to Greece stay too long in Athens', to concluding hints about *retsina*—'the average foreigner learns to tolerate the taste after about a gallon', and conversion tables for sizes of men's socks and women's dresses. He could not even resist a quiet gibe at his own subject, while defending its importance, in Athens museum: 'Through perhaps excessive research the great output of Greek pottery with painted decoration has been classified by styles and schools and even painters and so vase painting has become the best understood branch of Greek art.' And a sympathetic reflection on the changes in modern Greece: 'Greece is changing fast and the old-fashioned peasant is at last disappearing, lamented of course by irresponsible enthusiasts who do not have to endure his miserable existence and still less his wife's.'

Kathleen's death in 1979, soon after his retirement, threw him back on his own considerable resources, not least the domestic. His home in Wilberforce Road was well attended by Cambridge classicists, seniors and students, who could rely on at least adequate sustenance and Robert's special brand of comment on the world of scholarship, often deliberately provocative. However much he disapproved of the new trends in classical archaeology which were apparent not least in his own university, their proponents were always welcomed, and glad to be welcomed; even the ranks of Tuscany could not but acknowledge his quality as critic and friend. He died in Cambridge on 10 August 2000, shortly after his ninety-first birthday.

JOHN BOARDMAN
Fellow of the Academy

Note. Principal sources have been personal knowledge, A. M. Snodgrass, J. Reynolds, conversations and correspondence with family and mutual acquaintances.

TERRY COPPOCK

John Terence Coppock
1921–2000

TERRY COPPOCK was a pioneer in three areas of scholarship: agricultural geography, land-use management, and computer applications. Educated at Queens' College Cambridge, he spent his academic career at University College London and at the University of Edinburgh, where he was the first holder of the Ogilvie Chair in Geography. One academic session at the University of Ibadan in 1964–5 provided an opportunity for mapping out new directions and endeavours, and his time as Visiting Professor at the University of Waterloo in 1972 strengthened his convictions about the application of academic geography to tackling real-world problems. Terry occupied high office in the Institute of British Geographers, of which he was president in 1974. He received the Murchison Grant (1969) and the Victoria Medal (1985) from the Royal Geographical Society, and served as Secretary (1976–8) and then Chair (1978–80) of the Commission on World Food Problems and Agricultural Productivity of the International Geographical Union. His Edinburgh years were marked by allegiance to the Royal Scottish Geographical Society and by exceptional involvement in government committees dealing with recreation and rural affairs. He was elected Fellow of the British Academy in 1975, serving on Council and holding the post of Vice-President from 1985. Following the death of Sir Henry Clifford Darby in 1992, Terry became the father figure of the small group of human geographers in the Academy. In 1976 he was made a Fellow of the Royal Society of Edinburgh.

Upon retirement in 1986 he became Secretary and Treasurer of the Carnegie Trust for the Universities of Scotland, a post that he held until

Proceedings of the British Academy, **115**, 207–224. © The British Academy 2002.

the end. He was honoured by the award of a CBE in 1987. Twelve years later he received honorary degrees from the University of Glasgow (D.Litt.) and the University of Edinburgh (D.Sc.), and was especially delighted with the higher doctorate (D.Sc.) from the University of London that was awarded for a submission which included fourteen books and 66 articles or chapters. I was moved that my old tutor should have sought my advice prior to deciding on his final selection but this represented only half of his total published output of 24 books and 138 articles and chapters. In addition, he edited and contributed substantial portions of the 46 reports produced by his Tourism and Recreation Research Unit (TRRU) at Edinburgh. Terry also prepared numerous unpublished papers during his membership of the Land Data Committee of the Natural Resources Advisory Committee (1965–6), as Chairman of the Nature Conservancy's Land Use Panel (1968–71) and of the Facilities Planning Committee of the Scottish Sports Council (1984–7), and as a Specialist Advisor to the Select Committee on Scottish Affairs, whose report on land resource use contained a major personal input.

The first three decades

John Terence was born in Cardiff on 2 July 1921 and received his secondary education at Penarth County School. He left aged sixteen since it seems that his family lacked the resources to send him to university, nonetheless his brother experienced a long and costly training at medical school. In 1938 Terry entered the Lord Chancellor's Department of the civil service in the Rhondda Valley and in the following year performed very well in the administrative examinations that would have enabled him to enter the administrative grade without a degree. With the outbreak of war Terry joined the Welch Regiment and spent the war years as an intelligence officer in North Africa, receiving a commission in 1941. After demobilisation in 1946 he returned to the civil service, working first for the Ministry of Works and then for the Board of Customs and Excise. Whilst a bureaucratic career offered the promise of security and financial reward, it also carried with it intellectual frustrations and a profound wish to escape tedious routines. Professional advice was duly sought and his mentor suggested that a career in university teaching or research might be appropriate.

In 1947 he decided to read for a geography degree at Cambridge, where he was tutored by the orthodox economic geographer W. S. Thatcher, who had served as an administrator in India. He required three main qualities from his tutees: the ability to construct a logical and sustainable argument; the need to test the validity of all forms of evidence, whether quantitative or qualitative, official or unofficial; and an unfailing commitment to clear expression by the written and spoken word, and the use of statistics, maps, and diagrams. These points are embedded in Thatcher's now forgotten writing, which failed to capture the theoretical excitement that was enthusing some economic geographers but conveyed a great deal of practical common sense that would set any tutee and many a tutor in good stead. In due course, Terry would demand those same qualities from his own students, as I and many others remember only too well. With the benefit of sound tutorial advice from the lawyer Arthur Armitage at Queens' College, Terry worked with determination to make up for what he perceived as lost time. He performed brilliantly in both parts of the Geographical Tripos and graduated with a first class degree in 1949 after only two years at Cambridge. Then followed a year as departmental demonstrator and director of studies at Queens' before his academic career would truly begin.

The London years

In 1949 Henry Clifford Darby left the thriving department he had built up at Liverpool to succeed C. B. Fawcett as Professor of Geography at University College London. He determined that the small number of academic and support staff he inherited should be promoted elsewhere and set about assembling a completely new team. In this way, W. R. (Bill) Mead was brought from Liverpool to build up human geography and the physical geographer E. H. Brown arrived from Aberystwyth, the two having trained at the LSE and Kings College London respectively. As a graduate of and former lecturer at Cambridge, Darby took soundings among his former colleagues (J. Alfred Steers, Vaughan Lewis, Harriet Wanklyn, Jean Mitchell, and Margaret Anderson) with a view to acquiring a Cambridge man. Terry Coppock received whole-hearted support and in 1950 was duly appointed as assistant lecturer at an annual salary of £550, which was the maximum for that grade. Two years later he would be confirmed as lecturer, starting at £600 per annum, and would be firmly established in the rejuvenated UCL department that was set on a trajectory of rapid growth in the next two decades.

Bill Mead recalls that since Terry did not enjoy robust health he took him 'under his wing' in his large College apartment in Kensington. He became acquainted with the stream of Scandinavian and North American colleagues who stayed in the spare bedroom, maintaining contact with some of them throughout his life. This arrangement lasted until after Terry had married the classicist Sheila Burnett in 1953, who came from a Pontefract medical family and whom Terry met at one of the supper parties that Sir Ifor (later Lord) Evans held for young staff and students. Sheila eventually convinced Terry that they should put down a deposit on a home of their own and also buy a car. Even the perambulator for Terry and Sheila's first born had been delivered to Bill's bachelor flat. Darby required his young colleague to teach several aspects of geography, including biogeography, map interpretation, the British Isles, and some lectures on western and central Europe for which Terry prepared by cycling trips through Belgium, the Netherlands, and northern France. This experience led him to enunciate the principle that no matter which route one travelled, the prevailing wind would be in the opposite direction. However, it soon became clear that his forte was not Europe, about which he never published and which was passed to others to teach, but rather the economic, and especially agricultural, geography of Great Britain.

Early in the 1950s Darby conceived a regional project that would focus on an area close to London and which would galvanise members of the department, students and staff alike, through field investigations, research for higher degrees, and publications. The chosen area was the Chilterns, close to Darby's home in Berkhamsted, with Terry being entrusted with research into its land use and farming. Despite a number of master's degrees being completed, the regional project failed to materialise in its intended form. Nonetheless, for several years Terry organised cohorts of students to undertake a massive land-use survey as well as pursuing his personal research into rural changes in the Chilterns from 1870 to the middle of the twentieth century. His work combined the qualities of the Land Utilisation Survey that had been masterminded by L. Dudley Stamp in the 1930s and had won the admiration of Clifford Darby, with the historical dimension that Darby had developed to great effect in his personal work on the Fens, his evolving team project on the Domesday geography of England, and his edited volumes which comprised half of the Naval Intelligence Geographical Handbooks compiled during the Second World War.

In the middle 1950s Terry published a suite of journal articles in which he probed the reliability of agricultural returns and other statistical and cartographic sources, developed innovative mapping techniques to depict agricultural phenomena, and reported on radically changing distributions of arable and other land-use categories in the Chilterns due to the 'Feed Britain' campaign. These essays were, in effect, the first drafts of material that would contribute to his doctoral thesis. Like so many dissertations that were being written by young academics at the time, his research was under the nominal direction of the head of department but was, in effect, undertaken without supervision. Many years later, Terry wrote ruefully to Ron Cooke that 'Mine is a London Ph.D., ten years in the making! I think HCD was my supervisor, but we never discussed it!' (12 June 1987). With the assistance of an aged Austin Seven, which had the propensity to break down or to lose doors or vital parts at crucial moments, Terry marshalled his field assistants across the Chilterns, while at weekends and long into the night he assembled, abstracted, and processed statistical and cartographic evidence. Not surprisingly, he sometimes complained that this was drudgery. Throughout the 1950s he made abundant use of the department's first-rate drawing office whose staff produced literally hundreds of detailed maps for his thesis and for related publications, rivalling the output of Domesday maps drawn for his head of department.

Disaster struck when a drying oven overheated in a nearby office at UCL, occupied by the Egyptologist Margaret Murray (once Flinders Petrie's assistant), causing a fire which destroyed or badly singed many of Terry's documents, drafts, and finished maps. The 'curse of the Pharaohs' was blamed. Insurance covered some of the material losses but much work had to be prepared afresh and completion of the thesis was delayed until 1960. The first volume distilled Terry's critical review of source materials and methods of cartographic depiction, before exploring the structural background to agricultural change and conveying his meticulous reconstructions of the agricultural geography of the Chilterns in 1870 and 1951. Then followed an analysis of the mechanisms of change recorded during three component phases and then across the whole eighty-year span. The second volume formed a veritable atlas containing no fewer than 193 original maps and diagrams. Terry's methodology echoed the juxtaposition of temporal cross sections with process-orientated vertical themes that had been developed by Jan Broek in his study of *The Santa Clara Valley* (1932) and was much favoured by Darby, but Terry's thesis lacked the rigid symmetry that Darby was conceiving for his new volume on the historical geography of England that would eventually appear in 1973. Terry acknowledged that 'much helpful criticism and advice has been given by numerous friends and colleagues' (vol. I, p. 5) but made no direct mention of his head of department. He chose not to revise his vast corpus of material in order to produce a regional monograph.

After a decade of close attention to one region, Terry's interests began to broaden during the early 1960s, with respect to theme, time, and space. He wrote on matters related to conservation and recreation as well as to farming, recognising that geographers had much to offer planners and decision makers in terms of practical land-use management. Whilst always acknowledging the importance of the past in seeking to understand the present, he began to place growing emphasis on the future use of land resources. These issues were fully incorporated in his contribution to the new M.Sc. programme in Conservation devised by the botanist William Pearsall and Clifford Darby and delivered by their lecturing staff. As a university teacher, now in his forties and with a wife and two children but still on the lecturer grade, Dr Coppock compared his lot unfavourably with that of his former colleagues who had risen through the ranks of the civil service and with that of his neighbours who commuted from Hertfordshire to well-paid jobs in the City. His unflagging energies and punishing work routines were directed to a series of new writing and research assignments.

These included preparing a suite of articles that reviewed work in British agricultural geography and land-use studies in order to inform the Twentieth International Congress that would meet in London in the summer of 1964. Together with his UCL colleague Hugh Prince, he also edited *Greater London* (1964), whose fifteen chapters written by geographers and planners in the capital (and especially from UCL) brought together research findings on the conurbation past and present. Terry contributed three chapters that summarised physical resources and historical development, analysed commuting from dormitory settlements (with detailed focus on Radlett where he lived), and looked to the future challenges of managing London as a world city. His final words anticipated the decentralisation of work and housing into outer sections of the metropolitan region that would become so characteristic of the remainder of the twentieth century. It was, however, Terry's third new assignment that was set to break completely fresh ground.

After analysing evidence for individual farms and for the component parishes of the Chilterns, Terry wished to expand the scale of his work to produce an agricultural atlas for the whole of England and Wales that would exploit an enormous range of statistical sources including those available for the 350 National Agricultural Advisory Districts. The amount of material that would have to be abstracted and manipulated to produce such an atlas and an explanatory text far exceeded what might be expected of a lone researcher with pen, paper, slide rule, and calculator. Terry soon realised that the new experimental science of computerised data analysis and depiction might offer a solution, and he obtained enthusiastic support from UCL colleagues in electrical engineering and computer science. With the help of a few undergraduates (of whom I was one) during the summer vacation of 1963 for checking calculations and ensuring that information was 'centred' correctly for cartographic display, the atlas began to take shape. Its primitive printouts were far from camera-ready in quality and so the final maps were drawn by UCL cartographers who worked from machine-generated drafts. This was, indeed, a breakthrough and heralded Terry's profound interest in data handling, computergraphics, and remote sensing of information that would become so very important not only to academics but also to environmental managers in the later decades of his life. It is also a salutary reminder of how far and how fast the world of cartography has changed since the early 1960s.

A West African interlude

With all these projects under way and yet a desire to escape for a while, Terry accepted an invitation from Michael Barbour (a former geography colleague at UCL and subsequently Dean at the University of Ibadan) to spend a year as visiting senior lecturer in Nigeria. This offered him the opportunity to travel widely, to explore tropical aspects of rural geography and land-resource management, and to add the word 'senior' to his title, albeit only for twelve months. With Akin Mabogunje, Michael Thomas, and Michael Chisholm on the staff of geographers, Ibadan held exciting prospects for Terry, Sheila, and the children. Intensive blocks of teaching were interspersed with periods for local and more distant travel, set against a demanding schedule of proofreading, indexing and map checking, as well as assembling materials for future articles on Nigerian farming. Geography finalists at Ibadan were required to research a long essay on their home area, with Terry supervising those on farming topics. He arranged to go out with each of his tutees to see their home area. Terry's letters to Bill Mead at this time are filled with anxieties about cartographers, publishers, and proofs, as well as descriptions of the terrain, climate, and economy of Nigeria and of the ex-colonial university systems operating in various parts of Africa.

To quote his own words, Terry found Ibadan to be 'quite an extraordinary city—nearly a million inhabitants, the great majority living in single storey houses roofed with corrugated iron (the universal and unlovely roofing material), open drains and rutted roads. There is no public transport, but a vast number of taxis' (9 November 1963). As well as the extreme heat 'the two things we notice are the extreme stillness of the air, especially at night, and . . . the way sounds carry . . . It's surprising how you welcome the sudden breeze before a thunderstorm' (9 November 1963). January and February seemed to be 'climatically the least enjoyable time, before the rain cools things off; it's very hot and humid so that it's rather difficult to work up any enthusiasm for anything' (2 February 1964). Terry apologised for the quality of his typing, since 'it's a very hot and sticky day without a breath of wind, and which one just drips perspiration sitting quite still', notably while dealing with proofs and indexes (28 February 1964). Sheila assisted him with these tasks, joined other members of the university community in choral singing, and received distinguished visitors to supper. Fortunately, they had acquired the services of a 'very efficient cook/steward, which is a great blessing' (21 November 1963).

In November Terry reported that 'the pineapple season is just beginning (we even have some growing here in our garden) and I think there's little to beat a really good fresh pineapple for breakfast! We also have several paw-paw trees where we knock ripe fruit down with a large stick. The life has its advantages' (21 November 1963). During February, he visited various agricultural developments with USAID and FAO officials and organised complicated personal visits to farm settlements, research stations and plantations. He wrote: 'The difficulty is that official hours are 8 till 2, a relic of war and colonial times, so that you cannot visit anywhere in the afternoons. As some of these places are a 100 miles out of Ibadan it means a good deal of duplication in travel' (6 February 1964). Wasting time and wasting money—both scarce resources—were arguably Terry's pet hates.

The presence in Ibadan for six weeks of the distinguished agricultural physiologist Sir John Hammond FRS (1889–1964) as Nuffield Professor offered new opportunities, including a visit 'starting at the crack of dawn, to an experimental livestock centre 150 miles north of here in the savannah. . . . I was going to drive myself but when I heard he was going in a Ministry car, I scrounged a lift' (17 February 1964). Terry noted 'a couple of useful chats' with Sir John and was preparing himself for 'tomorrow's tour of the cocoa area' and 'on Thursday to a 30,000 acre ranch being run by the Western Region Development Corporation' (17 February 1964).

The routine was characteristically punishing with 'twelve hours in the sun today and motored 300 miles and feel pretty battered. How Sir John stood up to it at 75 I don't know. Tomorrow we are off to more cocoa farms' (18 February 1964). Subsequently, a most complex three-week programme of visits to thirty different institutions was arranged for Terry by the Eastern Region Ministry of Agriculture and could not be missed. This included a two-day trip by turbo jet launch into the mangrove swamps of the Niger delta. 'One by-product was that, sitting on top of the launch all day, I got badly sun-burnt for the first time since we landed in Nigeria almost six moths ago' (29 March 1964). Then followed a visit to the African Timber and Plywood Company at Sapele which exploited a 2,000 square mile timber concession that was 'being surveyed and mapped at a scale of 2 feet to the mile, at a cost of £3 400 per square mile, to locate all economic species and to plan exploitation' (29 March 1964). Despite Nigeria not being 'a country of fields and hedgerows', Terry reported being continually 'surprised at the variety I find, often confined to quite a small locality—live hedges of a variety of materials, many made of bamboos or sticks, earth banks and so on. The other day I suddenly came across a closed landscape of small fields surrounded by woven mat fences' (29 March 1964).

By mid-April he found that the climate was becoming more bearable, and wrote: 'The rains are beginning now and it's appreciably cooler—a ten degree drop in the maximum to the high 80s and a smaller drop in the minimum; it's like a tonic when a storm comes over and the wind gets up and the temperature falls suddenly. We had $2\frac{1}{2}$ inches in a couple of hours the other day—this is something you can't take a decent photograph of' (18 April 1964). With examining under control, proofs completed and three articles on rural Nigeria under way, based on 16,000 miles of travel throughout the country, Terry felt able to leave Sheila, Helena, and John in Ibadan in order to travel south to Salisbury, where the 'clear sparkling air' of early May was 'extremely refreshing' (3 May 1964). Then on to Swaziland which, although 'only about the size of Wales, . . . contains extraordinary contrasts and I have even been able to have a quick look at most of them' (16 May 1964). Finally, came five hectic weeks in South Africa when Terry 'hardly ever spent two nights in the same place, but all very interesting and enjoyable. I spent the last 24 hours in style on the 20,000 acre farm of a millionaire farmer whose grandfather was a Welsh drover who emigrated in the 1850s' (14 June 1964).

As well as reports on the joy of discovery and of work completed, Terry's letters to Bill Mead contained a nagging thread of anxiety about

his future at UCL. He believed that he should already have been made a
Reader and deeply regretted that Darby's public declaration of support
for promotion at a meeting of the Maconochie Foundation a couple of
years previously had not resulted in action (18 April 1964). He set about
applying for Chairs in Britain and overseas, but funds for flying in candidates were slight and he was not called back from Africa for interview. In
due course, the internal promotion came through and for the academic
session 1964–5 Terry held a Readership in the University of London.
With the *Agricultural Atlas of England and Wales* (1964) complete and
articles and chapters flowing apace, the idea of a Chair became all the
more appealing, but that would mean leaving UCL as many of his cohort
of colleagues would do in the years ahead as provincial chairs became
vacant and new departments were established. The newly-created Ogilvie
Chair in Edinburgh was announced in the Spring of 1965; Terry became
the first occupant, on the basis of his thoroughness and tenacity in
research, his appreciation of contemporary techniques, and his sympathetic and understanding approach to students. He had, however, very
limited experience of administration or of graduate supervision under the
firm regime of H. C. Darby.

The Edinburgh years

The Ogilvie Chair offered Terry new opportunities to expand his developing interests in public policy and to further his enthusiasm for devising
new methods for handling, interpreting and displaying vast quantities of
spatial information. His inaugural lecture on 17 May 1966, entitled 'The
Geographer and the Use of Land', was dedicated to the late Sir Dudley
Stamp, and traced Terry's career to date and his future plans. He recalled
his presentation to the conference of the Institute of British Geographers
at Keele in 1954 on the topic of 'Land-use maps: a plea for quantitative
data', and his conversation with Professor Alan Ogilvie in which he argued
that changes in land use should be recorded systematically to assist environmental planning. In a phrase that he liked to quote, he remarked that
'the map is to the geographer as the microscope is to the biologist and as
the telescope is to the astronomer, a means of converting material to a
more manageable scale' (p. 3). He praised Stamp's Land Utilisation Survey
of the 1930s and noted the utility of various historical sources to aid
reconstruction of past land-use conditions but regretted the lack of
proper land-use statistics in Britain, rendering it impossible to determine

accurately how much farmland had been taken for urban and other uses. Geographers, he maintained, had a vital role to play in environmental management, with their experience of critically evaluating sources, skills in interpreting air photographs, knowledge of spatial sampling methods, and growing appreciation of computerised techniques. Terry cited appreciatively the experience of the Canada Land Inventory that had assembled and correlated data on settled parts of the nation (effectively forming a proto-geographical information system) and he argued that there was great scope for extending this GIS approach in Britain, and especially in Scotland. With remarkable foresight he noted that even the Canadian facilities 'will seem modest if the vision of satellites recording and analysing land-use automatically becomes a reality' (p. 10).

To practise this new kind of geography would require technicians and computer laboratories as well as secretaries and libraries. The Ogilvie Professor greatly welcomed the expansion of computing facilities at Edinburgh and looked forward to collaborating with colleagues in economics, statistics, and agriculture, and to liaising with civil servants in St Andrew's House who he rightly anticipated would be more accessible than their counterparts in Whitehall. His proposed research agenda embraced studying recreation as a user of rural land, the march of urbanisation and afforestation in transforming the look of the countryside, and also the implications of on-going rural depopulation for landscapes and community life in remote areas. Terry argued that research should be given higher priority in geography departments in British universities, long overwhelmed by the demands of teaching undergraduates, that lectures should concentrate on issues of significance in the real world (while never ignoring their historical antecedents), and that geographers should focus 'on the examination of problems in regions rather than of regions themselves' (p. 19). In other words, they should give purpose to the rich but stifling legacy of regional geography. This was a revolutionary agenda for the mid 1960s.

Whilst being a sympathetic and understanding teacher, it must be said that Terry was not always the most fluent of lecturers. He could rise superbly to the grand occasion, such as his defence of 'the geography of agriculture' to a powerful audience of sceptical agricultural economists, but trying to retain the interest of a lecture hall full of occasionally reluctant undergraduates sometimes appeared to be an ordeal. Packing lectures together to suit his commitments could be simply disastrous, as I recall from four-hour lecture sessions at UCL prior to his departure for Nigeria. Terry's real teaching strength was in tutorials or personal supervisions when his energy could be sharply concentrated on the person and the work in hand. His ability to assimilate and synthesise vast amounts of information, to recognise key points, and to identify a way forward also made him an excellent and much sought-after *rapporteur*. These, if I may call them, 'editorial' skills were widely recognised in academic and policy circles since Terry could always be relied upon to produce a balanced report with amazing speed and accuracy. By virtue of his willing nature and quest for perfection and rapid delivery he never ceased to drive himself exceptionally hard. One wonders why he tolerated so many committees and so much travelling when he had a wife and children at home who would have welcomed his company. As Bill Mead recalled at Terry's memorial service, he was 'strong on responsibility, duty and loyalty—old-fashioned qualities which stood him in good stead'. He was blessed with having Sheila as 'a wonderful foil [who] could not always turn misfortune into fortune, but her infectious humour could counteract the stresses that Terry could suffer and allay his anxieties'.

As his inaugural lecture and the successful meeting with the agricultural economists had shown, by the mid 1960s Terry had established an exhausting agenda that would consume his personal energies and administrative skills for the rest of his life. Research, publication, advisory work on committees, and serving the scholarly community absorbed most of his waking hours. Not surprisingly, he was far from enamoured with the time-consuming routines of running a department, serving only once as head. After five years in the Ogilvie Chair and with his revolutionary agenda still buzzing in his head, he confessed that he still felt like an outsider in the department managed by Professor James Wreford Watson, of whom he never became a close friend, and a group of long-established senior lecturers. His reaction was to convert his knowledge of Canadian applied geography, which was closely tied to public service, into practical reality in Edinburgh. His appointment as a specialist adviser to the Select Committee on Scottish Affairs had reinforced this conviction and prompted him to create and direct an applied research unit which evolved into the Tourism and Recreation Research Unit.

This operation was both novel and controversial in British geography departments in the late 1960s which largely emphasised teaching of undergraduates and pursuit of individual, unfunded enquiry rather than becoming involved with contract research, external funding, and fixed-term support staff. The TRRU drew funds from numerous sources, including the Social Science Research Council, the Natural Environment Research Council and many Scottish agencies. It investigated the growing participation in outdoor recreation, the spatially variable supply of recreational resources, the implications of increased use of the private car to reach recreational sites, and the overall impact of outdoor recreation on the landscapes and communities of rural Scotland. A notable feature was the construction of a pioneering computer-based information system, known appropriately as TRIP (the Tourism and Recreation Information Package). The TRRU produced almost four dozen reports between 1966 and 1980, which often drew on the results of specially commissioned surveys that required Terry and his colleague Brian Duffield to assemble and organise teams of temporary field surveyors and squads of short-term analysts. Terry's experience with UCL staff and students in the Chilterns during the 1950s provided good training for such an enterprise.

Recreation in the Countryside: a spatial analysis (1975), written jointly with B. S. Duffield, not only summarised many results from the work of the TRRU but also firmly embedded study of recreation and tourism into an interdisciplinary academic context. This volume and many other TRRU initiatives owed much to the skills of Mona Robertson who was able to decipher Terry's amazing speed writing that spread at a sharp angle across the page. Every word began clearly enough with a few recognisable letters but then trailed off into a line, thereby presenting the reader (and in my case, the first-year undergraduate) with a formidable challenge. Electronic manipulation of data was an integral part of the work of the TRRU, with early examples of computergraphics figuring in its reports and in *An Agricultural Atlas of Scotland* (1976). This was modelled on the prototype for England and Wales but the final versions of the Scottish maps were produced mechanically rather than by draughtsmen with pen and ink. The second edition of *An Agricultural Atlas of England and Wales*, which appeared in the same year, also contained computer-generated maps.

In due course Terry was instrumental in setting up at Edinburgh University the first taught M.Sc. programme in Geographical Information Systems (later called Geographical Information Science), an initiative that would be emulated in numerous universities at home and abroad. In the 1980s he would found the *International Journal of Geographical Information Systems* (now *Information Science*) and edit it from 1986 to 1993 as part of his retirement project. Not surprisingly he preferred instructing small groups of committed masters students about the strengths and weaknesses of 'information' of all kinds to facing mass audiences of undergraduates. His real delight was the score of doctoral students he supervised on agricultural geography, recreation studies, computer mapping, and geographical information systems. Many now occupy senior academic positions. His schedule of meetings and committees was formidable and often required him to take the 6 a.m. train to London, returning late at night. Train journeys were preferable to flying since reading and writing could be undertaken *en route* and hence less time would be 'lost'. Meeting graduate students had to be accommodated somehow. The story of doctoral supervisions being conducted at Edinburgh Airport is probably apocryphal but one of Terry's students, now a Vice-Chancellor, has confirmed that some meetings were held over very early cups of coffee at Waverley Station.

Terry's productivity continued unabated throughout the 1970s and 1980s. Student needs were met by a textbook on the *Agricultural Geography of Great Britain* (1971), while a book embracing *Land Use and Town and Country Planning* (with L. F. Gebbett, 1978) provided sound advice to researchers. Terry presided over the annual conference of the Institute of British Geographers at Norwich in January 1974, delivering the keynote address and chairing the plenary session when distinguished academics spoke on the theme of 'geography and public policy'. His life-long habit of what is now called 'power napping' during lectures was displayed with memorable effect before a full auditorium but, true to form, he 'awoke' just in time to deliver the ever-perceptive first question. In his presidential address, entitled 'Geography and public policy: challenges, opportunities and implications', he developed the case he had made in his inaugural and set it in a wider spatial frame, with the support of some senior colleagues, and before the assembled body of his chosen profession.

He argued that environmental resource issues were of greater public importance than ever before. To study them offered an unparalleled opportunity for geographers 'to demonstrate both to the academic community and to government and the public that they have the necessary skills and concepts to contribute effectively to the solution of some of the major problems facing society. Moreover, if geographers do not respond, they will find that others adopt a role which they have traditionally regarded as theirs' (p. 1). He warned repeatedly that politicians and environmental managers beyond the geographical profession were largely ignorant of what geographers could do. In order to resolve this paradox, the profession needed to identify its capabilities (reinforced by computer applications, automated cartography and remote sensing), focus its research, rejuvenate its teaching, and enter into dialogue with those who advised on and implemented official policy at local, regional, national, and international levels. In short: the thinkers should become doers.

These arguments were reinforced and exemplified soon afterwards in *Spatial Dimensions of Public Policy* (edited with W. R. D. Sewell, 1976) which asked academics 'What are you contributing to the good of the society which supports you?' (p. xiii). Over a dozen essays by leading international scholars offered examples of geography in action, with Terry providing an analysis of the work of the TRRU. His conclusion was that geographers must acknowledge their potential and collaborate with other disciplines to tackle 'topics where the man in the street (and, it is hoped, increasingly the politician) recognises no disciplinary or sectoral boundaries, those which affect the earth as the home of man' (p. 262).

In characteristic fashion, Terry also convened a specialist session of the Rural Geography Study Group at the Norwich IBG meeting. He had energised this group since its inception as a working party concerned with agricultural mapping and then with agricultural geography more gener-ally, and had given generous encouragement to many young workers in rural studies. The specialist forum at Norwich focused on the environ-mental and social threats associated with the proliferation of second homes in parts of North America and continental Europe, and the grow-ing fear that such problems might reach critical proportions in the British Isles. A selection of conference papers plus commissioned chapters from researchers in the USA, Canada, Australia, and mainland Europe appeared in *Second Homes—curse or blessing?* (1977). Terry concluded the volume by looking to the future and anticipating the implications of the 'wired society' when he speculated that 'Perhaps the electronic age and the wonders of holography will obviate the need for second homes and make it a matter of indifference where we live, since we may be able to simulate our ideal environment (or in fact a whole family of environ-ments) in our own first home' (p. 214). As a contributor to and translator for that volume, I was truly amazed with the speed at which edited and completely retyped manuscripts came back to me. Undoubtedly the skills of Mona Robertson contributed to this 'return of post' efficiency.

After a remarkably productive quarter century from 1950 to the mid 1970s, Terry approached his second decade in the Ogilvie Chair with the same selfless determination and dedicated drive. Committees, co-ordination, and editorial work absorbed an even greater share of his time, while formal teaching retreated. In the years approaching retire-ment he was involved at a high level with the International Union for the Conservation of Nature, the International Geographical Union (Working Group on Environmental Mapping), the Royal Society (British National Committee for Geography), the Ordnance Survey, the

Scottish Field Studies Association, and the Scottish Sports Council as well as numerous local organisations in Scotland. All this was in addition to organisations mentioned earlier. Edinburgh colleagues never ceased to be amazed at the sheer stamina of this man who had been prone to physical ill-health throughout his life and was sometimes afflicted with self-doubt; the tidal wave of publications concealed such patches of darkness from all except his closest friends and collaborators.

Professor emeritus

Terry never really retired, with his translation to emeritus professor in 1986 merely involving a change in his title and in the range, but certainly not the volume, of his responsibilities. His professional commitment to the Carnegie Trust (which required frequent travel by bus and train from Edinburgh to Dunfermline) commenced in 1986, as did his position as editor of the *International Journal of Geographical Information Science*. He recruited an international editorial board to assist him with this ground-breaking journal, travelled to GIS conferences throughout the world, and exerted his enthusiastic influence on many scholars to obtain suitable articles. He was especially generous when dealing with submissions from authors whose first language was not English, always striving to find the best in such pieces and helping contributors to rewrite in a more comprehensible and relevant form. At times, he was caught between acting as a rigorous editor and functioning as a teacher who always wanted to help.

The number of committees and panels with which he was involved in retirement never declined, and there were always post-doctoral researchers and young academics to advise and encourage. Following Sheila's death in 1990 he immersed himself even more deeply in work, while complaining occasionally that there was not enough time to indulge his passion for listening to classical music. Moving from a large house to a small flat and having to dispose of most of his books and papers was a deeply traumatic experience, but one from which members of the Royal Geographical Society have benefited since the documents are now in its keeping. Up until 1997 he was a frequent traveller on the early train to London in order to attend afternoon meetings in the capital before setting off in the evening to return to Edinburgh. In 1987 he was made a Fellow of University College London and was often to be seen in the Department of Geography or in the Senior Common Room. As he drank his coffee and read a newspaper, it was almost as if he had never left the college. He was invariably accompanied by a large rucksack that contained proofs and manuscripts, and perhaps a suit if formal attire was more appropriate than his comfortably worn sports jacket and rather casual trousers. This life-long commitment to comfortable clothes was reinforced when he took up cycling to keep fit after a heart attack.

By the time of Clifford Darby's death in 1992, the memory of earlier personal difficulties had faded and Terry increasingly assumed his role as the leading geographer in the British Academy. After all, he had been called to contribute a chapter on 'The changing face of England 1850–c.1900' for Darby's *New Historical Geography of England* (1973), and I am led to believe that in 1976 Darby had favoured him as his successor at Cambridge—though that was not to be. Terry remained in close contact with Eva, Lady Darby, and acceded to her request to find a means of publishing Sir Clifford's methodological essays, around which his famous 'methods seminars' at UCL had been articulated. Enlisting the help of others, Terry produced an early draft of one of the contextual essays that surround Darby's own words in *The Relations of History and Geography* (edited by M. Williams, H. D. Clout and H. C. Prince, 2002).

Late in 1997 he fell ill with Lupus, which halted his output for a while but he continued to write and to edit for a further two years. His letters became increasingly difficult to decipher and were, perhaps, a little shorter than before. He continued faithfully to travel to British Academy meetings but confided that his apparent good health was really the result of medication. In the final weeks up to his death on 28 June 2000 he complained bitterly of technical problems affecting the computer he was using to type from his hospital bed. His intention to write the centennial history of the Carnegie Trust for 2001 would not be accomplished, nor would he see Darby's essays through to publication.

By virtue of remarkable insight and prodigious hard work, which took its toll on his health and family life, Terry Coppock made an enormous contribution not only to geographical knowledge and to the profession of geography but also to a wide field of scholarship both in Great Britain and internationally. His work on the countryside and land-use matters heralded our current concern with environmental issues, food supply, sustainability and the wise use of scarce resources. His ideas on policy-orientated research, involving teams of scholars and appropriate technologies, have been accepted so widely among geographers and members of related disciplines that they are now taken for granted. His early use of computerised cartography, geographical information systems and remote sensing made him a true pioneer in these rapidly expanding fields that extend beyond geography. His students at UCL and in Edinburgh recall his firm and friendly tutorial advice, just as members of government committees and panels will not forget his level-headed approach to problems and his clearly-written reports setting out the path ahead. Members of the Academy will remember his selfless dedication, high standards and unflagging energy with grateful affection.

HUGH CLOUT
Fellow of the Academy

Note. This essay owes a great deal to conversations with Terry Coppock's former colleagues at UCL: E. H. Brown, R. A. French. J. H. Johnson, W. R. Mead, H. C. Prince, and D. Thomas. I am very grateful to Bill Mead for allowing me to use material from his address at the Memorial Service for Professor Coppock, held in Edinburgh on 25 October 2000, and to quote from letters sent to him from Nigeria. Comments from Michael Williams are also acknowledged with gratitude. I have drawn upon obituaries published in the *Independent* (7 July 2000) by Dr Roger Kirby who was a colleague of Terry Coppock at Edinburgh, as well as having been one of his students at UCL, and by another Edinburgh colleague, Lyndhurst Collins, in the *Transactions, Institute of British Geographers* (2001) NS 26, pp. 263–4. A suite of short essays in the *International Journal of Geographical Systems* (1996) 10, pp. 3–15 pays tribute to his contribution to GIS. Three publications by Professor Coppock have been particularly useful: *The Geographer and the Use of Land*, University of Edinburgh Inaugural Lecture 29, 1966, 22 pp.; 'The geography of agriculture', *Journal of Agricultural Economics*, 19, 1968, pp. 153–69.; 'Geography and public policy: challenges, opportunities and implications', *Transactions, Institute of British Geographers*, 63, 1974, pp. 1–16.

FRANCIS HASKELL

Francis James Herbert Haskell
1928–2000

FRANCIS HASKELL was born in London on 7 April 1928, the eldest of three children. His father, Arnold, who invented the term *balletomane*, played a leading role in establishing the taste for ballet in Britain, first as a writer and subsequently as director of the Sadlers Wells Ballet School, later the Royal Ballet School. Arnold also took an interest in contemporary art and was the author of a book on Jacob Epstein. In the early years of their marriage he and his wife, Vera Saitsova, the daughter of a Russian émigré industrialist, talked to one another in French, so this was Francis's first language. His early familiarity with France was strengthened by a period at the Lycée in Kensington, between the ages of five and eight. From this experience he retained little beyond a vague memory of Pepin le Bref and Louis Le Fainéant, but later thought that it might account for his passion for French history. His family also spent their holidays in France, including a badly timed trip which left them stranded near Bordeaux in late August 1939, after the signing of the Nazi–Soviet Non-Aggression Pact. In the face of formidable problems, Arnold and Vera, neither of whom could drive, managed to bring their children back to the Channel by taxi. Arnold's observation, as they ate a marvellous roast chicken in the restaurant of the Hotel de la Poste at Rouen, that this would be their last good meal until the end of the war, was one that Francis never forgot. He was to return to France in 1945, when the experience of attending trials of collaborators in Paris gave him a sense of being present at the making of history, while nightly visits to the theatre, to see works by Giraudoux, Jules Romains, and others, provided further stimulation.

Proceedings of the British Academy, **115**, 227–242. © The British Academy 2002.

During his wartime schooldays at Eton, which he did not much enjoy, Francis specialised in science, with the intention of becoming a doctor, but changed his mind after a few months of medical training. Following his military service in the Education Corps, when he found himself, to his appalled amusement, lecturing troops on sexual hygiene, he went up to King's College, Cambridge, in 1948. In his first two years he read History, one of his teachers being Eric Hobsbawm, who was to be a lifelong friend, but changed to English in his final year. The ethos of King's in those years, with its strong emphasis on intellectual enquiry, liberal values and sociability, proved immensely stimulating and sympathetic, giving him a much more congenial milieu than he had experienced at school. As an undergraduate he took some interest in the history of art, reading the few general books then available, visiting museums and exhibitions and travelling abroad. He also attended the lectures given by the Slade Professor, Nikolaus Pevsner, which ranged from ancient Egypt to Cubism. Thus it was almost inevitable that when Francis was encouraged in 1951 to write a dissertation for a college Fellowship, doctorates then being scarcely considered seriously at King's, and thought of choosing a subject related to art history, he should have sought Pevsner's advice, even though he had never met him. The topic which Pevsner suggested was to explore the possible influence of the Jesuits on the art of Mannerism and the Baroque; and he also agreed to act as Francis's supervisor.

Francis's approach to his research was inevitably coloured by his previous experience, or rather lack of it. The idea of working on an Italian topic had an obvious appeal, not least because he had been astonished and delighted, on an early trip to Italy, to discover, while he was being given a lift in a lorry, that the driver talked to him about Michelangelo. But his interest in Italian art up to that time had been confined to the Renaissance, so the art that he was now set to study, on which almost nothing of substance had been written in English, and, in modern times, very little in other languages, was entirely new to him. Equally important, he had never had any formal training in art history and so had never acquired the habits of mind which this encouraged. In particular, he did not start from the idea that his main task was to study individual works of art and the craftsmen who had made them, nor was he preoccupied with style, which was then often thought to reflect in some way the 'spirit of the age', although there was a deep ambiguity about whether this applied most directly to the attitudes of the artists themselves, or of their patrons, whose social and intellectual background was usually very different. Both approaches have tended to place a high premium on subjective responses to works of art and have encouraged strongly deferential attitudes towards the views of supposed experts. But by temperament and training Francis was, and always remained, empirical and sceptical.

Pevsner evidently assumed that he would concentrate on style, exploring the possible parallels with the attitudes of Jesuits, as expressed in their teachings and theology. The idea was that he was to establish whether Jesuit ideals fitted better with Mannerism or the Baroque, and which of these styles they had promoted. But unaware of his supervisor's expectations, Francis adopted an entirely different approach. When he first arrived in Rome, and was acquiring a knowledge of Italian and looking for the first time at the art of the Baroque, he lodged with a well-connected Catholic family, who helped him to gain access to the Jesuit archives. Here he discovered the answer to the problem that Pevsner had set him. It turned out that the Jesuits had little or no say about the art that decorated their churches, simply because in their early years they were extremely poor and therefore had to follow the wishes of wealthy benefactors, which often did not coincide with their own preferences. Seen in this light, the Jesuit style turned out to be a myth.

The experience of writing the dissertation was decisive in many ways. It introduced Francis to types of art at which he had never looked closely before and which he found immensely exciting and sympathetic. It gave him a taste for research in libraries and archives which he never lost. It showed him that some art-historical problems could be solved by straightforward historical enquiry of a kind that very few of those professionally involved in the subject were then doing. Most important of all, it introduced him to a new culture, that of Italy, which was profoundly different from what he had known in England. Thus in the family with whom he lodged it was unthinkable for the daughters to leave the house unchaperoned; and when he moved into a flat with two young Italian art historians, Luigi Salerno and Alessandro Marabottini, who was to remain one of his closest friends, he was surprised to discover that as a matter of course they employed a maid who looked after the house and prepared their meals. Francis also soon learned about the power which Italian professors had over their young assistants, and about the ferocious feuds which dominated Italian art history, a topic on which he remained a well-informed and fascinated observer.

He had already been introduced to Marabottini and Salerno in England by Rudolf Wittkower, who was then on the staff of the Warburg Institute. As Francis himself later wrote, the influence of the émigré scholars who worked there, including also Otto Kurz and Ernst Gombrich,

was to be of fundamental importance for his later career. Not only did
they have a far greater familiarity with baroque art than virtually any
British scholar of that time, they were also generous with their advice and
in encouraging him to make use of the unique resources of their library,
not least the wonderful collection of early source material in the history
of art. Equally important, their own interests and approaches were very
different from those then dominant in the British art-historical world,
which was centred on the connoisseurship that was so important in museums as well as the art trade. But the Warburg Institute also had another
strong attraction. At a time when fuel was short, it was extremely warm,
because it shared a heating system with an adjacent building that had to
be maintained at a high temperature.

When he was completing his fellowship dissertation in 1953 Francis
found a job in the Library of the House of Commons, on the strength of
a single interview. This was work that he greatly enjoyed, involving as it
did pure research on a huge variety of topics; and late-night sittings also
gave him the opportunity of reading Gibbon. At the same time he was
occupied with a task that proved far less congenial, a translation of
Franco Venturi's *Roots of Revolution*, which finally appeared in 1960. His
career in the Commons library was very brief, because in the summer of
1954 he was awarded a Fellowship at King's on the strength of his dissertation and accordingly returned to Cambridge, where he was to remain
until 1967. It was expected that he would turn his dissertation into a
book, but Francis himself did not believe that the subject would have
much appeal to the public, and soon decided, with the agreement of the
college authorities, to undertake a more general study of art and patronage in seventeenth- and eighteenth-century Italy. This finally appeared in
1963 under the title *Patrons and Painters*, and at once established him as
one of the leading art historians of his generation.

The idea of tackling so immense a subject, even restricting the focus
largely to seventeenth-century Rome and eighteenth-century Venice, now
seems so ambitious as to be entirely foolhardy. Yet Francis's intellectual
ambitions were evident to his contemporaries from his earliest years at
King's. Admittedly, in the 1950s the study of baroque art was still un-
developed, and most of the scholarly literature was concerned with problems of attribution and chronology. Major discoveries could still be made
by reading the primary sources, while the archives, which were less fre-
quented and more accessible than today, were still largely unexplored,
especially from the perspective of patronage. But to make some sense of
such a vast field still called for exceptional energy and insight. Even today,

the book remains astonishing for the amount of ground that Francis covered and for the sureness of his judgement. It also demonstrates the extent of his first-hand knowledge of and admiration for the art he was discussing, the result of years of assiduous sight-seeing, partly by public transport and partly in the company of friends with cars; for Francis wisely recognised that he was temperamentally unsuited to driving. He explained his priorities in a letter to his friend and driver, Willy Mostyn-Owen, in a letter of 1953, 'You're the only person I really enjoy travelling with, as, like me, you want to see everything. This isn't flattery, as I don't think that it is a virtue: it comes from a form of puritanism, of the same type that makes me loathe skipping the pages of a book, even when they are dull.'

In his dissertation he had shown how a knowledge of patronage helped to resolve a specific historical problem. In extending this approach to the whole Italian art world of the seventeenth and eighteenth centuries he was not attempting to advance a particular theory, but to understand what had happened. The general conclusion that he reached could hardly have been more tentative: 'Inevitably I have been forced to think again and again about the relations between art and society, but nothing in my researches has convinced me of the existence of underlying laws which will be valid in all circumstances. At times the connections between economic or political conditions and a certain style have seemed particularly close; at other times I have been unable to detect anything more than the internal logic of artistic development, personal whim or the workings of chance.' For all the modesty of the tone, the implications of Francis's comments could hardly have been larger. Most obviously, he was challenging the then influential Marxist approach of historians such as Friedrich Antal, in his *Florentine Painting and its Social Background* (1948). More generally, he was emphasising that the relationship between art and the society in which it was produced was far more complex than many scholars of all political persuasions were then willing to admit. Given his deep suspicion about all large theories of history or politics, this was a finding that cannot have caused him surprise or dismay. Yet, paradoxically but characteristically, he only added a conclusion at the urging of his friend Benedict Nicolson.

Francis may not have found a single pattern underlying baroque patronage, but he did reveal an immense amount about the circumstances in which the art of the period was produced, as well as about the personalities and motives of those who paid for it. He was later to claim that he saw the purpose of history as bringing the past to life, and in this he triumphantly succeeded. His descriptions of the leading patrons, as well as of a host of minor figures, are vivid, economical and convincing, not least because he did not claim that the most perceptive patrons were necessarily admirable in other ways. Up to that time most art historians had only been concerned with the motivations of the artists themselves, and such accounts as they had provided of patrons tended to be schematic and one-dimensional. *Patrons and Painters* inspired a vast amount of new research, as other scholars tried to fill in the gaps in Francis's account, increasing our knowledge of specific commissions and of the activities of individual patrons and collectors. But no one has attempted to look again at the subject as a whole, so his book remains the point of departure for all discussions of patronage, as well as the most readable and illuminating introduction to the topic of Italian art and society of the seventeenth and eighteenth centuries.

At the time, and subsequently, Francis was criticised for neglecting eighteenth-century Rome in favour of Venice. But he consistently defended his choice, for two reasons: firstly, that the mechanisms of patronage established in Rome in the seventeenth century remained virtually unchanged in the later period, whereas the social circumstances of Venice were very different, thus providing a basis of comparison; secondly, that in terms of quality painting in eighteenth-century Venice was unmatched anywhere in Italy. The shift in his focus from Rome had one unforeseen consequence which was of far more than professional importance to him. One evening in 1962, while he was working in Venice, Francis's friend Alessandro Bettagno took him to dinner at the Ristorante Malamocco, where he introduced him to Larissa Salmina, curator of Venetian drawings at the Hermitage. She had been sent to Italy as Commissar of the Russian pavilion at the Biennale, and because of some bureaucratic confusion had been obliged to remain in Venice until the exhibition closed. Francis realised after their first meeting that he wanted to marry her, and Larissa was equally smitten, but the problems that they faced were formidable. Pessimistic by nature, seemingly wholly unpractical, as well as being a constantly anxious traveller and at that time unable to face flying, Francis nonetheless succeeded in meeting Larissa in Yugoslavia and Russia and finally in obtaining permission to marry in 1965, in the Soviet Palace of Weddings in Leningrad. Without Arnold Haskell's prestige in the world of ballet and the access this gave him to the Russian authorities, the necessary consent, a matter which supposedly involved even the Central Committee, could never have been obtained. The whole romance had been conducted with extreme discretion, and when Francis arrived in Stockholm a few days after his marriage, his visa having expired, an old friend he met there, on learning that he had just been in Leningrad immediately said that he bitterly regretted not having given him an introduction to a charming curator in the Hermitage, only to be told by Francis that this was unnecessary, as he had married her less than a week before. A few months later Larissa was granted a visa and was finally able to come and live with him in Cambridge, where he served as an outstandingly effective librarian of the Department of History of Art. In 1967, following his appointment as Professor of the History of Art in Oxford, with a Fellowship at Trinity College, they moved to a house in Walton Street, a few yards from his department and from the Ashmolean. This was to remain their home for the rest of his life, repeatedly converted and modified to accommodate a vast and constantly growing library.

The success of *Patrons and Painters* led to many offers from publishers, all of whom wanted Francis to write essentially the same book, but he decided instead to turn his attention to French painting of the nineteenth century. This was a subject on which he was required to lecture in Oxford; it was also an entirely different and still largely unexplored field, about which he knew relatively little. Initially he hoped that it would provide the kind of surprises, in the form of unjustly neglected artists, that had followed the reassessment of the Italian Baroque, but later conceded that this turned out not to be the case. Characteristically, he was particularly intrigued by the growth of the idea, in the second half of the nineteenth century, that leading artists would, and perhaps should, initially be rejected by the public, a phenomenon, which, as he observed, had no obvious precedent in the history of European art, although it had often been claimed, for example, in the case of Caravaggio. Whereas in his work on Italian Baroque patronage he had had the field virtually to himself, he soon discovered that there were other scholars, particularly in France, equally interested in recovering the forgotten masters of the nineteenth century, as one can see today in the Musée d'Orsay. Francis's own research led immediately to various articles, some of which were later collected in *Past and Present in Art and Taste* (1987). It also led him to transform the department of the History of Art at Oxford into one of the major centres for the study of French eighteenth- and nineteenth-century art anywhere in the world, at first through the typically astute purchase of a remarkable collection of early Salon criticism; and he soon attracted a number of gifted graduate students working on the topic.

Whereas his previous work had been concerned primarily with attitudes of patrons and the wider public to the art of their own time, his next major book, *Rediscoveries in Art: Some Aspects of Taste, Fashion and*

Collecting in England and France, published in 1976, for which he won the
Mitchell Prize for Art History, instead focused on changing perceptions
of the art of the past, which was henceforth to be his major preoccupation. It was based on the Wrightsman Lectures he had given at the
Institute of Fine Arts in New York in 1973. Despite the qualification in
the subtitle, the book was an extraordinarily wide-ranging account of
changes in the taste for Old Master paintings, particularly in England and
France, from the French Revolution until about 1870, a period which saw
the most dramatic reversals in artistic values ever recorded. During the
eighteenth century many collectors may have preferred, for example,
Dutch art to that of the canonical Italian masters, but scarcely anyone
had tried to argue that the former was superior to the latter. By 1870 the
early Italian and Flemish had almost entirely eclipsed the painters of the
seventeenth century, and even within individual schools the old hierarchy
had been overturned, with Vermeer supplanting Dou and El Greco
replacing Murillo. Such revaluations had usually been seen by historians
as a relatively straightforward consequence of an increase in knowledge,
or as a reflection of responses to contemporary art. But while conceding
that the growth of knowledge was at times an important factor, Francis
realised that this was far from being the whole story. The availability of
particular types of painting on the market, a desire for novelty on the part
of certain collectors, dislike as much as admiration for contemporary art,
even changing political and social ideals were all factors that came into
play at different times and in different ways. While explicitly rejecting the
idea of 'total aesthetic relativism', he demonstrated 'that history itself
can—at certain moments—only be understood at the price of a certain
abdication of those value judgements which art lovers (rightly) esteem so
highly'. Francis himself took far too much pleasure in art to reject those
value judgements, and he was well aware that it was virtually impossible
to do so; but he was temperamentally sceptical enough to take pleasure in
contemplating that they would almost certainly be overturned by changes
in fashion and historical circumstances in ways that are entirely unpredictable. Indeed, as he pointed out, this was evident enough in the way
in which museum acquisitions were made; and as an active and highly
valued member of the committee of the National Art Collections Fund
he championed the purchase of works by unfashionable and neglected
artists, realising that sooner or later their turn would come. What mattered,
in his opinion, was to trust one's own judgement in selecting objects of
the highest quality and historical importance, rather than those of merely
parochial interest.

Francis's interest in changes in taste, and in the preconceptions on which taste is so often based, led him not long afterwards, while spending a few days with Larissa at Versailles, to escape a heatwave in Paris, and strolling round the park, to the recognition that many of the once famous ancient statues that were visible there in reproductions, as indeed they are in palaces and formal gardens throughout Europe, were now virtually unknown even to specialists, including himself. Soon afterwards, he and his friend Nicholas Penny, who was then working on the impact of classical art on English sculpture, decided to write a short illustrated pamphlet for art historians, with the intention of providing a summary of the discovery and subsequent history of a hundred celebrated ancient statues. They thought that the job could be done in a few weeks. In the event it occupied them for three years, and resulted in *Taste and the Antique* (1981), which retained the approach they had originally envisaged, but which involved far more research than they had anticipated.

The book itself was immediately recognised as fundamental for the understanding of European art from the middle of the sixteenth century until at least the time of the French Revolution. It marked the rediscovery of an important chapter in the history of taste, as well as illustrating one of the most profound and irrevocable changes in artistic fashion that has ever occurred, one that was illustrated by Francis himself in a letter written in 1953, in which he said that having just revisited the Elgin Marbles he would never again take the classical section of the Vatican Museum seriously. Without changing his preferences, he did of course take it very seriously indeed, while recognising that many of the sculptures he studied are never likely to recover their former prestige. The removal of baroque restorations by archaeologically-minded museum directors has ensured that in some cases this is impossible, since their appearance has been irrevocably altered. *Taste and the Antique* itself contributed greatly to bringing that practice into disfavour.

In his next book, *History and its Images: Art and the Interpretation of the Past*, published in 1993, Francis shifted his focus once more, to examine the use and, more often, the misuse that historians had made of art as historical evidence, or, as he put it, to provide 'a study of the impact of the image on the historical imagination'. In a sense this marked a return to a problem that he had been forced to confront in his thesis on the supposed Jesuit style, since his starting point there had been a hypothesis that a particular artistic style was somehow revelatory of the attitudes of a religious order. The equation of the Jesuit style with the Baroque, indeed, had been popularised by Taine. But whereas in his earlier work Francis

had examined how an idea about history had been taken up by art historians, now he turned to the work of historians themselves. He had been
struck by the almost ubiquitous modern practice of illustrating history
books with reproductions of works of art, and he had also been amused
by some of the strange identifications proposed for the Roman statues
that he had studied in *Taste and the Antique*. But the immediate catalyst
was a paper he was invited to deliver on Gibbon and the visual arts, in
which he had been surprised by the fact that although Gibbon had certainly looked at works of art with the diligence expected of a cultivated
eighteenth-century tourist, and although the original impetus for *The
Decline and Fall of the Roman Empire* had, famously, come to him when
he contemplated the ruins of the Forum, in his book the visual arts
scarcely figured at all; and when they had been mentioned, Gibbon had
subscribed to the view, already present in Vasari, that the decline in the
power of the Roman empire had coincided with a change, and a perceived decline, in the visual arts, despite some clear evidence to the contrary. Gibbon, he realised, had been a decisive influence on Seroux
d'Agincourt, who provided the first extensive illustrated survey of the
visual arts from the Roman empire to the Renaissance. The publication
was delayed for many years, which meant that d'Agincourt's original
intention of providing a complement to Gibbon's masterpiece was largely
overlooked.

Francis's approach to his vast topic was necessarily selective, and, as
usual, more descriptive than analytical. Starting with the antiquarians of
the Renaissance, he moved on to Paolo Giovio and the fashion for collecting historical portraits, then to the discovery of the images in the Roman
catacombs, and, via Voltaire, Caylus and Montfaucon, to Lenoir's establishment of the Musée des Monuments français, an institution which had
already figured in *Rediscoveries in Art*. Dealing also with the use of
medieval manuscripts and gargoyles for the study of popular culture, and
the types of historical reconstructions used to illustrate popular works of
history, he discussed the ideas of Burckhardt, Warburg, and Huizinga, as
well as the notion, influential in the early years of this century, that art
could somehow be prophetic of social or political change.

What emerged most strongly from this survey was the extreme slow-
ness with which most historians came to appreciate the potential value of
visual evidence, and the apparent naivety with which they almost always
used it. Some of the reasons are easy enough to understand, most notably
the lack of reproductions and the absence of secure historical evidence
about the objects themselves. But gradually the more perceptive scholars

became more conscious that the purpose for which such objects had been made was seldom merely illustrative, that art had its own conventions, which changed over time. With this realisation came the idea, shared for example by Gibbon and d'Agincourt, that the visual arts were somehow symptomatic of larger social changes; but estimates of how this might work in practice varied very widely. According to Francis, the historian who used the evidence of art in the subtlest and most imaginative way was Huizinga, who based his reinterpretation of Flemish culture in the late Middle Ages on a highly personal response to the art of the fifteenth century, but who later expressed strong reservations about the validity of his approach.

As a study of the intellectual history of Western Europe, *History and its Images* is wide-ranging and immensely impressive, with a huge cast of characters portrayed with authority and an obvious familiarity. It casts a new light on ways in which the past was perceived by historians over a long time-span, as well as on ways in which art itself was understood by a series of highly intelligent and learned scholars. Equally importantly, it underlines the fact that the study of large areas of European art, from late antiquity to the early Renaissance, had largely been initiated by historians, who used visual material as a source of historical information about social customs, or as evidence of cultural change. What emerged most strongly from this survey was just how elusive the evidence provided by art has proved to be. The seductive notion that it is in some sense equivalent to written sources is profoundly misleading, and its interpretation presents us with problems which even the most acute of past historians have consistently failed to solve, and which in most cases do not permit a definitive solution. The book in this sense is a cautionary tale, and, now that visual evidence is used more extensively than ever before, one that historians, and art historians, need to ponder.

One of the topics that Francis discussed in the later part of the book was the growth of exhibitions of Old Master paintings, and in particular the impact of a major exhibition of Flemish 'primitives' on the thought of Johann Huizinga. His final book, *The Ephemeral Museum*, completed just before he died, was a study of the development of this phenomenon. It is entirely typical that here, once more, he should have discovered a theme of central importance for the understanding of the art of the past and its place in cultural life, and one that had never previously attracted the attention of historians, at least in a systematic way. His own views about the phenomenon were predictably ambivalent. On the one hand, he was attracted by the possibility of seeing, under one roof, huge selections of works of art that had never previously been brought together, and he was personally deeply involved in organising several of these exhibitions, such as *The Genius of Venice*, held at the Royal Academy in 1983, and the Council of Europe's neoclassical show of 1960. Yet he deplored not only the risks that such enterprises involved, in the transport of irreplaceable and fragile objects, but also the ways in which such exhibitions distorted the development of scholarship, leading to a focus on the kinds of object that could be lent and encouraging, through the publication of massive catalogues, a superficial and bland type of analysis; and he recognised that the motives that prompted the organisation of such manifestations often had little to do with the interests of scholarship, but were instead all too frequently involved with cultural propaganda of the most dubious kind, as in Mussolini's promotion of the famous exhibition of Italian art held at the Royal Academy in 1930. He also observed that, in bringing together works of widely different periods by a single artist, they also permitted us to see these works in ways that had never been anticipated by those who had made them.

In addition to his books, Francis also wrote a large number of articles and reviews. Most are focused on the seventeenth, eighteenth, and nineteenth centuries, and deal with the same kind of issues as he explored in his major books. If there is one single feature that unites all his published work, it is a reluctance to address the most common topics of art history, the study of individual artists and the works that they produced. Francis instead preferred to concentrate initially on the circumstances in which art was made and the motives of those who paid for it, and later on the ways in which the art of the past was understood, appreciated and collected by later generations. That process was so complex and unpredictable that it would not be surprising if he had believed that his own interpretation of what the works had meant to those who created them was bound to be subjective and, in the last analysis, profoundly partial. As I have already indicated, his reluctance to adopt a traditional approach was certainly not because he was insensitive to the power of art. On the contrary, he was always an enthusiastic and discriminating collector, a passionate sight-seeer and an assiduous visitor to museums and exhibitions. But, unlike most art historians, he evidently did not believe that his own aesthetic responses constituted historical evidence of a reliable kind, except about himself. Everything that he wrote suggested just the opposite, and in this sense his work was powerfully subversive.

This cannot have been a source of dismay to Francis, who was keenly alert to pomposity and more strongly still disliked all forms of dogmatism.

By temperament he was suspicious of received opinions, ideologically motivated positions or anything that smacked of theory. As he once put it in connection with *Patrons and Painters*, he was trying to write Marxist history without Marxism; and while he believed strongly in ideas, he regarded theory as congealed or dead ideas. He was also convinced that individuals were important, and for this reason he tried to discover as much as he could about those he chose to study. He enjoyed their eccentricities while admiring their insights and sometimes their productive or revealing errors. He believed that the greatest challenge to the historian was to bring the past to life; and that meant getting to know the protagonists of his books in the same way as he knew his own friends and acquaintances. Not that he supposed that the past was like the present, or that all societies worked in the same way. That, after all, was part of the appeal of Italy; and he was fascinated to discover, in his early days there, when invited to tea with a local dignitary, that it was appropriate to address him as 'Your excellency', just as it would have been in the seventeenth century. Throughout tea Francis's companion noticed that he used the expression whenever he could, just to see what it felt like.

As a scholar Francis was as partial as any to delving into small, well-defined problems, finding out exactly what had happened by following up countless leads in archives, but his most characteristic medium of expression was the book, rather than the article. He was primarily interested in the broad questions of the history of art, and his detailed investigations were always part of a larger enquiry. He had the great gift of knowing how far to carry his research. And it was precisely because he was not deeply preoccupied by the minutiae of the subject that he usually avoided the scholarly controversies that are so characteristic of the subject. This was certainly not because he was ever reluctant to express contentious or unfashionable views, or did so only in a qualified way. In his writing, as in conversation, he was entirely without such inhibitions, seeing his role as that of mapping out new territories by raising new issues, advancing hypotheses that others might enrich or modify on the basis of further research.

Francis defined his own political attitude as one of pessimistic liberalism. Entirely uncensorious, he valued above all else personal and professional honesty, candour, and tolerance, and he was committed to the idea that everyone should have equal access to art and education. It was typical too that when the government of the day refused to provide funds to buy a painting by Poussin that had been owned by the disgraced Anthony Blunt, Francis should have urged the National Art Collections, of which he was a member of the executive committee from 1976, to contribute to the purchase. His pessimism was profound, in that he felt that the values he believed in were under constant threat, and, in his early years, that he was not equipped to achieve happiness, although this changed when he met Larissa. His marriage brought him security, companionship, and reassurance of a kind that he had never expected or indeed thought possible. Up to that time his friends had always felt that he needed to be looked after. Afterwards, Larissa fulfilled that role, and from the time of their marriage they were almost never apart. Inevitably he remained anxious about the practical problems of life, constantly expecting that carefully planned arrangements would go wrong, or worrying about his health, but this type of anxiety was such a deep aspect of his character that he would have not have been able to function without it. Certainly, it did not prevent him from acting extremely effectively as an administrator and on committees, when he thought it was important to do so, or even, in his later years, from mastering the challenge of computers, to his surprise and satisfaction.

In his youth Francis's appearance of diffidence and impraticality was certainly helpful in gaining him access to archives and libraries; he had the gift of persuading people that they could and should help him. At the same time, this diffidence could easily be mistaken for shyness, to which he was not subject. On the contrary, he was the most sociable of scholars, with a vast network of friends which extended far beyond his circle of professional colleagues. He was an alert and subtle observer of social situations of all kinds, equally at home at smart dinner parties as among old friends. He was also a marvellous and generous host, welcoming to students no less than to his contemporaries, all of whom were treated with the same informality and attention. Young foreign scholars, in particular, were often overwhelmed by his accessibility and kindness. Francis did not believe in hierarchy; he encouraged a critical attitude to the work of all scholars, and his lack of discretion about their follies made many of them seem less intimidating. Most important of all, he believed and managed always to convey the idea that to study the past was the most enjoyable thing that one could do; his vast curiosity and his evident delight in what he did always left his friends and students with the feeling that to be an art historian was a great privilege.

For many of his friends, one of the great pleasures of life was to travel with him and Larissa. Encyclopedic in their knowledge and indefatigable in their enthusiasm, they were eager to see, and see again, every significant building and collection in Europe, although the Middle Ages was relatively low on their list of priorities. Because Francis persisted in his inability to drive and for some reason of his own did not entertain the idea of Larissa doing so, they needed drivers, but there was no lack of people happy to oblige, since they were such ideal travelling companions, unerring in their ability to discover obscure but wonderful things, encouraging to the chauffeur and also careful to ensure that the rigours of the journey were moderated by good meals and a decent level of comfort. Although he claimed to be a nervous passenger, and invariably insisted on sitting in front, he would soon forget his fears if informed that it might just be possible, by driving flat out, to see just one more museum before closing time. In later years, after Francis had conquered his fear of flying, he and Larissa became more ambitious in their plans, extending their range to Turkey and Egypt, and towards the end of their life were planning a trip to China, where they were to be entertained by a student who had written a thesis on his work.

While Francis was still unable to fly, his travel plans usually involved the most elaborate advance planning, and he often insisted on arriving at the station in time to catch the previous train to the one on which he had booked. On one occasion, when asked to attend a conference in New York, he unwittingly used up the entire travel budget by organising an itinerary that enabled him to go by boat, via the West Indies. Later, America became a fixed stage on his itinerary, particularly the Getty Center in Los Angeles, where he could often be seen, wrapped in scarves and clutching a gin-and-tonic by some swimming pool. The incongruities of southern California had a great appeal to him, such as the sight of the San Francisco Gay Men's Choir singing God Rest You Merry Gentlemen on television, but so did the resources of the Getty Center and especially its Provenance Index, an initiative which he championed from the first, as he did another major project of scholarly collaboration, the publication of the Paper Museum of Cassiano Dal Pozzo, of which he was an editor.

Francis's huge influence on his contemporaries was exerted not just through his many publications but also through his lectures, which were delivered in French and Italian as well as English, in a slightly histrionic tone, a relic of his experience as a student actor in Cambridge. Equally important for the diffusion of his ideas was his friendship with art historians from every country in Europe, as well as from North America, who were constantly entertained in Walton Street, with Francis dispensing whisky and Larissa providing marvellous and abundant food. He was usually not particularly forthcoming about the details of his latest research, but he always enjoyed discussing general questions about the history of art, in a provocative, probing way, or exchanging gossip, which he loved, and which in his case was never coloured by moral judgements. Conversation with Francis was always exhilarating, because of his wit, his exceptional intelligence, and his candour.

Francis was elected to a Fellowship of the British Academy in 1971, and in 1985 was awarded the Serena medal for Italian Studies. He was also a Trustee of the Wallace Collection, a Foreign Honorary Member of the American Academy of Arts and Sciences, a Corresponding Member of the Accademia Pontiana in Naples and Foreign Member of the Ateneo Veneto. His contribution to scholarship was also acknowledged in 1999 when he became a chevalier of the Légion d'Honneur.

In November 1999 he received the news that he had inoperable liver cancer with exemplary stoicism. At first he thought of spending his last months rereading authors such as Molière and Shakespeare, and watching again his favourite French films, but soon decided instead to devote his efforts to completing the *The Ephemeral Museum*. While he did so, friends came to visit him from all over the world. He died at home on 18 January 2000, spared what he had always feared most, having to face life without Larissa.

CHARLES HOPE
Warburg Institute

MARTIN HOLLIS

James Martin Hollis
1938–1998

JAMES MARTIN HOLLIS (always known simply as Martin) was born on 14 March 1938 into a family well-known for its commitment to public service. His father was a senior diplomat; one of his uncles was the MP Christopher Hollis; another was Roger Hollis, the head of MI5. Following a well-trodden mandarin path, Martin attended Winchester College as a Scholar, and duly went on to win the expected Classical Scholarship to New College, Oxford. Before going to University he did his national service in the Royal Artillery. This was a period of his life about which he seldom spoke, but it evidently left its mark, if only by turning him into a heavy smoker for many years.

At Oxford Martin was taught by two philosophers for whom he always professed the highest regard. One was A. J. Ayer, whom Martin particularly admired as a teacher. Ayer, he would say, invariably treated even the most unpromising remarks of his students with complete respect and tried to find some truth in them. This experience too must have left its mark, for Martin's own teaching was inspiring and encouraging in a very similar way. The other Oxford philosopher about whom Martin always spoke with admiration was P. F. Strawson, to whom Martin acknowledged a debt for the way in which he had formulated his account of the role of rationality in explanation. This was to become a master theme—almost an obsession—of Martin's own philosophical work. Martin's belief in the power of reason was unshakeable, and he viewed all manifestations of religious sentiment with a sense of amused disbelief. He was never in the least abashed by critics who complained that his own

Proceedings of the British Academy, **115**, 245–255. © The British Academy 2002.

commitment to the ideal of rationality was so fervent as sometimes to seem unreasonable. As always, he merely relished the irony.

After gaining a First Class in PPE in 1961, Martin took up a Harkness Fellowship at Berkeley and Harvard Universities. While at Harvard he clearly fell under the spell of W. O. Quine, but he nevertheless decided against an academic career. He sat the civil service examinations, passing out top, and joined the Foreign Office in 1963. With his long string of youthful triumphs behind him, he now seemed set for an equally triumphant public career.

Very soon, however, Martin found himself drawn back to philosophy. He began to combine his work at the Foreign Office with teaching back at Oxford, and in 1964–5 he held a lectureship attached to Balliol College. He was not finding the civil service especially challenging, and his employers soon found themselves accused of behaving irrationally, always the worst sin in Martin's book. Having sent him to Heidelberg to learn German, they announced that his next posting would be to Moscow. A further reason why this prospect seemed out of the question was that in 1965 Martin had married Patricia Wells, whom he had met while they were both Harkness Fellows in the United States. Martin resigned from the Foreign Office in 1966 and embarked on an academic career instead.

Patricia and Martin both obtained lectureships at the fledgling University of East Anglia in 1967, and there they both stayed. They quickly became prominent in the local community as well as in the university. Martin served as a JP between 1972 and 1982, while Patricia joined, and later led, Norwich City Council. Martin took immense pride in the fact that it was Patricia who went on to combine her distinguished academic life with a career in politics, a career that culminated in her appointment to a government post in the House of Lords as Baroness Hollis of Heigham after the General Election of 1997.

Meanwhile Martin pursued his own academic career with a remarkable combination of intensity and steadiness. He proved to be extremely prolific, writing with a seemingly effortless ease and lucidity, and by the 1990s he had gained an international reputation. He made a visit to China in 1996, and was much in demand as a visiting lecturer in Europe and in the United States. His own university was not slow to recognise his gifts, and he was promoted to Senior Lecturer in 1972 and to the Chair of Philosophy ten years later. Although he always appeared genuinely indifferent to academic honours, the mark of recognition that perhaps gave him the greatest pleasure was his election in 1990 to the philosophy section of the British Academy.

Although Martin was unremitting in his dedication to his research, he also liked to run things. He was editor of the Anglo-German journal *Ratio* from 1980 to 1987, and did much to broaden its coverage while at the same time sustaining its high standards. He was President of the Aristotelian Society in 1986, and in the early 1990s was exceptionally active as a Fellow of the Academy, acting as chair of the Philosophy section in addition to serving on Council. His university was likewise fortunate in being able to call on his administrative talents, and he gave unstinting service, acting in turn as Head of Philosophy, Dean of his School between 1983–6 and Pro-Vice-Chancellor between 1992–5.

Martin disclaimed any ambitions as an administrator, but his exceptional intelligence, combined with his deeply ingrained sense of civic duty, made him a highly effective one. All letters and memos were instantly answered in neat handwritten notes, and only by the faintest tones of irony did he ever convey that one might be wasting his time. Unusually for someone of such preternatural quickness, he was remarkably tolerant of colleagues whose superegos were less well developed or who simply thought and worked at a slower pace. He himself was steely in his efficiency, utterly to be trusted and utterly to be relied upon to do whatever he had promised to do, come what may.

Although he always worked hard, Martin was devoted to his family and domestic life. While incapable of speaking boastfully about himself, he took tremendous pride in Patricia's achievements and in those of their two gifted sons. Visitors to the house were always welcome, and when the children were young there was a motor-cruiser on which one would be taken for trips on the Norfolk Broads. There were certain snares, however, for unwary guests. One was that Martin liked to throw off the modest observation that he enjoyed a bit of chess. (He was an extremely strong and competitive player.) Another was the delight he took in setting puzzles for his guests to solve. He himself adored brainteasers, and for some years contributed a weekly column of logical puzzles to the *New Scientist*, publishing a selection of them in 1970 under the title *Tantalisers*. This was considered by aficionados to be a work of real originality, although Martin failed to mention it in his list of publications in *Who's Who*.

What Martin really enjoyed was philosophical conversation, or better still argument. Best of all he liked to throw off epigrams that left his interlocutors unsure about their relevance to the question in hand. This quizzical and deeply pedagogic aspect of his character is nicely captured by Malcolm Bradbury—another eminence from the University of East Anglia—in the Preface to his last novel, *To the Hermitage*. 'Martin Hollis', he writes, 'contributed greatly. A believer in the cunning of reason, he often led me, wandering and peripatetic, up the Enlightenment Trail, aiming for the pub at the top, The Triumph of Reason. I fear we never reached it.'

After thirty years at the same institution, there were signs in the mid-1990s that Martin might be ready for a change. He thought about Chairs elsewhere, and there was talk of his becoming the Head of one of the Cambridge Colleges. But it was not to be. The last academic occasion on which he was able to take part outside his own university was in February 1997, when he helped to organise and lead a *conversazione* at the Academy on 'Philosophy and its History'. Although he read his own contribution in his usual impeccable style, it was clear that something was wrong, for in the course of a long discussion he sat almost silent, a thing unknown. A brain tumour was diagnosed shortly afterwards, and proved resistant to treatment. Most heartbreakingly for such a lord of language, his linguistic powers were the first to go. Before the end of the year he was bedridden, and thereafter he was devotedly nursed by his family at home, where he died on 27 February 1998.

It was possible to know Martin well for many years without feeling that one really knew him. He was always thoughtful and generous, and always wonderfully witty company, but he maintained a considerable reserve. Even in the midst of social occasions it sometimes seemed that (humming to himself the while) he had somehow withdrawn. With his reserve went a genuine stoicism. He never complained about his life, which he recognised as privileged, nor about his colleagues, feckless though many of them must have seemed if judged by his own relentless standards of efficiency. He was not without intellectual aggression, but he was totally devoid of malice. His courtesy was invariable, and he extended it equally to everyone. Even *in extremis*, these qualities of equability never deserted him. A colleague who visited him shortly before he died remarked that university life was becoming so harassing that one was probably better off in bed. By then Martin could no longer speak, but he was still able to give his inimitable smile.

A memorial occasion in Martin's honour was held at the University of East Anglia on 5 May 1998. The university theatre was packed with well-wishers who had come from several countries to pay their respects. The occasion was a wholly secular one but was made intensely memorable by the way in which Martin's immediate family commemorated him. His wife Patricia spoke finely of his intellectual brilliance (and of his domestic incompetence); his younger son Matthew read out one of his own poems, a moving meditation on his sense of loss; and his elder son Simon quoted passages from Martin's philosophical works that left the audience alternately reflecting on the argument and helpless with laughter at the wit.

At the heart of all his work was a passionate and unwavering rationalism. Starting from the assumption that there is an 'epistemological unity of mankind', the idea that there is, in P. F. Strawson's words, 'a massive central core of human thinking which has no history', he devoted his scholarly energies to exploring, often in close collaboration with social scientists in a variety of disciplines, the meaning and scope of rationality. Are the criteria of truth and rationality universal and objective? Should we accept a picture of rational agents as pure calculators of the consequences which best satisfy their given preferences? Can reason extend to a concern with the rationality of ends? Can we accept that social norms are a source of reasons for reasonable persons without sliding into relativism? Can we aspire to a single account of practical reason for all species of rational action or single definition of rationality for all purposes of social science? Such were the questions he repeatedly and insistently addressed as his thought evolved and deepened over three decades.

His serious engagement with the social sciences and collaboration with their practitioners was both characteristic and distinctive. His first book, *Rational Economic Man* (1975), was co-authored with the economist Edward Nell and he subsequently published an Oxford book of readings on *Philosophy and Economic Theory* (1979) with Professor Frank Hahn, who has remarked that he was 'one of the few non-economic theorists I know who had a serious understanding of the subject; indeed, a good deal superior to that of many economists'. His last collaboration was the strikingly successful collective work, *The Theory of Choice: A Critical Guide* (1992), co-written with four colleagues in the School of Economic and Social Studies at the University of East Anglia, three of them economists and one a Professor of Politics. Another early collaboration was with Steven Lukes. Their widely-discussed edited volume *Rationality and Relativism* (1982) brought together influential essays by philosophers, sociologists of science and anthropologists. His *Models of Man* (1977) addressed issues central to contemporary sociological theory. And with another colleague from East Anglia, Professor Steven Smith he wrote *Explanation and Understanding International Relations* (1990). He also wrote an engaging *Invitation to Philosophy* (1985) and a (very demanding) 'introduction' to *The Philosophy of Social Science* (1994) and two major works which develop and synthesize his thoughts: *The Cunning of Reason* (1987) and the posthumously published *Trust within Reason* (1998). He also wrote many lively and interesting papers, on all these and other subjects, some of them collected in his *Reason in Action*.

His first writings were stimulated by the debate in the 1960s opened up by Peter Winch's Wittgenstein-influenced *The Idea of a Social Science* and his much-debated article 'Understanding a Primitive Society' which, discussing Zande witchcraft and Nuer symbolism, maintained that standards of rationality could be plural. According to Winch, 'standards of rationality in different societies do not always coincide': thus Professor Evans-Pritchard had misunderstood the Zande by 'pressing their thought where it would not naturally go'. In a series of articles and chapters Martin firmly rejected this apparently relativist line of thought, which can also be found in the work of the so-called 'Edinburgh School' in the sociology and history of science, whose 'strong programme' consisted in denying any form of knowledge a 'privileged status' and in tracing the local modes of cultural transmission, socialisation and social control as constituting the specific local causes of beliefs being held. The anti-relativist case can be argued either on empirical grounds (along Humean lines: that mankind is 'much the same in all times and places') or on a priori grounds. Martin firmly took the latter course. He saw the problem of interpreting the beliefs and practices of other cultures as merely a colourful version of the problem of Other Minds and maintained that all understanding presupposes a 'bridgehead' of true and rational beliefs: that 'some assumption about rationality has to be made *a priori*, if anthropology is to be possible; and that we have no choice about what assumption to make'. On this issue he never wavered though his thought became ever more nuanced in successive discussions of the hermeneutic circle. His settled views on the relations between rationality and relativism were as he set them out in *The Philosophy of Social Science*:

> The first step towards charting a world from within is to understand what its inhabitants believe. When one is convinced that a belief is both true and held for good reason, no further step is required. False beliefs which are held for good reason can be understood by relating them to 'bridgehead' beliefs. Bad reasons, however, call for explanation at a causal level, which supplies an external structure to account for them. Rationality thus comes first but relativism then has its turn.

A second major theme in his writings was the issue of how to conceptualise personal and social identity: how to account for autonomy and individuals' relations to their social roles. This theme was first treated extensively in his *Models of Man* whose argument is structured around the contrast between the two models of 'plastic man' and 'autonomous man' and proceeds by taking up the idea, following on from that just indicated, that reasons are 'the explanation but not the cause of rational action', so that 'fully rational action' is 'its own explanation, given the context and the actor's identity', concluding with the idea that social action is to be understood as 'the rational expression of intention within rules' and 'where models of rational action give advice which actors do not follow and call for skills which they do not have, two kinds of explanation co-exist'. This theme was carried further in the chapter on 'Reasons and Roles' in *The Cunning of Reason* in an ingenious discussion of how to explain action by reasons by using two frames of reference in seeking to explain bureaucratic behaviour:

> One is the role-playing frame, where the reasons for action derive from normative expectations. That a situation is of a declared sort makes it the particular responsibility of those in some set of offices. They thereby have a reason for doing something appropriate about it. A Bureaucratic Politics model is excellent for pinning down this point and spelling it out. The other frame is a problem-solving one. It will not do to come up with any old appropriate solution. The problem calls for a best, or at least, a good one. A rational actor model is excellent for studying those aspects of decision-making which are fairly independent of normative context.

Roles, he insisted, are not 'fully scripted in advance of every situation', must always be interpreted and so call for judgement of what in particular is required of social actors who are best seen, not as impersonating but as personifying characters—an older idea and one 'closer to the roots of drama than the idea of dressing up and pretence'. We are 'rational stewards', he liked to say, not players of our social roles. The rule-governed games of social life are not like the strategic interactions of game theory. This was his version of *homo sociologicus*:

> The games we play become open-textured and our motives or real reasons for making our moves can be distinguished from the intentions expressed in the act of making them. But this leaves an ambiguity, if we, the actors, hoped to emerge as persons whose identity is not defined by any or all of the games of social life. Talk of motives or real reasons may signal only a deeper level of intentions, as when a chess master who seems to be merely defending against a threat is really setting a trap. Or where motives are external to the game of the moment, they may still belong to another game.

He turned a last time to the topic of autonomy in the chapter devoted to it in *The Theory of Choice*, in which he argued that rational choice theory, concentrating upon internal coherence among preferences, among beliefs, and between preferences, beliefs, and actions, cannot give a satisfactory account of autonomy, which, he thought 'must take on moral shape', for the satisfied fool's and the happy slave's autonomy are illusory:

> Self-direction becomes the moral independence which goes with individuality in Mill, especially if Kant's connection is made between a free will and a will made under moral laws.

Which leads us directly to the third major theme of his writings: an elaborate and deeply thought-out critique of rational choice thinking and its extensions, which explored the instrumental notion of practical reason central to microeconomics and critical for 'economic' theories of social action at large. His work on economic theories began with his first book, written with Nell, *Rational Economic Man*, in which he endorsed the idea, also found in von Mises, that the formal abstractions of economic theory constitute a priori knowledge, furnishing 'Kantian conditions a priori of the possibility of finding a kind of describable order in social experience'. He continued to hold this view and explicitly endorsed it in later writings, but his critique of rational choice does not require acceptance of this admittedly contentious position. That critique is complex and rich, but its bottom line is characteristically Hollisian: an objection to the Humean idea that reason is the slave of the passions.

The critique is most fully developed in *The Cunning of Reason*. This begins with an exceptionally lucid presentation of the elements of rational choice theory and game theory. He shows how it presumes desire, rather than belief, as the only motor of action; that the theory of efficient choice is unconcerned with the ends pursued; and that belief is assimilated to information and deliberation to its processing. He then challenges all three presumptions, at length and in detail, arguing that the decision-theoretic model of human action and interaction—in which 'the agent is simply a throughput' and individuals are interchangeable computing units who differ only in their preferences or individual sources of satisfaction—cannot account for the phenomena of trust and morality in social life. Extended discussions of rational expectations and of 'maximising' and 'satisficing' lead back to the idea of social actors as rational role players.

Martin's last book, *Trust within Reason* takes up the theme of trust and the inadequacies of 'current versions of reason' to account for it. It merits a somewhat more extended treatment here, since it represents Hollis's mature and, sadly, his final reflections upon the themes we have considered, gathering them together in addressing a central and pressing contemporary question. Why do we keep our promises, obey the law, honour contracts, vote in elections, pick up hitchhikers, give blood, and so on? Why do people play their part in social life (rather than 'defecting') and is it rational to do so? Martin's objective is to show that it is, by 'defining reason aright'.

He begins with a memorably vivid parable of a proposed journey of Adam and Eve 'through smiling uplands along the Enlightenment Trail', lined with six inns ('The Rational Choice', 'The Social Contract', 'The Foole', 'The Sensible Knave', 'The Extra Trick' and 'The Triumph of Reason'). They agree to end their walk at one of them and to take turns in deciding where to halt or walk on. Each of the two would-be travellers, armed with different preference-orderings, will, starting from the last of the inns, which they both much prefer to the first but rank differently, foresee the other's defection and so, through backward induction, they will never get going. Rational choice precludes the journey to the Triumph of Reason.

First, he considers rational choice theory and the attempts within that tradition to answer objections and fix things by modifying assumptions and making technical improvements. He judges such attempts as failures, the central problem being that 'the standard theory of rational choice defines rationality by reference to the agent's own expected utility, whereas trust requires that we can expect people to ignore this siren call' or, in game-theoretic terms, that trust requires 'out-of-equilibrium play—strategic choice which is not a best answer to the other player's move'. Neither Hobbes's attempt to rely on negative sanctions nor Hume's appeal to sympathy can solve the problem which resides in part in the assumption of philosophical, rather than psychological egoism and in part on exclusive reliance on forward-looking reasons. For these moves can only change the balance of reasons while leaving their character unchanged and thus can only render 'rational' people more trustworthy under favourable circumstances. Nor can we solve the problem by reconceiving utility as a purely formal notion, 'bleaching' it of all psychological content, thereby depriving it of motivational and thus explanatory force. Nor can we solve it by injecting probability considerations or by positing a series of games of infinite or indefinite or unknown length. We can reduce defection in these ways, but we cannot remove it while 'reasons for being amiable remain only forward-looking'. This version of reason still leaves 'many occasions to rat and would undermine people with irrational motives'. As Hume put it, 'the sensible knave' may still 'think that an act of iniquity or infidelity will make a considerable addition to his fortune, without causing any considerable breach in the social union and confederacy'.

But what about subordinating instrumental rationality to a higher kind, namely Kantian reason? This would render Adam and Eve's journey possible but only because they both adopt the moral point of view, acting on universalisable maxims, on categorical and not hypothetical imperatives, and casting aside concern for consequences and mutual self-interest. But this, Martin argues, misses 'the secret of trust': it requires too ruthless an abstraction of individuals from social life, from 'personal ties' and 'particularised social relations', since it posits that people 'recognize one another as selves distinct from their human and social peculiarities and treat one another impersonally and fairly, as required by the universal maxims that guide moral action'. It would not, for instance, explain why people used to leave their doors unlocked. Such a social norm has moral content and yet could not plausibly be construed as a universal maxim: it is grounded in social relations and is also strategic, depending on how trustworthy others are.

Nor does a contractarian perspective on reason help, for this, according to Martin is rooted in mutual self-interest and is thus not combinable with a Kantian perspective. What is needed, and missing in all contractarians, is an account of why, if A has helped B, C owes something to D. Here too the persistent question remains: why rational persons are morally bound to keep their covenants when prudence dictates otherwise?

Nor, finally, can a Wittgensteinian version of reason in terms of the 'games' of social life solve the problem, suggesting that, since understanding advances in finding rationality in what is understood, what is rational derives 'from the rules followed'. But there are many 'forms of life' that cannot be endorsed as 'reasonable'. For, self-evidently, although a mafioso and a cannibal have reasons 'internally and intersubjectively', one cannot forsake the 'right and ability' to question their social relations from the outside and the need for a 'universal standpoint from which to discriminate between different ways of embedding the self in social relations'. For we cannot avoid keeping 'a space for questioning institutions at large; and asking what are 'the social relations that reason can endorse'.

Adam and Eve never reached their destination, but, we may ask, did Martin Hollis reach his? Did he arrive at 'a different idea of practical reason, deeper than prudence and morally charged' that unlocks 'the secret of trust' and 'illuminates the bond of society after all'? His readers will decide. What he has certainly left them with, in this and other works, is a series of thought-provoking negative injunctions and positive suggestions.

Among the negative injunctions are: distrust individualist theories of human nature and practical reason; reject consequentialist views that exclude backward-looking motivations; view with suspicion the distinction between procedural and substantive values, between the right and the good; reject accounts of the social sciences that lend themselves to social engineering, promising to reconcile the interests of each with the interests of all. Among the positive suggestions are: think about fully generalised reciprocity, by reflecting upon team spirit, and on Titmuss's account of blood donors in Britain where 'creative altruism is local and conditional—a matter of there being enough members for a joint undertaking'; think about how Rousseau's account of how individuals are transformed into citizens, where preferences are both consulted and constructed; imagine schemes of generalised reciprocity that 'offer to settle who we are and where we belong' but 'do not define us immutably' and 'are not beyond criticism'; and 'regard the social world as an interpretative fabric spun from shared meanings which persist or change as we negotiate their interpretation among ourselves.'

STEVEN LUKES
Fellow of the Academy
QUENTIN SKINNER
Fellow of the Academy

JOHN KENT   *British Museum*

John Philip Cozens Kent
1928–2000

JOHN KENT was Keeper of Coins and Medals in the British Museum from 1983 to 1990 and was the world's leading authority on the coinage of the late Roman empire. His achievement was to present the coinage of that complicated period in a modern and systematic way, credible to historians and archaeologists as well as to numismatists. This wider audience will be aware of his massive eighth and tenth volumes of *Roman Imperial Coinage* (*RIC* VIII and *RIC* X). Otherwise his characteristic output was the dense and pithy article, often in an obscure place of publication.[1] Sometimes it might be no more than a few pages long, even though the issue might be complex. The reader was expected to work hard.

John Kent was born on 28 September 1928 in Palmers Green, London, the only child of a senior railway official and a civil servant. While at school, one day towards the end of the war, he narrowly avoided being hit by a V2 rocket, and, having been awarded an Andrews Scholarship in Arts, went on to university at University College London. After his BA in 1949, he immediately embarked on a Ph.D. thesis, and on its completion in 1951, he proceeded to National Service, initially with the Middlesex Regiment. When limited sight in one eye precluded service in Korea, army logic saw him commissioned into the Royal Army Service Corps and despatched to serve as a Pay Officer. Later he was posted to an advanced battalion where he was responsible for the administration of a large company. On demobilisation he was appointed in 1953 as an

[1] For a full bibliography of his work, see A. Burnett, *Numismatic Chronicle*, 162 (2002), forthcoming. We would like to thank Roger Bland for his help in preparing this obituary.

Proceedings of the British Academy, **115**, 259–274. © The British Academy 2002.

Assistant Keeper in the Department of Coins and Medals in the British Museum.

His love of coins dated from his childhood, but his choice of period was influenced by two men, J. W. E. Pearce and A. H. M. Jones. The latter, a familiar name to all historians, held the chair at UCL where Kent was an undergraduate; Jones was then the supervisor of his Ph.D. thesis, on *The Office of the Comes Sacrarum Largitionum* (the chief imperial finance officer of the late Roman empire). Pearce is less well known, but, though a schoolmaster by profession, his knowledge of late Roman coinage was extraordinary. The ninth volume of *RIC*, published under Pearce's name in 1951 after his death, belies his contribution and only hints at his profound knowledge and instinct for the subject. Like Kent's own contribution— and surely not coincidentally—Pearce can be seen at his best in the series of incisive articles that he wrote in the 1930s, work that has not been replaced. Both in period and style the elderly Pearce had a lasting impact on the young Kent, who later dedicated his *RIC* VIII to him.

His career might have gone in a different direction, archaeology. His first publication, at the precocious age of nineteen, was 'Monumental brasses: a new classification of military effigies',[2] for which the year before he had been awarded the Reginald Taylor Prize and medal of the British Archaeological Association. The classification remains in use, and Kent was always pleased, many years later, at the surprise of colleagues when they realised that he was the author of this classic piece, and that it was not written by some ancient antiquarian after a lifetime of studying brasses. Throughout his life he kept up a lively interest in archaeology, building on early friendships with people like John Mann, John Emerton, John Wilkes, George Boon, and Ralph Merrifield. This interest in archaeology had three main products. First, he was active in the archaeology and excavation of greater London, especially in neighbouring Hertfordshire, excavating at Pancake Hall in Welham Green, Perrior's Manor, Cheshunt, and South Mimms castle. He was also a keen supporter of local societies in Hertfordshire, including—nearest to his home in Hadley Wood—the Barnet Local History Society, of which he was president for the last twenty years of his life. He played an active role during the difficult years of the London and Middlesex Archaeological Society, being its President in 1985–8, and was a long-serving member of its archaeological research committee.

---

[2] 'Monumental brasses: a new classification of military effigies', *Journal of the British Archaeological Association,* 12 (1949), 70–97.

Secondly, he was always ready to use coins to bear on archaeological problems and sometimes solve them. He took a new harder look at the evidence of coins for the Roman occupation of Britain, reviewing in particular the contribution of coins to our understanding of Hadrian's Wall, the end of Roman Britain, and in the reassessment of 'barbarous radiates'. Barbarous radiates are crude and locally made imitations of late Roman coins, and it was thought that they were produced in the 'Dark Ages' of the fifth and sixth centuries after the Roman withdrawal from Britain just after AD 400. Kent was one of the first to overturn this dating, and demonstrate convincingly that the coins in question were in fact contemporary products, thereby removing them from any attempt to date archaeological sites to the later period. Equally important was his work leading to the dating of the Sutton Hoo ship burial (see further below). Thirdly, he was very interested in related methodological questions. The best example of this is probably his article on 'Interpreting Coin Finds', first published in 1974 and reprinted more or less verbatim 14 years later,[3] in which he demolished the assumptions that geographical patterns of the places in which coin hoards were deposited could be connected either with areas of fighting or with areas of wealth. It remains sad, however, that outside the British audience, his strictures have not had the lasting effect that they deserve.

RIC VIII was published in 1981,[4] and focuses on the coinage from the death of Constantine the Great in 337 to the accession of Valentinian I in 364. Much of Kent's work of the previous twenty-five years was preparatory. Articles on hoards, such as that ironically titled CHAOS,[5] and studies of rare individual pieces took their place alongside the definitive laying to rest of the old chestnut: the use of the mint mark CONS by mint of Arles rather than Constantinople; or the non-existence of one Carausius II, a supposed British usurper some 70 years after the Roman admiral who did indeed proclaim himself emperor alongside Diocletian. He also approached the work of producing a definitive catalogue with specific studies, and with more general considerations. He insisted, for example, following the great Austrian scholar of the early twentieth century Otto Voetter, that the way to study late Roman coinage was by the

---

[3] 'Interpreting Coin Finds', in J. Casey and R. Reece (eds.), *Coins and the Archaeologist*, British Archaeological Reports 4 (Oxford, 1974), pp. 184–200; reprinted with some additions in second edition (1988), pp. 201–17.

[4] *The Roman Imperial Coinage*, vol. VIII, *The Family of Constantine AD 337–64* (1981).

[5] The intentional acronym of 'Constantinian hoards and other studies in the later Roman bronze coinage', which he published with R. A. G. Carson in *Numismatic Chronicle*, 6th ser. XVI (1956), 83–161.

chronological classification of the reverse designs by mint, and not by imperial effigy. This represented a major step away from the standard reference work then in use, Henri Cohen's *Description historique des monnaies frappées sous l'Empire romain*, which presented the coins in order of emperor and then alphabetically by the inscription on the coins' reverses. Cohen's order, though hallowed by usage and of convenience to collectors and antiquarians, obscured the proper chronological order and hence proper development of the coinage, thereby rendering it useless for historical interpretation and reducing its value for archaeological dating. The publication in 1960 of *Late Roman Bronze Coinage* killed off the use of Cohen for the bronze coinage. In *LRBC* Kent collaborated with his BM colleagues Robert Carson and Philip Hill to produce an extremely concise account of the bronze coinage of over 150 years in an astonishingly short 114 pages. The book requires several tutorials for the uninitiated to use and understand, was frequently reprinted and became a bible not only for numismatists but especially for archaeologists, who were delighted to find that a book costing only about £5 could tell them everything they needed to know to identify more than fifty per cent of the coins they would excavate from a site, thereby freeing them from the impossible task of searching through the endless specialist literature. Though the coin lists were replaced by more up-to-date ones in the later *RIC* VIII and X, *LRBC* remains an indispensable and much-loved tool for anyone trying to identify coins in the field. Copies have been spotted as far afield as Sri Lanka and Turkmenistan!

Further studies, on Magnentius, Julian, and medallions, were accompanied by his superbly illustrated general work on Roman coins and by catalogues of the Dumbarton Oaks collection and the British Museum exhibition, *Wealth of the Roman World: Gold and Silver AD 300–700*.[6] The exhibition was held in 1977, and Kent greatly enjoyed, *inter alia*, the trip from Cyprus in an RAF transport to accompany the Cyprus treasure on its way to London. The conclusion of all these works and studies fed into *RIC* VIII, which was eventually published in 1981. 'Eventually' because cataloguing was not Kent's natural forte, and Robert Carson, his colleague and editor, had to cajole him to complete the manuscript, and its completion was facilitated by a year in the Institute for Advanced Study at Princeton. This was followed by several problems in the production of

---

[6] *Roman Coins* (with M. and A. Hirmer) (1978); *Late Roman Gold and Silver Coins at Dumbarton Oaks: Diocletian to Eugenius* (with A. R. Bellinger, P. Bruun, C. H. V. Sutherland), *Dumbarton Oaks Papers*, 18 (Washington, 1964); *Wealth of the Roman World: Gold and Silver AD 300–700* (1977) (with K. Painter).

the book. The result, however, rose above the problems (apart from the poor plates, but that too is now being rectified with the current reprint), and the book came out to lead to Kent's appointment as Keeper of Coins and Medals at the British Museum in 1983 and his election as a Fellow of the British Academy in 1986.

Twenty years later it is easy to take *RIC* VIII for granted. But it represented two great achievements. First, it enabled those who were not numismatists to appreciate what the coinage can, and just as importantly cannot, contribute to our understanding of the period from the death of Constantine in 337 to the accession of Valentinian I in 364. With the notable exception of the reign of Julian ('the Apostate') this is not a period which has attracted a great deal of interest from historians, since the written sources are thin and since it falls between the great periods of Constantine and Theodosius. But Kent could show how the period foreshadowed a number of the developments in the financial and administrative systems of the later period. Second, in terms of the coins and the *RIC* series itself, the volume represented a great advance—and not just because it weighed several kilos more than any previous volume! The additional length was, in part, accounted for by the complexity of the period, with multiple Augusti and Caesars in power and recognising or not recognising each other in a complicated pattern. But Kent also wanted to encapsulate as much relevant information as possible in one place, thereby making the book a truly effective work of reference. That does not mean that useless details were included, or excessive material repeated from previous studies, but rather he wanted to give a full account that would be comprehensible on its own terms (and hence remedying some of the problems in Pearce's *RIC* IX), while enabling the specialist to follow up the argument elsewhere.

In parallel to his work on the late Roman coinage, and almost as an interlude between *RIC* VIII and *RIC* X, Kent also took up the study of late Iron Age numismatics. He took over this role from Derek Allen. Allen, both as an Assistant Keeper in the BM and as Secretary of the British Academy, had been the leading light in the subject, and his death in 1975 left a void, specifically for the completion of the catalogue of Celtic coins, for which he left an unpublished manuscript. It would be wrong, however, to suggest that Kent merely took over Allen's work, since although he edited two European volumes of the projected five-volume catalogue,[7] he transformed the discussion. A natural sceptic, he was

---

[7] D. Allen (ed. J. P. C. Kent and M. Mays), *Catalogue of Celtic Coins in the British Museum*, vol. 1, *Silver Coins of the East Celts and Balkan Peoples* (1978); D. Allen (ed. J. P. C. Kent and M. Mays),

unimpressed by what he regarded as the loose level of argumentation
which he encountered in Celtic numismatics, and wanted to establish
more clearly the limits of knowledge. He did this by organising careful
distribution maps, rather than relying on traditional 'tribal' attributions,
and by being much more careful with dates than had previously been the
case. He did not publish much about British Iron Age coins, even though
his knowledge was very detailed. But he had the same concerns with the
British material as he did with the European, and was specially uneasy at
what he saw as the disjunction between Iron Age archaeology, which had
developed very fast, and Iron Age numismatics, which was still using an
older set of concepts. As a result he became an ardent supporter of
'down-dating', even though at heart he remained fundamentally uncon-
vinced about any of the so-called fixed points of the chronology.[8]
Although he maintained his interest in the subject during the 1980s, he
was content to hand over the mantle of Iron Age numismatic studies to a
new and more numerous generation of scholars, preferring to return to
his major interest in the Roman empire.

His second major contribution to the *RIC* series was volume X, published shortly after his retirement from the British Museum in 1990.[9] This
dealt with a much longer and far more difficult period than *RIC* VIII. It
covered the coinage from the division of the empire on the death of
Theodosius in AD 395 until the fall of the western empire in AD 476, or, as
Kent preferred, in AD 480.[10] The coins are much more difficult, partly
because they are often rare and very poorly preserved,[11] partly because
the typology became partially immobilised, and partly because the various people who took over parts of the empire (the Vandals, Visigoths,
and Ostrogoths) made imitative coinages. The analysis of their style is the
only significant way of distinguishing these non-Roman products from

---

Catalogue of Celtic Coins in the British Museum, vol. 2, *Silver Coins of North Italy, South and Central France, Switzerland and South Germany* (1990).

[8] 'The origin and development of Celtic gold coinage in Britain', *Centenaire de la mort de l'Abbé Cochet, 1975. Actes du colloque international d'archéologie* (Rouen, 1978), pp. 313–24; 'The origins of coinage in Britain', in B. Cunliffe (ed.), *Coinage and Society in Britain and Gaul* (1981), pp. 40–2.

[9] *The Roman Imperial Coinage*, volume X, *The Divided Empire and the Fall of the Western Parts, AD 395–491* (1994).

[10] 'Julius Nepos and the fall of the Western Empire', in R. M. Swoboda-Milenović (ed.), *Corolla Memoriae Erich Swoboda Dedicata* (Graz/Cologne, 1966), pp. 147–50. He argued that the recognition by Theoderic of Nepos after Romulus' death in 476 indicated that, until his death in 480, Nepos was regarded as the western emperor.

[11] *RIC* X includes over 300 unique pieces; anyone who has ever tried to get to grips with the fifth-
century bronze coinage will know well the great difficulty of finding legible pieces.

their Roman prototypes or cognates, and Kent had an unrivalled eye for them, which he developed over a period of twenty-five years.[12] Much of his thinking on all these issues was developed and expressed as a series of five Presidential Addresses to the Royal Numismatic Society (1985–9), in which he took the picture back to Diocletian's reforms, discussing metrology and mint organisation, the extent to which it is helpful to think that late Roman coinage 'declined' and how we can approach the 'barbarian' coinages. The last was a typically dense Kent publication of only a few pages and a handful of illustrations, yet every word and picture has a broader significance, generally implicit.[13] Once, when challenged on a point, he would refer the correspondent to this article; when the response came that nothing was said on the point, he replied, 'but just look at the pictures!', as if the difficult point was obvious to all.

He would apply a similar methodology to his studies of the fifth- and sixth-century coinage. A sketch of the relevant aspect or period would be given in a few sentences, based on a wide knowledge of the written sources; this would be followed by a concise presentation of the coin material. The latter would be presented as a series of conclusions, with little attempt to argue the point. Readers, some of whom were irritated by this somewhat *ex cathedra* style of presentation, were expected to do what Kent had done: to make a painstaking collection of material from the great museums and from much material garnered from coins illustrated in sales catalogues, and then make a detailed stylistic analysis of it. The record cards on which these studies were based are now a valuable part of the British Museum's archive. Particularly good examples of this approach can be seen in his study of the coinage of Arcadius and Valentinian III,[14] as well as his treatment of the western coinage of Valentinian's successors.[15]

The climax of all these studies was *RIC* X, a book which astonishes by its breadth of coverage. The encyclopaedic and detailed knowledge of the coinage is matched by a sure grasp of the political and administrative

---

[12] His first such study was the identification of Vandalic silver in the name of Honorius: 'Un monnayage irrégulier du début du Ve siècle de notre ére', *Cercle d'Études Numismatiques. Bulletin*, 11, no. 1 (Jan.–March, 1974), 23–9.

[13] 'The President's Address', *Numismatic Chronicle*, Proceedings, 149 (1989), iii–xvi.

[14] 'The coinage of Arcadius', *Numismatic Chronicle*, 151 (1991), pp. 35–57; 'Solidi of Valentinian III: a preliminary classification and chronology', in H.-C. Noeske and H. Schubert (eds.), *Die Münze: Bild—Botschaft—Bedeutung. Festschrift für Maria R.-Alföldi* (Frankfurt am Main, 1991), pp. 271–82.

[15] 'Style and mint in the gold coinage of the western Roman empire, AD 455–61', in M. Price, A. Burnett, R. Bland (eds.), *Essays in Honour of Robert Carson and Kenneth Jenkins* (1993), pp. 267–75.

history of the period. 'Bear traps' are effortlessly passed by (which Eudocia or which Theodosius?), and many new systematic presentations are made of material which was previously inaccessible, such as much of the bronze coinage, where many new discoveries—mostly known to Kent alone—greatly revised the picture painted in *LRBC*. Of greater importance is the way he arranged the catalogue. Previous volumes of *RIC* had already abandoned the nineteenth-century arrangement by emperor in favour of arrangement by mint, and this would have been an obvious option for volume X. But this would not have worked so well for the later period, given the complex political history with many short-lived emperors and usurpers taking the stage in an empire that was, in any case, divided into two. So Kent divided the book between east and west and then by period, thus enabling the user to have a much clearer view of the development of the coinage and its relationship to events. The result is that, a collector keen on the coins of, say, Honorius would find them scattered throughout the volume (depending on who recognised him and made coins for him), and—typically for a Kent publication—the reader has to work much harder to follow what is going on, but the advantages of this approach are very considerable. As remarked by one reviewer, 'where the coins of the . . . fifth century had seemed impenetrable, now they have been laid out with lucidity'.[16]

RIC X had much longer introductory chapters than was usual in the series, and these do much to alleviate the paucity of written work on the coinage of the period. As well as a masterly summary of the monetary system and a lucid presentation of the designs and legends used on the coins, he presented an extensive discussion of over 150 pages of the development of the coinage by reign. This is one of the few accounts of the subject that gives a clear sense of the changes and indeed subtleties of what had previously seemed an inaccessible and confusing body of material. It represents some of Kent's best work.

Kent's experience and knowledge of the coinage of the post-Roman period led to his being asked to undertake the study and publication of the Merovingian coins from the purse in the Sutton Hoo Mound 1 ship-burial. The site had been excavated in 1939 but the war and the difficult period thereafter meant that it was only in the early 1960s that the preparations towards final publication, led by Rupert Bruce-Mitford, got fully under way. Although other numismatic scholars had given their views on the coins when they first came to light, significant advances had been

---

[16] T. V. Buttrey, *Journal of Roman Archaeology*, 9 (1996), 587–93.

made in Merovingian numismatic studies in the interval, particularly by French researchers such as Jean Lafaurie, and it was clear that a fresh start had to be made. Kent's approach was characteristic: an unusually perceptive application from first principles of traditional numismatic method combined with scientific investigation chosen for its potential in the specific context. He saw that a key to the numismatic chronology here lay in the fineness of the gold used for the coinage which related the many regally anonymous issues to the few coins that bore the names of historically datable persons. It had long been recognised in general terms that the gold content of the Merovingian coinage had declined during the seventh century but no coherent framework had ever been devised. Appreciating that results would be statistically viable only if a wide body of material could be tested, the cooperation of cabinets outside that of the British Museum (in particular the French national collection) was required, and it would be forthcoming only if the coins were not to be damaged in any way. He saw that the specific gravity method, although seriously flawed in dealing with other alloys, was the answer here where the coins could not be sampled and were essentially of gold-rich binary alloys. He had the ready cooperation of his colleagues in the Research Laboratory in the British Museum, particularly Andrew Oddy and Michael Hughes, who developed a refined SG technique for use with the Sutton Hoo material. Contacts made through his own helpfulness with others' projects, together with his well-known talent for persuasion, overcame considerable difficulties in arranging the wider programme. It should be emphasised that analysis alone would not have brought about the successful outcome, and did so only because it was allied to his masterly re-ordering of the complex numismatic evidence.[17] Whereas the Sutton Hoo coins had been dated to the third quarter of the seventh century Kent concluded that the latest coin to enter the Sutton Hoo purse was minted c.620–5.[18] He was always most insistent that his role was to provide the terminus for the coins, not to date the burial, but his work revolutionised the interpretation of Sutton Hoo Mound 1 and its historical context, opening up the possibility of its identification as the grave of

---

[17] Preliminary studies: 'Problems of chronology in the seventh century Merovingian coinage', *Cunobelin*, 13 (1967), 24–9; 'Analyses of Merovingian gold coins' (with W. A. Oddy, M. J. Hughes, R. F. Coleman, A. Wilson, and A. A. Gordus with contribution by R. L. S. Bruce-Mitford), in E. T. Hall and D. M. Metcalf (eds.), *Methods of Chemical and Metallurgical Investigation of Ancient Coinage*, Royal Numismatic Society Special Publication No. 8 (1972), pp. 69–109.

[18] 'The coins and the date of the burial' (with S. E. Rigold, W. A. Oddy and M. J. Hughes) in R. Bruce-Mitford, *The Sutton-Hoo ship-burial* (1975), pp. 578–678.

Redwald, the greatest of East Anglia's kings. His results also had important consequences for the chronology of the Merovingian and early Anglo-Saxon coins generally, and for dating archaeological contexts in which they are found. It has recently been suggested that the terminus for the Sutton Hoo coins may be a few years earlier still, but conclusive proof is lacking either way and the attribution to Redwald remains the most likely and authoritatively favoured.[19]

Although the medieval period had its own specialists in the museum throughout his career, the breadth of his interests and scholarship allowed him not only to contribute helpfully to discussions of its problems but to intervene decisively on occasion. Often a challenger of received wisdom, he could be equally resolute in its defence against unjustified revision, for example in decisively demolishing a reattribution of a gold Carolingian coin in the British Museum to Charles the Bald when it bore titles which he knew could belong only to Charlemagne.[20] Another of his early medieval papers discussed the derivation of Anglo-Saxon coin designs from Roman originals,[21] the choice of specific imperial prototypes informed, among other things, by his close familiarity with the issues most likely to have been available in Britain, considerations not always appreciated by those inspired to follow his lead in this area. An article on the surprising subject of farthings of Richard II[22] was prompted by an important reference to them in City of London records which had been overlooked by previous specialists.

The coinage and medals of the modern period from 1485 onwards was part of Kent's brief when he first joined the Department of Coins and Medals. He brought energy and fresh insights to several series within it which had been rather neglected, the English Civil War issues for example having become largely fossilised in the orthodoxies of a couple of generations earlier and the later eighteenth- and nineteenth-century issues hardly deemed, in some quarters, worthy of academic study at all. He produced a number of useful papers dealing with this period including an important one on Newark siege pieces,[23] but his output was dominated by

[19] W. A. Oddy and A. Stahl, 'The date of the Sutton Hoo coins', in R. Farrell and C. Neuman de Vegvar (eds.), *Sutton Hoo. Fifty years after* (American Early Medieval Studies, 2, 1992) pp. 129–47; M. Carver, *Sutton Hoo. Burial Ground of Kings?* (1998).

[20] 'Charles the Great or Charles the Bald?', *Numismatic Chronicle*, 7th ser. VIII (1968), 173–6.

[21] 'From Roman Britain to Saxon England', in R. H. M. Dolley (ed.), *Anglo-Saxon Coins. Essays presented to Sir Frank Stenton* (1961), pp. 1–22.

[22] 'An issue of farthings of Richard II', *British Numismatic Journal*, 57 (1987), 118.

[23] 'Newark siege money and Civil War hoards', in *Newark Siegeworks*, Royal Commission on Historical Monuments (1964); reprinted in *Cunobelin*, 15 (1969), 22–5.

the publication of treasure trove of the sixteenth to twentieth centuries (plentiful even before the advent of metal detectors). In the later milled series Kent broke new ground in investigating the phenomenon of the counterfeit coinages of the eighteenth century.[24] Issues from the territories of the British Empire were not forgotten and he threw new light on the Madras fanams of the seventeenth and eighteenth centuries.[25] It is a pity, though inevitable, that the increasing demands of his work on the Roman coinage soon crowded out further detailed research in this period but he maintained an interest in the later English and British series throughout his career. His early faith in the validity as evidence of an illustration in a contemporary merchant's book showing an unrecorded variant type of the rare George noble of Henry VIII was vindicated when one turned up seventeen years later and was acquired by him for the museum.[26] More recently he published two papers on the circulation of foreign coins in England,[27] and he also enjoyed returning to this more modern period of coinage during the preparation of his retirement study of the coinage and currency of London (see below).

Kent had considerable interest too in the later Byzantine coinage which was developed in a memorable series of advanced extra-mural lectures but he did not have the opportunity to work up more than a few topics for publication.[28] His expertise in this area is conspicuous in the incisive reviews of publications by other British and overseas scholars in the field.[29] Less widely known was his work for the Barber Institute in the University of Birmingham. His happy and fruitful association was initially prompted by the augmentation of its existing strong holding of Roman coins by the bequest of the scholar's Byzantine collection built up

[24] He did not publish this work in detail although an abstract of his May 1957 paper was published in R. N. P. Hawkins, ed. E. Baldwin, *A dictionary of makers of British metallic tickets, checks, medalets, tallies and counters 1788–1910* (1989), pp. 892–8.

[25] 'Madras fanams of the seventeenth and eighteenth centuries', *Numismatic Circular*, vol. 70, no. 6 (June, 1962), cols. 133–4.

[26] 'A lost variety of the George noble', in 'Five Tudor notes', *British Numismatic Journal*, 32 (1963), 162–3. 'A new type of George noble of Henry VIII', in A. Detsicas (ed.), *Collectanea Historica: Essays in Memory of Stuart Rigold*, Kent Archaeological Society (Maidstone, 1981), pp. 231–4.

[27] 'The Circulation of Portuguese coins in Great Britain', *Actas do III Congresso Nacional de Numismática, Sintra 1985* (Lisbon, 1985), pp. 389–440; 'Continental Coins in Medieval and Early Modern England', in M. Castro Hipólito, D. M. Metcalf, J. M. Peixoto Cabral, M. Crusafront i Sabater (eds.), *Homenagem a Mário Gomes Marques* (Sintra, 2000), pp. 361–76.

[28] 'The Italian silver coinage of Justinian I and his successors', in S. Scheers (ed.), *Studia Paulo Naster oblata* I (Louvain, 1982), pp. 275–86.

[29] See, for example, his review of W. Hahn, *Die Ostprägung des römischen Reiches im 5. Jahrhundert (408–491)*, *Numismatic Chronicle*, 150 (1990), 284–8.

by Philip Whitting which Kent was anxious to see properly curated and used. As honorary adviser, his diplomatic skills were invaluable in helping the cabinet through a number of difficulties as was his expert advice and support in securing conservationally sound storage for the coins and advancing a programme of cataloguing. He also produced a short book-let[30] on its Byzantine collection, but his main contribution lay in the university lectures and seminars on a range of numismatic topics which he gave weekly during one term each session for many years, continuing into retirement and only giving up when the pre-dawn starts and long journeys became too much for his failing health. All this work he did without payment except for expenses which he kept to a minimum by purchasing a single on the first outward journey and returns from Birmingham thereafter as fares were cheaper that way round.

He spent much time identifying large numbers of coins from excavations, regularly deciphering apparently blank discs which had defeated others. Becoming concerned at unhelpful under- and over-conservation in some quarters, he welcomed the opportunity to participate in a conference which discussed the problem followed by a publication which established guide-lines for future good practice.[31] He was also keen to ensure that site-finds and coins should be properly evaluated and wrote a classic paper on their interpretation.[32] In recognising modern counterfeits he was in a class of his own. He was among the first to condemn the Beirut forgeries of late Roman and Byzantine gold coins and gave evidence in the famous Dennington forgeries case at the Old Bailey in 1969. His judgement on questions of authenticity was accepted by academic colleagues, collectors, and dealers worldwide.

He was a superb lecturer to audiences of every type. He gave a great deal, perhaps even too much, of his own time running evening classes in his earlier days and, throughout his career, lecturing to both national and local numismatic and archaeological societies as well as at several universities. He regarded these activities as part of his duty to his subject and profession, believing that they made an important contribution to the wider understanding of coinage as historical evidence, and in demonstrating the approachability of the British Museum's curators and the

---

[30] *A Selection of Byzantine Coins in the Barber Institute of Fine Arts, Birmingham* (Birmingham, 1985).

[31] 'The numismatist and the conservator—conflict, co-operation and education', in P. J. Casey and J. M. Cronyn (eds.), *Numismatics and Conservation. University of Durham, 1978* (Durham, 1980), pp. 10–14.

[32] See above, n. 3.

accessibility of its collections to all *bona fide* enquirers. As Keeper he encouraged his junior colleagues to maintain these traditions.

Kent was appointed to the British Museum as an Assistant Keeper in the Department of Coins and Medals on demobilisation in 1953. The old Coin Room was still in ruins after being hit by an enemy incendiary bomb in 1942 and the collection, returned from its wartime cave in South Wales, was inconveniently housed in the East Residence. He was involved in its move back to the restored department in 1959. Under the keeper, the senior curatorial staff then numbered only four so that being 'at the receipt of custom' (dealing with all the general public enquiries in person and by letter for a week) occupied a considerable proportion of his time. He was promoted to Deputy Keeper in 1974.

In 1977 Kent was responsible for the first coin gallery in the museum since the war, '2000 years of British Coins' and its accompanying booklet.[33] Mounted in cases originally designed for Near Eastern antiquities and intended to be only temporary, no one regretted more than he that it remained in place ten years later with still no prospect of money being available for a replacement. It was during this time that he began his campaign to persuade other departments that coins should be part of their cultural and historical displays. With their cooperation, this has become an established feature of the museum's antiquities galleries alongside the permanent HSBC Money Gallery opened, two keepers later, in 1997.

Kent became Keeper of Coins and Medals in 1983, holding the post until his retirement in 1990. He was a strong keeper, but made himself constantly available to his staff, and was generous in his academic support. Shortly after he took over, the entire collection and library again moved, this time down into the basement while the department's accommodation was being expanded, and then back to its refurbished premises. Always a good delegator, he left the organisation to his capable deputy, and he was more directly responsible for the planning of the new accommodation, including enhanced security measures and better facilities for staff and student visitors alike. It was during his keepership that in 1986 London was host to the International Numismatic Congress with 600 world-wide delegates and this was organised within the department. To coincide with this event the department mounted a major exhibition entitled 'Money' which was accompanied by an innovative thematic catalogue.[34] Kent also encouraged departmental participation in an

[33] *Two Thousand Years of British Coins and Medals* (1978).
[34] J. Cribb (ed.), *Money. From cowrie shells to credit cards* (1986).

increasing number of large-scale museum exhibitions, loans to other institutions and the expansion of the department's role in the museum's education programme.

He was an active member of many societies both local and national serving on their councils and holding their highest offices. Among the presidencies he held were those of the Royal Numismatic Society 1984–90, the British Association of Numismatic Societies 1974–8, and he served on the International Numismatic Commission 1986–91, being elected an honorary member in 1991. He was elected a Fellow of the Society of Antiquaries in 1961 and of the British Academy in 1986. Recognition of his achievement was marked by the world's leading awards for numismatic studies including the medals of the Royal Numismatic Society in 1990, the Huntington medal of the American Numismatic Society in 1994, and the British Academy's Derek Allen Prize in 1996.

If the publication of *RIC* X in 1994, shortly after his retirement, was the climax of his publications on Roman numismatics, he nevertheless pursued several directions of research during his retirement. One was writing up some of the odder aspects of numismatics which had fascinated him for many years such as the inscriptions on coins. He was always particularly interested in mistakes; his favourite was a coin of Vespasian inscribed *Iudaea navalis* and apparently (but not really) referring to a naval battle in Vespasian's war to crush the Jewish rebellion of AD 66–70, perhaps that on the lake of Gennesareth which is mentioned by Josephus.[35] He had a long-standing interest in the way Latin was used on coins and what coins could tell us about late Latin usage. An early article solved a puzzle of coins of the emperor Gallienus with the apparently oddly gendered inscription *Gallienae Augustae*. Later on, he presented a more general discussion of the linguistic forms used on coins and the way they reflected different Latin usages.[36]

The second project on which he embarked was the preparation of a new British Museum catalogue of 'sub-Roman' coins. This was partly

---

[35] As he pointed out *Iudaea Navalis* is a conflation by a die engraver of two separate coin inscriptions: *Iudaea capta* and *Victoria navalis*. See his article 'Getting it wrong; some errors of Roman die-cutting and their significance', in *Festschrift für Katalin Bíró-Sey und István Gedai zum 65. Geburtstag*, eds. K. Bertók and M. Torbágyi (Budapest, 2000), pp. 209–20. He was alternately enraged and amused by the fact that he had not been sent proofs of this article and it contained numerous printer's errors!

[36] For the former, see his 'Gallienae Augustae', *Numismatic Chronicle*, 7th ser. XIII (1973), 64–8, where he showed it was a hyper-corrected form of the vocative; for his more general treatment, see 'Coin inscriptions and language', *Bulletin of the London Institute of Archaeology*, 29 (1992), 9–18.

intended to replace Wroth's flawed *Catalogue of the coins of the Vandals, Ostrogoths and Lombards, and of the empires of Thessalonica, Nicaea and Trebizond* (1911), but also to give it a greater focus by concentrating on the earlier period down to the eighth century and increasing the coverage to include missing groups like the Visigoths, Suevi, and Merovingians. This is an area of coinage which is very difficult to deal with but which he knew well, and much better than anyone else. Unfortunately, however, although he had spent much time rearranging the trays of the relevant coins in the BM, he had not committed anything to writing, and his death led to a permanent loss to our understanding of this difficult area of monetary history.

His attention became increasingly focused on the preparation of his book *Coinage and Currency in London* based on, but greatly expanded from, his presidential addresses to the London and Middlesex Archaeological Society. This brought into play many of his wide-ranging lifetime interests and involved much original research in and beyond the city archives. It has resulted in a book which is uniquely informative on subjects not to be found in standard histories of the coinage. His typescript had gone through several drafts and was already complete when he died on 22 October 2000. It is being edited by his daughter and will be published shortly.

His outside interests were many: cricket, medieval architecture and music, the history of monumental brasses, early medieval music, archaeology, railways (both real and model), Restoration poetry and drama, and the songs of the Victorian and Edwardian music hall. His ability to talk long and learnedly—and with a relish for the ironic use of the cliché—on any of these topics was well known among his wide circle of friends and acquaintances; his colleagues were as well informed on the impact of the railways on the development of London in the nineteenth century as they were on the finer points of the mint attributions of the bronze coinage of Zeno. Those same colleagues presented him with a portrait medal (by Avril Vaughan) to mark his retirement. The reverse by his own choice bears the inscription *nil sine labore* which he enjoyed mistranslating as 'no sign of work'. In the centre is a rather enigmatic pyramid, a motif which he always declined to explain saying that its meaning should be obvious. After retirement he remained, in his words, 'a regular if unobtrusive' visitor to the department to which he had given so many years.

John Kent was a scholar of international standing who made a major contribution to the advancement of numismatic and historical knowledge.

His learning extended far beyond his own specialisms and he was generous with his time and ideas. His service to the British Museum, the academic community and the public was distinguished. He had an irrepressible enthusiasm for all he did and many occasions were enlivened by his infectious good spirits. He was devoted to his wife Pat (née Bunford) whom he married in 1961, their son and daughter and four grandchildren.

ANDREW BURNETT
The British Museum
MARION ARCHIBALD
The British Museum

STEPHAN KÖRNER

Stephan Körner
1913–2000

STEPHAN KÖRNER was one of the leading late twentieth-century British philosophers. His work ranged widely, from the philosophy of science and mathematics to that of ethics, law, and politics. In *Conceptual Thinking* (Cambridge, 1955) he drew a fundamental distinction between exact and inexact concepts. In his textbook *The Philosophy of Mathematics* (1960; New York, 1986) he showed how the exact concepts of pure mathematics arise from the idealisation of inexact concepts. The distinction between the logics of exact and inexact concepts again plays an important part in his book on the philosophy of science, *Experience and Theory* (London and New York, 1966). In later works, for example *Experience and Conduct* (1976) he extended his investigations of how we negotiate between idealisations and empirical practice to other fields of philosophy, such as ethics and law. Together with the physicist M. H. L. Pryce he edited an influential volume *Observation and Interpretation* (1957), the record of a conference he organised at Bristol which brought together many of the leading physicists and philosophers of science at that time. From 1972–4 he organised each year a Bristol Conference on Critical Philosophy which attracted leading philosophers in the chosen fields—*Practical Reason* (Oxford, 1974), *Explanation* (Oxford, 1975), *Philosophy of Logic* (Oxford, 1976). In addition to his scholarly work he did significant expository work. His Penguin book *Kant* (1955) played a major part in making that notoriously difficult philosopher accessible to students, and *What is Philosophy?* (1969), also for Penguin, brought philosophy to a wider audience. He played a leading role in the post-war development of the University of

Proceedings of the British Academy, **115**, 277–293. © The British Academy 2002.

Bristol and its Philosophy Department where he held the Chair from 1952 to 1979. He also held a chair of Philosophy at Yale University from 1970 to 1984 and visiting professorships at several other universities in the USA. After he retired from the University of Bristol he held a Chair of Philosophy at the University of Graz, Austria.

Stephan was born in Ostrava, Czechoslovakia on 26 September 1913 the only son of Emil Körner and Erna Maier. From an early age he wanted to become a philosopher, but his father, a devoted secondary school teacher, whom he greatly admired, advised him to read law in order to earn a living. Stephan accepted this advice but it proved to be doubly wrong—events forced him to abandon his legal career and he made a good living as a philosopher. He went to school at the classical gymnasium in Ostrava from 1923 to 1931. He had a happy childhood, growing up at ease in two languages, Czech and German, and at home in two cultures. He later added Russian, French, Italian, and English to the languages with which he was familiar and even learned Hebrew to read the writings of Spinoza. (Of course this was biblical Hebrew and he created considerable amusement in Israel by addressing people in the language of the prophets.) This gave him a cosmopolitan approach to scholarship, which enabled him to transcend the restrictions imposed upon concepts developed against a mono-cultural background. Although he came from the German speaking part of Czechoslovakia and his schooling had been in German he chose deliberately to go to a Czech speaking university, the Charles University in Prague. In accordance with his wishes his substantial personal library went to Charles University after his death. He studied there from 1931 to 1935, graduating as a doctor of law and political science. He entered a legal practice and was delighted to win his first case, not least because the senior partner thought it was hopeless. In 1936 when he was called up for military service another piece of paternal advice proved more useful. His father said that he would be ordered to mount a horse and if he stayed on he would be accepted into the cavalry, if he fell off he would be relegated to the infantry. Some time later Stephan was able to repay his father. Leading his mounted troop through the streets he astonished his men by ordering them to give a royal salute to two passing pedestrians, his parents. He acquired such equestrian skill that he claimed to be able to ride one horse over a jump while leading three other horses beside him.

After the Nazi invasion of Czechoslovakia in 1939 Stephan fled the country, having been warned by one of his father's former students, now an SS officer, that he was to be arrested the following day. Unfortunately his parents chose to remain in Czechoslovakia and both perished in concentration camps. Stephan arrived in England thanks to the sponsorship of an Englishwoman who had never met him but to whom he was eternally grateful. He joined the Czechoslovak division of the British Army but, because there was a lengthy lull in the fighting in Western Europe he was given extended leave which enabled him, aided by a small grant, to study at Cambridge. He abandoned law and pursued his dream of studying philosophy. He was amazed, but was profoundly grateful to the university, and particularly to Professor Richard Braithwaite, for admitting him to study for a doctorate in a subject in which he had no formal qualifications. He always remembered the kindnesses great and small that were shown to him as an impoverished foreigner ('Körner, we have just been given some continental sausage. Could you show us how it should be dealt with?').

While he was at Cambridge he met his wife, Edith Laner, at a social gathering of Czech émigrés in London. Edith, known as Diti to friends and family, was born in Czechoslovakia, daughter of a prosperous corn miller. She came to England in 1939 as a schoolgirl, but her parents, like Stephan's stayed in Czechoslovakia and died in concentration camps. She used her command of English, Czech, German, French, and Italian to monitor foreign broadcasts for a news agency. Company policy forbade the employment of women but her services were so valuable that her sex was concealed from upper management until her marriage and subsequent pregnancy made this impossible. She also supplemented her income by teaching English to Czech refugees. She then in two years obtained an honours degree in economics at the London School of Economics. She claimed to have never attended a lecture, because she was too busy teaching to support herself; she passed all her examinations just by studying the reading list. Stephan and Diti were married in 1944 when Stephan was back on leave but were separated almost immediately afterwards when he was recalled to take part in the campaign after the D-Day landings. It was a matter of intense personal pride that, when faced by so great a test, he proved that he had the courage and ability to play his part as an infantry sergeant in some of the bitter fighting which led to the defeat of the enemies who had devoured his country. His experience of English ways was unexpectedly useful when he returned to the army. A Czech regiment was on the verge of mutiny after having been given some 'bitter jam' and he was called in to explain that the English regarded the marmalade as a special treat. He and Diti attempted to familiarise themselves with the culture of their new homeland by reading through the whole of English literature. Whilst he was in hospital behind the lines the doctor saw that Stephan was reading Dickens. 'We must give you an extra 24 hours here to let you finish.' During that 24 hours the Czech army was involved in a particularly ill-planned and bloody attack in which several of his friends were killed. On the anniversary of that day he would always sit somewhere by himself and remember his comrades. Like many of his generation he and Diti considered every day of their lives as the result of an unexpected reprieve.

When he was demobilised in 1946 Stephan briefly took a lowly job at Cardiff University, helping students with their German. Later in that year he was appointed to an Assistant Lectureship in Philosophy at the University of Bristol. At the interview the vice-chancellor anticipated one possible objection and ended the interview by asking 'Finally, Dr Körner, where did you learn such excellent English?' He joined a university with little more than a thousand students, and a department of three people. That was when I first met him; I was appointed Assistant Lecturer in Mathematics at the same time. We were at opposite ends of the age range; I was 20 he was 33, but his growing reputation and ability resulted in rapid promotion, and only six years later, he succeeded Guy Field as professor and head of department. By then the university had doubled in size, but the philosophy department still had only four members of staff. When he retired in 1979 he had built it up to a productive department of eleven. He was an efficient head of department who believed in delegating as far as possible and leaving his staff free to get on with their own work without interference. He was very supportive of our efforts in the mathematics department to build up a group of mathematical logicians. He believed that the study of philosophy was particularly relevant to the development of other disciplines, and set up several joint degrees. In view of his interest in logic and the philosophy of mathematics it was natural that a degree in Philosophy and Mathematics was the first of these. He had no interest in university politics for its own sake, but his intellectual eminence and transparent honesty resulted in his serving as Dean of Arts, 1965–7, and Pro-Vice Chancellor, 1968–71. His negotiating skills were invaluable during the difficult days of student sit-ins of the late 1960s and early 1970s. At one point he was approached by a group of students from his own department who presented their demands. 'First we want more continental philosophy.' 'That should be easy, already half the staff can't speak English.' His distinguished service to the university was recognised in 1986 by his election as an Honorary Fellow of the University, one of the university's most important honours.

He was an enthusiastic backer of adult education. In his early years in Bristol as an Assistant Lecturer he found the fees a useful addition to his income; he claimed to have used them to buy a stove, which he named the Hopkins stove after the tutor in the Department of Extra Mural Studies who arranged his lecture courses. But he continued to attract good audiences at his extramural lectures until after his retirement, and he gave the department strong support through his membership of Senate and other university committees. He was delighted by Tom Stoppard's portrait of a philosopher in *Jumpers* and he and the playwright enjoyed a friendship cemented by a mutual love of the intellectual life of old Vienna.

He was in great demand as a speaker at conferences and as an invited lecturer at numerous universities. He held visiting professorships at Brown (fall 1957), Yale (fall 1960), Texas (fall 1964), and Indiana (fall 1967). He was elected to the British Academy in 1967 and in that year gave their Dawes Hicks lecture on 'Kant's Conception of Freedom'. In 1971 he gave the Eddington Memorial lecture in Cambridge on 'Abstraction in Science and Morals'. From 1970 to 1984 he held a regular professorship at Yale as well as Bristol, and thereafter returned for some weeks each year to check the progress of the doctoral students whose dissertations he was directing. He had many students in his seminars there and they were especially enthusiastic about his range of expertise—from logic and mathematics to political theory and categorial frameworks—as well as his capacity for clarity and concern for students. This post at Yale was made even more attractive by the presence there of the eminent mathematical logician Abraham Robinson. Stephan and Abraham had been refugee students together in Cambridge and now set up a seminar on the philosophy of mathematics. Although many people attended the seminar it was clear that the two organisers would have been just as happy in each other's company had no one else turned up. Stephan also had a long association with the Institut für Philosophie of the Karl-Franzens University in Graz, Austria. He visited there in the summer term of 1980, was appointed an Honorary Professor in 1982 and from then until 1987 visited every summer term, teaching a broad range of lecture courses and seminars and participating in a joint discussion group with the department of philosophy of law. Stephan's lectures had an additional attraction for native German speakers since he spoke beautiful 'pre-war academic German' with clauses, sub-clauses, and verbs all in exactly the right place. In 1984 the University of Graz awarded him an Honorary Doctorate of Philosophy, in 1981 the University of Belfast awarded him the Honorary Degree of Doctor of Literature, and in 1991 his old college in Cambridge, Trinity Hall, made him an Honorary Fellow. This honorary fellowship was a delight to Stephan, not only because of the kindness of the College in taking him as a student when he was an unknown refugee, but because his son Tom was a fellow in mathematics there. He was president of the British Society for the Philosophy of Science, 1965–6, of the Aristotelian Society, 1966, of the International Union for the history and Philosophy of Science, 1968–70 and of its division for Logic, Methodology, and Philosophy of Science, 1968–72 and 1983 when he presided over its Seventh International Congress in Salzburg, and of the Mind Association 1973. He was the editor of *Ratio*, 1961–80, and of the philosophy section of Hutchinson's University Library since 1969, a member of the editorial board of *The British Journal for the Philosophy of Science*, *Analysis*, and *Metaphilosophy*, and a member of the council of the Royal Institute for Philosophy.

Cambridge philosophy, when he went there in 1939 as a postgraduate student, was influenced by Wittgenstein, to such an extent, he said,[1] that

> C. D. Broad eventually gave up attending meetings of the Cambridge Philosophical Society. For whatever subject was being treated, the discussion was completely dominated by Wittgenstein. The guest speakers from Oxford and other universities often brought only apparently new ideas to Cambridge— mostly they were ideas which in the neighbourhood of the Vienna Circle were so well known that they seemed hardly worth mentioning. Even A. J. Ayer's book *Language, Truth and Logic*, which many English teachers and students of philosophy saw as a revolutionary new approach, was in fact only a popularisation of Austrian Logical Positivism. I sometimes ask myself why—apart from the kindness of my supervisor R. B. Braithwaite—I was accepted as a research student despite my low philosophical qualifications. The answer to this question seems to be that at that time my philosophical knowledge had at least the merit of being almost completely derived from the writings of the Vienna Circle; and so my English sounded Austrian to the English . . .

He certainly did not accept the Wittgensteinian thesis that there are no genuine philosophical problems, only puzzles:

> Wittgenstein taught me to see that one of the tasks of philosophy is to describe modes of thought or, as he calls them, language games, and that this description is an empirical undertaking or, in his words, belongs to natural history. While taking into consideration the importance of this anthropological branch of philosophy one must not—and I do not—follow Wittgenstein also in the assertion that this is the only legitimate task of philosophy. When Wittgenstein for example condemns speculative metaphysics as 'language running idle', he forgets that many metaphysical theories—such as the atomistic theory of

---

[1] In his acceptance speech for his Honorary Doctorate at Graz 1984.

Democritus—which began as a speculation, were later incorporated into scientific theories.

He was much more influenced by his supervisor, R. B. Braithwaite; and his Ph.D. thesis *Propositions asserting relations of entailment* was an exercise in symbolic logic extending C. I. Lewis's work on Strict Implication. It was as much mathematics as philosophy with proofs of formal theorems. Further work on entailment followed and then in 1951 he published in *Mind* his first article 'Ostensive Predicates', on the importance of the distinction between exact and inexact concepts:

> PHILOSOPHERS frequently fail to distinguish between the precise description of imprecise relationships and the replacement of imprecise relationships by more precise ones. A failure to make this distinction seems to strengthen two opposite mistakes in philosophical method. These are the misdirection of inexact relationships as if they were exact and the erroneous belief that imprecise relationships require imprecise descriptions. The purpose of this article, which is mainly to describe imprecise relationships in a precise manner, is to consider the logic of ostensive predicates for its own sake and to show its relevance to some wider philosophical questions.

Quite a lot of his subsequent work is devoted to this same purpose, showing the relevance of the logic of inexact predicates or concepts to the philosophies of mathematics, of science, of ethics, and law. Ostensive concepts are those like 'table' ('is a table' is the corresponding predicate) which are defined or determined by giving examples of tables and non-tables. However many examples are given there will always be borderline cases, e.g. a small stool. Most of the concepts of ordinary experience (like 'red' or 'tree') and law (like 'conspiracy' or 'fraud') are inexact, have borderline cases, unlike the concepts of mathematics, such as 'even integer'. So inexact predicates cannot be dealt with using classical logic with its two truth-values 'true' and 'false' but need at least a third truth-value 'neutral'. Indeed if the gradation is continuous a fuzzy logic using all real values between 0 (false) and 1 (true) would appear to be a more precise tool. This would now be a fashionable way to proceed but it is only a theoretical possibility; actually assigning such truth-values would be unfeasible. Even for concepts such as 'wealthy' or 'near' which could in some way be numerically measured, the actual way truth values might be derived from these measures is fairly arbitrary. For most concepts the best you could do would be to rely on a voting system, giving the proposition 'This small stool is a table' a truth value equal to the proportion of people in some chosen group who agreed that it was true. Stephan did not follow that unrewarding route in search of greater precision[2] but chose to stay with the simpler classification into three truth-values: true, false, and neutral. The truth of compound propositions was governed by two principles. Firstly, 'p and q' is false if one or more of p, q is false, and 'p or q' is true if one or more of p, q is true. Secondly, once a compound proposition has been evaluated as true or false, this value is unchanged when any neutral component is sharpened to true or false. That is sufficient to determine the truth tables for 'and' and 'or'. He did not investigate the mathematical properties of this three valued logic any further than he needed in order to discuss the relevance of inexact concepts to philosophical problems but J. P. Cleave did much work on the logic of inexact concepts.[3] In 1955 in *Conceptual Thinking* Stephan studied the impact of this inexactness of concepts on a very wide range of problems. As examples of 'conceptual thinking' he gives:

> The person who expounds a mathematical proof and equally the person who follows the exposition is thinking conceptually. So is the person who is engaged in any kind of classification; as also the judge who applies a legal statute to a state of affairs. Any child who uses a colour-word correctly proves himself thereby a conceptual thinker.

Later he suggests a minimal definition of 'conceptual thinker' as 'accepter of ostensive concepts'. Of course they will also accept some non-ostensive concepts, e.g. mathematical ones such as integer or ellipse, and philosophical ones such as proposition, concept, judgement. Stephan offers an account of how we may move from ostensive concepts to non-ostensive ones and back again to the world of experience. He contrasts the sharpening of ostensive concepts by adding new rules with the replacement of ostensive concepts by non-ostensive ones. If all the exemplifications of 'raven' qualify as 'black' by the existing rules then we can without inconsistency add a new rule that nothing is to be called a 'not-black raven'. But if the exemplifying sets of 'visual circle' and 'visual ellipse' overlap then we cannot consistently add a new rule to the effect that nothing is to be called both a 'visual circle' and a 'visual ellipse'. If we want to move towards the exact non-overlapping concepts of 'geometrical circle' and 'geometrical ellipse' we must at some stage replace an ostensive concept

---

[2] But with the mathematician Ali Fröhlich he started work on a book *A Mathematical Theory of Ostensive Predicates* using topological methods. That seemed to be a fruitful and more appropriate approach than fuzzy logic, but the book never appeared and the project seems to have been abandoned.

[3] See Cleave 'Logic and Inexactness' in Jan T. J. Srzednicki (ed.), *Stephan Körner—Philosophical Analysis and Reconstruction* (Dordrecht, 1987), pp. 137–59.

by a non-ostensive one. For Stephan the exact concepts of pure mathematics arise from the idealisation of those inexact concepts that can be applied to experience. His 1960 textbook on the *Philosophy of Mathematics* focuses on the metaphysical question how applied mathematics is possible:

> To sum up our discussion of applied mathematics: the 'application' to perception of pure mathematics, which is logically distinct from perception, consists in a more or less strictly regulated activity involving (i) the replacement of empirical concepts and propositions by mathematical, (ii) the deduction of consequences from the mathematical premises so provided and (iii) the replacement of some of the deduced mathematical propositions by empirical. One might add (iv) the experimental confirmation of the last-mentioned propositions—which, however is the task of the experimental scientists rather than the theoretical.

Stephan's book *Kant* (1955) was one of the first post-war books to attempt to make the ideas of that notoriously difficult philosopher accessible to English-speaking students. In his foreword A. J. Ayer wrote:

> What he has achieved is to give, in a remarkably small compass, a general conspectus of Kant's thought and to relate it to some issues in contemporary philosophy.

Indeed Stephan himself suggested it might also serve as a general introduction to philosophy. He saw the centre of Kant's philosophy to be his attempt to derive the possibility of intelligible experience from built-in features of our conceptual system. This view (which in effect sees the canonical introduction of Kant to be Kant's own *Prolegomena*) is not perhaps the only possible interpretation of Kant or of the whole of Kant. Stephan's central objection to Kant's metaphysics was that while Kant was correct in believing that we require an overriding conceptual framework in order to make sense of our experience, his mistake was to suppose that we may single out just one such framework from a number of competing possibilities. Much of Stephan's later work was devoted to the investigation of the structure and function of the possible variety of such frameworks. This started in 1966 in the first chapter of his book on the philosophy of science *Experience and Theory,* and was developed in more detail in 1969 in chapters 11–13 of *What is Philosophy* where he introduced the term *categorial framework*. In the 1970 monograph *Categorial Frameworks* he expounds the notion:

> The steps leading to the definition of a categorial framework are first, a discussion of the classification of all entities with special emphasis on the difference between arbitrary classes and natural kinds; second, a preliminary examination of the relations holding, on the one hand, between the 'categories' or maximal kinds of a natural classification and, on the other hand between the maximal

kinds and their subordinate genera; third, a general characterization of the attributes the joint possession of which is a necessary and sufficient condition of an entity's being a member of the maximal kind, and of the attributes the joint possession of which is a necessary and sufficient condition of an entity's being a distinct, individual member of a maximal kind; fourth, a discussion of the logical assumptions involved in the categorization of all entities into maximal kinds and of the constitution and individuation of their members.

Kant's 'Transcendental Deduction of the Categories' can be regarded as a 'proof' that a particular categorial framework involving twelve Categories is necessarily employed in making objective empirical judgements. In his article 'The Impossibility of Transcendental Deductions'[4] Stephan generalises this notion of transcendental deduction to include any 'logically sound demonstration of the reasons why a particular categorial schema is not only in fact, but also necessarily employed, in differentiating a region of experience', and shows that no such transcendental deduction can be successful. He felt the tendency to attempt such demonstrations was still deplorably widespread, and examined some recent versions in 'Transcendental Tendencies in Recent Philosophy'.[5] Although he felt that time had shown Kant to be wrong on this issue, he considered himself part of the Kantian tradition. Other philosophers whose point of view he found particularly sympathetic included Leibniz and Cusanus but he read philosophers of many different traditions and schools with undisguised pleasure.

The Colston Research Society Symposium *Observation and Interpretation* which Stephan organised in Bristol in 1957 was an important meeting which brought leading philosophers and physicists together to discuss the philosophy of physics. Most of the discussion was about the philosophy of quantum mechanics, which was at that time in an active state of development, particularly in Bristol. In 1955 the young polymath Paul Feyerabend had, on the strength of recommendations from Karl Popper and Erwin Schrödinger, been appointed to a lectureship in Stephan's department and was working on the philosophy of quantum mechanics. David Bohm was working on hidden variable theories of quantum mechanics in the physics department where the Nobel Prize winner Cecil Powell had built up a world famous school of nuclear physics.

Stephan's own contributions to the philosophy of science started in 1953 with 'On Laws of Nature' (*Mind*, 62, 216–29) and continued with

---

[4] *Monist*, 51 (1967), 317–31.
[5] *Journal of Philosophy*, 63 (1966), 551–61.

many more articles and the 1966 book *Experience and Theory*. As noted above that starts with the observation that there are many different ways of differentiating the world of empirical experience or, as he puts it, many different categorial frameworks. For example one might use categories of movable things and immovable spatial regions, alternatively of spatial regions with certain qualities such as distributions of densities, gravitational or electromagnetic fields. He goes on to argue that all empirical propositions are inexact by virtue of involving ostensive concepts, and hence to deny the common view that the predictions of scientific theories are empirical propositions:[6]

> It is usual to picture a hypothetico-deductive system as a hierarchy with the logico-mathematical and substantive postulates at the top, and at least some empirical propositions at the bottom. The predicates of the system are similarly either formal or substantive—the substantive predicates being again either empirical or non-empirical. In other words a hypothetico-deductive system which unifies a field of experience contains, on the orthodox view, three kinds of propositions and concepts, namely formal, empirical and theoretical ones.
>
> The hierarchy is, according to received opinion, directly linked to experience (to the empirical world of observation and experiment) for the simple reason that at least some of the propositions and concepts at the basis are assumed to be empirical.
>
> . . . Two main propositions are defended: Either (i) theoretical propositions and concepts are held to be reducible to logical functions of empirical ones; or (ii) theoretical propositions and concepts are regarded as not reducible to logical functions of empirical ones, but as merely auxiliary notions without empirical meaning.
>
> . . . It should, I think be clear by now that I reject both these doctrines in favour of the view that all concepts and propositions which occur in scientific theories are theoretical, since the (unmodified) two-valued logic, in which scientific theories are embedded, admits no inexact or internally inexact predicates. This rejection, however, must be qualified in two respects and so protected against any charge of pedantry. Firstly for dealing with most, if not all, scientific and with many logico-philosophical problems it is not necessary to distinguish between, say, an inexact resemblance predicate and its exact theoretical counterpart. An inquiry which is concerned with scientific and extra-scientific thinking can safely ignore this distinction, once it is acknowledged. Moreover scientific inquiry is unlikely to suffer by ignoring it altogether.

Thus a scientific theory can make predictions about mathematically idealised rigid bodies, but not about the rigid objects we encounter, though for most practical purposes we can assume they apply to these.

---

[6] *Explanation and Theory*, pp. 88–9.

Experience and Conduct (1979) is Stephan's account of practical think-ing, how we make or should make decisions about courses of action involving concepts such as morality, justice, welfare, or prudence. This is a very searching investigation into the logical relations between preferences, attitudes, and beliefs about such courses of action and between them and principles of morality, legality, and prudence. It is distinguished by the depth of the analysis. He sees one source of the conflict between practical attitudes, which corresponds to logical inconsistency between beliefs, to be the way in which practical attitudes may themselves become objects of other practical attitudes. So he stratifies a person's attitudes into levels, attitudes of the $(n+1)$th level being attitudes towards nth level attitudes. For example a person might have a second level anti-attitude towards his first level pro-attitude to smoking. This could be a practical attitude, i.e. one that he is capable of implementing, for someone who is undergoing aversion therapy against smoking. But it would by his own standards be irrational. This stratification gives rise to a very complex structure with many different ways in which attitudes may conflict with each other; Stephan distinguishes opposition, discordance, incongruence. He argues that stratification affects and vitiates accounts of combining individual preferences into social welfare. 'Thus it is simply a gross error to regard the principle of the maximisation of first level preferences as the supreme prin-ciple of rational conduct.' For example he rejects Arrow's famous theorem on the impossibility of combining individual preferences into a social ordering satisfying certain conditions which seem to be intuitively obvious, on the grounds that one of the conditions 'is immoral or unclear'. That condition is the Pareto principle to the effect that if the alternative x is preferred to y by every individual then the social ordering must rank x above y. It would be immoral if applied only to the first level preferences of a society where all members of the society had a first level preference for smoking which conflicted with their higher level moral principles. If it attempted to take account of both first and higher level preferences of the individuals it would be unclear whether the first level preference shared by all individuals or the higher level moral preference should become the social preference. [Though one could apply it separately to both and come to the conclusion that the society, like all its members, had an irrational conflict between its first and second level preferences.]

He sees a parallel between the way a scientific theory replaces inexact empirical concepts by exact idealizations in such a way that treating the empirical concepts as if they were the idealized ones is justifiable in certain contexts, and what he calls 'practical idealization'. That is a way of making greater harmony between one's morality and one's conduct by the imaginative replacement of one's actual by an ideal way of life that can to some extent be approximated by one's conduct. The influence of his early training as a lawyer is evident in much of his philosophy but it makes his discussion of the way legal and public moral institutions modify each other and the extent to which it is reasonable break the law to express moral disapproval of the social order which it protects, particularly informative.

Stephan wrote one or two articles on the philosophy of religion from his humanist viewpoint. In 'On Making Room for Faith'[7] he discusses the problem of the compatibility of science with morality and religion. He ends up with the view that belief in free will is neither supported nor contradicted by science, since the applicability of science to experience is limited to contexts in which decisions play no part. However:

> Although belief in science is compatible with the belief in moral responsibility and in God, as the creator of the world, it is not compatible with the belief in miracles. For this belief implies that there are no laws of nature in the strict sense, but only alleged laws of nature the full formulation of which requires the additional clause: 'Provided that no miracle happens'. The religious person, of course, has no qualms about adding this clause. For to be religious is to hold, among other things, that whatever is incompatible with one's religious beliefs, is false.
>
> To me, if I may conclude with a personal remark, the main value of any religion consists in its moral teaching. If God exists, and has the perfections which are ascribed to him, then he must be much more concerned with man's fulfilling his moral duties and following worthy ideals, than with his religious belief, disbelief or agnosticism.

However in order to reach these conclusions Stephan felt the need to explain the notion of exact and inexact concepts and their role in scientific theories. This obviously bewildered the editor:

> The foregoing paper demonstrates some of the difficulties to be encountered when we ask for a dialogue between philosophy and theology to be established as part of the curriculum of a modern British university.

Stephan's last book, *Metaphysics: its Structure and Function* 1984, is, apart from a short chapter on aesthetic attitudes ('the sketch of a book which is unlikely to be written'), a wide ranging survey of his latest views on metaphysics as it relates to ethics, politics, mathematics, science and even, with gently sceptical sensitivity, mystical religion. He adopts the traditional terminology that distinguishes between 'immanent' and 'transcendental' metaphysics:[8]

---

[7] J. Coulson (ed.), *Theology and the University* (1964), chap. 6, pp. 236–47.
[8] *Metaphysics: its Structure and Function*, pp. 47–8.

> The term 'immanent philosophy' is here, in accordance with traditional termi-
> nology, understood as referring to inquiries into the supreme principles gov-
> erning one's own and other people's beliefs about the world of intersubjectively
> interpreted experience, as well as one's own or other people's attitudes towards
> this world. . . . The term 'transcendent philosophy', on the other hand, refers to
> attempts at grasping the nature of this reality and at answering questions which
> cannot be answered without a grasp of it.

A person's metaphysical beliefs will be based on his supreme cognitive
and practical principles and hence on his categorial framework and general morality. Stephan here reiterates his early view that there is a plural-
ity of such categorial frameworks and moralities. He exhibits their
general structure and shows that a great many of them share common
cores. He argues that the fact that people can understand other people's
categorial frameworks shows that different categorial frameworks can—
in a more or less distorted manner—be represented by each other, and
that this suggests that each of them is a distorted representation of transcendent reality. Unlike most philosophers he took great care to distinguish between his account of the possible variety of metaphysical systems
and the one he adopted himself. It seems appropriate to end this very
brief sketch of his philosophical work with the description of his own
metaphysics with which he ends this last book:[9]

> The logic underlying my categorial framework is finitist and inexact, admitting
> of various kinds of idealizing exactifications and infinitization. Its maximal
> kinds are persons, animals and inanimate things—linked to the results of the sci-
> ences. . . . My personal morality implies a preference for representative democ-
> racy, approval of any strengthening of institutions which protect society from
> violations of personal freedom, from illness, political oppression, economic
> exploitation and undereducation. . . .
>
> My transcendental metaphysics is a version of perspectivism according to
> which various categorial frameworks are different perspectives of transcendent
> reality. . . .
>
> As to the issue between determinism and indeterminism, I believe (and am
> pleased) that a good case can be made for a strong sense of human freedom and
> for a conception of man as Goethe's 'little God of the world' rather than a
> completely programmed *homunculus.*
>
> I am agnostic about the existence of a perfect being and of immortal souls
> because I do not understand the key terms used in statements and arguments in
> which their existence is asserted or allegedly proved. I do not, however, deny the
> possibility that some future experience of a wholly new kind may give meaning
> to these terms.
>
> . . .

[9] *Metaphysics: its Structure and Function*, pp. 232–3 and 221.

I, naturally, sometimes wonder how understanding and accepting a belief in the existence of a perfect being and of immortal souls would affect my categorial framework and my morality. Since I would probably regard these beliefs as speculative interpretations of experiences which, at best, can be characterized only negatively or analogically, the new framework would, I assume, not differ greatly from my present one. My morality would, I think, not change in content, though I might be enabled better to overcome any moral weakness. My transcendent metaphysics would, very likely, change out of all recognition. And the mere possibility of a theodicy would help to alleviate any feelings of despair and inadequacy in the face of human misery and wickedness and would serve as a most welcome ground for cosmic optimism.

Stephan was a very handsome man with an old fashioned Central European charm of manner, a droll sense of humour, and very regular habits. His students could set their watches by his time of arrival in the morning and at lectures, and he always took coffee at a local café with friends and colleagues at 11 a.m., leaving promptly at 11.50. In Austria he regularly had Wiener Schnitzel, defending his habit with Wittgenstein's dictum that 'It doesn't matter what it tastes like, the main point is that it is always the same.' He had an abiding delight in philosophy and up to the end of his life regularly attended staff research seminars. He will be remembered by his friends for his generosity and warmth of feeling. His devotion to his wife Diti was one of the most endearing things about him. He used to say, 'Diti does everything, but leaves the philosophy to me'. She had a very distinguished career in voluntary work. She became chair of the south western regional health authority in 1976 and was chosen in 1980 to chair a full-scale review of health service information. The resulting system of information management bears her name. It earned her a CBE in 1984. She also chaired the magistrates' bench in Bristol 1987–90. The University of Bristol awarded her the Honorary Degree of Doctor of Laws in July 1986. They were very proud of the achievements of their children and when Ann's husband Sydney Altman was awarded a Nobel Prize for chemistry Diti had a T-shirt printed with the words 'My son-in-law is a Nobel laureate'.

Stephan's philosophical views in *Experience and Conduct* were echoed in his own conduct. The philosopher Broad wrote an autobiographical note in which he gave an unsparing account of his own inner life. Stephan's son Tom remembers his father saying that the note gave him even more respect for Broad who had always managed to behave well in spite of inner urgings to unworthy conduct. Stephan distinguished carefully between things which were important like his family, friends and the life of the intellect and things which might be enjoyable (and which should therefore be enjoyed) but which were ultimately unimportant. He took great pleasure in the comfortable home that Diti provided for him but when he lived alone in Yale his rooms had a monastic simplicity. He greatly relished ice cream and recognition (in about equal measure) but could have relinquished either without a moment's regret. Both he and Diti had a strong sense of public duty, but this was combined with a feeling that individuals were to be valued as individuals. They treated everybody from beggars to government ministers and from children to Nobel Prize winners as equals.

His actions were always informed by the spirit of the enlightenment but there was more of the romantic about his feelings than generally appeared. He knew much of classic German poetry by heart (he could also sing every popular German song of the 1920s and 1930s) and wrote poetry in his youth. (Even afterwards, in accordance with continental custom, he would write a poem for Diti on each of her birthdays.) Diti was a very witty woman and they shared a keen sense of the ridiculous. Tom remembers a home filled with love and laughter. When Stephan and Diti discovered that she was suffering from a terminal illness they chose to die together. They were both deeply committed to a clear-eyed view of life and death. Tom says Stephan held three important philosophical principles. 'The first was Aristotle's view that one should do right because it is in one's nature. The second was from Kant, who said to do only that which you wish to be adopted in universal law, and the third was the utilitarian principle of the greatest good for the greatest number. My father felt that if what you wanted to do agreed with all three then do it. And he disagreed with Kant that it was wrong to take one's own life.' And so on 18 August 2000, they made sure their affairs were in scrupulous order, procured some tablets and, for the last time, did what they thought was proper. They left detailed instructions for the funeral at a local crematorium attended by their family and very many friends from the university, the health service and the judiciary. In accordance with Stephan's final wishes Schubert's *Trout Quintet* was played. This was the favourite piece of music of Stephan and his father. Professor Kenneth Ingham gave a moving address, Tom read a passage from Leibniz and, although they were non-believers, Diti had asked for the Kaddish (Hebrew prayer for mourners) which was read by Sydney Altman. We left saddened by the sudden loss of two very good friends but heartened by the memory of two lives so full of achievement.

JOHN SHEPHERDSON
Fellow of the Academy

Note. I am most grateful to Stephan's son Dr Tom Körner for contributing information about Stephan's life and lending me copies of obituaries and commentaries; to Professor Kenneth Ingham for permission to use material from his moving funeral oration, to Dr Andrew Harrison, for allowing me to use material from his obituaries in the *Guardian* and *Erkenntnis*, to Professor John E. Smith for information about Stephan's time in Yale, to Professor Werner Sauer for material about his time in Graz, and to Ted Waring for telling me about his extra-mural work.

Obituaries appeared in *The Times*, 23 August 2000, the *Guardian*, 30 August 2000, by Andrew Harrison, and in *Erkenntnis,* also by Andrew Harrison. Two commentaries on his works, and his reply to them were:

Haller, Rudolf (ed.), *Beiträge zur Philosophie von Stephan Körner* (Amsterdam, 1983).
Körner, Stephan, Some clarifications and replies, *Grazer Philosophische Studien*, 27 (1986), 1–25.
Srzednicki, Jan T. J. (ed.), *Stephan Körner—Philosophical Analysis and Reconstruction* (Dordrecht, 1987) contains bibliography, pp. 161–7.

DON MCKENZIE

Donald Francis McKenzie
1931–1999

Don McKenzie was Professor of English Language and Literature in Victoria University of Wellington, and later Professor of Bibliography and Textual Criticism in Oxford. One of the most stimulating teachers of his generation, he gave to bibliographical study new purposes and insights, and argued for its place at the centre of literary and historical understanding. In a lifetime divided between his native New Zealand and Britain, he sought to influence national values in both countries, whether in bibliography, theatre, publishing, or librarianship. A quick critical intelligence, an almost intuitive gift for friendship, personal sensitivity and a striking liveliness in his appearance, all informed his professional and private life alike.

He was born on 5 June 1931 in Timaru, South Canterbury, New Zealand, the son of Leslie Alwyn Olson McKenzie and his wife Millicent Irene. He was the eldest of four brothers and a sister. His father, a boot-maker, was restless; and as the family moved about so Don moved also: when he reached Palmerston North Boys' High School he had attended about a dozen primary and secondary schools. But by the time he left Palmerston North he had made a lifelong friend in Iain Lonie, who became a distinguished poet and whose premature death in 1988 caused him great distress.

On leaving school in 1948, and a summer job in a meat freezing plant that turned him into a vegetarian, he joined the staff of the Post Office, as a cadet. There he was appointed to the Public Relations Department in Wellington, a situation that both provided a living and permitted him to

Proceedings of the British Academy, **115**, 297–315. © The British Academy 2002.

enrol part-time at what was then still Victoria University College. At this time he met Don Peebles, an artist from Christchurch, who introduced him to a world of art, film, and theatre of which hitherto he had little or no inkling: the two also became lifelong friends. In this world he married Dora Haigh, slightly older than himself, more widely cultured, and likewise sharing an interest in the theatre. Among those who taught him was Keith Maslen, later of the English Department at Otago, whose understanding of the history of printing proved to be a formative part of Don's subsequent work. As a part-time student, his road to a degree was slow. In 1954 he took his BA, and in 1955 (uncertain of a career) a diploma in journalism. In 1957 he graduated MA with first-class honours in English, his thesis being on Compositor B's role in the second quarto of *The Merchant of Venice*.[1]

He had joined the Post Office as a public servant, a title of which he was proud: 'a public servant, devoted not only to my own job but to the political philosophy that seemed to me then to inform our society, in its concern for full employment, good and free health care, free education, and help for the old and ailing to live out their lives with dignity'. If some of his memory was idealistic, other aspects were real enough. McCarthyism, the Korean War, and domino theories about the spread of Communism all affected public opinion. For failing to stand for the national anthem in the cinema, and for discussing republican ideas with his workmates at the Post Office, he attracted the attention of the New Zealand secret intelligence service, who also discovered that he kept books by Marx, Lenin, and Trotsky, as well as the Communist Manifesto (all, in fact, prescribed for a course in political science he was following at university) in his home. It was further noted that he had received an invitation from a Russian organisation to see ballet films.[2]

Don maintained the principle of political liberty, and for a while was to consider standing for Parliament; but though he learned to keep his politics more to himself, he felt uncomfortable in the employ of so inquisitive a state. When, therefore, he was invited by Ian Gordon, Head of the English Department, to teach temporarily at Victoria, he was doubly glad to accept. A few months later, supported with a Unilever scholarship to study at Cambridge, he embarked with his wife and baby son Matthew to begin at Corpus Christi College in autumn 1957.

[1] Published in *Studies in Bibliography*, 12 (1959), 75–89.
[2] Speech on receiving an honorary doctorate from Victoria University of Wellington, 10 Dec. 1997. A few copies of this speech, with the associated ceremonies, were later printed in Wellington for private circulation.

The tale of his period as a research student in Cambridge in the late 1950s is one to make most students, and most supervisors, blench. He had family responsibilities. His initial project grew out of interests nurtured partly by his wife Dora, in early English drama. Under Philip Gaskell's guidance he embarked on a study of the working conditions of English printers in the late sixteenth and early seventeenth centuries. This took him naturally to the archives of the Stationers' Company, and in due course his first book. He was still working on other parts of that extraordinary and still under-exploited archive at the time of his death. But, for the purposes of his thesis, he found himself in a blind alley.

The discovery of the extent of the late-seventeenth- and early eighteenth-century records of Cambridge University Press came therefore as a godsend. Although they were not completely unknown, having been referred to by S. C. Roberts in his history of the Press published as long ago as 1921, they had never been investigated in detail, and they had been only summarily arranged. They seem to have been introduced to him partly by John Oates, of the University Library; but this was no simple matter, in that the papers were not in the Library, where they might easily be visited, but still in the University's central administrative offices where they were guarded by a formidably protective University Archivist. Somehow, with Oates's help, Don was accepted, and he not only transcribed a vast body of material, but also analysed it and brought everything into shape within the space of just two years—all the time that remained with his scholarship money after the false start.

His thesis, published as *The Cambridge University Press, 1696–1712; a bibliographical study*, appeared in two volumes in 1966, the first an analysis of the organisation and (to a rather lesser extent) the policy of the Press, together with a detailed bibliography of its output at this time, the second a transcript of the surviving documents: not just the formal records of decisions made, and the annual balance sheets, but also the weekly tallies (in sometimes minute detail) of all the miscellaneous equipment required. The records are unequalled in any printing-house in Britain before the nineteenth century, and they have the advantage of being close in date to the first English printer's manual, Joseph Moxon's *Mechanick exercises on the whole art of printing* (1683–4). Moxon has, inevitably, to bear the burden of being used as a commentary on printers and printing up to a century previously, the generations of Shakespeare and his immediate successors and the period to which most bibliographical and editorial work was devoted until the 1960s; but *Mechanick exercises* also reflects Moxon's own preferred interests; it is far from comprehensive, and Moxon himself was no printer. On some activities and equipment, he is obsessively detailed; on others, he offers little or nothing. But in all matters his statements could now be tested against the Cambridge record of daily reality.

The Press had been re-established at the instigation of the classical scholar Richard Bentley (not yet Master of Trinity College), and in due course it printed his editions of Horace (1711) and of Terence (1726). Thanks to Bentley, who contrived to extract from its reluctant author a revised second edition (the first having been published in London) the Press also printed Newton's *Principia* in 1713. With the exception of *Psyche*, a long poem by Joseph Beaumont, Master of Peterhouse, it printed little English poetry, and there was no drama. To some subsequent students of sixteenth- and seventeenth-century English literature this seemed a disadvantage. Not only was this not a London press, but as a learned press it also had a quite different kind of list when compared with those emanating from the modest premises that had produced the plays of Shakespeare, his contemporaries and successors, or the poems of Elizabethan, Jacobean, and later seventeenth-century England. However, while acknowledging the differences, Don argued that the similarities were more important, pointing out that though the University Printer was a Dutchman (Cambridge, like Oxford and John Fell before it, had had to import the skills and equipment necessary for a learned press), many of the other staff—journeymen and apprentices—were English, some from London itself. There was no intrinsic difference that could be confidently attributed to country rather than town working practices. In his view, it followed that much (though not all) of what he had discovered concerning the management of a press fifty miles away from London was not only applicable to London but also, to a great extent, to London of a century or so earlier. The records of the operation of a small, loss-making, university press were relevant to the production and therefore editing of many renaissance texts.

These two volumes on the details of men and work at Cambridge University Press between 1696 and 1712 led to a transformation of bibliographical studies, demolishing and blowing away some of the more imaginative theories of textual bibliography based on examination of individual books alone. Don demonstrated conclusively the fundamental importance of concurrent production: not only that several books passed through the printing house at one time, but also that each could be shared often haphazardly among several workmen. As David Fleeman expressed it in reviewing the work, here was 'a salutary reminder that no book can be properly analysed in isolation'.[3] In 1963, Charlton Hinman had enunciated a comparable lesson in his account of *The printing and proof-reading of the First Folio of Shakespeare*, demonstrating how the First Folio was printed over an unexpectedly long period, at the same time that other books were passing through the hands of Jaggard's workmen. Don, setting documentary evidence beside surviving copies of the finished books, showed how very much more complicated the process was even than Hinman had realised.

To the end of his life, it remained a wonder to Don that the Cambridge English Faculty agreed to pass a thesis so evidently linked to economic history, supervised in its last year by Peter Mathias. They condoned Don's work only after vigorous arguments on his behalf by his supervisor. This was, after all, the faculty that contained not just Muriel Bradbrook and F. R. Leavis (of whose work Don helped compile a check-list in 1966[4]), but other factions besides. Gaskell, with the help of his father-in-law H. S. Bennett, a senior member of the faculty and one sympathetic to historical bibliography, and also sustained by Bruce Dickins, tutor in charge of graduate students at Corpus Christi College, pressed support for Don's work at crucial moments. His two examiners were adamantly in favour, and this most unlikely body consisting mostly of literary critics agreed the case.

In fact, and as Don knew, the application of responsible bibliographical principles to critical understanding was to be a protracted battle. In 1958, Fredson Bowers delivered his Sandars lectures at Cambridge, home to a particular kind of literary criticism that generally set little value on understanding how printed texts were made, reproduced, and recreated. Don's review of these lectures, commissioned by John Oates (a man with whom he shared a very similar sense of humour) and published in *The Library*, was frank as to the practical difficulties.

> Whereas in the past the literary editor with a little learning in textual matters could always justify his position in a university by undergraduate teaching, the textual bibliographer is pedagogically useless except at research level. University promotion of textual, let alone analytical, bibliography is therefore all too likely to be opposed, as it is at Cambridge. My point is simply that the problem requires discussion in terms wider than those of critical nescience.[5]

[3] *The Library*, 5th ser. 23 (1969), 76.
[4] D. F. McKenzie and M. P. Allum, *F. R. Leavis: a check list, 1924–1964* (1966).
[5] Review of Fredson Bowers, *Textual and literary criticism*, in *The Library*, 5th ser. 14 (1959), 208–13.

Don's roots were in New Zealand. Though his strong affinities with English scholarship were now bound by new friendships, he always expected to return home. Having obtained his Ph.D., in 1960 he returned to Wellington, first to a lectureship in the English Department and then advancing until in 1969 a new Chair was created for him in his department. As a lecturer, he was irresistible, and his ability to galvanise students, taking them into interests of which they had little previous idea, remained throughout his career. His passion for theatre, for acting, and for the use of the voice all contributed to his mastery at the podium (which he treated almost as a stage) and in class, while his evident commitment to students' work made him a teacher who was also widely cherished.

During his time at Wellington, theatre, printing, and publishing were everyday components of the way in which he saw the Department and his duties. From 1964 he was a member of the University's Publications Committee, and he worked to establish Victoria University Press in its own right. From 1970 to 1973 he served as Dean of Languages and Literature, taking the opportunity to foster more understanding and teaching of Maori. Don also took up his old connections with local theatre, and in 1964 became a foundation member of the management committee of the new professional Downstage Theatre. In this capacity he took a key part in building the Hannah Playhouse, and seeing Downstage into it. Between 1968 and 1970 he served on the Indecent Publications Tribunal, but his hopes for changes in attitude withered in the face of increasing amounts of commercial pornography. His concern for libraries made him an obvious choice as a trustee of the National Library, where he argued vigorously (and latterly in the face of contrary management policies) for the continuing importance of both the National Library and the Turnbull Library (including its great collection of John Milton) as research collections, entrusted with the collection and maintenance of the original material (in whatever format) on which responsible historical enquiry depended. In 1970, he took an initiative on Victoria's Professorial Board which was to lead in 1979 to the establishment of the University's own library school, and he worked to ensure that students there had sufficient understanding of older books that might come under their care.

Initially as an adjunct to teaching, but increasingly as a project in its own right, in 1962 he established the Wai-te-ata Press, naming it after the road in which it was situated but also relishing the link between the Maori *wai* (waters) and the Water Lane Press in Cambridge that had served as a bibliographical teaching press under the aegis of Gaskell in the 1950s. There was a further connection. In 1953, Cambridge University Press had lent to the Water Lane Press an early nineteenth-century Stanhope iron hand-press.[6] Encouraged by Gaskell, he now persuaded the Press to agree to transfer its loan to Wellington. Don was proud of the Wai-te-ata Press's claims to historic authenticity: 'as antiquated and as obsolete as diligent inquiry and dust-disturbing visits to old newspaper offices and defunct printing shops can make it'.[7] It obliged students to make an effort of imagination; but any lessons could not easily be forgotten. Gradually, some machinery was added as well. As he scoured the local printers for type and other equipment, so the garages in which the Press was housed filled up. From them there emerged not just a series of student exercises, but also a distinguished list of authors including the poets Peter Bland, Alistair Campbell, Iain Lonie, and Bill Manhire. To this was added music publishing, including the work of Douglas Lilburn.

Informal and pressing invitations to leave New Zealand and settle in America, with a view to succeeding Fredson Bowers at Virginia, were flattering, but they held little appeal. The lessons of his thesis were taking a while to sink in amongst the scholarly community. In his great paper on 'Printers of the mind',[8] as well as in the irritation that can be sensed in his much later paper on what he called the 'spaced-out comps',[9] Don drew on his documented proof to demonstrate some further follies of more recent textual bibliography. In May 1963 he lectured at the Universities of Illinois, California (Los Angeles), and Virginia, and over the next few years developed an article of 75 pages based on work prepared for this tour. 'Printers of the mind: some notes on bibliographical theories and printing-house practices' took its text from T. S. Eliot: 'All our knowledge brings us nearer to our ignorance.' While making due obeisance to Bowers, who insisted on bibliography's claims to be a scientific discipline, he reflected that it was more often the case in some recent work that so-called scientific proofs were in fact no more than conjecture, and that the norms alleged of editorial and printing-house conditions were so irrecoverably complex that bibliographical knowledge was still only partial and theoretical. In response to this, he demanded a 'new and rigorous scepticism'. Drawing on the

[6] James Mosley, 'The Stanhope press', in Horace Hart, *Charles Earl Stanhope and the Oxford University Press*, ed. James Mosley (Printing Historical Society, 1966), pp. xix–xxxiii.
[7] *The Wai-te-ata Press, 1962–1992* (Wellington, 1992). After Don's departure to Oxford the Press was less used, until it was revived for new purposes in 1995: see Sydney Shep, 'A new dawning; Wai-te-ata Press and letterpress printing in New Zealand', *The Book Collector*, 45 (1996), 457–75.
[8] *Studies in Bibliography*, 22 (1969), 1–75.
[9] 'Stretching a point: or, the case of the spaced-out comps', *Studies in Bibliography*, 37 (1984), 106–21.

evidence gathered in his work on the Cambridge records, but alluding also to other documentation from the sixteenth to the eighteenth centuries, he demonstrated the fallacies of some prized current bibliographical theories: of workmen's output, of edition sizes, of the relation between composition and presswork. Most of all, the fact that concurrent production was normal in printing houses of all sizes (the Cambridge press frequently had two presses or fewer at work) meant that no book could be studied in isolation. It was a lesson requiring repetition.

In the face of the programme such a conclusion implied, it was small wonder that he wrote, 'I must confess to a feeling of mild despondency about the prospects for analytical bibliography.'

> Bibliography will simply have to prove itself adequate to conditions of far greater complexity than it has hitherto entertained. To do so, it will inevitably be obliged to use multiple and ingenious hypotheses, to move from induction to deduction, simply because a narrow range of theories is less likely to embrace the complex possibilities of organization within even a quite small printing house. A cynic might observe that the subject is already characterized by multiple and ingenious hypotheses, but too many of these have been allowed to harden into 'truth'. A franker acceptance of deductive procedures would bring a healthy critical spirit into the subject by insisting on the rigorous testing of hypotheses, and the prime method of falsification—adducing contrary particulars—would impose a sound curb on premature generalizations (pp. 60–1).

His emphasis on understanding the relationship between the archival record (where it existed) and the printed artefact extended to enquiries into the personnel of the printing trades. Ever since Edward Arber had published the registers of the Stationers' Company for the sixteenth and early seventeenth centuries, in 1875–94, the archives of the Company had gradually been brought before the public. Since, by its Charter of 1557, the Company was set at the centre of the English book trade, these records have a unique status. Don had relished being able to set names to tasks in the Cambridge printing-house. His earliest work as a graduate student had taken him into the archives of the Stationers' Company, and from them he had written one of his earliest articles, as well as *Stationers' Company apprentices, 1605–1640*, published by the Bibliographical Society of the University of Virginia in 1961. As a student, he had pointed out that, bleak though compositor analysis seemed, it was necessary to take matters further, to discover more about printers' social and educational backgrounds as well as their apprenticeship training.[10] To

---

[10] 'Compositor B's role in *The Merchant of Venice* Q2 (1619)', *Studies in Bibliography*, 12 (1959), 75–89, at p. 89.

him, bibliographical study always depended on the endless variety of human action. Or, as he put it in his presidential address to the Bibliographical Society some years later, 'The book as physical object put together by craftsmen—as we all know—is in fact alive with the human judgements of its makers.'[11] It was therefore natural that he should draw from the Stationers' Company a list of all apprentices, a sequence unique of its kind and providing the basis for what he hoped would one day become a prosopography of English printing and bookselling. Between 1961 and 1978 he saw published three volumes, surveying all the apprentices, their origins and their masters, between 1605 and 1800.

With the Stationers' Company, he extended into the eighteenth century, and he was always eager to refer to the archives of the London printers William Bowyer, father and son, which he delighted in seeing edited and published after many tribulations by Keith Maslen and John Lancaster in 1991. In an edition of a single surviving ledger of Charles Ackers, printer of the *London Magazine*, for 1732 to 1748, he worked with John Ross to place before the world further evidence of the procedures of a printing-house.[12]

His primary interests remained in the seventeenth century. A paper on 'The London book trade in 1668'[13] was written quickly, to make up for an article that had failed to arrive, but it was based on a characteristically painstaking survey of an extremely high percentage of surviving publications from that year. It presented a viewpoint that he had come to hold more and more firmly: that if the printing and publication of literature was to be understood, then this could only be achieved by considering the wider production, regardless of subject and format. Comprehensiveness and the urge to collect, displayed most obviously in national libraries, thus led not only to enumerative bibliography, but also to a social *raison d'être* for librarianship, and, with it, much of the artefactual diversity in printing sought by Don. In this way, the article also hinted at his developing awareness of the relationship between libraries and bibliography, a nexus he was to develop gradually into an argument for national strategy.

> Paradoxically, this diversity was both a strength and a weakness. The strength lay in its comprehensive responsibility to classify not merely literary documents but all books, to develop techniques for studying the elements common to

---

[11] 'The sociology of a text: orality, literacy and print in early New Zealand', *The Library*, 6th ser. 6 (1984), 333–65, at p. 335.

[12] *A ledger of Charles Ackers, printer of the London Magazine*, ed. D. F. McKenzie and J. C. Ross (Oxford Bibliographical Soc., 1968)

[13] *Words; Wai-te-ata Studies in Literature*, 4 (1974), 75–92.

them, particularly type and paper, and to foster the study of regional printing and publishing as an essential means of determining the origin and date of the individual editions. The weakness lay in the innocent assumption that the locus of bibliography as subject was *the* book—any book—as a physical object. For this assumption has had two consequences. First, it accounts for our current failure to accept into the discipline artefacts which are not books but which serve a comparable function. I mean any message-bearing document. Manuscripts may qualify, although Greg felt obliged to argue the case; printed music is acceptable, if not quite central; prints and drawings, if not photographs, have been given a home; but magnetic sound and video tapes, gramophone records, films, and much archival material, are still perhaps regarded as embarrassingly extraneous . . . Paradoxically therefore, the emergence of bibliography as a coherent subject has been inhibited, not promoted, by its restriction to books, and by the very diversity of motive and interest which books serve (p. 76).

On this occasion, Don restricted himself to the output of the press— books, pamphlets, newsbooks, broadsides, and other ephemera. His calculations were confessedly founded on inadequate statistics; but the real extent of that inadequacy was immeasurable thanks to the losses of history.

He was to return to these themes later. They informed his early support for the *Eighteenth-century short-title catalogue* when it was being planned at the British Library in the 1970s under the management of Robin Alston. They also influenced his work on the early imprints programme in Australia and New Zealand, designed to survey holdings in both countries of books published before 1801: it was some measure of his leadership and energy that the only part of this project so far to appear in print in New Zealand surveyed the Wellington libraries, those closest to home.[14]

Meanwhile he turned to William Congreve, the editing of whose plays for Oxford University Press were to occupy much of his time for the remainder of his life. He succeeded to this task after the death of Herbert Davis in 1967, and was able to approach it by his own route. This was partly laid out in his Sandars lectures, delivered at Cambridge in spring 1976.[15] In these, he offered what he described as a tentative preliminary enquiry into the triple relationship of political history, the book trade and dramatic literature. After beginning with Ben Jonson, whose explicit

---

[14] *Early imprints in New Zealand libraries; a finding list of books printed before 1801 held in libraries in the Wellington region* (Alexander Turnbull Library, Wellington, 1995).

[15] *The London book trade in the later seventeenth century.* These have not been published. Typescript copies are available in Cambridge University Library (850.b.188), the British Library (Ac.2660.m(28)), the Bodleian Library and elsewhere.

treatment of these subjects made him a ready witness, he moved in his second lecture away from the restrictions of bibliography as he saw it currently practised, and offered a phrase to which he was to return, 'the sociology of the text'. On the one hand he contested the 'reductive sterility of much that has ... been done in Greg's name'; and on the other he advanced the necessity of looking at texts not simply as written or printed, but as theatre, film, or other media. From this, he turned to a closer examination of the late seventeenth century, so departing from Greg's main areas of study in the late sixteenth and early seventeenth centuries, to suggest that in concern for proofreading, and the coalescence of printing and publishing to serve particular needs, there emerged new textual conditions. In particular, he drew attention to the partnership between Congreve and his publisher Jacob Tonson, and the ways in which Congreve's plays were given new form and new status by their joint determination to accord to the plays a classical status that not only offered a revision of earlier versions, but also set the plays in a European context. The collected edition of Congreve's *Works* (the title was warning enough), published in 1710, broke new ground in matters quite apart from its bowdlerisation. Where earlier it had been a widespread custom to issue such collections in folio, this was in octavo—a smaller format than the quarto in which the plays had first been published. It was a format modelled on editions of classical texts, designed to sit neatly on the shelves of gentlemen's libraries. Internally, typography, both in 1710 and further in the edition of 1719–20, was used to present entirely new emphases, by the use of centred speech-heads, italicisation and typographical ornament. These and cognate matters were developed in a paper offered at a conference at Wolfenbüttel, 'Typography and meaning: the case of William Congreve' which in its published form achieved wide acknowledgement and influence on the continent as well as in the English-speaking world.[16]

It was a topic that stretched back to the beginning of printing, but one that for English literature had its most obvious and explicit earlier parallels in Ben Jonson's works. The fact that both Jonson and Congreve turned to the design of the printed page to present in print what had been originally prepared to be spoken on stage, was of fundamental significance. In the conjunction of the two media, oral and printed, Don found the kind of textual cross-fertilization of which he wrote in 1974. In

[16] In Bernhard Fabian and Giles Barber (ed.), *Buch und Buchhandel in Europa im achtzehnten Jahrhundert* (Hamburg, 1981), pp. 81–125.

drama, the issue was further enriched by such matters as staging, scenery, costume, and music. For all kinds of literature, the relationship of speech, manuscript, and print underlay its communication and publication. This extension of bibliographical activity was, for Don, one of honesty to scholarly responsibilities: he was ever the most moral of critics in this respect. The issues were as obvious in Milton's *Areopagitica* as in L'Estrange's censorship, and in 1990 he developed them in a further article, 'Speech—manuscript—print'.[17]

By the time, therefore, that he came to prepare his influential Panizzi lectures in 1985, many of his thoughts were already assembled.[18] The lectures had been founded anonymously by Mrs Catherine Devas, and were intended to provide for the new British Library a platform for bibliographical studies comparable to that provided by the Sandars and Lyell lectures for Cambridge and Oxford respectively. Don was an obvious choice as the first to give the lectures, and he deliberately chose a topic that would have general applications. Terminology was a conspicuous problem, and he persuaded himself only slowly of the validity of the phrase he had coined some years before and that now became part of his title, 'the sociology of texts'. The lectures, mostly written in Cambridge while he was on leave, puzzled over as he paced the corridors of the University Library, and as usual rewritten and revised up to the moment he went on stage, represent the *comble* of one part of his work. In them, he sought to come to terms with some of the more fashionable French theoreticians, of whose influence he was all too well aware. He also returned (using an example from the work of W. K. Wimsatt and M. C. Beardsley) to some of the follies of Anglo-American New Criticism— content apparently to work with inaccurate texts even where textual authority was the subject of study. His emphasis was on printed texts, but in the course of the lectures he referred to theatre, film, computer-based texts, maps, and the Australian landscape. If there was an historic base to his stress on the social aspects of texts, in the work of late-eighteenth-century philologists such as Wolf and Eichhorn, and some of his argu-

---

[17] Dave Oliphant and Robin Bradford (eds.), *New directions in textual studies* (Austin, Tex., 1990), pp. 87–109.

[18] *Bibliography and the sociology of texts* (1986). Reviews included those by Hugh Amory (*The Book Collector*, 36 (1987), 411–18); T. H. Howard-Hill (*The Library*, 6th ser. 10 (1988), 151–8); Jerome J. McGann (*London Review of Books*, 18 Feb. 1988, 20–1) and G. Thomas Tanselle in his 'Textual criticism and literary sociology', *Studies in Bibliography*, 44 (1991), 83–143, at pp. 87–99. The Panizzi lectures were translated into French (*La bibliographie et la sociologie des textes* (Paris, 1991)), with an introduction by Roger Chartier, and into Italian (*Bibliografia e sociologia dei testi* (Milan, 1999)) with an afterword by Renato Pasta as well as with (again) Chartier's essay.

ments followed on from those of Marshall McLuhan, he applied himself to them with a new finesse and new imagination.

But he began with a simple proposition, one that grew out of his earlier work and that considerably advanced the assumptions that had controlled bibliographical practice since the days of W. W. Greg.

> The principle I wish to suggest is simply this: bibliography is the discipline that studies texts as recorded forms, and the processes of their transmission, including their production and reception. So stated, it will not seem very surprising. What the word 'texts' also allows, however, is the extension of present practice to include all forms of texts, not merely books or Greg's signs on pieces of parchment or paper. It also frankly accepts that bibliographers should be concerned to show that forms effect meaning. Beyond that, it also allows us to describe not only the technical but also the social processes of their transmission. In those quite specific ways, it accounts for non-book texts, their physical forms, textual versions, technical transmission, institutional control, their perceived meanings, and social effects (p. 4).

The implications for literary criticism were far-reaching: that such activity had inescapably to take account of historical and textual bibliography, a discipline that had in the course of the twentieth century developed a quite independent momentum. Here, at last, was an expression of the kind of reconciliation between new bibliography and critical practice at which he had grasped in 1959. Of the three lectures, the first two were concerned with concepts of text: the first with what could be claimed to be authorially sanctioned; the second with the open-ended fate of a text, 'unstable, subject to a perpetual re-making by its readers, performance or audience'.

The lectures deliberately ranged widely; but in his presidential lecture delivered to the London Bibliographical Society in February 1983 Don had already found space to explore some of these questions in the context of New Zealand. In *Oral culture, literacy and print in early New Zealand; the Treaty of Waitangi*[19] he reflected on the conflict of understanding that underlay the negotiations and agreement of the treaty on which was based all subsequent relations between the Maori and the colonial power: between a people to whom literacy and its implications were totally unfamiliar, and an authority to whom the written and printed word were not merely long familiar, but were parts of its very foundation. In such circumstances, the spirit of the Treaty was, in his words, 'only recoverable if texts are regarded not simply as verbal constructs but as social products'.

---

[19] First published as 'The sociology of a text: orality, literacy and print in early New Zealand', *The Library*, 6th ser. 6 (1984), 333–65; republished under its new title by Victoria University Press and the Alexander Turnbull Library (Wellington, 1985).

In arriving at such a conclusion, and so contributing to a lively contemporary debate in New Zealand, he had re-examined not just the circumstances of the 'signing' of the treaty, but also available contemporary evidence of how early missionary printing had been received and understood. It incidentally brought out the best of Don's constant insistence that printing depended on the individuality of human responses as much as on mechanical processes; but when it was published in New Zealand the lecture was criticised both by Maori and by Pakeha historians, who were uncomfortable at the intrusion of a bibliographer into the subject.

Don was elected a Corresponding Fellow of the British Academy in 1980. His work had always been divided between duties in New Zealand and research leave in Britain, with occasional forays into the United States. A further period of leave took him to Cambridge in 1982, and his marriage was breaking up. He was in England again in 1983, when he served as President of the London Bibliographical Society, and then again in 1984 and 1985. Partly in order to work on Congreve, in 1984 he reduced his appointment at Victoria to part-time. David Foxon had retired as Reader in Textual Criticism at Oxford in 1982, and the position was unfilled. It seemed only natural that in 1985 he should allow his name to go forward as Foxon's successor. He arrived in 1986, and was elected to a Fellowship at Pembroke College. He was among friends, some of them fellow-New Zealanders, but the Oxford landscape was no match for New Zealand, where he always kept a house. More cheerfully, he discovered amongst the research students ample opportunities to explore the implications of bibliographical principles for film and other twentieth-century media. Now (settled in Britain, and thus eligible under a different rule) elected Fellow of the British Academy, he soon afterwards joined the British Library Advisory Council as the Academy's representative. At Oxford, he delivered the Lyell lectures in 1988, on the seventeenth-century book trade.[20] More honours followed. He was elected an Honorary Fellow of the Australian Academy of Humanities and awarded the Marc Fitch gold medal for bibliography in 1988, and the gold medal of the Bibliographical Society in 1990. With his marriage in 1994 to Christine Ferdinand, Librarian and Fellow of Magdalen College, the broken pieces of his life could be seen firmly and happily reordered.

In his third Panizzi lecture, he had addressed the implications for bibliography as it was currently practised. It will already have become apparent that Don had a keen interest in the practices and responsibilities

---

[20] These have not been published, but Don used them as a quarry for his other work.

of librarianship. Indeed, early in his career attempts were made to recruit him to the staff of Cambridge University Library. Recalling that the lectures were named after the greatest of all nineteenth-century librarians, who had been responsible for establishing the British Museum Library as the unequalled international (not merely national) library, Don turned his attention to questions of national librarianship: not just of books, but of film and of electronic publication. At the time of writing, the archiving of both film and computer-based work lagged still further behind that for the more traditional forms of text than it does today. But Don also emphasised the difference between public responsibility and private convenience. 'I stress public because commercial considerations rarely bear upon the past with much responsibility to historic depth.'

> A principle of economy in the service of private interest renders all records vulnerable. Why keep them if the demand year by year diminishes to the point where they are seldom consulted and it becomes unprofitable to maintain the structures which house and service them? Even in the public realm, some texts are more equal than others, a principle of frequency of use is invoked, and policies of selective retention constantly advocated (pp. 62 3).

As he viewed the conflict developing in national libraries between the needs of existing collections and needs for and of new technologies, he argued for extentions to bibliographical understanding. Even the history of the book, to which he had devoted so much energy, suggested limitations that required both acknowledgement and accommodation. To acknowledge the instability of texts, whether because of their different media, their metamorphoses in publication, or reception, was also to acknowledge that 'histories of the book cannot tell the full story: they cannot fully account for our parallel use of manuscript even to the present day, the texts lost to history by their failure to survive, the import and export trade in books, the second-hand trade, the metatextual foundations of libraries, the number and nature of successive readings and partial readings, the concurrent production and circulation of graphic images, and formal and informal oral texts'. Electronic texts add to these issues, but they do not fundamentally transform them. Don reached tentatively at questions of the relationships between the digital worlds and the worlds of the codex. Had he lived, he would certainly have attempted to reconcile the two, despite environments of library management that gave him little comfort. Meanwhile, in his centenary address to the Bibliographical Society he rested content with contrasting what, notwithstanding his usual strictures, he termed the durability of books, a quality that 'ultimately secures the continuing future of our past', with the 'evanescence' of new forms. To him, this was 'the most critical problem for bibliography and any further history dependent upon its scholarship'.

For national libraries, forced to develop strategies of limitation, the most critical question seemed to him to be the ways by which forms of texts were being changed in order to be offered to readers, as paper-based stocks became unwieldy and expensive. The ubiquity of substitutes— paper, film or electronic—was not in itself cause to be ungrateful:

> But with every replication we have to balance the immediate social gains of availability and utility against the loss of the historical evidence every original contains—and our natural instinct, given our training, is to resist and regret the new prohibition against reading books with our fingers. Once we accept the premise that the forms themselves encode the history of their production, it follows that to abstract what we're told is their 'verbal information content' by transferring it to another medium is to contradict the very assumption that the artefact is the product of a distinctive complex of materials, labour, and mentality. . . . Any simulation (including re-presentation in a database—a copy of a copy) is an impoverishment, a theft of evidence, a denial of more exact and immediate visual and tactile ways of knowing.[21]

With issues concerning the future of the book in mind, and with the publication of the four-volume *Histoire de l'édition française* edited by Henri-Jean Martin and Roger Chartier (Paris, 1983–6) before him, Don turned his attention to a history of the book in Britain from Roman times to the end of the twentieth century. Such a project (by no means limited just to what had been produced in Britain) would both provide a survey of what was thus far known, and an opportunity to emphasise the place of the book at the centre of social activity.[22] It would also be a place in which to emphasise the necessity of accommodating different means of communication, including electronic media, to the history of the manufacture and use of manuscript and print. In 1988 a proposal for a seven-volume work, under the general editorship of Don, David McKitterick, and Ian Willison was accepted by Cambridge University Press: the volume covering the years *c.*1400 to 1557 appeared in 1999, edited by Lotte Hellinga and J. B. Trapp. Gradually, too, Don watched other national histories being discussed, most rewardingly in New Zealand, where it was only natural that he should press vigorously for a similar project. His own work had concentrated on the earliest printing there, and on the late

---

[21] *'What's past is prologue'; the Bibliographical Society and history of the book* (Bibliographical Soc., 1993), p. 24.
[22] 'History of the book', in Peter Davison (ed.), *The book encompassed; studies in twentieth-century bibliography* (Cambridge, 1992), pp. 290–301.

nineteenth-century printer Robert Coupland Harding, whose vision and international frame of reference made him naturally attractive to Don. Harding formed the subject of a lecture delivered in honour of Keith Maslen in Melbourne in 1991.[23] As in some other countries, a coherent single history for New Zealand proved impracticable. Instead, within an astonishingly short time, contributors were assembled for a collection of essays on many aspects of the subject, published at Wellington in 1997.[24] Don viewed the term used in its title, 'print culture', with some unease, mainly because it seemed to him to avoid the complexities of the relationships of print to other media. But his admiration was clear for the energy that had produced something so comprehensive, even if rather different from that for which he had argued.

In 1996 he retired from Oxford, though it was difficult to see any difference to the pace of his life as he continued to write, attend meetings in London, support his students with innumerable references, and push forward with the two major projects, his edition of Congreve and the Cambridge *History of the book in Britain*. In spring 1997 he gave the Clark lectures at Cambridge, using the opportunity to present Congreve as a person of integrity in two senses: on account of the coherence of his work over about forty years, and secondly on account of 'the honesty and humanity of the values which, at least to my mind, inform it'.[25] The lectures offered a foretaste of matter to be included in the Oxford edition. They also represent the closest Don came to reconciling critical and editorial values, the puzzle he had set himself as a research student. But his friends, and he, knew that he was asking too much of his body, even after major heart surgery. As he put it more than once, as he threw himself into new arguments, 'The trouble is that I cannot help getting involved': for Don, that meant more energy than many can muster even in full health. In the event, the task of completing Congreve had to pass after his death to others. The seventeenth-century volume of the history of the book, edited jointly with John Barnard of Leeds University, will appear imminently, edited now also by Maureen Bell. Don died of heart failure on

---

[23] 'Robert Coupland Harding on design in typography', in R. Harvey, W. Kirsop, and B. J. McMullin (eds.), *An index of civilisation; studies of printing and publishing history in honour of Keith Maslen* (Clayton, Vic., 1993), pp. 187–205.

[24] Penny Griffith, Ross Harvey, and Keith Maslen (eds), *Book & print in New Zealand; a guide to print culture in Aotearoa* (Wellington, 1997).

[25] *The integrity of William Congreve* (1997). This is unpublished, but copies are in the Bodleian Library (shelf-mark M97.C01782) and in the library of Trinity College, Cambridge.

22 March 1999 in the Taylorian Library. Characteristically, he was pursuing a query for someone else at the time.

Don's restless upbringing left its mark, and though the journey between England and New Zealand was hardly to be faced with relish, his taste for travel did not diminish with age. In the early years, the long sea voyage allowed time for uninterrupted work. Latterly, even the New Zealand journey could be lightened by a pause in California, to visit the Los Angeles libraries or Christine's family. He visited New Zealand for the last time in January 1999, to deal with family obligations. In his last few months, Picasso's ceramics at the Royal Academy and a visit to the Mark Rothko exhibition in Paris each refreshed his energies and enthusiasms. A few months before that, a visit to an all but forgotten painting of Congreve in Leuven[26] combined his delight in the visual arts and his love of drama. On another occasion, he sent an excited postcard announcing that he had at last not only seen the eighteenth-century theatre at Drottningholm, but had actually had a chance to work the thunder machine there as well. His enjoyment of life in such circumstances, and in the last few years particularly in the company of Christine, was almost tangible.

His need to be in England for the sake of its libraries, its archives, and the historic wealth on which he worked was always in conflict with his love of his own country. Once on one side of the world, he ached to be on the other. It was only in his last years that he found expression for his feelings:

> Thy firmness draws my circle just,
> And makes me end where I begunne.

He quoted Donne's words when in 1997 he received an honorary doctorate from Victoria University. It was a distinction that he prized above all others: not simply because it recognised his contributions to knowledge, and to the life of New Zealand and Wellington in particular, but because it implicitly acknowledged the ways in which he had sought to apply the gains of bibliographical and critical enquiry to wider literary, historical and social issues. Though he died in Oxford, his ashes were scattered on the sea off the little North Island holiday settlement of Paekakariki, as he wished.

DAVID McKITTERICK
Fellow of the Academy

---

[26] 'Richard van Bleeck's portrait of William Congreve as contemplative (1715)', *Review of English Studies*, NS 51 (2001), 41–61.

Note. In preparing this, I have been greatly helped by the existence of a number of memoirs by his friends, in particular Keith Maslen, 'Donald Francis McKenzie, 1932 [*sic*]–1999', *Bibliographical Society of Australia and New Zealand Bulletin*, 23 (1999), 3–10; Kathleen Coleridge, 'Donald Francis McKenzie, born 5 June 1931, died 22 March 1999', *New Zealand Libraries*, 49 (1) (1999), 24–7; Nicolas Barker, in *The Book Collector*, 48 (1999), 445–50; Harold Love, 'The intellectual heritage of Donald Francis McKenzie', *The Library*, 7th ser. 2 (2001), 266–80. The obituary notice in *The Independent*, 25 March 1999, was reprinted with various alterations in the *Turnbull Library Record*, 32 (1999), 5–9 and in *The Library*, 7th ser. 1 (2000), 79–81. I am also grateful for help of various kinds to Christine Ferdinand, Hugh Amory, John Barnard, Kathleen Coleridge, Douglas Gray, Penny Griffith, Harold Love, Matthew McKenzie, Keith Maslen, Don Peebles, Ian Willison, Wallace Kirsop, and my wife Rosamond. For a selective bibliography of his work, see D. F. McKenzie, *Printers of the mind and other essays*, ed. Peter McDonald and Michael Suarez (University of Massachusetts Press, 2002).

KATHLEEN MAJOR   *Bassano & Vandyk*

Kathleen Major
1906–2000

KATHLEEN MAJOR was born on 10 April 1906 at 54 Penn Road, Holloway, a short distance north of the Caledonian Market. Her father, George Major, a potato merchant in partnership with brothers, had married her mother, Gertrude Alice Blow, in April 1902. George's father Robert had been a master mariner in the East India trade. It was perhaps Robert's retirement to Yorkshire which led George to make the acquaintance of the Blows whose home was at Goole in the West Riding. George Major does not seem to have had any formal religious attachment, but the Blows were Congregationalist, and it was at their Congregationalist Christ Church in Goole that Kathleen was baptised on 20 June 1906, to be followed six years later by her sister (and only sibling) Eileen, born in February 1912. When Kathleen went up to Oxford in 1925 she was registered as Church of England.

The potato and vegetable business prospered and before the end of the First World War George Major had bought the agricultural estate of Whaplode Manor near Holbeach, in the Holland division of Lincolnshire. Abbott's Manor in Holbeach became the family home. His daughters were educated at private schools, regarding which Kathleen was oddly reticent. Her last school, Wilton House in Reading, must have done a good job, because in 1925 she won a commoner's place to read history at St Hilda's College, Oxford. Had the Majors remained in London we might doubt whether their elder daughter would have become a noted medievalist. At Whaplode, however, her home was close to a remarkable cluster of large parish churches dating variously from the twelfth to the

Proceedings of the British Academy, **115**, 319–329. © The British Academy 2002.

fifteenth century—Whaplode itself, Holbeach, Gedney, Long Sutton and others—while the flat countryside bore ample evidence, in its dykes and commons, fens and drains, of a long-drawn-out and essentially medieval enterprise whereby potentially rich land was recovered from the sea.

At St Hilda's an outstanding tutor Agnes Sandys (Mrs Leys) steered KM firmly towards the middle ages and a love of documents; her special subject was medieval boroughs, the sources for which brought the student face to face with the interpretation of highly technical Latin records. In 1928 she took a Second Class in Modern History and embarked on study for the B.Litt., having been introduced by Mrs Leys to F. M. (afterwards Sir Maurice) Powicke, newly appointed to the Regius Chair. Powicke was wrapped up in a study of the intellectual and spiritual development of Stephen Langton; he suggested to the young KM that she should collect and edit the *acta* of Langton as archbishop of Canterbury (1207–24). The formal result was a volume published by the Canterbury and York Society in 1950; the longer-term result for the editor herself was the acquisition of an unrivalled knowledge of the cathedral and diocesan archives of England and Wales. KM became aware that at many cathedrals rich stores of archival material lay unsorted, uncatalogued and in some cases seriously neglected. This was a lesson she never forgot; it underlay the fervour with which in later years she campaigned for adequate archive administration and protection, not only for ecclesiastical but also for secular records.

After graduating, KM became librarian at St Hilda's, and she began the serious study of diplomatic with Vivian Galbraith, who had been made Reader in Diplomatic in 1928 after some years as a keeper in the Public Record Office. While searching for Langton *acta* at Lincoln in 1930 KM met the astonishingly learned and energetic scholar Canon C. W. Foster, chief founder (in 1910) of the Lincoln Record Society and of the Lincoln Diocesan Record Office. Canon Foster, busy rural parson as he was, had dedicated his life to the cause of preserving and publishing the medieval records of Lincoln Cathedral and diocese. She fell under Foster's spell and in 1935 he secured her appointment as chief officer of the Lincoln Diocesan Record Office (which after the Second World War became the Lincolnshire Archives Office). On this matter Foster sought the help of his old friend Professor F. M. (afterwards Sir Frank) Stenton at Reading, who had been one of Kathleen's B.Litt. examiners. 'It seems to me (Stenton wrote) that [she] has every qualification for the post' and he advised that she should start at £300 p.a. Stenton added: 'Miss Major is a piece of sheer good luck.' Only a few days before his sudden death in

October, Foster wrote to George Major 'we consider that we are very fortunate in securing Kathleen for the work at Lincoln, and her appointment is specially gratifying to myself'. Already in 1932 and 1933 KM had published, in the *Associated Architectural and Archaeological Societies' Reports and Papers*, vol. 41, 'Some early documents relating to Holbeach' and 'An unknown house of Crutched Friars at Whaplode'. In these short papers we can still be astonished at the confidence with which the recent BA and B.Litt. edits the texts of original charters and cartulary copies of papal bulls, perhaps spurred on a little by the knowledge that the documents she was making public dealt with lands around her home. Many years later, in a booklet published at her own expense *The D'Oyrys of South Lincolnshire, Norfolk, and Holderness 1130–1275* (Lincoln, 1984), KM went over much of the same ground in an extended study of a family originating in the department of Marne, whose descendants ramified widely across Norfolk and south east Yorkshire, although their first settlements north of the Channel were in the territory around Holbeach.

KM's self-confidence and self-assurance must, of course, have been enormously enhanced by the love and support she received from her parents. Her father, in this respect ahead of his time, believed that women should enjoy as much independence as men. He had a fine house built at 21 Queensway, Lincoln, which he made over to Kathleen and which became her home from 1937 until her death 63 years later. She liked expensive clothes, good plain food, comfortable hotels when travelling, and from an early period in her life owned and drove a motor car. A revealing letter written to her parents from 21 Queensway on 16 November 1941 shows a mixture of confidence, ambition, and diffidence as she is clearly preparing herself for a serious career as historian. She has been in Bromley, London, and Oxford, and she has been consulting, or at least speaking with, Rose Graham, Dorothy (Whitelock?),[1] Agnes Leys, the Powickes, Robin Humphreys (the distinguished Latin American historian whose parental home was in Queensway, Lincoln, just opposite Kathleen's house), Arnold Toynbee—these both were keen to recruit KM for Chatham House—and finally the Stentons. She has made up her mind to stick to medieval history: 'So that I feel my course is all set for work for twenty years ahead. It is so exciting to have so much to do and to find that the eminent think me equal to the task, though I am not so sure of that

---

[1] In an important lecture on diocesan records given at Lincoln in July 1941 (*Lincolnshire Architectural and Archaeological Society Reports and Papers*, ii, pt. 2, p.129) KM thanks Dorothy Whitelock for helpful criticism.

myself, but it is nice to be told so, and I can't tell you how grateful I am to you for making it possible. All these excitements are very exhilarating, but I am quite humble really.'

KM's appointment at Lincoln in no sense severed her links with St Hilda's or with Oxford. She was an elected member of the college council from 1935 to 1940. In 1945 she was appointed university lecturer in diplomatic (within three years to be Reader) and elected to a college Research Fellowship (eventually a Professorial Fellowship). Only a year before her appointment Vivian Galbraith had left the chair of history in the university of Edinburgh to become director of the Institute of Historical Research, and only two years later Galbraith succeeded Powicke in the Regius Chair at Oxford. It was important for KM's tenure of her Readership that one of the foremost medieval historians actively teaching in the university was someone who had the greatest respect for her scholarship and judgement. She and Galbraith held complementary classes for postgraduate medievalists, the one on diplomatic (immensely thorough and wide-ranging), the other on the sources for English history from the eleventh to the fifteenth century. (My own MS notes of KM's lectures run to 124 quarto pages, from 15 October 1948 to 10 June 1949.)

The corollary of KM's Readership was supervision of postgraduates embarking on research, normally aiming at the degree of B.Litt. In this work the standard she set was strikingly higher than what was then, and long remained, the Oxford norm. She saw her pupils regularly once a fortnight, allowed ample time for a thorough discussion of their work, and insisted on the production of written drafts or summaries to ensure that the student remained on course and did not drift.

Some months before his death in October 1935 Canon Foster invited KM to collaborate in the editing of volume IV of *Registrum Antiquissimum of the Cathedral Church of Lincoln*, intending that she should complete the task if he did not survive. The volume duly appeared in 1937, dedicated to Foster's memory and containing an eloquent appreciation by F. M. Stenton. For KM it was the beginning of a commitment which lasted thirty-six years, and entailed the meticulous editing of most of volume IV and eight further volumes, six of texts and two of facsimiles. The total number of documents printed is 2,980 serially numbered, over 3,000 if supplementary material is included. By any standards *Registrum Antiquissimum* must be accounted one of the great enterprises of English historical editing of the twentieth century. Volumes 1 to 5 appeared within a decade, despite the outbreak of war in September 1939 and KM's responsibilities in overseeing the microfilming of the pre-1812 registers of 299 Lincolnshire parishes. The war and the move to Oxford led to a ten-year gap between volume V and volume VI. Volume VII appeared in 1953 and VIII five years later (the last to be printed at the *Hereford Times*). There was then another ten-year gap, to be explained in the following pages, before volume IX (the first of four to be printed in Gateshead at the Northumberland Press), followed in only five years by the final volume and the facsimiles. This would have been an astonishing achievement even if KM had been a solitary scholar dedicating all her waking hours to one *magnum opus*; but, as will be seen, she bore a wide range of educational and scholarly responsibilities and, until 1971, took her share of family responsibilities as well, in seeing that her mother was looked after and able to lead as comfortable a life as age and disabilities allowed.

From the 1930s onward the archivist and the historian in KM were balanced equally. This is clear both from her work and from her correspondence. As David Vaisey acknowledged in an address to the Society of Archivists published in the society's *Journal* (vol. 22, no. 2, October 2001, p. 231), KM's career marked a critical stage in the process by which adequate local record offices and diocesan record offices were established across England. Just as she was consulted by graduates who aspired to enrol for the archives course at the Bodleian Library, so also her advice was sought by many cathedral authorities (e.g. Chichester, Ely) and local authorities anxious not only to preserve their records but also to make them accessible to a public increasingly eager to consult them. KM's advice, always practical, was given unstintingly. On the historical side, KM's voluminous correspondence with Sir Charles Clay, Lewis Loyd, the Stentons, and Christopher Cheney (to name but few) brings out the historian, especially the family historian and local historian, in her intellectual make-up.

In 1955 KM—invariably Miss Major both at home in Lincoln and at Oxford—was appointed Principal of St Hilda's. She succeeded Julia de Lacy Mann, who had run the college virtually single handed for 27 years. KM 'moved quickly to modernise the college, establishing a proper college office and an administrative system that really worked'. Her experience as a governor of Lincoln College of Education proved especially valuable since in 1955 St Hilda's had become a self-governing institution. The position of bursar was critical, for Miss Mann (though an economist) had no head for figures. KM encountered difficulties which could not be overcome at once. As she noted somewhat acidly, 'the arrangements in 1951 gave [the bursar] an assistant who not only had no positive qualifications for bursarial work but the positive disqualification of no simple arithmetical ability and an unwillingness to handle money' [KM papers]. She was determined to meet the challenge of expansion and the need to provide more undergraduate places. In her time as principal, St Hilda's acquired the Milham Ford building, thus uniting the two separate parts of the college's grounds, and through the munificence of the Wolfson Foundation added the Wolfson Building, largely the work of Sir Albert Richardson, as a residential block. This meant that for the first time St Hilda's could accommodate all its undergraduates, a situation which did not last. A further addition shortly before KM took charge had been a handsome principal's lodging, also designed by Richardson.

During her principalship KM fought more than one crucial battle to save St Hilda's from disaster. The Oxford city planning authorities put forward a scheme for a 'relief road' through Christ Church meadows, or alternatively proposed a dual carriageway road down the edge of Christ Church playing fields, passing within 35 feet from the Wolfson Building. The words KM spoke at one of the public enquiries deserve to be quoted in full:

> Thus we have been able to create, not only for Oxford but for the whole nation, an asset which can and ought to be preserved. If this road is built there will be lost to future generations of women undergraduates something of rare value which they might so easily have enjoyed. We feel it our duty to demand that this sacrifice shall not be imposed on them unless it is proved beyond doubt that it must be made for the preservation of Oxford as a whole. The ruin of this college, for the sake of enabling some motorists to make a slightly more convenient journey, would stand as a monument to the false values of our age.

The relief road was abandoned, which must be reckoned not the least among the debts which the city and university of Oxford owe to the redoubtable Miss Major.

It was inevitable that KM's principalship should have involved a measure of collision between a generation of young women, intelligent, self-confident, and conscious of the sexual revolution which came with the contraceptive pill and a fundamental shift in social attitudes, and a dignified but shy scholar brought up on strict principles and possessing what must already have seemed a rather old-fashioned outlook. (There is no doubt that in a number of respects KM *was* old-fashioned. It is, for example, inconceivable that she would ever have used the expression 'OK'). To many undergraduates she seemed rather formidable, even daunting. Some, whose conduct proved to be incompatible with college life, were required to leave, but to them KM was invariably helpful, even sympathetic. To anyone within the college who might be in need of help, financially or otherwise, she was a ready, generous, and anonymous benefactor, as she has been publicly to the college as a whole.

KM was elected principal of St Hilda's by a senior common room which included a number of fellows whose eminence in scholarship was equal to her own, e.g. Dorothy Whitelock, Beryl Smalley, Menna Prestwich, and Helen Gardner. The consternation of some of these fellows when the new principal showed that she had very clear ideas about what the college needed and single-mindedness in carrying out her policies may perhaps be compared to the dismay of Sir John Falstaff and his cronies when Prince Hal became King Hal. There is no doubt that KM suffered some persistent opposition and criticism; her approach could seem authoritarian, even autocratic. Nevertheless, Beryl Smalley, by then Vice-principal, could write in the college report for 1964–5 'Miss Kathleen Major retired at the end of July after ten years of office which have been constructive in every sense of the word.'

It has been said by a subsequent principal that KM's achievement at St Hilda's 'was to turn a small, inward-looking college, run from the outside, into a genuinely self-governing, self-confident organisation'. She was largely instrumental in bringing about the enlargement essential if St Hilda's was to play a proper part, as it clearly has, in the expansion of university education for women.

It should be borne in mind, when we consider the calls upon KM's time and the pressure of work to which she subjected herself, that until their mother's death in 1971 she kept to an agreement with her sister Eileen, who lived with Mrs Major in Nottingham, that in vacations Kathleen would undertake the responsibility of looking after the old lady, who could be very demanding. This meant that, even when her mother could stay in the principal's lodging, KM had few if any real holidays and that many opportunities for travel which she would have greatly enjoyed were denied her.

The affection KM felt for her mother, however, is not in any doubt. In October 1960 she was a guest of honour at the dinner celebrating the 250th anniversary of the Spalding Gentlemen's Society. She drove there from Oxford on the day of the dinner, stayed the night and drove back the next day, a Sunday. She still had the energy to write her mother a long letter telling her all about the dinner and naming everyone present who had asked after Mrs Major—and what their families were doing. The very next day she was to face an exhausting session with city planners over the Wolfson Building and the letter concludes, not surprisingly, 'Must go to bed, much love, Kathleen.'

At the end of KM's ten year principalship it was a lucky encounter on the Paddington–Oxford train in 1966 that led to the next stage in her academic career. Professor Sir Fred (afterwards Lord) Dainton, Vice Chancellor of Nottingham University, finding himself sharing the journey with KM, took the opportunity to invite her to become a part-time professor in the history department for the next five years. Professor J. C. (afterwards Sir James) Holt, who had attended KM's diplomatic class in the late 1940s, was about to leave Nottingham for a chair at Reading, and Professor Donald Bullough had not yet been appointed to succeed him. The university had already awarded KM the honorary degree of D.Litt. in 1961. Her Nottingham professorship, a 'special chair' in medieval history, gave KM a wholly fitting and congenial closing phase to her formal academic career. She enjoyed teaching again and supervised several postgraduates working for a doctorate, the last of whom was Professor David Smith, for long director of the Borthwick Institute of Historical Research at York. She served on the council of the Royal Historical Society, of which she was made an honorary Vice-President in 1981, and she was also Vice-President of the Canterbury and York Society and a member of the British Academy's committee for the publication of English episcopal *acta* (1973–89). In 1977 she was elected a Fellow of the British Academy.

To mark her retirement at Nottingham in 1971 some fifteen friends and former pupils collaborated to present her with a *Festschrift*, edited by D. A. Bullough and R. L. Storey, *The Study of Medieval Records* (Oxford: at the Clarendon Press, 1971). At the end of this volume a list compiled by Dr Arthur Owen gives the particulars of some 33 articles and booklets published by KM between 1932 and 1971, as well as of eight editions of texts and two of facsimiles. To this list at least six further items may be added (see below, p. 329). It is a formidable achievement for someone so deeply immersed in administrative work and in teaching.

Kathleen Major was notably generous with her time and her erudition. Dr Alison McHardy recalls that in 1967 her supervisor Dr Roger Highfield introduced her to KM with a letter of recommendation, whereupon a lifelong friendship ensued. 'She would invite me to dinner. It was plain . . . but very good quality. I remember lovely steaks, which an impoverished research student could not afford, and excellent sherry beforehand. After dinner she would say: "Now, is there anything you would like to ask me?" And so I got a free research supervision from the person who knew the Lincoln diocesan archives better than anyone else.' Nor was it only professional historians who could count on her help. A wide range of local history societies, tourist bureaux, branches of the Women's Institute, local government offices, and other worthy bodies benefited from her advice. From the 1960s the Friends of Lincoln Cathedral published a series of pamphlets, of which the first eight were edited by KM, who was herself author of *Minster Yard*, no. 7 of the second series (1974). Eighteen years later she published at her own expense an 81-page booklet on Lincoln Minster for the use of 'guides and others concerned in the service of the Cathedral'. She gave a copy to each guide. Her devotion to the cathedral and its long history did not entail automatic admiration for the learning, dedication, or wisdom of its clerical dignitaries. Many of her surviving letters bear witness to her exasperation in the face of senior ecclesiastical ignorance and obtuseness. KM's heroes were Canon Foster and Canon Srawley—for her they represented Anglican erudition at its best:

> Good Dons perpetual that remain
> A landmark, walling in the plain—
> The horizon of my memories—
> Like large and comfortable trees.

No-one who knew Kathleen Major could suppose for a moment that in retirement, given reasonable health, she would not pursue her own studies with pertinacity or help others to pursue theirs. As *Registrum Antiquissimum* proceeded to its final three volumes the editor's attention was inevitably directed to the many hundreds of urban properties, scattered across the city of Lincoln's twenty-nine parishes, from which rents were paid or land and buildings conveyed to the Common Fund and to chantries administered by the chapter. Thus KM became an enthusiastic urban archaeologist. She had long been a friend of Sir Francis (Frank) Hill, the author of a highly successful history of *Medieval Lincoln* (Cambridge, 1948, repr. 1965), and he (who served for some years as mayor of the city) encouraged a co-operative campaign to identify and record the old houses and other buildings before they were swallowed up by modern development. The result was a substantial co-operative enterprise, *The Survey of Ancient Houses in Lincoln*, which was recorded in four volumes, *Priorygate to Pottergate* (1984), *Houses to the south and west of the Minster* (1987), *Houses in Eastgate, Priorygate and James Street* (1990) and *Houses in the Bail: Steep Hill, Castle Hill and Bailgate* (1996), by Stanley Jones, Kathleen Major, Joan Varley, and Christopher Johnson. KM provided the preface to each volume, and in the last she wrote 'I will close by recording how very enjoyable and interesting the collection of material has been over this period.' She was already 78 when the first volume appeared and 90 when the enterprise was completed—a remarkable testimony to her indefatigable energy and devotion to Lincoln and its history.

Until the last few years of her life KM delighted in excursions to some historic church or castle or country town, invariably accompanied by a substantial picnic or visit to a good restaurant. Her knowledge of that older rural England which still survived in her younger days was extensive and reliable. With that knowledge went her delight in such details as that Sir Frank Stenton's father was admitted solicitor in 1837 and owned strips in the open fields of Eakrigg, or that her friend Joan Wake, immensely and fruitfully learned with regard to the early records of Northamptonshire, 'had no more education in her childhood than the governess in the school-room at Courteenhall'. KM could be stoical in the face of illness, luckily uncommon until her last years, and of personal setbacks. In October 1985, for example, she could write 'The burglars took my remaining silver (most went last year) and all my jewellery which was not much and mostly of no great value other than sentimental. But the thieves had house-breaking implements and had gone all over the house. Mercifully they had not thrown my file cases and card indexes about, only the papers in my desk.'

To many who knew her well, KM will be remembered as kindly, hospitable and generous. They will readily concur with the tribute paid by Anne Whiteman in her preface to the *Festschrift* presented to KM in 1971: 'All who have worked with her, as pupils or colleagues, have learnt to respect the extent and depth of her knowledge, her sound judgment, and her unshakeable scholarly integrity.'

Kathleen Major died at Lincoln on 19 December, 2000. At the funeral service in the Minster, presided over by the bishop, an address was given by the Vice-Chancellor and Librarian of the cathedral, Dr Nicholas Bennett. In it he outlined the 'three causes, above all others, of which she was a tireless advocate', namely the cause of women's education, the study of medieval records and the history of the cathedral and diocese of Lincoln. At the very well attended memorial service held at Oxford on 17 March 2001, in the university church of St Mary the Virgin, Mrs Mary Moore, herself a former principal of St Hilda's, spoke of KM's outstanding contribution to the life and work of her college, her achievement as archivist and historian, and of how 'her friendship always embraced the whole family; the fortunes of her friends' children, and *their* children and grandchildren were always of interest'.

G. W. S. BARROW
Fellow of the Academy

Note. Dr Nicholas Bennett kindly allowed me access to the personal papers of Kathleen Major at Lincoln, of which he had made a preliminary arrangement. Professor David Smith at York and Mrs Jeannette Davies of Andrew and Co., solicitors, Lincoln, have readily answered many questions. Mrs Mary Moore provided much valuable information and gave me the text of her address at the memorial service on 17 March 2001. In the memoir, unattributed passages within quotation marks are taken from this address. Miss Maria Croghan, librarian of St Hilda's College, Oxford, helped greatly with material relating to Kathleen Major's college career and with personal correspondence files. Others whom I wish to thank for assistance and information readily given are Molly Barratt, Julia Barrow, Mary Bennett, Elizabeth Boardman, Hilda Brown, Pierre Chaplais, Eleanor Davis, Barbara Emerson, Susan Hall, Barbara Harvey, Caroline Hill, Alison McHardy, Arthur Owen, the late Dorothy Owen, Margaret Rayner, and Jane Sayers.

Bibliographical Note

A full bibliography to 1970 by A. E. B. Owen was published in *The Study of Medieval Records*, ed. D. A. Bullough and R. L. Storey (Oxford, 1971), 322–7. Other items are given below.

1939–40:

The nature of diocesan records. *Lincolnshire Architectural and Archaeological Societies Reports and Papers*, ii, pt. ii, 129–40.

1968:

Sir Frank Merry Stenton. In *The Registrum Antiquissimum of the Cathedral Church of Lincoln*, ix, pp. xi–xii.

1972:

Doris Mary Stenton, 1894–1971. *Proceedings of the British Academy*, lviii, 525–35.

1974:

Minster Yard. Lincoln Minster pamphlets, Second Series, no. 7, pp. 3–31.

1975:

Joan Wake. *Archives*, xii, no. 53, 28–29.

1984:

The D'Oyrys of South Lincolnshire, Norfolk and Holderness, 1130–1275 (Lincoln). Pp. 80 + maps and genealogical tables.

1986:

Houses in Minster Yard, Lincoln: Documentary sources. In *Medieval Art and Architecture at Lincoln* (British Archaeological Association), 146–7.

1992:

Lincoln Cathedral. Some materials for its history in the Middle Ages, for guides and others concerned in the service of the Cathedral (Lincoln). Pp. i–iv, 1–81.

For *The Survey of Ancient Houses in Lincoln* (1984–96) see above, p. 327.

MICHAEL ROBERTS   *Hepburn & Jeanes*

Michael Roberts
1908–1996

'To BEGIN WITH, I seemed a sufficiently unlikely historian', Michael Roberts began a personal memoir in 1991.[1] His father, Arthur Roberts of Lytham St Anne's, built steam-engines for the Lancashire cotton-mills and Michael, an only child born on 21 May 1908, spent 'a very middle-class, provincial boyhood' during which he developed a lifelong interest in test cricket and learned to play the piano. He also excelled as a child soprano.[2] 'We were not a bookish family', he later recalled: 'one bureau-bookcase sufficed, and it was dominated by a large octavo edition of the complete works of Thackeray.' He nevertheless developed an abiding love of English literature: he knew long passages of Dickens by heart and could also quote extensively from Jane Austen, Trollope, Waugh, Wodehouse, and many others.[3]

Roberts's interest in history developed almost by accident. 'The influences which made me a historian', he declared near the end of his life, 'were (a) *Puck of Pook's Hill* and (b) H. G. Wells (an intelligent Assistant-Master at my prep-school had made available to his charges H. G. Wells' *Outline of History*, re-issued in twenty-four monthly parts)'.[4] Thus fortified, his parents sent him to a boarding school, Brighton College (partly, he later alleged, in order to 'cure' his Lancashire accent), where he acquired 'reasonable

---

[1] M. Roberts, 'Retrospect', *The Worcester College Record 1993* (Oxford, 1993), 61–71.
[2] He once wrote: 'My effective participation in music came to an end when my voice broke: until then, for range, clarity, facility of executing the most difficult baroque cadenzas, I have never heard my superior, or even my equal' (MR to Alan Hall, 10 Nov. 1996). In fact, Roberts continued his 'effective participation' in music throughout his life (see below).
[3] 'Retrospect', 61; G. H. Le May to GP, 3 June 1997.
[4] MR to Alan Hall, 10 Nov. 1996.

Proceedings of the British Academy, **115**, 333–354. © The British Academy 2002.

Latin, execrable French, and poor science'; but he excelled at history and, in 1927, won a scholarship to Worcester College, Oxford. His father paid him a generous allowance so that, with his scholarship, he could enjoy university life to the full. He made good friends, played sports (golf, squash, and especially fives) and made music. Curiously, for a historian who would write much on war, he hated the OTC. Looking back sixty years later, the luxury of his life as an undergraduate impressed him most (meals individually cooked, his fire lit every day) and his musical endeavours afforded the fondest memories (one summer he made a pilgrimage to Bayreuth). He also remembered with gratitude his history tutor at Worcester College, P. E. Roberts (no relation), on whose teaching methods he modelled his own.[5]

He performed spectacularly well in his final exams in 1930. He modestly ascribed this to the fact that 'I could count myself exceptionally fortunate to find, in the nineteenth-century English paper, a question on the importance of the novels of Charles Dickens to the social historian'; but there was more. Twenty-one years later, one of his examiners still recalled the originality of Roberts's answer to the question on the General Paper: 'Which of the arts has had the greatest influence on the history of its times?' Roberts wrote on 'the art of war'. He took the best first-class degree of his year and won the Gibbs Scholarship, the Amy Mary Preston Read Scholarship, and the Jane Eliza Procter Fellowship, which allowed him to spend a year at Princeton University.[6] There, encouraged by Professor W. B. Hall, he identified a promising topic for his doctoral dissertation: English party history in the early nineteenth century.

Back at Oxford, partly to improve his chances of winning a college fellowship, in 1932 he decided to compete for the university's Gladstone essay prize; and this brought another outstanding success.

> The regulations for the Gladstone Prize laid it down that the subject prescribed for the essay should, in alternate years, be one connected with Mr Gladstone, and one on some other historical topic—a provision which firmly defined Mr Gladstone's importance in relation to the general scheme of things. It unluckily happened that this was not a Gladstone year, and the prescribed subject was 'The reign of David I and its significance in the History of Scotland'. Of Scotland I knew little, and of David still less—not even his dates; but there was no help for it: David it had to be.[7]

[5] 'Retrospect', 61; MR conversation with GP, New Year 1985.
[6] M. Roberts, 'The naïve historian: an undelivered inaugural', *Comment*, XVIII (Winter, 1995), 2–11, at p. 3; G. H. L. Le May to GP, 31 Aug. 2001 (the examiner was Sir David Lindsey Keir, who praised Roberts's Tripos prowess in 1930 when Le May—Roberts's former student—arrived at Balliol in 1951.)
[7] 'Retrospect', 63.

His essay won the prize, but a College Fellowship still eluded him and so Roberts taught as a lecturer and tutor in history at Merton College (1932–4), and then as an Assistant Lecturer at Liverpool University (1934–5). Meanwhile he sought to apply the revelations of Sir Lewis Namier on eighteenth-century English politics to the early nineteenth century. Although he soon realized that Namierite structural analysis did not fit a generation in which elementary party organisations, with distinctive ideas and ideals, had already become an essential element in politics, he completed a finely nuanced dissertation under the supervision of Professor G. S. Veitch of Liverpool University.[8] Namier accepted a revised version of the thesis for publication as the first volume in what he intended to be a series of nineteenth-century studies: *The Whig Party: 1807–1822* (London: Macmillan, 1939; reprinted 1965).

Roberts acknowledged Namier as the second great influence on his formation as a historian (the first being P. E. Roberts). Sir Lewis would 'read the text [of *The Whig Party*] with great care, and again and again would stop short and say: "What do you mean?" And I would tell him what I meant. And he would reply: "But you don't say so!" I have never forgotten that question and that answer.'[9]

By then, Roberts had decided that his future did not lie in English history. He had discerned that 'the way to historical fame was to choose a field that had never been ploughed before, and then plough it in such a way that it would never require to be ploughed again'; yet 'in all periods of English history the competition was fierce; and vested interests existed upon which it would be presumptuous for a beginner to intrude'. By contrast, few British historians ventured into European history and he therefore searched for areas with an obvious lack of information available to those who read only English.

> There was no difficulty in identifying three or four such areas. For a time I was tempted by eighteenth-century Portugal; or again, by eighteenth-century Tuscany; but in the end the choice seemed to reduce itself to some seventeenth-century topic in the history of either Poland or Sweden. Poland was in fact better provided for than I suspected; but Sweden was scarcely provided for at all. I took what seemed to me a practical step towards resolving my hesitation. One Friday I went into Blackwell's bookshop and simultaneously bought myself a

[8] Roberts worked with Veitch, making 'expensive pilgrimages' to Liverpool for his supervisions, only because the History Faculty could find no one suitable for him to work with in Oxford. ('Retrospect', 64.)

[9] 'Retrospect', 64; MR conversation with GP, New Year 1985. Roberts would later apply Namier's approach, which saw personal ambition as more important than parties and ideology, to both South African and Swedish political history: see pages 339 and 342 below.

> *Teach Yourself Polish*, and a *Teach Yourself Swedish*. A weekend's inspection of
> these volumes was sufficient: by Sunday evening I had decided that Poland was
> not for me.

Instead, Roberts saw that the reign of Gustavus Adolphus and Sweden's
dramatic intervention in the Thirty Years' War constituted the major
'field to plough' in seventeenth-century Swedish history and began to buy
Swedish books and printed sources on the subject, which he read with the
aid of a dictionary.[10]

Then a contact at Rhodes University College in Grahamstown, South
Africa, persuaded him to apply for its chair of history. The position was
not his first choice—he retained hopes of a fellowship at Oxford; he
applied unsuccessfully for a lectureship at Glasgow—but it offered many
advantages. Although he had published nothing at the time, Rhodes
offered a salary of £700 per year—enough to finance a comfortable life-
style—and a yearly voyage by Union Castle steamship back to England.
Roberts therefore accepted the chair of Modern History and, aged 27 (the
youngest professor appointed to that date), moved to Grahamstown in
1935.

Rhodes was then little bigger than a large Oxford College—about 500
students—and Roberts threw himself into university life. He acted in
student dramatic productions (giving a magisterial performance as King
Magnus in Shaw's *The Applecart*) and served as president of the undergraduate Dramatic Society; he played squash with the students and participated in Saturday night dances in the College Great Hall. He served as
Warden of Milner House, a student residence, and took his meals at the
high table in its refectory. He also built up an impressive record library,
which he deployed at soirées for his colleagues and students, played the
piano and sang. He even took up the trombone in order to provide a brass
component in the orchestra for a production of *Iolanthe*, one of three
Gilbert and Sullivan operettas that he staged (and performed in) at
Rhodes. Years later, a former student recalled:

> Between the Warden and those students of Milner House who did not enjoy
> music there was an amiable mutual tolerance. Skirmishes on matters disciplin-
> ary were few and far between. A recalcitrant offender, no matter how eminent
> on the sports field or in student politics, would find himself reduced to less than
> the dust by the barest glance from a pair of baleful blue eyes under eyebrows

---

[10] 'Retrospect', 65. In a conversation at New Year 1985, MR noted that he had lost his bet,
because before long he had to master materials in both languages. Roberts's library at that time
still contained well-worn copies of *Teach Yourself Polish* and *Teach Yourself Swedish*, both bearing the same date of purchase—1934.

raised in distress and amazement at his misdemeanour: eyes which would focus their vision down the full length of a slender nose, past a firmly shut and disapproving mouth and powerful chin, to the fingers that were busy with the far more important matter of filling the professorial pipe. When the words came they were few and flaying.[11]

Roberts also revelled in his teaching. Although not physically big, he exuded a remarkable 'stage presence' that immediately captivated his lecture audiences. A student enrolled in his first-year history course in 1939 recalled almost sixty years later that 'at the very first lecture [I] was struck, not to say dazzled, by the effortless articulateness and the urbane, ironic style of the lecturer'. He and his fellows immediately realized that:

> This was a different order of performance from any we were accustomed to, not only because we were fresh from high school and were glad not to be talked down to, but because a more sophisticated level of intercourse seemed to be taken for granted. The speaker's vocabulary, and the degree of comprehension assumed, flattered us. We had been promoted.

Another likewise recalled 'the (apparently) effortless flow of exquisite language (he did not use notes), the irony ... I had the heady feeling that I was being treated as an intellectual equal.' In 1941, Roberts married Ann Morton, the sister of a Rhodes colleague, whom he had met on one of his voyages back to England. Years later, he looked back on his first period at Rhodes as 'the happiest years of my life' and he remained close to several students from that period. In 1968, he dedicated a book to two of them, both then professors.[12]

Amid so much social and pedagogical activity, Roberts's research on Swedish history languished somewhat. Nevertheless, he worked on his languages on the boat trips to and from Europe and he published an article on 'The constitutional development of Sweden in the reign of Gustav Adolf'. He also undertook a translation of Nils Ahnlund's *Gustav Adolf den Store* [Gustav Adolf the Great]. The American-Scandinavian Foundation agreed to publish it; Ahnlund—Sweden's leading historian at the time—approved; and in 1940 the book duly

[11] See the hilarious account of Guy Butler, *Bursting world: an autobiography 1936–1945* (Cape Town, 1983), 36–9, on MR as Warden and trombonist. Butler spent 1937–8, his second year at Rhodes, in a room directly opposite the Warden's flat. He wrote his recollections between 1977 and 1982; MR read and critiqued them.

[12] Alan Hall to GP, 30 Sept. 1997; G. H. L. ('Copper') Le May to GP, 31 Aug. 2001; Paul Maylam, 'Michael Roberts: a profile', *South African historical journal*, XXXVI (1996), 269–76, at p. 272. The dedication of *The early Vasas, 1523–1611* (Cambridge, 1968) reads 'To Copper and Alan'.

appeared. This labour of love planted in Roberts a fascination with the craft of translation that he never relinquished.

In 1943, Roberts joined the South African Intelligence Corps. At first he served at Headquarters in Pretoria, but soon secured permission to travel northwards in the wake of the South African First Division. He spent Christmas in Khartoum with a former pupil and from there flew to Asmara in Eritrea, where torrential rains stranded him for six weeks. Two things happened to Roberts at Asmara. First, he had time to study 'The English Road', built by the Anglo-Indian troops of Sir Robert Napier for the Abyssinian expedition of 1867–8, on which he would write a fine article. Second, he received an invitation from the British Council to serve as its Representative to Stockholm, an accident that finally determined which historical field he would plough. In the summer of 1944, Michael and Ann Roberts travelled to Stockholm.[13]

The British Council intended its Representatives to familiarise the countries to which they were assigned with what was then called 'the British way of life'; and, although life as the Representative in Stockholm bore little resemblance to life as it was lived in Britain in 1944, Roberts expounded what it had been and might one day be again. For the next two years, he ran a reading-room, a small library and a record collection in Stockholm and toured the entire country giving lectures on Britain's literature, music, institutions, social assumptions, and social policies to various Anglo-Swedish Societies. In the end, he thought he had covered over three quarters of the country's extensive rail network.

In 1946, after his two years in Sweden, Roberts returned to Grahamstown determined to make that country's history his principal research field, although he realised it would not be easy.

> There remained formidable bibliographical problems, and small chance of returning to Sweden to fill the gaps within a reasonable time. For the moment, the difficulty was relieved by the extraordinary benevolence of Uppsala universitetbibliotek, which for three or four years after the war was generous and trusting enough to send me consignments of books on loan, a dozen at a time, with the sole proviso that I should not keep them for more than a month. That meant, of course, hard labour on the arrival of each parcel. But what other library anywhere, at any time, would have been liberal enough to lend books to a reader six thousand miles away?[14]

---

[13] Roberts had originally responded favourably to a circular from the British Council 'enquiring whether anybody would be interested in teaching English to the offspring of Arab sheiks somewhere in the Middle East'. At the last minute, the Council changed the location to Stockholm. ('Retrospect', 65–6.) On the 'English Road', see Roberts's account 'A little war' (typescript). Roberts also kept a fine diary of his East African odyssey (also in typescript).

[14] 'Retrospect', 68–9.

Roberts again participated fully in the intellectual life (pedagogical, musical, and dramatic) at Rhodes, staging more Gilbert and Sullivan (playing the judge in *Trial by Jury* and Sir Ruthven Murgatroyd in *Ruddigore*). He also inspired another generation of talented young historians, six of whom would later become professors in South Africa or elsewhere: Rodney Davenport, Andrew Duminy, Jeffrey Horton, Basil Le Cordeur, John Omer-Cooper, and Leonard Thompson. Some he steered consciously towards the political history of nineteenth-century South Africa, seeking to apply to it the techniques developed by Namier for eighteenth-century Britain. He, too, wrote on South African history, using sources in both English and Afrikaans (a language he had learned in Grahamstown before the war). *The South African Opposition 1939–1945: an essay in contemporary history* (with A. E. G. Trollip, London and Cape Town, 1947) constituted the first scholarly study in English of the South African Nationalist Party.

His main historical project throughout this period nevertheless remained seventeenth-century Swedish history, and in 1953 he published the first volume of his massive study: *Gustavus Adolphus: a history of Sweden, 1611–1632*. Its favourable reception secured Roberts's appointment as professor of Modern History at the Queen's University, Belfast, in succession to the formidable G. O. Sayles. When he arrived in Belfast in January 1954 his new department numbered only six. Almost at once, however, a rapid and sustained rise in student numbers began and Roberts faced the task of guiding and controlling a major transformation of the History School. New posts arose to cope with the growing numbers and he took advantage of this to increase the number of specialized courses and to extend the range of choices open to students. Two other developments stood out. First, as at Rhodes, Roberts firmly believed in promoting the study of 'local' history, and he insisted that the existing lectureship in Irish history be raised to the rank of a Chair and a second lectureship established. He also gave constant and effective encouragement to postgraduate work in the subject, and played a vital role in creating the university's Institute of Irish Studies. Second, he worked out a novel use for the munificent endowment recently gifted to the department by Mrs Janet Boyd to establish the Wiles Lectureship, in memory of her father. As an *ex officio* member of the Wiles Trust, and as the person mainly responsible for organising the lectures, Roberts devised a unique format. Every year, a distinguished historian delivered public lectures on four consecutive evenings, each followed by a more intimate seminar attended by both Queen's faculty and specially invited guest historians who could (and sometimes did) tear the speaker to pieces as they sipped Bushmills and nibbled Stilton. Roberts maintained an 'unobtrusive discipline in these gatherings and displayed, in his own contributions, a remarkable (at times almost terrifying) versatility of mind and range of knowledge'.[15] Herbert Butterfield inaugurated the series of Wiles Lectures in November 1954, later published under the title *Man on his Past.* Most subsequent lecture series also appeared in print soon after they were delivered, and the format Roberts established remained unchanged after his retirement—a fact that gave him great satisfaction.[16]

Three months later, Roberts delivered his most influential lecture— one of the most influential inaugural lectures ever given: 'The military revolution, 1560–1660'. He began with a modest disclaimer that he felt the topic of his own research to be too obscure.

> I concern myself with a small country, peripheral to the main centres of European development; its history neglected, and almost unknown to English scholars; its language untaught in our schools, and unblessed, I am afraid, by any very high priority in our universities. In these circumstances, the cultivation of Swedish history is bound to be something of a purely personal hobby; and that is one reason why I have felt it better not to take it as my subject for this lecture.

Instead, Roberts deployed his daunting knowledge of early modern European history (in many languages) to select four critical changes in the art of war in the century following 1560. He reviewed in turn the 'revolution in tactics' (the replacement of the lance and pike with firepower), the growth in army size and the adoption of more ambitious and complex strategies, ascribing most of these transformations to the military innovations wrought by Maurice of Nassau, prince of Orange, and Gustavus Adolphus of Sweden. He then examined the impact of the new-scale warfare upon Europe's political and social development.[17]

Like so many inaugural lectures, probably even this novel contribution would have passed into oblivion had Sir George Clark not singled it

---

[15] *Essays presented to Michael Roberts*, ed. J. Bossy and P. Jupp (Belfast, 1976), viii.

[16] He attended the 1987 Wiles lectures which 'I was glad to note, ran on precisely the lines I laid down 33 years ago; the feeding was good; Geoffrey Elton, as always, was the last to leave the Common Room bar every night, and the first to get up every morning'. All was clearly well with the world. (MR to GP, 4 Nov. 1987.)

[17] *The military revolution, 1560–1660: an inaugural lecture delivered before the Queen's University of Belfast* (Belfast, 1956), quotation from p. 3. It has been frequently reprinted, most recently in *The military revolution debate. Readings on the military transformation of early modern Europe*, ed. C. J. Rogers (Boulder, CO, 1995), 13–35. Later in 1955, he also delivered a complementary lecture, 'Gustav Adolf and the art of war', printed in M. Roberts, *Essays in Swedish History* (1967), 56–81.

out for special praise as the new orthodoxy in his 1956 Wiles Lectures, published two years later as *War and society in the seventeenth century*. For a quarter of a century, almost every work on early modern Europe that mentioned warfare included a paragraph or two that summarized Roberts's argument. Then, from 1976, a plethora of books and articles by various historians discussed the 'military revolution' of early modern Europe, and in the 1990s strategic analysts began to compare it with the 'Revolution in Military Affairs' which they perceived in the wake of the Gulf War. All of them took that 1955 lecture as their starting point. Forty years later, Roberts observed with characteristic modesty, 'It is a sobering thought that an obscure inaugural in a provincial university should provide the pretext for forty years of debate. I can't help feeling that for once in my life I did *invent* something.'[18]

Roberts's research on early modern Sweden now appeared in print at a rapid pace. The second volume of *Gustavus Adolphus* came out in 1958, to universal acclaim. 'The author weaves a complex military, political and diplomatic narrative in the old-fashioned grand manner', wrote Christopher Hill in *The Spectator*, 'but he combines this with first-class analytical chapters which recreate the economic, social and intellectual life of Sweden, and set Gustavus Adolphus's achievement in a deep historical context.'[19] His achievement led to Roberts's election as Fellow of the British Academy in 1960 and as Honorary Fellow of Worcester, his old Oxford College, in 1966. He also became a Fellow of the Royal Irish Academy. Eight more books on Swedish history followed, starting with *Essays in Swedish history* (a collection of his previously published articles and book chapters) in 1967; and *The early Vasas: a history of Sweden, 1523–1611* and *Sweden as a great power, 1611–1697: government, society, foreign policy* (a collection of translated documents) in 1968. Five years later, he brought out both *Gustavus Adolphus and the rise of Sweden* (an abridged version of his great biography, republished in 1992 as *Gustavus Adolphus*); and *Sweden's age of greatness, 1632–1718* (a collection of essays, most of them translated from Swedish into English by

---

[18] MR to GP, 9 Jan. 1995. For a succinct review of writings on the Military Revolution in the 1980s, see Rogers, *The military revolution debate*, 4–5; for the expanding debate in the 1990s, see C. J. Rogers, '"Military Revolutions" and "Revolutions in Military Affairs". A historian's perspective', in *Towards a Revolution in Military Affairs? Defense and security at the dawn of the twenty-first century*, ed. T. Gongora and H. von Riekhof (Westport, CT, 2000), 21–35. For one example of the article's impact, see I. A. A. Thompson, *War and society in Habsburg Spain* (Aldershot, 1992), ix: 'My interest in the historical study of war [was] inspired by Michael Roberts's seminal essay on "The Military Revolution"'.

[19] *The Spectator*, 8 Aug. 1958. I thank Paul Maylam for this reference.

Roberts).[20] In 1979, he published his own Wiles lectures, *The Swedish Imperial experience, 1560–1718*, which provided a brilliant concise survey of the subject; and in 1986, *The age of Liberty: Sweden 1719–1772*, a 'Namierite' view of men and politics in which personal ambition prevails over party organisation, ideas and ideals. Finally, in 1991, he published *From Oxenstierna to Charles XII. Four studies*, a collection that contained one of Roberts's finest articles (which had served for many years as a stunning public lecture): 'The dubious hand', an investigation of the mysterious death of Charles XII of Sweden. 'All that one needs to pronounce judgment', he once jested, 'is expertise in folklore, ballistics, forensic medicine, tactics, geology and the history of costume.' Thanks to the mastery he acquired in these skills, his 'judgment' has stood.[21]

Roberts also transcribed, translated, and edited the dispatches of two Swedish diplomats sent to Republican England in the 1650s, and he translated for a colleague the letters and journal of Johan Wahlberg, a Swedish naturalist who in the mid-nineteenth century travelled around South Africa, and subsequently in Namibia, until an elephant trampled him to death.[22] His last intellectual tribute to Swedish history was an article on the visit to England in 1809 of the Swedish luminary Erik Gustav Geijer, whose sharp eye and ear picked up such things as the popular interest in the extra-marital affairs of the duke of Clarence, one of George III's sons, which reached such a pitch that instead of calling 'heads or tails' gamblers began to call 'duke or darling'.[23]

---

[20] He expressed amazement at the success of the abridged *Gustavus Adolphus*, commenting that Longmans had made 'an incredible offer of £1,000 advance royalties. Nobody ever offered me advance royalties before.' (MR to GP, 19 July 1991.) Full citations for all Roberts's publications between 1935 and 1975 may be found in *Essays presented to Michael Roberts*, 179–83; references to his subsequent works are provided in the footnotes below.

[21] MR to GP, 7 Nov. 1980. Roberts took his title from a poem on the subject by Samuel Johnson, *The Vanity of human wishes* (1749): 'His fall was destined to a barren strand/A petty fortress and a dubious hand . . .'

[22] *Swedish diplomats at Cromwell's Court, 1655–1656: the missions of Peter Julius Coyet and Christer Bonde* (Camden Society, fourth series, XXXVI, 1988:); J. A. Wahlberg, *Travel journals (and some letters), South Africa and Namibia/Botswana, 1838–56*, ed. A. Craig and C. Hummel (Cape Town, 1994: Van Riebeeck Society, 2nd series, XXIII). The initiative came from Hummel, a colleague in the Rhodes History Department. As it happened, Roberts had acquired a microfilm of the Wahlberg papers in the 1970s. He produced a complete translation between 1989 and 1992, which Hummel then edited. In addition to the articles and book chapters on Scandinavian history reprinted in *Essays in Swedish history* and *From Oxenstierna to Charles XII*, Roberts also wrote 'Sweden and the Baltic, 1611–1654', in *The New Cambridge Modern History*, IV, ed. J. P Cooper (Cambridge, 1970), and numerous reviews of books on Swedish history (above all for the *English Historical Review*).

[23] M. Roberts, 'Geijer and England', *Scandia*, LX (1994), 209–30 ('duke or darling' at p. 217).

Roberts's prodigious output on early modern Sweden had a tremendous impact. A subject that had scarcely featured in earlier historical debate in the English-speaking world now entered the mainstream and has remained there ever since. Indeed, Roberts made available so much information about his subject with such authority that it diverted attention from other Baltic powers, especially from Denmark and Poland. As Robert Frost commented in his excellent new synthesis of early modern Baltic history:

> History, it is often suggested, is written by the winners. Yet losers also write history; they just don't get translated. Thus Anglo-Saxon historiography is dominated by accounts of the period from the Swedish viewpoint in the seventeenth century, and from the Russian viewpoint in the eighteenth.

As Göran Rystad, doyen of Swedish historians put it: 'When it comes to making Swedish history known in the Anglo-Saxon world, I believe Michael achieved single-handedly more than all other historians together.' One can think of few other twentieth-century scholars who, single-handedly, have had a comparable influence on the historical study of a foreign country.[24]

The impact of Roberts's work stemmed not just from its quantity and quality, but also from the remarkable vigour of his style. Throughout his life, Roberts strove to make his prose vivid and arresting, whether in lectures or in writing (for he spoke as he wrote and not the other way round). He had a sure command of syntax and tone; he would blend the mandarin and the demotic to mischievous and ironic effect; he was skilful at parody (like W. H. Auden, he believed that the ability to parody is the surest indicator of literary command). On this subject, he gave no quarter.

> No one teaches us the craft without which we are not fitted to be good historians: the craft of letters. Many of us do not care to apply ourselves to it, and few expect instruction in that matter from their supervisors; with the consequence that (in the unkind words of Mr. Philip Guedalla) 'Historians' English is not a style: it is an industrial disease'. Yet in history, as in so much else, 'le style, c'est l'homme'; and just as Lord Dunsany once warned us never to trust a man with elastic-sided boots, so I take leave to look askance at the historian with elastic syntax and grammar. If a man will not take pains with his sentences, he cannot expect me to put unlimited faith in the accuracy of his footnotes.[25]

---

[24] R. Frost, *The Northern Wars. War, state and society in northeast Europe, 1558–1721* (2000), 14; G. Rystad to GP, 17 Oct. 2001. Unlike John Elliott and some other British historians of early modern Europe, Roberts created no 'school'. As he observed in 1991: 'I never in my whole life had a student prepared to do research in Swedish history': 'Retrospect', 69.

[25] Roberts, 'The naïve historian', 8–9. No doubt MR derived enormous pleasure from his inclusion as an authority in the *OED*: the entry on 'poliorcetics', for example, ends with a quotation from the second volume of *Gustavus Adolphus*.

Roberts's reputation never rose as high in Sweden as in the English-speaking world, even though most of his major works appeared in Swedish translation.[26] In part, of course, this arose from the fact that many native historians wrote about early modern Sweden and so Roberts's view was just one among many; but it also reflected methodological differences. Until at least the 1980s, Swedish academic historians remained committed to deep archival research and the construction of interpretive models that dwelled heavily on economic and social imperatives and the emergence of what Sven A. Nilsson of Uppsala University styled 'the military state'. It was 'all Methodology, Marx and Models' Roberts once observed.[27] He, by contrast, constructed his analysis around a strong narrative core. Nevertheless, Sweden honoured him with a knighthood in the Order of the North Star, an honorary degree, and membership of both its Academy of Letters and its Academy of Science. He subsequently wore with pride the distinctive Swedish black livery and top hat on academic occasions. The university of Lund proved especially welcoming, thanks largely to the determination of its leading historians to internationalise the context of Sweden's past. After one delightful research trip to Lund, Roberts reflected 'I could live there happily, if it wasn't such a regimented and bureaucratized country'. He persisted in liking it even after the Chief Archivist informed him 'In Sweden, you are regarded as *a living myth*'![28]

Looking back in 1991, Roberts expressed three regrets concerning his engagement with Swedish history. First, it was a lonely subject for anyone but a Swede: 'The number of Scandinavian historians in the United Kingdom was very small indeed, and the relative isolation of Belfast made contact with any of them—for instance, with Ragnhild Hatton—comparatively rare.' Second, 'Swedish history occupied only a minuscule place in the schools of modern history at British universities, though Swedish language and literature (with some encouragement from Svenska

---

[26] *Essays in Swedish history* appeared as *Sverige och Europa: studier i Svensk historia* (1969), the first two sections of *The early Vasas* as *Gustav Vasa* (1970), *The Swedish Imperial experience* as *Sverige som stormakt* (1980), and *The age of liberty* as *Frihetstiden* (1995). MR took great pains over these editions: of *Sverige som stormakt* he wrote 'I have just finished an extensive revision, designed to make it palatable to the Swedish General Reader' (MR to GP, 2 Oct. 1979)—and in this he triumphed for, according to Göran Rystad, that work remains 'in Sweden probably the most widely read of Michael's books' (G. Rystad to GP, 17 Oct. 2001).

[27] MR to GP 26 April 1982.

[28] MR to GP, 15 Nov. 1986 and 9 May 1988; and G. H. L. Le May to GP, 31 Aug. 2001. The Chief Archivist swiftly amended his accolade to 'a living legend' and Roberts 'took this very kindly'.

Institutet) was occasionally a subsidiary subject for departments of German,' and so he could never train students in his own discipline. Above all,

> Anything like genuine archival research seemed precluded by my domestic cir-
> cumstances, to say nothing of the expense involved. . . . With *The Early Vasas* I
> seemed to have typed myself as a synthesizer, a political historian, a narrative
> historian—labels which at that time still carried no serious pejorative sugges-
> tion. But to myself I seemed to be simply an interpreter who busied himself
> with trying to make available to an English public information which they
> might otherwise have found difficult of access: a service-industry, perhaps,
> though hardly a public utility.

One day, he overheard himself 'dismissively referred to as "not an archive historian". I was stung; I bristled. Shades of Namier!'[29] He immediately resolved to change his subject once more to something that would allow him to deploy his palaeographic skills.

Roberts had kept up his reading and teaching on eighteenth-century England, and he noted both that the history of British foreign policy in the two decades after 1763 remained strangely neglected and that Anglo-Swedish relations became unusually significant in international affairs during the first of those decades. He had already drawn attention to the topic, and identified the main themes, in a pioneering article published in 1964, entitled 'Great Britain and the Swedish Revolution, 1772–3'. He now worked on the relevant British manuscript collections and accumulated miles of microfilms from foreign archives. The first fruits were a series of studies that revealed the central role of the Baltic in British foreign policy during the mid-eighteenth century. In 1970, he published his Stenton Lecture on 'Splendid isolation, 1763–80'—almost as influential in its field as 'The Military Revolution'—and a chapter on Anglo-Danish-Russian relations; followed five years later by a study of Lord Macartney's mission to Russia.[30] The crowning glory came with *British Diplomacy and Swedish Politics, 1758–1773* (1980), which displayed mastery of an unusual range of primary sources. To the obvious British and Scandinavian archival material, Roberts added manuscript and

---

[29] 'Retrospect', 69–70. The colleague he overheard was Ragnhild Hatton, who made no secret of her view that although MR was a fine scholar, since he only used printed sources he was not a 'true historian'.

[30] 'Great Britain and the Swedish Revolution, 1772–3', *Historical Journal*, VII (1964), 1–46; *Splendid isolation, 1763–1780* (Reading, 1970); 'Great Britain, Denmark and Russia, 1763–1770', in *Studies in diplomatic history*, ed. R. M. Hatton and M. S. Anderson (1970), 236–68; *Macartney in Russia* (English Historical Review Supplement, VII, 1975).

printed material from Austria, France, the Netherlands, Prussia, and (via
Michael F. Metcalf) Russia. He managed, unlike many students of international relations, to relate foreign policy developments to domestic
affairs in each of the countries involved—partly through the skilful use
of reports by foreign diplomats to their home governments. The book
exemplified the three qualities that marked all Roberts's writing:

> A complete mastery of the sources; an ability to reach beyond his sources and
> give an interpretation of events and individuals that is both vivid to the general
> reader and accurate to the specialist; and a literary style which at its best is in
> the tradition of Gibbon or Macaulay.

The reviewer for *The Times Literary Supplement* hailed it as 'probably
the most thorough study now available of any aspect of British foreign
policy during the eighteenth century.'[31]

Roberts did much of the research and writing for these works while
serving as head of department at the Queen's University, Belfast, aided by
a few fellowships and sabbaticals (he particularly enjoyed a spell at All
Souls and another at the Villa Serbelloni); but he devoted much of the rest
of his time—as at Rhodes—to administration and teaching. He left his
mark on both. Although his department became one of the largest in the
Faculty of Arts, Roberts made many important contributions to the general academic life of the university, especially through the Library
Committee, which he chaired for many years during a period of change
and expansion. He also fulfilled the traditional role of an old-style professor by teaching at all levels, from the first-year outline to the final year
Special Subject, and for the General Degree as well as for Honours.[32] He
took his share of tutorials and, while maintaining a steely professionalism
(and ceaselessly lighting, cleaning and puffing on his pipe), pointed out
errors with gentleness and good humour. ('*Very* interesting theory, Miss
Campbell. It's such a pity it doesn't fit the facts.') He shared his students'
excitement when they dug something new out of the sources (for example
in his popular Special Subject on 'The Interregnum, 1649–1658'). He

---

[31] Quotations from Peter Jupp's obituary in the monthly bulletin of the QUB History department (in fact, Jupp referred to Roberts's first book, *The Whig Party* but, as he correctly stated,
those same qualities 'marked all his subsequent work'); and *TLS*, 27 Mar. 1981. For the scale of
Roberts's achievement in this field, see also the review article of H. M. Scott, 'British foreign
policy in the age of the American Revolution', *International History Review*, VI (1984), 113–25.
[32] At QUB in 1961, the first history lecture heard by George Boyce was from MR on the impact
of the French Revolution. 'It was history as we had not yet encountered it: sweeping, yet detailed
and exact; and we emerged from the lecture wondering "how one small head could carry all he
knew"' (George Boyce to GP, 21 Aug. 1997)—a striking parallel with the reaction of Alan Hall
and Copper Le May at Rhodes over twenty years before: see page 337 above.

VIOLATION OF NEUTRALITY, MAY-JUNE, 1960.

"SO YOU SEE — YOU'VE LOST EVERYTHING."
"NOT MY DOLE."

Source: Cory Library for Historical Research, Rhodes University: Michael Roberts Collection.

ensured that they received the material support they needed, asking about difficulties in getting hold of books and persuading the university library to buy duplicate copies when bottlenecks occurred. He also brought student representatives onto the Department Board (the first at Queen's to do

so) and, in every timetable change or innovation, the welfare of the students remained paramount. As one former student put it: 'My impressions
of Michael, as I look back, are of a man who had always time to listen'.[33]

Roberts won the respect of all sorts and conditions of students who
came to Queen's, whether Protestant or Catholic and whether hard-
drinkers or week-end retreaters (a division perhaps no less significant in
Ulster than religion). Between 1958 and 1960 one of them produced a
series of cartoons of departmental life featuring Roberts (and sometimes
his colleagues) in mock adversarial positions—for example as 'Kaiser
Bill', leaning heavily on his 'examiner's blue pencil', while the student
impotently wields his 'examinee's pen' (see figure). Roberts treasured
copies of these cartoons and wished one to accompany this notice. He
also got on very well with his departmental colleagues. As two of them
commented upon his retirement:

> He was able to maintain the friendly atmosphere [in his department] that had
> come easily enough whilst most matters could be settled by mutual agreement
> among the few people concerned but that might easily have perished in the
> more formal meetings that the expansion of the staff now made necessary.

When he retired, his colleagues at Queen's presented him with two
Festschrifts: one published, *Essays presented to Michael Roberts*, edited
by John Bossy and Peter Jupp (Belfast, 1976); the other a personal tribute, 'Words and Music: an entertainment for Michael Roberts', a collection full of private jokes on subjects that interested him. Nothing could
better reveal the depth of their affection.[34]

This collegiality owed much to Michael Roberts's shrewd ability to
judge job candidates. He held that one could assume a certain level of
professional flair and competence from candidates who made a short-list;
what really mattered was temperament, and choosing someone whom
everyone could live with, and enjoy doing so. Outsiders attending the
Wiles lectures always returned impressed by the collegiality as well as the
erudition of the Queen's faculty whom they met. Looking back, one of
Michael's former colleagues recalled:

> We seemed to laugh a great deal. When the political troubles came to Northern
> Ireland in 1968 the department held together to a man and a woman for more

---

[33] James Casey (an undergraduate at QUB 1961–5) to GP, 26 June 1997. Most former students
and colleagues recalled Roberts's pipe rituals with great affection.
[34] *Essays*, vii. The 'Michael Roberts Collection' at the Cory Library, Rhodes University, contains a copy of 'Words and Music: an entertainment for Michael Roberts', as well as copies of
the cartoons.

than a decade and a half, and those who joined it hold together still in friendship and affection.

That, too, was an important part of Michael Roberts's legacy to Queen's in particular and to Northern Ireland in general.[35]

When Roberts reached retirement age in 1973, he and Ann decided to move back to Grahamstown. Since he intended to retire, he reluctantly broke up his magnificent library (housed in a special extension to the house at Ballynahinch), and sent many of his books on seventeenth-century Europe to the Institute of Historical Research in London (where readers can admire his austere, neat signature). But he found he could not stop writing. In addition, he served as Director of the newly founded Institute for Social and Economic Research at Rhodes for three years and as a member of the Rhodes Council for over a decade. As one of the relatively few lay assessors resident in Grahamstown, he was much in demand on committees, especially Selection Committees, where (according to a colleague) he displayed his customary 'breadth of academic experience, independent judgment, [and] a nose for knavery however carefully concealed'.[36] He made excellent use of the Institute's resources in order to continue his publications on both Britain and Sweden in the eighteenth century; and he kept up his reviewing, especially for the *English Historical Review*, which had published his first articles in 1935. He also returned to another old interest: translation.

Roberts always loved poetry, and wrote a lot of witty light verse in younger days ('Not all of which', he later admitted, 'was retained').[37] This may explain his remarkable facility at rendering eighteenth-century Swedish verse into English, for at Grahamstown he translated many of the 'Epistles and Songs' written by Carl Michael Bellman, as well as some duets for drinkers by Gunnar Wennerberg, several poems by Anna Maria

---

[35] Deborah Lavin to GP, 17 July 1997. Nevertheless after leaving 'the Province', at least, MR revealed his sympathies: at Grahamstown he wore an orange tie on 12 July.

[36] From Rodney Davenport's address at the Memorial Service for MR, Grahamstown, 27 Jan. 1997, quoting Calvin Cook. He also played a key role in developing the Trevelyan Fellowships during a period as Visiting Fellow at the University of Durham in 1982 (Deborah Lavin to GP, 17 July 1997.)

[37] Some of Roberts's pre-war light verse appeared in two Rhodes University publications, *The Rhodeo* and *The Rhodian*. Other works met rejection, including a scatological poem inspired by his landlady in Grahamstown whose immediate reaction to the events of September 1939 was to order a hundred dozen rolls of toilet paper 'to see her through the war'. Roberts's poem ended with a curse that she might be

Compelled to use, in self-despite,/The whole twelve hundred in one night;
And hence to earn a grisly lustre/As the world's champion Bronco-buster.

Lenngren and some pieces by Birger Sjöberg. He had them privately printed and bound for his friends (and anyone else whom he thought might enjoy them) and would sing them when requested by interested visitors. He was delighted when, in honour of his eighty-fifth birthday, Swedish Radio broadcast a concert of his translations of Bellman and others.[38]

From Grahamstown, Michael Roberts also maintained contact with a huge circle of friends, including many former students. He planned his trips deliberately so he could visit them.[39] In between, he wrote them a stream of letters on a battered 1936 Remington typewriter (modified with some special keys to produce Swedish diacritics). In these he recounted recent events and the progress of his books in a shapely, sequential form, full of sharp observations and elegant turns of phrase, punctuated by a few well-aimed malevolent barbs. Keeping up with his friends must have consumed many hours, but he still found time to maintain his Swedish, to start learning Spanish, and to follow cricket. Gradually, however, his medical problems multiplied. He had a laminectomy in 1984, and thereafter needed to wear a brace, and from 1987 he depended on a pacemaker. These did not prevent him from travelling—later that year he went all round the United Kingdom with a Rail Pass—but in 1991 his tear ducts dried up and for a time he feared for his sight. He had to cancel a planned visit to Lund. His doctors even forbade watching cricket matches on television, though he occasionally violated this prohibition: in 1994, he gloated as he 'watched S. A. lick the boastful Aussies twice running'.[40] By then, his hearing had also deteriorated and he struggled to find a hearing-aid and a record player that were compatible.

Despite these afflictions, he always remained ready with advice and help—as I know better than most. I first became familiar with Roberts's 'Military Revolution' while completing my thesis on the Spanish Army of

---

[38] MR to GP, 18 Aug. 1993. The volumes are: Gunnar Wennerberg, *The Boon Companions: twenty-four duets from* Gluntarne *newly done into English by M. R.* (Grahamstown, 1976); Carl Michael Bellman *Epistles and Songs translated into English by M. R.* (3 vols., Grahamstown, 1977, 1979, 1981); Anna Maria Lenngren, *Fifteen poems from* Samlade Skaldeförsök *translated into English by M. R.* (Grahamstown, 1980); and Birger Sjöberg, *Seven pieces from* Fridas bok *done into English by M. R.* (no place, no date).

[39] For example, his last trip to Britain (in 1987) revolved around visits to Copper Le May in Oxford, his QUB friends in Belfast, Iain Adamson (another ex-QUB colleague) in Dundee, and his former students James Casey in Norwich and George Boyce in Swansea: MR to GP, 4 Nov. 1987; MR to Alan Hall, 11 Nov. 1987.

[40] MR to GP, 18 Jan. 1988 ('I never neglect my Swedish'); 9 Sep. 1989 ('I rashly decided that it was time I learned Spanish'); and 22 Feb. 1994 (on Australia's Test Match downfall).

Flanders between 1567 and 1659 and, although bowled over by the erudition and the broad sweep, wondered why my data did not match his. For
example, in 1634, at the battle of Nördlingen, Spanish troops who exhibited none of the 'revolutionary' characteristics described by Roberts
routed Swedish forces that epitomized them. Further research in Spanish
sources seemed to cast further doubts on Roberts's argument, and I
addressed them in the last chapter of my thesis, entitled 'A Military
Revolution?' With characteristic grim humour, the Degree Committee of
the Cambridge History Faculty appointed Michael Roberts to serve as
my external examiner. They scheduled my viva in the rooms of Charles
Wilson at Jesus College and I apprehensively arrived early, to find a small
but athletic man purposefully pacing the quadrangle. To my horror, I
recognised the volume under his arm as my thesis and fled until the
appointed hour. I need not have worried: although Roberts devoted a
good part of the exam to discussing that chapter (and spent much of the
rest criticising my appalling style), he agreed with my critique of his
'Military Revolution' theory and even suggested ways to strengthen it. He
recommended, however, that I could find a more appropriate conclusion
to my work when I turned it into a book, and that I should publish my
critique separately, perhaps as an article, once I had further developed the
argument.

I followed this advice, and the article duly appeared in 1976. There the
matter might have rested had Trinity College Cambridge not invited me
to deliver the 1984 Lees Knowles lectures on a topic—any topic—in military history. I decided to revisit 'The Military Revolution', partly because
I had learned a lot more about the conduct of war in early modern
Europe, by both land and sea, and partly because I suspected that
changes in that conduct played an important role in European overseas
expansion. I gave my four lectures at Trinity in November 1984 but could
not decide what to do with them. I had two concerns. First, did the lectures amount to a book, or should they appear as separate articles (a
Trinity don who had heard some of the lectures opined that they would
not merit a book)? Second, how would Roberts feel about a whole book
devoted to qualifying his original idea? I sent Roberts the lecture texts
and resolved to visit him in Grahamstown to discuss my second concern
in person. We spoke at length at New Year 1985, and I returned to Britain
re-assured that he would not take offence at my choice of subject. He
promised to re-read my text and three weeks later delivered his verdict.

> [Chapter] II was good, but basically unsurprising, except for its richness of
> illustration; as to [chapter] I, I still think that it might be more sharply focussed

> (and does your siege-theory for the Military Revolution in the West fit with your revelation of the Far Eastern salvoes, which you incautiously refer to as the eastern Military revolution?); but III is fine and IV, sensational. . . . The *total* experience of the lectures makes me think that much would be lost if they were dissected and distributed: they need to make their impact together.

With that letter, a book was born. Roberts also provided numerous references to strengthen my case and expressed great delight when the work duly appeared and received favourable notices. I can think of few other scholars who would display such remarkable generosity to a tiresome ploughboy disturbing a field that they had ploughed before.[41]

Although Michael Roberts frowned upon those who devoted their energies to discussions of historical theory and method, he did commit to paper his own views on how the discipline should be practised. He did so in 1954, in preparation for his inaugural at Queen's, but 'at the last moment my nerve failed me' and he decided on 'The Military Revolution' instead. 'The undelivered inaugural was consigned to the archives and forgotten' until, in 1994, he 'fished it out, re-read it, and found to my surprise that I still thought (by and large) what I thought in 1954.' Some excerpts from this historical testament, which he delivered at Rhodes University in March 1995 to mark the sixtieth anniversary of his appointment there, form a fitting epitaph for one of the most erudite, prolific, and influential British historians of the twentieth century.

> All historical enquiry starts with the question 'what happened?'; goes on to the question 'how?'; and ends up with the far from simple question 'why?'; but if we were to suspend our activities until the philosophers reached agreement on the meaning of 'why', the chances are that we should never embark upon them at all. A determination to establish first principles is notoriously inhibiting to constructive activity. It seems to me that there is a certain morbidity in the preoccupation of some modern historians with the justification of their own existence and the rigorous scrutiny of their intellectual intestines. Self-consciousness may at last stifle creation . . .
>
> There are certain qualities which are common to all historians, of whatever colour: an unflagging desire to know and understand the past; an imaginative sympathy which overleaps the centuries; a personal engagement which is strong enough to bear up under the labours of the enterprise. However we may rationalise it, however 'scientific' the methods we may employ, historiography at bottom is not a rational activity, any more than writing an opera is. Historiography is generated by a species of emotion; and a main problem of the historian is to keep emotion under control. . . . It is vain to wish for impartiality: class-feeling, patriotism, religion, so far from being weaknesses to be deplored, or stifled, or

---

[41] MR to GP, 27 Jan. 1985. G. Parker, *The military revolution. Military innovation and the rise of the West, 1500–1800* (Cambridge, 1988; 3rd edition, 2000; dedicated to Michael Roberts).

disguised, are necessary trace-elements without which history grows feeble and chlorotic. What matters is not an unattainable impartiality, but honesty and fair-mindedness.

It is a commonplace that history involves a continual act of selection: this is, indeed, crucial to the whole business of writing history. It is an agonizing operation. Anybody who has ever engaged in an extended piece of historical writing will vividly remember how much of his material never got into the book at all. Was he right to leave it out? right to prefer this example to that, the one testimony to the other? ought not his decisions as between them to have been justified in a fairly-argued footnote? After all, it is with history as with icebergs: it is the submerged part which is the larger, and also the more dangerous to passing mariners. For my part, I confess to a conviction that very few historians select their material in accordance with clear, logical and philosophical principles. Most of us (I think) select it according to the issue of innumerable conflicts within ourselves, conscious, half-conscious or unconscious: conflicts between mind and heart, prejudice and fair-mindedness, austerity and abandon, utility and ornament, rigour and style. . . .

The Recorded Past, it seems to me, is the material out of which historians are made. When we study history, or attempt to write it, the object of our attention is, quite simply, the materials from which history can conceivably be written, together with the histories which have in fact been based upon them. In the sense in which I use the word, 'history' is the effective communication, in speech or writing, of some information retrieved from the Recorded Past: without the historian, there is no history. In itself, history does not exist, it is *made*: made by the historian, or by tradition, or by the folk-memory, or even by the bard. Extraneous circumstances—material prosperity, social misery, foreign conquest, messianic notions, or whatever it may be—have from time to time led historians to write in ways which reflected those circumstances, and hence have appealed to a majority of their contemporaries; others, less sensitive to the prevailing climate, have written histories that failed and were (for a time) forgotten. But no history exists until it has been written, or otherwise narrated.[42]

GEOFFREY PARKER
Fellow of the Academy

Note. In compiling this memoir, I have drawn on four principal sources. The 'Retrospect' written by Michael Roberts for *Maktpolitik och Husfrid: Studier i internationell och svenska historia tillägnade Göran Rystad* (Lund, 1991), 1–26, and reprinted in *The Worcester College Record 1993* (Oxford, 1993), 61–71; an interview with Paul Maylam six weeks before his death, used by Professor Maylam in 'Michael Roberts (1908–1996): a profile', *South African Historical Journal*, XXXVI (1997), 269–76; a series of conversations with MR over New Year 1985; and reminiscences of

---

[42] MR to GP, 21 June 1994; 'The naïve historian', 6–7. MR updated some references in his original text and had it retyped before delivering and publishing it.

Michael Roberts kindly communicated by Jeremy Black, John Bossy, George Boyce, James Casey, Rodney Davenport, Andrew Duminy, Alan Hall, Peter Jupp, Deborah Lavin, Basil Le Cordeur, G. H. L. Le May, Paul Maylam, Michael F. Metcalf, Pepé and Ian Morton, Joanna Parker, Jane Roberts, Göran Rystad, Hamish Scott, and Shirley Stewart. I thank them all.

Professor Roberts bequeathed his Scandinavian books, microfilms and other materials, and a part of his academic correspondence, to Worcester College, Oxford, and the rest of his papers and some memorabilia to the Cory Library of Rhodes University, Grahamstown, South Africa, where they form the 'Michael Roberts Collection'.

ROBERT ROBINS

Robert Henry Robins
1921–2000

ROBERT HENRY ROBINS, Professor Emeritus in the University of London will be remembered as one of the pioneers in the establishment of linguistics (as distinct from the related but older discipline of philology) as an academic subject in Britain. More specifically and especially in his later life, he was recognised as the leading scholar throughout the world in the history of linguistics.

He was a well loved, if somewhat unworldly and old-fashioned, figure known affectionately by all of his friends and many of his colleagues simply as 'Bobby'. He died suddenly (and alone) in Caterham, Surrey on 21 April 2000 at the age of seventy-eight.

He was born in Broadstairs, the son of a GP, on 1 July 1921. He tells, in an autobiographical account, of his interest in language from an early age. He learnt Latin and French at school and his father had taught him the Greek alphabet before he was introduced to Greek at the age of nine. He was fascinated by the intricacies of Latin grammar (especially the mysterious 'ablative absolute'), by the idea that 'French came from Latin' and the suggestion that English was 'like French but also like German in a different way'.

He won a scholarship to Tonbridge School in 1935 and was placed in the Classical Upper Fifth and the Classical Sixth Form the following year. As was usual in those days his education at Tonbridge consisted almost entirely of a traditional study of the grammar of Latin and Greek and the reading of classical texts, but he continued his personal interest in linguistic issues, especially the relationship between Latin and Greek, which

Proceedings of the British Academy, **115**, 357–364. © The British Academy 2002.

led him to look up etymological entries in the relevant major dictionaries and even (somewhat uncomprehendingly) to read Otto Jespersen's
Language in 1940.

He won a scholarship for classics to New College, Oxford in 1939
and took the courses for Honour Moderations from 1940 to 1941 (during
the Battle of Britain), achieving a First Class degree. He often stated
later that he regarded the study of the Classics, with its considerable
emphasis on the language itself (and its grammar in particular) as the
finest training for a career in Linguistics. Moreover, he added to his
interest in, and knowledge of, the relationship between languages by
attending a course of lectures entitled 'The Comparative Philology of
the Greek and Latin languages', given by the Professor of Comparative
Philology, G. K. Braunholtz. Bobby adored Braunholtz and was proud
that he achieved a 'straight alpha' in the 'Mods' examination. Yet he was
somewhat critical of Braunholtz's lectures in that they failed to discuss
the predecessors of the Neogrammarians and, although they introduced
topics such as sound laws, analogy, and borrowing, they did not address
any of the theoretical issues associated with them (and even did not
mention the term 'Neogrammarian').

He resumed his studies in 1945 and was awarded a First Class degree
in Literae Humaniores ('Greats') in 1948. At that time this course consisted of Ancient History and Philosophy and Bobby saw both subjects as
relevant to his future career—ancient history as a basis for his interest in
the history of linguistics (discussed below) and philosophy as relevant to
linguistic theory. He must have been influenced by A. J. Ayer and the
logical positivists, and by the sceptical criticism of them by his tutors
Isaiah Berlin and Herbert Hart. It was also the period of the dawning
of 'ordinary language philosophy', which later found disciples among
linguists.

From 1942 to 1945 he served in the RAF. In 1942 the War Office came to
realise that knowledge of foreign languages was an essential part of the war
effort, and that, in particular, there was complete ignorance of Japanese.
So Bobby was sent to a rather traditional short course of Japanese, was
then given a commission and sent to the School of Oriental and African
Studies in London to teach Japanese to service personnel, under the formidable J. R. Firth. According to what may well be a somewhat apocryphal story, the War Office discovered that the Japanese Air Force was
able to send all their operation messages in clear, because no-one understood Japanese (and the Americans had detained all their citizens of
Japanese origin). So they approached a Department of Japanese for help,

only to be told that a course in Japanese would take four years! By some flash of inspiration, they then approached Firth, who realised that all that was needed was the ability to recognise a very small section of the spoken language (what he called a 'restricted language') and that this could be taught in a matter of months. There can be no doubt that Bobby's experience in teaching Japanese (with the emphasis on the spoken language and this notion of a restricted language) under Firth was quite the most influential on his later work in Linguistics.

After the war the Scarbrough Commission recommended expansion of work in Oriental and African languages. Firth was appointed to the Chair of General Linguistics at SOAS (the first such chair in any British University) in 1946 and proceeded to gather around him a band of young scholars who were willing and able to follow him. When Bobby had finished his degree at Oxford, Firth invited him to apply for a lectureship in his Department of Phonetics and Linguistics, and appointed him in 1948.

He was a very fine tutor and lecturer, explaining the intricacies of what was then a completely new subject in a clear and lucid manner. Indeed, one of his main tasks in his early years was to give a course of lectures at 11 a.m., immediately after lectures by Firth (which attracted a large audience from outside SOAS). He often said that his main function in these lectures was to explain what Firth had said to a largely uncomprehending audience. For Firth, for all his originality and knowledge, presented his ideas in a very discursive, unsystematic way and often used a sarcastic tone to indicate the matters that he disagreed with, much to the confusion of the overseas students in particular, who would often conclude that Firth was saying the opposite of what he actually intended!

His enthusiasm for his subject never waned, for he continued with part-time teaching in the Universities of Luton and Cambridge right up until his death. He also boasted that he would never decline an invitation to a conference after his retirement, for fear that he might be thought to be 'past it' and so not invited again. Indeed, he returned from one in Cyprus less than two weeks before his death. He often announced that his main aim in life was that of 'advancing the subject'. This he certainly achieved by the publication of one of the best ever introductions to Linguistics— his *General Linguistics: an introductory Survey*, first published in 1964 (fourth edition 1989). The word 'General' is important in that he believed that the inevitable specialisation in the subject should not mean that it could not be presented as an integrated whole. Moreover, for him linguistics was always 'descriptive', i.e.; based upon research into actual languages. This was partly through the influence of Firth and Bobby's experience with teaching spoken Japanese, but it also derived from the fact that the department was in SOAS, for all its members, like the members of all the other departments, were expected to undertake research in little-known languages (or their institutions) and encouraged to take paid study leave to do so. After some research in London on Georgian, Bobby chose to work in California on Yurok, a Native Language of America, and later worked, in London, on Sundanese, a language of Indonesia. He wrote a number of excellent articles on all of these languages.

Firth's views on linguistics were highly original, marked particularly by his opposition to what was then known as 'American Structuralism' and to phonological analysis in terms of the phoneme, as presented by both the American linguists of the time and by Daniel Jones, who had been the Head of the Phonetics Department at University College London. Firth had been a lecturer there in the 1930s and had been required to teach phonemics, though his publications indicate early dissatisfaction with the theory. Yet members of Firth's department were expected to follow and develop his ideas (notably his theory of 'Prosodics', 'collocation' and 'context of situation'), and even to submit all their research papers to him for approval. However, Bobby, unlike most other members of the department, always maintained his interest in the American work, probably through the influence of American scholars whom he met in California while researching Yurok. Most importantly he (rightly) provided a detailed exposition of it in his lectures, thus somewhat balancing Firth's complete dismissal of it. Two of his best articles were published early in his career—'Noun and verb in universal grammar' (1952) and 'In defence of WP' (1960). The first of these was published in the American journal *Language* and anticipates one of the most important issues to be much discussed later, mainly after 1980 and mostly in America under the heading of 'linguistic typology'. The second relates directly to a discussion in America on the merits of 'Item and Arrangement' and 'Item and Process' as the two possible models of grammatical description, but advocates neither, arguing instead for 'Word and Paradigm'. Both were excellent, scholarly, works, but neither of them has much relevance to the issues that Firth was pursuing. It may also be said that he was probably less enthusiastic than other members of the department about Firth's phonological theory of 'Prosodics'. His one descriptive article, 'The phonology of the nazalised forms of Sundanese', shows less enthusiasm for prosodics as well as less originality than some of the crusading articles written by other members of the department, while his more general article on prosodics, 'Aspects of Prosodic Analysis', takes a fairly detached view of the theory, discussing it in relation to other linguistic proposals. It may also be significant that, unlike others, he did not continue to publish on the subject after Firth's retirement. But, of course, the fact that he was less inclined than others to follow Firth blindly is more a sign of his independent thought than a criticism of his scholarship.

Most of his publications in the twenty or so years after Firth's retirement were concerned with general linguistic theory. The most important was his *General linguistics: an introductory survey*. This, as already mentioned, is one of the best introductions ever written, but there are three comments on it when seen from today's perspective. One is that, as in some of his articles, he was influenced more by American work than by Firth's views. For instance, he devotes almost thirty pages to the (American) phoneme and only ten to Firth's prosodic analysis. The second is that there was very little on semantics apart from a section on 'The structural treatment of linguistic meaning' and a chapter entitled 'Grammar: grammatical semantics'. This neglect of semantics he inherited from both the Americans and Firth. Thirdly, there was nothing on Chomsky's Transformational-generative grammar, although Chomsky's *Syntactic structures* had been published seven years earlier. Although this omission was remedied in later editions, it is clear that Bobby, like so many others in both Britain and America, had failed at the time to realise its importance and to realise that, post-Chomsky, American structuralism would no longer be the dominant theory. He was, no doubt, encouraged in his theoretical work by the fact that Firth's successor was C. E. Bazell, himself an outstanding theoretician. In addition to the two articles already mentioned and the book, he wrote articles on a variety of subjects, such as the merits of formal grammar and its place in linguistic theory, syntactic analysis, the structure of language and the Sapir–Whorf hypothesis (that one's grammar determines one's view of the universe), as well as more general papers concerned with language and the status of linguistics as a science within a liberal education. None of them was outstandingly original, but their excellent presentation must have helped in Bobby's stated desire to 'advance the subject'.

Yet Bobby will be best remembered as the pioneer and for years the leading scholar in a subject that had been almost completely neglected — the history of linguistics. He published a little book entitled *Ancient and mediaeval grammatical theory in Europe* in 1951, the outcome of an invitation to Firth by Marjorie Daunt to give a short series of lectures at Birkbeck College which Firth passed on to Robins, stating firmly that any classicist worth his salt had read Priscian. That challenge led him to develop an area of research which, founded on his love of ancient history, gradually claimed ever more of his energy and affection. In 1967 he published *A short history of linguistics*, a textbook which provided a coherent and accessible account of western linguistics from Plato to the present. Although not the first book on the subject in English, it was the most comprehensive in its scope, and certainly the first to pay more than lip service to the medieval and early modern epochs. It was characterised by a Firthian concern for "context of situation", in that the relevant cultural and intellectual context was outlined in a few pages at the start of each chapter. This was a wise precaution in the light of the widely differing educational backgrounds of the international community of students at SOAS, and one which ensured that the book would continue to find an audience in Britain decades after such terms as 'Hellenistic' and 'Scholastic' ceased to be common knowledge amongst undergraduates. Studies on individual scholars and themes in the history of linguistics came to occupy the lion's share of his time: particular favourites were Priscian, William Bullokar, Sir William Jones, and of course J. R. Firth. Also dear to his heart were the grammarians of Byzantium, and he tried to break through the deplorable silence of Byzantinists on the subject in his last book, *The Byzantine grammarians: their place in history* (1993). This is probably his most original contribution to the subject, offering as it does a series of sketches of the work of the principal figures, with generous quotations from sources available in print (he never indulged in manuscript work). He was particularly proud of his two doctoral students in the history of linguistics, Geoffrey L. Bursill-Hall and Francis P. Dinneen, both of whom went on to become scholars of note in the field. Not surprisingly, when the Henry Sweet Society for the History of Linguistics was formed, he was chosen as its President.

He stayed in the Department of Phonetics and Linguistics until his retirement, in 1986, deservedly and expectedly becoming a professor in 1966 and its head in 1970, after the retirement of Bazell. Although this was the first university department in Britain with 'Linguistics' in its title, a number of other departments were established in the sixties, and Bobby was always happy to point out that most of the Heads of these departments had started their careers in London. Yet he himself did not apply for any of the vacant chairs. This may have been due, in part, to lack of ambition for purely personal advancement and reputation, for he was always modestly content with his lot, though always quite devoted to pursuing his academic interests. It may also be due to the fact that everyone knew that he would eventually be appointed to what had once been Firth's chair.

He will also be remembered for his close association with the Philological Society, the oldest linguistic society in Britain. He was its Secretary for eighteen years and then its President for three and, when he retired from that presidency, he was awarded the unique honour of being made President Emeritus. His eminence in scholarship was widely acknowledged. Many honours were bestowed upon him nationally and internationally. Most notably (in addition to being elected a Fellow of the British Academy in 1986), he was made a life member of the Linguistic Society of America and a member of the Academia Europaea. He also served as President of the European Linguistic society, the Societas Linguistica Europaea and of the Comité International Permanent de Linguistes. Indeed, his standing was probably even greater overseas than in his home country, as shown by his election to the presidency of the SLE (for he had never had any interest in it and had never even been a member) and by the award of life-membership of the LSA quite early in his career.

He was presented with two Festschrifts, both concerned with the history of linguistics, and was justly proud that he had been so honoured by his colleagues. Even since his death his eminence has been recognised. The Philological Society has set up an annual Robins Prize open to all, while the University of Luton has established the R. H. Robins Memorial Prize awarded annually to its best student in Linguistics.

Something must be said of the man himself, for he was a quite unique 'character'. To those who knew him only as the very distinguished Professor Robins he probably appeared to be a rather aloof patrician figure. Yet even this won him many admirers. At the business session of the International Congress of Linguistics in Japan in 1982, which was chaired by him as President, a distinguished American woman professor was quite ecstatic about his performance as Chairman, his wonderful command of English and his beautiful accent. He was, she said, 'the perfect English gentleman-scholar'. It is certainly true that he could present himself with dignity and confidence when required, as could be seen when, at the same Congress, the Japanese Crown Prince and Princess unexpectedly decided to accept an invitation to attend the official reception. Bobby and his wife Sheila were perfect hosts at this most prestigious occasion. (As an aside, it might be added that it was a most enjoyable event, because, in honour of the royal guests, the hotel in which it was held put on a magnificent offering of food and drink, at its own expense!)

To those who knew him well, those for whom he was always just 'Bobby', he appeared to be uncomplicated, with an almost child-like simplicity and even a little other-wordliness. He was generous, courteous and quite incapable of making enemies or thinking ill of anyone—except when he was incensed by the threatened closure of 'his' department after his retirement and by subsequent unfortunate events that involved some of his most valued former colleagues. He was a supreme optimist who could always look on the bright side. He was held in great affection by many, though that affection was occasionally tinged with kindly amusement at what were seen as actions or remarks that were typical of him.

Yet his life was affected by great sadness. His two elder brothers had died when he was young, so that he was virtually an only child of aged parents. When he married Sheila Fynn, a fellow lecturer at SOAS, in 1953, he would speak openly and with pleasure about the blessings that 'le bon Dieu' would bring to them, but, unfortunately, they were not blessed and remained childless. Yet Sheila was a wonderful influence on him. Not only did she support him in his academic life, but she also made him extremely happy, relaxed and even domesticated. She died not very long after they celebrated their silver wedding anniversary. It was typical of Bobby that, although he spoke openly about her final, terrible, illness, he did not show his enormous grief, even to those who shared it, but involved himself in his work right up until the day he died. Yet his love for her never waned: shortly before his death he said 'I'm not afraid of death, for either I shall just go to sleep for ever, or I shall see my beloved Sheila again'.

F. R. PALMER
Fellow of the Academy
VIVIEN LAW
Fellow of the Academy

Note.   Vivien Law was seriously ill when she contributed to this memoir, and died before its publication. She will be greatly missed.

ALAN TYSON

Alan Walker Tyson
1926–2000

FEW COMPOSERS HAVE ATTRACTED so much critical, scholarly, and analytical attention as Haydn, Mozart, and Beethoven. Despite inevitable changes of emphasis, the classic status accorded them even by contemporaries has proved extraordinarily durable. Until relatively recently their music stood at the heart of the concert repertory and was widely accepted as a touchstone of excellence. As early as the mid-nineteenth century important biographical and musical studies of Mozart and Beethoven initiated traditions of research which still retain their momentum. Alan Tyson's contribution to their continuing vitality can scarcely be over-estimated. By the time he entered the field the main questions of authenticity and chronology seemed to have been settled in so far as the evidence allowed, and reasonably satisfactory texts established. Yet it was precisely in these fundamental matters that he was to make his most remarkable discoveries, some of which brought with them fresh insights into the composers' working methods. The originality of his achievement was great; it can perhaps be paralleled only by the singularity of the path that led him to musical scholarship in the first place.

Tyson took some pride in having three Scottish grandparents, but the Tysons themselves were Cumbrian, and although born in Glasgow he and his brothers were brought up in London, where their father was Surmaster of St Paul's School. In 1940 Tyson went to Rugby. He specialised in Classics; many years later he claimed to have wanted to take science, but it is unlikely that any firmly expressed preference would have been over-ruled. In any case, he pursued Classics with enthusiasm and success. At

Proceedings of the British Academy, **115**, 367–382. © The British Academy 2002.

Rugby too he learned the viola, which apparently suited him better than the piano, and he much enjoyed playing in the school orchestra. His parents encouraged his musical interests; towards the end of his school days his father gave him Tovey's *Essays in Musical Analysis*. However, he seems not to have been taught any music theory. He never became entirely at home with standard musical terminology, although that set no constraints on his intuitive understanding of music or his astounding musical memory.

On leaving school in 1945 Tyson decided to do his two-year stint in the armed forces before going up to Oxford. He took a naval short-course, as it happened in Oxford, which should have led to a commission, but when at a late stage he presumed to question a long-established point of navigational procedure he was judged unsuitable. He made out the rest of his time as a postman seaman, a position that gave him plenty of practice in palaeography. Having contributed to and edited the *New Rugbeian* at school, he continued to exercise his talent for light verse in his new surroundings, as he was later to do in Oxford. One example was published in *Blighty*, a humorous weekly distributed free to the forces overseas and listing Churchill among its patrons.[1] But most of his efforts would scarcely have filled the bill: some parodied verses that would have been unfamiliar to much of the readership, some were in Latin, and others (for instance a couple of verses beginning 'O atom bomb, where are you bombing?') would have conflicted with the editors' morale-boosting brief.

The naval interlude seems to have left very little impression on him. In 1947 he followed in his father's and grandfather's footsteps to Magdalen, as his two brothers and a nephew were later to do. He had won the top open scholarship in Classics, and was to end up with a double first. Meanwhile he pursued many interests and was already noted among fellow undergraduates for qualities that many were to associate with him later: great sociability, good humour, kindness, interest in others and wit without malice. There were walking holidays in Greece, France, and Tuscany, and for three seasons he engaged seriously in mountaineering. In the summer of 1949 he spent nine days with his next eldest brother in the Arolla district where they climbed intensively every day, ending with the Dent Blanche. On a different occasion, when he and a friend were climbing the Schreckhorn with a guide, something went wrong. They were delayed, were obliged to spend a second night in the alpine hut, and returned to

---

[1] 'Clippie', by P/S A. A. W. Tyson, HMS *Royal Arthur*, in *Blighty*, NS no. 376 (28 Dec. 1946), 15. Authors of more substantial contributions were awarded two guineas, but versifiers could normally expect no more than half a guinea, which is what Tyson got.

the valley only on the third day. Tyson said very little about the incident, which seems to have shaken him; it may have been in his mind when a little later he wrote a brief appreciation of the mountaineering writings of Leslie Stephen,[2] who in 1861 was the first to climb the Schreckhorn. After 1950 he was obliged to give up climbing because of the degeneration of a hip through Perthes' disease, which he had contracted as a child.

With his graduation in 1951, Tyson reached the first of two turning points in his life when he had to face difficult decisions. On the face of it there was nothing unusual in his hesitation over the choice of a career, nor in his parents' anxiety at his indecision. His distinction in Classics and his father's profession pointed in an obvious direction which he was initially prepared to explore, if half-heartedly. He turned down a job at Harrow immediately after graduating, and tentative feelers at Winchester came to nothing. Applications for university posts at Manchester and Cardiff were unsuccessful, which discouraged him. But there were other factors at work. As early as 1951 he was reacting against the narrowness of school life and thinking of a career in psychotherapy as a possibility. When asked years later how he came to take up psycho-analysis, he replied that, as was the case with most analysts, he had begun by feeling the need to understand himself better. Whatever his difficulties may have been, the attempt to solve them opened up new horizons.

As soon as his finals were over Tyson made a proposal of marriage which was rejected. Apparently soon afterwards he struck up the first of his more durable relationships with an Afro-American graduate of Smith College called Marie Wills (later Singer). Sixteen years older than Tyson she was an accomplished pianist with an interest in jazz who accompanied her own singing; later in life she took up painting with considerable success. In 1950 she had joined Anna Freud's Hampstead Child-Psychotherapy Course. She was to qualify in 1954 and move to Cambridge, where she became well known as a psychotherapist and teacher, and was elected a Fellow of Clare Hall. Whether or not Tyson had already thought of being analysed before he met Wills, she played a large part in directing his steps. It is not difficult to understand how her responsible guidance may have helped to counteract the sense of oppression he seems to have experienced in relation to well-intentioned parental expectations and indeed family life in general.

Three important developments date from the following year, 1952. Tyson obtained at the second attempt a Prize Fellowship at All Souls and

---

[2] 'The Playground Revisited', *Oxford Mountaineering* (1953), 41–4.

announced his intention to work on psychology. He began analysis, probably at Wills's instigation, with Ilse Hellman-Noach, who was closely associated with Anna Freud's Hampstead Clinic; this was evidently a preliminary step towards his training as an analyst at the Institute of Psycho-Analysis, for when he started there in 1953 Hellman was his training analyst. And to earn a little money he coached Ralph and Frances Partridge's son Burgo for university entrance. This job, though not important in itself, had an important outcome. When Frances Partridge engaged him on 1 May, she wrote in her diary that he was 'training to be a psycho-analyst', and added: 'Perhaps that will come in useful, as I have just agreed to index the complete works of Freud for James's translation'.[3] It was thus, it seems, through the Partridges that Tyson met or became better acquainted with James Strachey, and was enlisted in the same year as one of the four editors of the Freud *Standard Edition* along with Anna Freud and Alix Strachey. At that time he knew no German, so he set about learning it and in due course contributed several of his own translations to the edition, including the study of Leonardo da Vinci and the *Psychopathology of Everyday Life*.[4] In September 1955, after checking his Leonardo translation, Anna Freud wrote to him that she was most impressed by it. She suggested some corrections involving shades of meaning, but it is extraordinary that he should have been able to tackle so soon texts in which everything depended on precision of that kind.

For the next few years Tyson's life settled into a relatively stable pattern. Initially psycho-analytical circles deprecated the distraction of his Oxford connections, and there were those at All Souls who wished he would abandon psycho-analysis altogether. Chief among these was the new Warden, John Sparrow, with whom his relations were always to remain uneasy. However, both parties soon found that they had to accept Tyson as they found him. As part of his training he was temporarily attached in 1954 to the nursing staff at the Cassel Hospital and he underwent a second analysis with Charles Rycroft, one of his supervisors at the Institute. It is of some interest that at the end of their lives both Hellman and Rycroft remarked quite independently that they did not feel that their analyses of Tyson had progressed very far. He qualified as a lay analyst in 1957 and practised until 1963.

Meanwhile he had decided that his prospects would be improved if he were able to work as a psychotherapist in the Health Service, for which a

---

[3] *Everything to lose: diaries 1945–1960* (1985), p. 155.
[4] As an offshoot of the work on the Freud edition Tyson published, in collaboration with James Strachey but as first-named author, 'A Chronological Hand-List of Freud's Works', *International Journal of Psycho-Analysis*, 37 (1956), 19–33.

medical doctorate was an essential qualification. Never having done any science he had no exemption from the First MB. So he took a course to rectify that in 1959–60, and then proceeded to the five-term course for the Second MB at University College London. All this presented him with as little difficulty as had the German language, but his mostly much younger fellow students at University College found the work considerably more arduous than he did, and were perhaps less bothered by the authoritarian teaching style, which was quite unlike anything he had been used to. His frustration showed and put him at odds with some of the staff. But he stayed the course, and at the end of it was invited to remain at the college and take a degree in a related subject such as bio-chemistry, an offer extended only to students of outstanding ability. However, he preferred to move on to clinical studies at University College Hospital Medical School. There he founded and edited a fortnightly duplicated magazine called *Probe*, which ran for a year in 1963–4. Because of its unofficial status it was able to air matters, especially about staff–student relations, which were not raised publicly elsewhere. It ruffled feathers and achieved a regular circulation of over 350 copies. After being obliged to resit his gynaecology and obstetrics examination Tyson obtained his MB and BS in 1965. He held house officer posts in medicine and surgery in London at New End Hospital, and was registered with the General Medical Council in 1967 at the age of forty.

Tyson's career now took an unexpected turn. It seems that satisfaction at acquiring his qualifications outweighed any strong desire to use them: the goal achieved, his interest waned. His first move was not to seek the kind of post in clinical psychiatry for which he had spent so much time equipping himself, but to apply successfully for a visiting lectureship in psychiatry at the Montefiore Hospital in New York for the year 1967–8; he could claim relevant experience, for he had lectured at various times to students in the Hampstead Child-Therapy Course and in the Tavistock Clinic Child-Therapy Course, and also on Freud and related fields in the sub-faculty of psychology in Oxford. Nor did he return to clinical work in 1968. For the next two years he was lecturer in psychopathology at Oxford, and during the same period took part in an introductory course for students at the Institute of Psycho-Analysis. In 1972 he was honoured with membership of the recently founded Royal College of Psychiatrists. But after 1970 he held no position of any kind concerned with psychological matters. Instead he devoted himself full-time to musicology.

Such radical steps are not taken easily. For many years Tyson must have thought of his musicology as a scholarly hobby, in no way a threat to his psycho-analytical career even if scarcely less important to him. Its origins lay a long way back. Whether, as seems likely, his studies for Greats first directed his attention towards the theoretical aspects of psychology, the seeds of his musicological work were, as he himself testified, sown even earlier by his introduction to textual criticism in the Mods course. The subject appealed to him strongly. His first idea was to work on Shakespeare, but he quickly realised that the ground had been too thoroughly worked over to afford a newcomer much scope, and he turned to music. This came about in an unusual way. The decisive factor was not the natural aptitude that enabled him to play jazz and Broadway songs by ear at the piano, strum the guitar, and quickly recognise the characteristic harmonic features of the newly emerged Beatles, essential to his work as such innate musicality may have been. Nor was it the habitually wide-ranging curiosity that led him, for instance, to acquire at some point a couple of square pianos dating from the period in which he specialised. It was something much more unexpected: he was a born collector.

Somewhat unfocused bibliophilia may be traced as far back as his undergraduate days, for his library contained early editions, presumably picked up at that time, of philosophical and political works that would have been required reading for Greats. Possibly no later he began collecting antiquarian printed music. Since he never noted dates of acquisition the growth of his collection cannot be charted at all precisely, but the general picture is not hard to reconstruct. After the war English musical publications of the late eighteenth and early nineteenth centuries were plentiful and for the most part cheap. Purcell and Handel seemed obvious cases for investigation. Tyson bought a few editions, including some earlier ones, but soon saw that nothing new was to be extracted from them. By contrast, although many of the editions of Haydn, Mozart, and Beethoven had appeared in their lifetimes and each composer had had well-documented contacts of one kind or another with England, the possible consequences for textual transmission had never been investigated. This prompted a line of enquiry that led to all Tyson's earlier discoveries, either directly or by divergent paths along the way.

The importance for Tyson of his collection needs to be emphasised, for few readers of his work will have guessed the extent to which it nourished his earlier scholarship, or even known of its existence: he only occasionally needed to mention that a particular edition was in his own possession, and locations of rarities cited in catalogues and bibliographies do not attract much attention. From the 1950s the collection grew fast. Tyson bought continental first and early editions of the Viennese classical composers as an essential complement to English ones. And his English purchases often brought with them a wide variety of other publications, because it was the custom in England at that time for amateurs to have their favourite songs, piano pieces, or chamber music bound in substantial composite volumes. Each volume bought for the sake of one item was a lucky dip that might contain in addition something of unexpected interest among the trivia. So almost by accident the collection began to reflect the whole spectrum of contemporary English musical taste, and the various ways in which the many publishers sought to exploit or shape some aspect of it. Far from turning a blind eye to what lay outside his primary concerns, Tyson noticed and followed leads that resulted in important research; his work on Clementi is an outstanding example.

For thirty years or more Tyson maintained the same patterns of collecting, though the scope widened as he began to travel abroad more frequently. He built up probably the finest private collection of the post-war period for primary and secondary printed sources of the music on which he worked most closely. At the same time the attraction of the ancillary and the peripheral never lost its hold on him. He brought together music by his composers' teachers, pupils, associates and prominent contemporaries of every kind. Various types of publication might provide useful background in particular contexts: a quantity of popular dances for piano intended for the same public as potboilers by Beethoven and Schubert; theatrical and literary year-books and almanacs occasionally carrying important musical supplements; librettos and the plays on which they were based; little word-books apparently printed for concert-goers; pocket histories of Vienna and guides with maps for tourists of the day, and a street directory.

Moreover, Tyson's interests ranged far beyond what originated in Vienna or London, or in the classical period: he had first editions of many of the most eminent composers right up to his own time, though fewer and with relatively little supporting material. And he could never resist anything from any time or place that seemed in some way musically or bibliographically anomalous. Thus a certain proportion of the collection, which by the later 1980s contained, quite apart from the literature, over 3,500 items of printed music and some seventy manuscripts, had no bearing on his scholarly work. However, the dividing line between the actually or potentially useful and the demonstrably irrelevant is a very fuzzy one. Unexpected connections or analogous situations might crop up at any point, and when they did Tyson was likely to have at least some of the evidence to hand. Even the first editions from later periods reflected continuities and changes in publishing practice that might prove instructive, though examples may also have been useful in seminars, and collecting for its own sake may have played a part as well. It was Tyson's wish, most generously honoured by his family in 1998, that the British Library and the Bodleian Library, in that order, should eventually receive anything they might want from his collection before the remainder was dispersed. The gift has been of enormous benefit to both institutions.[5]

Although Tyson's early collecting gave the impetus for his first musicological undertakings, it could naturally not answer all his needs. He had to search for further material in many libraries, above all in the music library of the British Museum (later transferred to the British Library). An essential source of information in his work on English editions was provided by the registers at Stationers' Hall, where publishers had to submit any publication for which they wished to claim copyright on the day of publication. Of the institutions to which registration copies were distributed the Museum was most easily reached while Tyson was training in London; it was only a short walk from University College Hospital, where he would fill every spare moment studying music. The Museum had other advantages. In relatively recent times considerable effort had been put into improving the representation of continental editions of the Viennese classics; after the acquisition in 1946 of the Paul Hirsch Library, which was particularly rich in that respect, the Museum could offer a range of editions hard to match outside Vienna. Especially valuable for Tyson were the apparent duplicates, for the engraved plates from which a particular work was printed would often be corrected, damaged, or both, between printings. With the Museum copies and his own for comparison he was well placed to trace the vicissitudes through which a text had passed, even if a trip to Vienna on his Lambretta motor scooter (later upgraded to a Volkswagen Beetle) became necessary at some point. An early essay on Steiner's publishing of Beethoven gives striking evidence of his sharp eye in such matters.

Tyson had never published on music until his first year as a medical student, but he soon made up for lost time: by 1967, when he was registered, he had produced some twenty articles, several of the earlier ones grouped round a book on the authentic English editions of Beethoven. This was a notable achievement. It was known from correspondence that

---

[5] See O. W. Neighbour, 'The Tyson Collection', *British Library Journal*, 24 (1998 [2000]), 269–77; P. Ward Jones, section headed 'Music', *Bodleian Library Record*, 16 no. 5 (April 1999), 432–3. Tyson's working papers have been placed in the Bodleian.

Beethoven had tried over many years to arrange simultaneous publication of his works on the continent and in London. Tyson was able to show by reference to the Stationers' Hall registers that the London editions were in some cases the first to appear; moreover, much more important, they were usually textually independent, having been prepared from manuscripts copied and sent over for the purpose. The continental editions sometimes benefited from the composer's last minute changes, but where errors were missed the English ones could often supply the correct readings. The practice of simultaneous publication in more than one country also gave the English editions of Mendelssohn and Chopin textual value. Tyson never published his work on them, though he sent information to other scholars. But through his familiarity with publications of the time he realised that many English publishers' plate numbers could be dated with a fair degree of confidence; with the help of a collaborator he put together a useful book of dated lists.

It was typical of Tyson that alongside all this he should find time for other important work. In his very first article, of 1961, he proved that two piano trios invariably included among Haydn's were by Pleyel, and a little later he removed six string quartets known as Haydn's Opus 3 from his canon. He drew attention to the role of Stephen Storace in bringing new works by his friend Mozart to London. He dispelled much of the uncertainty surrounding the early works of Field, at the same time suggesting his authorship for two small anonymous compositions (perhaps because of his psychological training he was always particularly interested in composers' beginnings). And he produced a definitive thematic catalogue of Clementi. Here he showed the same ability as in his Beethoven book to recognise the importance of neglected evidence. In the course of achieving international popularity Clementi's works were reprinted by numerous continental publishers who assigned their own conflicting opus numbers to them and sometimes regrouped them. Tyson noticed that the less widely circulated English editions of the great majority were entered at Stationers' Hall, that they were the primary sources for the texts, and that they carried the composer's own opus numbers reflecting their chronology. Much else remained to be done, but the framework was there. The resulting catalogue presented for the first time an authoritative overview of Clementi's complete output and cleared the way for future assessment.

It happened that about the time when Tyson was finally free of his house officer work a slight change of emphasis took place in his musicological research. Hitherto he had worked mostly with printed sources.

However, in the case of Beethoven, who was still his main concern, the texts evolved continuously from sketches, through a complete autograph, to later stages at any of which the composer might make further changes: a copyist's manuscript for the use of the engraver, publisher's proofs, and one or more published issues, not to mention the question of parallel publication. Tyson was able to study important sketches and copyists' scores in the British Museum, but in the nature of things associated sources were widely scattered in other institutions or private collections. His own collection could not help here because, although he occasionally bought manuscripts which might throw light on textual transmission, sources close to the composer, if they ever came on the market, fetched prices far beyond his means. In his only early manuscript study he had pointed out, on the basis of the printer's copy in the Museum, important departures from Beethoven's intentions in all current editions, and hence performances, of the Violin Concerto. He now published a more detailed sequel involving Viennese sources that was in all probability the direct outcome of greater freedom to travel following his release from hospital work.

The demands of the new lines of enquiry that were now opening up before him undoubtedly explain, at least in part, his hesitation over returning immediately to clinical work. A hospital appointment would allow too little leave for him ever to visit the innumerable places in Europe and the United States where manuscripts of Beethoven or, to anticipate a little, Mozart had come to rest, and although private practice might appear to offer greater flexibility, patients dependent on his help could not be abandoned for long. As a consequence of the growing international reputation of his scholarly work he obtained in 1969 a visiting professorship in music at Columbia University, which he managed to fit in between his other lecturing. This brought home the realisation that he could earn as much for a series of musicological lectures in the United States as for a year's work in a National Health Service hospital. It was becoming plain that musicology might offer him an alternative means of livelihood, and that the claims of the rival careers were incompatible; one would have to give way. Eventually, in 1971, the award of a Senior Research Fellowship at All Souls allowed him to follow his preference.

Why did musicology triumph? His lack of enthusiasm for resuming the practice of psycho-analysis did not result from a loss of faith in it: without keeping up with the literature he continued for some time to grant occasional interviews at the request of a friend to give a general opinion, though he was anxious to avoid as far as possible any follow-up work. But Tyson was an impatient person. It would not be surprising if he tired of dealing with patients who, as he understood well, never responded by the book and took their time about it. Yet it is curious that although he was noted as a theorist he never published anything substantial in that line.[6] Theory, of course, involves speculation, and it seems that ultimately the speculative did not satisfy him: he liked to solve problems, to get things right. The kind of musicology he pursued offered that possibility. Even in his early years as a psycho-analyst he was thought of as a perfectionist who wanted things to be precise. There was perhaps in addition another, rather different, reason for his retreat from clinical work. He hated to be tied down or have his freedom of action restricted in any way. Obligations irked him beyond measure, and he was not slow to complain about them. He could be utterly ruthless in his behaviour towards anyone, including his parents, who had served their turn in his own scheme of things, any impartiality that his training might have been expected to inculcate deserting him. Although he could enter happily into a domestic situation for which he had no final responsibility, he shunned any long-term commitment. He bitterly regretted having let slip an opportunity of marriage in the 1960s, but only after it was irretrievably lost.

To dwell on such things would be to give an unrecognisably distorted impression. To most of Tyson's friends inner tension betrayed itself only through occasional irascibility that was apt to erupt with scarcely discernible cause and quickly subside again. Such moments counted for little. Recollections are all of his geniality, sense of humour, warmth, thoughtfulness, personal and scholarly generosity, and his total lack of self-importance or any affected parade of the opposite. Witty, hugely sociable and widely informed, he was welcome in many circles.[7] His conversation raised the quality of intellectual life at All Souls whenever he was in residence. His stance tended to be that of an observer rather than

---

[6] He did write reviews from time to time until relatively late, for instance of books on Freud by Philip Rieff (*Observer*, 24 Jan. 1960) and Paul Roazen (*New Statesman*, 26 March 1976), and of a group of books by R. D. Laing (*New York Review of Books*, 11 Feb. 1971, followed by correspondence on 1 July).

[7] He became famous for his jokes, which he enjoyed as much as anyone and had an endearing habit of retelling. Two are recorded (with a rather misleading description of him) in Alan Bennett, *Writing Home* (revised edition, 1997), pp. 189, 203, and others in the address given at Tyson's memorial service (a copy of the text is at All Souls). For many years it was his task to sing the college's Mallard Song, which is sung by tradition at certain college dinners. Each time he produced a humorous penultimate verse of his own, alluding to a topical event or some eminent guest at the dinner; these verses are also preserved at All Souls.

a participant, as was noticeable when he became involved with the group of people who founded the *Universities and Left Review* in the aftermath of the Hungarian uprising of 1956, or when he was present at discussions among founders of the Social Democratic Party in 1981. This detachment was habitual, and he was conscious of it. When he was once asked how he had managed to study Classics, train as a psycho-analyst and medical doctor, translate Freud and achieve international recognition as a music-ologist, he is reported to have replied that 'he found it all the same thing: thinking about what people did, wrote and said, and how and why they did so'.[8] The inference here for his musicology is not that he wanted to psycho-analyse composers of the past; he thought that impossible and never attempted it. It was rather a matter of gaining insight into psychological probabilities, in that sphere as in any other.

During his time in New York at the Montefiore Hospital and Columbia University Tyson made many friends and became a central figure in social gatherings which included various well-known people outside musicology or analysis.[9] This made his visits to the country in which his work was attracting most attention all the more enjoyable. It was a fortunate moment. Leading scholars among his contemporaries were also working on Beethoven, and students were following on. The series of articles that he published at this time made a deep impression. One, rather unusually, was biographical, interpreting major works of 1803–5 as Beethoven's reaction to his increasing deafness. Others, like those relating to the Violin Concerto, were textual studies initially prompted by manuscripts in the British Museum. One of these attempted to recover as nearly as possible the first version of the oratorio *Christus am Oelberge*, another sorted out the handwritings of five of Beethoven's copyists with their approximate dates of activity, and a third dealt with sketches for the Piano Trio Op. 70 No. 1. Such pieces typify Tyson's methods. He preferred to take a single topic that had caught his interest and explore it pragmatically through the interconnections of biography, codicology, the state of texts, and any-thing else that might be suggested by the matter in hand. In the process he would often find new uses for such evidence, but as a by-product. Only in the case of paper-studies did he reverse the emphasis and take general principles as his subject: having discovered their possibilities in working on particular problems himself, he thought they should be more widely understood.

---

[8] Neal Zaslaw's obituary in the *Independent*, 14 Nov. 2000.
[9] e.g. Penelope Gilliatt, John Lahr, Thomas Nagel, Robert Silvers, Lionel and Diana Trilling.

His first essay of that kind, on reconstructing Beethoven's sketch-books (1972), was written in collaboration with Douglas Johnson. That was symptomatic: in response to the interest aroused by his work the perpetual spectator became the participant and collaborator as well. He made personal contact with Beethoven and Mozart scholars throughout Europe and the United States, and corresponded indefatigably with any whose work overlapped or bordered on his own; although he was never dependent on the stimulus of exchange, he knew its value and enjoyed it. With the sketchbooks he was making a fresh start, no sustained study of them having been attempted for a century. They had been horribly mistreated by their nineteenth-century owners. Very few of them were in their original state. Most had had leaves torn out and given away or had extraneous leaves inserted in them; others had been entirely dismembered and the contents scattered. Naturally much had been lost. Reconstruction depended on many kinds of evidence. Watermarks could establish the original make-up of integral sketchbooks; stitch-holes could associate leaves from a home-made book consisting of various papers. Rastrology also served to identify batches of paper, because machines ruled staves in different groupings and with differing dimensions. Contiguous leaves could be traced by matching notches where they had been separated along the folds, or by the offset of smudges or blots (this was known familiarly, though not in print, as 'Blotforschung'). Writing instruments, ink colour, and sketch continuity all played their part.

Tyson's work on Beethoven culminated in the 1985 publication, with Johnson and Robert Winter, of a reconstruction of the complete corpus of identifiable sketchbooks. It fell to him to deal with a sequence of seventeen books spanning the years 1801 to 1817. Meanwhile he had produced at various times detailed accounts of several of them beyond the scope of the more comprehensive compilation. Tyson was not among those who looked to sketches to suggest or support analytical or aesthetic readings. He preferred, characteristically, to extract evidence that shed light on the genesis or growth of a work, or its date. Thus he was able to demonstrate that the third Razumovsky string quartet had been put together rather hastily by comparison with its two companions, and that the 'first' *Leonora* overture was not composed till 1807, after the other two. And on manuscript evidence of a different kind he showed that Beethoven was only partly responsible for the quintet arrangement published as his Op. 104. Some of these findings were published in one or other of three volumes of *Beethoven Studies* that Tyson edited himself between 1974 and 1982. In one of these too he set out guiding principles for the complete edition of Beethoven's correspondence that the Beethovenhaus in Bonn eventually published in 1992–4.

While working on papers in Beethoven manuscripts Tyson was not neglecting those used by Mozart, who was eventually to displace Beethoven as his main object of study. The types of evidence that he looked for here were the same, but the context was rather different because most of the Mozart autographs were not sketches but complete manuscripts, whether the works contained in them had been completed or left in a fragmentary state. It is no surprise to find that Tyson's first results, published in 1975, involved, though not exclusively, autographs in the British Library or on loan there from the Stefan Zweig collection (subsequently donated in 1986). From 1980 his work was greatly facilitated when about 120 Mozart autographs and several Beethoven sketchbooks which had been missing from the Berlin Staatsbibliothek since World War II became available for study in the Biblioteka Jagiellońska in Kraków; Tyson was one of the first to gain access to them.

His Mozart findings were of many kinds. His study of the autograph scores of *La Clemenza di Tito*, *Le Nozze di Figaro*, *Così fan tutte,* and *Don Giovanni* showed that Mozart did not compose them straight through from beginning to end. Sometimes, for instance, he preferred to tackle ensembles before solo arias if he did not yet know the capabilities of the singers who were to take part. Comparison of the autographs of *Figaro* and *Così* with early manuscript copies brought to light cuts and revisions made in early productions very probably, and in some cases demonstrably, by Mozart himself, though whether such changes reflected his wishes or were forced upon him by circumstances there was no knowing. Tyson even restored to *Così* thirteen bars that had never appeared in print until the new complete edition followed his lead. Mozart is often said to have composed his music very largely in his head, so that writing it down was a purely mechanical process. But on his own admission the 'Haydn' and 'Prussian' sets of string quartets cost him much trouble, and Tyson's study of the papers bears him out: he finished some of them only after long delays and dodged back and forth from one quartet to the next. There are false starts to quartet movements on separate leaves which the paper showed to have been traditionally associated with the wrong completed works. The dates guessed for many other works and fragments proved equally fallible.

Not every work that did not progress very far can be regarded as a false start. It emerged that Mozart would often begin more piano concertos than he needed for a particular season and leave one as a fragment until there was some reason to finish it a year or two later; four very well-known concertos came into being in this previously unsuspected way. No doubt many other works survive as fragments only because an occasion for their completion never arose. Several other discoveries of Tyson's were no less startling: four famous piano sonatas formerly thought to have been composed in Paris in 1778 should probably be placed as much as five years later; several fragmentary mass settings given early dates turn out to have been written about 1788, suggesting that Mozart was hoping for a church appointment at that time; the accepted conclusion of the Rondo for piano and orchestra K. 386 was in fact the work of Cipriani Potter, Mozart's last forty-five bars having been lost until Tyson rediscovered them; the D major Horn Concerto, far from having been begun in 1782, was a very late work of 1791 left unfinished at the composer's death, the version of the finale always heard being an elaboration and expansion of his draft by Süssmayr.

By the end of the 1980s the importance of Tyson's work was very widely recognised. Having been elected a Fellow of the British Academy as early as 1978, he now, in 1989, was awarded a CBE and an honorary doctorate at St Andrews University (and also made an honorary member of the British Psycho-Analytical Society). In the United States, where he had lectured extensively and held positions at Columbia, Berkeley, Princeton and the City University of New York, he was named corresponding member of the American Musicological Society in 1991. But by that time all was not well with him. For some years he had been displaying signs of growing eccentricity; his horizons were narrowing perceptibly, as was his vocabulary. By 1991 he could no longer read an article, although rather strangely he could still put together a lecture or an essay on a subject he knew well. Life became increasingly difficult for those around him at All Souls until his retirement in 1994, and in the next few years dementia overtook him entirely. However, 1992 saw the publication of his most ambitious single undertaking. He had compiled over a number of years a catalogue of the paper-types in every Mozart manuscript accessible to him, so that the approximate period of Mozart's use of each type could be assessed, and the dating of undated individual manuscripts correspondingly aided. He had distinguished over 100 watermarks; moreover the paper containing any one of them might subdivide into two or three distinct paper types in accordance with the rastrology. Wherever he might be working, it had been essential never to let accuracy of measurement or alertness of observation falter for a moment. It was an immense labour, and it is some consolation that the results of his phenomenal determination and persistence should have appeared while he could still understand the importance of his own achievement.

OLIVER NEIGHBOUR
Fellow of the Academy

Note. I am extremely grateful to the many people who provided information for this memoir or directed me to others who could do so. In particular I should like to thank Tyson's brothers John and Donald, Noel Bradley, Robin Briggs, Julian Bullard, Pauline Cohen, Jennifer Crickmay, Douglas Johnson, John Lahr, Judith Milne, Peter Partner, Katharine Rees, Philip Skelsey, Peter Ward Jones, and Neal Zaslaw.

A complete bibliography of Tyson's musicological writings and his Freud translations is contained in S. Brandenburg (ed.), *Haydn, Mozart & Beethoven . . . Essays in honour of Alan Tyson* (Oxford, 1998), pp. 301–9. Two contributions to Japanese publications should be added. A talk given in 1991 at the International Mozart Symposium at Kunitachi College was published as 'Konnichi no mōtsuaruto kenkyū no hōhōron' in *1991 kokusai mōtsuaruto shinpojiumu hōkoku* (Tokyo, 1993), and an article commissioned by Shōgakukan appeared in no. 15 (1993) of the booklets accompanying the Japanese issue of Philips's complete recording of Mozart's works under the title 'Jihitsufu no yōshi ni yoru nendaigaku'. Tyson's titles for the original texts were respectively 'Methodology of Mozart Research today' and 'The Help of the Watermarks in the Leaves of Mozart's Autographs: they might often suggest when he wrote them'; typescripts of both are among his papers in the Bodleian Library, but neither contains anything not covered in his previous writings. Some miscellaneous pieces are mentioned in notes 1, 2, 4, and 6 above.

JOHN VAREY

John Earl Varey
1922–1999

I

JOHN VAREY was one of the greatest of twentieth-century hispanists, and the history of the Spanish theatre as a major research area was in large measure his creation. Serious study of puppets and other popular entertainments in Spain was due to him. These and other aspects of his scholarship are assessed by Melveena McKendrick in the second part of this memoir.[1] Yet his scholarship—enough to fill a long and active life for most academics—is only half of the story. He founded a new department, with minimal resources, and built it so skilfully that within twenty-five years it was one of the top two or three in the country in research quality. He founded a publishing house that became one of the most important and influential publishers in its field anywhere in the world. He was Principal of Westfield College in the last years of its independent existence, and succeeded, to an extent that no one else could have managed, in preserving much of Westfield's quality in the eventual merger. He was one of the most energetic and dedicated members of the University of London's governing bodies. And at the age of twenty-two, before he

---

[1] See also the assessments by Charles Davis in *Golden Age Spanish Literature: Studies in Honour of John Varey by his Colleagues and Pupils*, ed. Charles Davis & Alan Deyermond (Dept of Spanish, Westfield College, 1991), pp. 23–8 (a bibliography of Varey's publications is on pp. 29–38) and by José María Ruano de la Haza in *Bulletin of Hispanic Studies* (Glasgow), 77.1 (Jan. 2000: *Calderón 1600–1681: Quatercentenary Studies in Memory of John E. Varey*, ed. Ann L. Mackenzie), 25–31. A revised and amplified bibliography is provided by Charles Davis and Alan Deyermond in the latter volume, pp. 33–47.

Proceedings of the British Academy, **115**, 385–408. © The British Academy 2002.

had completed his degree, he had, as a navigator in Bomber Command, looked death in the face many times and not flinched.

John Varey was born on 26 August 1922 into a solidly middle-class, modestly prosperous Lancashire family where education and the life of the mind were valued: his father was a headmaster, his mother had been a teacher until her marriage. Like many such families, this one had reached a comfortable level thanks to the struggles of the preceding generations, a fact of which John was always conscious. His high intelligence and his appetite for knowledge were encouraged by his parents, and he spent eight years at Queen Elizabeth's Grammar School, Blackburn, before winning an Open Exhibition to Emmanuel College, Cambridge. He remained tenaciously, even fiercely, loyal to his native town and to its football team, and throughout his life would accept Saturday commitments only after consulting the Blackburn Rovers fixture list. Another childhood enthusiasm that stayed with him was puppets: he wrote his thesis on the subject, he staged puppet shows for his children's birthday parties, and he printed the family's Christmas cards with puppet designs.

He had considered reading English at university, and his Exhibition was in English and Spanish, but even before he arrived in Cambridge he was discouraged by the bitter factional quarrels that divided the Faculty of English, and he chose to read Spanish, at first with Italian and then alone. Yet his love of English literature persisted (perhaps all the more strongly because he never had to take a side in the quarrels), and it enriched his teaching and research in Spanish. And from the Cambridge of Leavis, Empson, and Richards he learned close reading, and his criticism combined attention to textual detail with a creative interpretation of imagery.

After a year as an undergraduate John joined the RAF, training in Canada before being commissioned as navigator in 1943 and serving in Bomber Command and then in Transport Command. To be a navigator in a bomber over Germany required not only technical skill of a high order but also a particularly durable sort of courage: on one occasion John looked up to find that another bomber was immediately above him, with its bomb-bays open. He was demobilised as Flight Lieutenant in December 1945, and returned to Cambridge the following term. It was in the war years that he renewed his friendship with Micky (officially Cicely Rainford) Virgo, whom he had known in childhood (their grandmothers had taught in the same school), and who in the early 1940s was working in the Bank of England. Friendship ripened into love, and John and Micky became unofficially engaged.

John received his BA degree in 1946 under war emergency regulations, and began his doctoral research in 1947. After a year of graduate work he was invited to give tutorial teaching for a number of colleges, and he and Micky could afford to marry. He enjoyed teaching and did it well, so he was in constant demand, though he was less successful in handling his press coverage: because he insisted on using the Cambridge term 'supervision' for a tutorial, a Blackburn newspaper published his photograph with the caption 'Local lad supervises five Cambridge colleges'.

The thesis, on 'Minor Dramatic Forms in Spain, with Special Reference to Puppets', required a great deal of work in Spanish libraries and archives, and it was in this period that John formed the habit of regular visits to the Madrid archives and of making use of every hour that they were open. His industry and his patience were inexhaustible: he once sprained his wrist by the constant turning over of thousands of pages of documents. A. E. Housman, writing a memoir of a Cambridge colleague over seventy years ago, said: 'A scholar who means to build himself a monument must spend much of his life in acquiring knowledge which for its own sake is not worth having and in reading books which do not in themselves deserve to be read.' Housman had no dealings with ancient account books and contracts, all in difficult handwriting, or he might have expressed himself even more strongly. John's boredom threshhold was extremely high, and as he made his way through the many irrelevant documents he was rewarded, time and again, by the finding of a document that filled a gap in his knowledge and shone light into a dark corner of theatrical history. It was in these first years that lasting friendships with Spanish scholars began—mostly with fellow-investigators of the Golden Age theatre, and mostly with the young (senior Spaniards were not then, with a few admirable exceptions, as inclined as they are today to welcome researchers from other countries). One such friendship was with the City Archivist of Madrid, who had a taste for the best hand-made shoes, and asked John to order him a pair in London. John pointed out that it was difficult to execute the commission unless the shoemaker was able to measure the customer's feet. 'I've thought of that', said the Archivist, 'and here is a plaster cast of my foot'. It was not easy for John to explain this unusual piece of luggage to a British Customs officer.

Having completed his thesis in the minimum time of three years, John assumed that his examiners would be equally prompt. They were not. The University had appointed as external examiner the man of letters Walter Starkie, then living in Madrid, and Starkie, never slow to see an opportunity, insisted on first-class travel. The University countered this ploy by agreeing to a viva in Madrid, but the plan collapsed when the internal examiner refused, on political grounds, to set foot in Franco's Spain. The deadlock continued for a year, and in the end John was set a written viva (I believe this to be the only one in the history of British hispanism). This was academic comedy of the finest kind, more David Lodge than C. P. Snow (though one of the protagonists appears as Eustace Pilbrow in Snow's *The Masters*). John saw the humour of it in later years, but at the time the strain on a talented, energetic, and ambitious young man, already held back by war service, must have been hard to bear.

There was some compensation even for that frustrating year: it meant another year in Cambridge, where he and Micky were very happy; he was appointed a full (though temporary) member of the Faculty of Modern and Medieval Languages, he was invited to continue his tutorial teaching even after he left Cambridge, and he began to supervise his first research student, Norman Shergold, a fellow-enthusiast for the history of the theatre.[2] This teaching experience must have helped as much as his research when he applied for a Lectureship in Spanish at Westfield College in 1952. The post was, unusually, within the Department of French. Since 1948 Spanish had been taught for a few hours each week at Subsidiary level by a retired Lecturer from King's College, Janet Perry. This experiment was successful, and Denis Elcock, Professor of Romance Philology and Head of the Department of French, wanted to expand the teaching, eventually to Honours level. He had, however, no wish to see the creation of a Department of Spanish, and assumed that the new lecturer would know his place. There was a strong field of candidates, and John emerged victorious. Westfield was still a small college, and all of the students and most of the staff were women; the college was not wholly prepared for what it got. John was as successful a teacher in London as in Cambridge, and after two years the college recognised the growing demand and agreed not only to the introduction of Honours teaching but also to the foundation of a Department of Spanish.

The appointment to a lectureship had given John and Micky the opportunity to settle down to something like a normal family life, after years of a hand-to-mouth student existence. They lived for a time in a rented flat near the college, but were soon able to move to a spacious unfurnished flat on the campus. For the first time, they had all the space they needed, and they could offer to colleagues, students, and visitors from other universities the hospitality that soon became legendary. They could also afford to have

[2] Their collaboration is described in Melveena McKendrick's part of this memoir.

children, and their first son, Christopher, was born, but their happiness was short-lived: the healthy baby caught a rapidly fatal infection in the maternity hospital. It was a shattering blow, despite the support of the close-knit college community. The pain never quite disappeared, but it was soon alleviated by the birth of another son, then a daughter, and then a third son. The two boys, Nicholas and Michael, grew up to share their father's love of Spain, where they settled for many years, and the girl, Alison, continued the family's academic tradition by becoming a lecturer (though not in Spanish) at Napier University in Edinburgh. In 1959 a timely legacy enabled the family to move to a house in Platts Lane—semi-detached, but big enough for two post-war detached houses rolled into one. They were now ideally situated, two minutes' walk away from Hampstead Heath and five minutes' walk from college. John could indulge his taste for gardening and home improvements, and Micky cooked superb meals. Groups of students were regularly and frequently invited for coffee, and for many years there was an end-of-session buffet supper for undergraduate and graduate students and staff, and a Christmas supper for staff and graduate students. The food was magnificent, the wine unlimited (the most respectable undergraduate of his year was once found in the small hours, sleeping peacefully in a front garden half-way down the hill).

The Department of Spanish opened for business in October 1955 with John at its head, presiding over one assistant lecturer (myself) and no secretary—the college had one part-time secretary, who was able to devote half a day a week to each department except Spanish (too newly established to need secretarial help). We had three Honours students in our first intake, giving us a staff–student ratio of 1:1.5, but statistics, as so often, masked the truth, because between us we had to cover the whole range of language and literature courses, and it was exhausting. John taught half the language courses, Golden Age drama and prose, and modern literature (Latin-American literature had not yet been discovered in Britain). He was a good lecturer, but was at his best in individual tutorials and, after the reform of the London syllabus about 1960, in Special Subject seminars. He was good at language classes, but did not miss them when pressure of other teaching commitments led him to withdraw from them. He could not, on the other hand, have been easily parted from his Special Subject seminars on the novelist Galdós (see below, p. 407), and he continued to take History of the Theatre seminars even after his election as Principal in 1983 ended his other teaching.[3]

---

[3] In his last year as Head of Department he negotiated a research collaboration agreement with the equivalent department in the University of Valencia, leading to joint Westfield supervision

That, however, was far in the future when the department was launched. John was thirty-three when he became Head of Department, the age at which Constance Maynard became the founding Mistress of Westfield College in 1882.[4] It had been decided that a Readership in Spanish should be established, but although the post was advertised and interviews held, no appointment was made. This was in part because another ambitious young hispanist, Roy Jones of King's College, also applied, and the committee was unable to choose between them. This, which caused lasting distrust between John and Roy Jones, may not have been the whole story: I suspect that a more important factor was a feeling among some senior academics and administrators that John was in too much of a hurry and that he should be restrained. John was deeply hurt, though he tried not to show it—as I got to know him, I realised that a good deal of his nervous energy (and quite possibly of Micky's, too) went into maintaining his phlegmatic Lancashire exterior. Pressure from outside the college soon produced the right result, and John became a Reader in 1957. Six years later the title of Professor of Spanish was conferred, and in 1967 an established chair was created, and John was appointed to it. He remained the Head until he was elected Principal in 1983. The idea of a rotating, elective headship did not attract him: this was his department, he had created it out of nothing, and his energy and vision, together with the fact that he alone had risked his life in the war, gave him unrivalled authority. This had its drawbacks, but they were much outweighed by the advantages (among them, the vigour and tenacity with which he defended any colleague or student who was under threat from outside the department). It is significant that in the twenty-eight years of his reign only two members of staff left for other universities, whereas in the eighteen succeeding years nine have done so.

John had high ambitions for his department, and rightly so. In the first three years, the student intake was very small but of remarkable quality: out of eleven students, four won Firsts (this was in the years when Firsts were a rarity), and went on, under his supervision, to gain Ph.D.s. His early appointments to the staff were not uniformly successful, but in the mid-to-late 1960s three high-flyers were appointed: Ralph Penny (now Professor of Romance Philology), the Trinidadian Premraj Halkhoree,

---

of Valencia theses, visits by staff in both directions, and publication of a growing number of volumes by young Valencian scholars on the history of the city's theatre.

[4] See Catherine B. Firth, *Constance Louisa Maynard, Mistress of Westfield: A Family Portrait* (1949).

whom John regarded as the brightest of us all (he left after nine years for the University of Ottawa, and died of leukemia two years later), and the American Dorothy Severin (now Gilmour Professor of Spanish at Liverpool). It is difficult for someone who has spent his whole working life in a department to assess it objectively, but objectivity may be found in the record: this is the only department of Spanish to have been chosen by the Nuffield Foundation for its survey of innovatory teaching methods (1964), it is the only one to have won a New Blood post (Charles Davis was appointed in 1983 to work with John on the History of the Spanish Theatre Project), it is one of only two to have two FBAs at the same time (Oxford is the other), and its average Research Assessment Exercise scores place it equal first with Cambridge. Such achievements come from team work, but teams need leaders, and without John's leadership they would have been out of reach.

It is strange now to look back to the early days, when John saw his Westfield appointment as an interlude before he returned to Cambridge (though his commitment to the college was total). He would have been an excellent choice to succeed Edward M. Wilson as professor at Cambridge, and would have given that department a more active leadership than suited Wilson's temperament.[5] He wanted the job, planned his career to that end, and was badly disappointed when Roy Jones was chosen. When Jones died suddenly after only a year in the Cambridge chair, much of the fire had gone out of that particular ambition, and John saw that Westfield gave him more scope than Cambridge for what he wanted to do.

One of those things was the running of his own publishing house, Tamesis Books. He told people that he founded Tamesis because no other publisher would carry the burden of his series Fuentes para la Historia del Teatro Español, sources for the history of the Spanish theatre.[6] This was certainly true of British publishers, but a Spanish publisher could probably have been found. He told himself and those close to him that Tamesis would strengthen his claim to the Cambridge chair. There was some truth in both these stories, but I think there was a simpler explanation: he was attracted to the life of a publisher, he saw something that needed to be done, and he knew that he could do it. There were no businessmen in his immediate ancestry, but he would have been a good full-time businessman,

[5] See A. A. Parker & D. W. Cruickshank, 'Edward Meryon Wilson, 1906–1977', *PBA*, 68 (1982), 643–66.

[6] Never wholly sound on bibliographical method, he insisted on treating this as a multi-volume book, even though the Tamesis catalogue listed it as a series, and he was surprisingly ungrateful when it was given its correct bibliographical treatment.

and when he mixed with those who were he valued their praise more highly than that of fellow academics.

The first impetus for the foundation of Tamesis was a conversation between John and the Spanish publisher Germán Bleiberg. Encouraged by the great London foreign-language bookseller Frank Cutler, they took the irrevocable step, and in 1963 Tamesis Books came into being as a publishing house dedicated entirely to Hispanic studies, in which both young and established hispanists published monographs and editions.[7] At first with Bleiberg, later alone, he ran both the business and the editorial side for thirty years, corresponding voluminously with authors and reading the proofs of each volume. The list grew rapidly in size and prestige, and in 1975 the Real Academia Española awarded Tamesis the Nieto López Prize. On the debit side, Bleiberg, a poet who still suffered from the effects of years in Franco's prisons, for part of the time under sentence of death, had an idiosyncratic approach to business that imposed considerable strain on John, and in 1985 caused a financial crisis that might have brought about the collapse of Tamesis if Frank Cutler had not provided fresh capital out of his own pocket. In the mid-1990s the burden of running the company as well as the editorial side became too much even for John, and Tamesis, with over two hundred volumes published, became an imprint of Boydell and Brewer, but still under his editorial guidance. That arrangement continues today, with John's chosen successors in the editorial role.[8]

Within the college, John's energy and administrative skill made him the obvious candidate when the post of Dean of the Faculty of Arts was created in 1966. Some people, nervous that an overly energetic Dean might disturb the even tenor of their ways, adopted the slogan 'Vote No for Dean' (a little unfair to the other candidate). This election was a perfect example of democratic participation: every elector voted in a secret ballot, and a substantial majority voted for John. He held the office for a two-year term, and did not seek re-election because of his appointment

---

[7] See the brief account of the the history of Tamesis Books in *25 años de Támesis*, ed. A. D. Deyermond, J. E. Varey, & Charles Davis (Tamesis Books, 1989), pp. 5–7. The book contains assessments by scholars from Britain, Spain, and Canada of Tamesis's achievement in six areas of hispanism. For Frank Cutler, see my obituary in *The Independent* (2 August 1999), Review section, p. 6.

[8] The association with Boydell and Brewer was particularly fitting. Soon after the foundation of Tamesis, the Chaucerian scholar Derek Brewer, later to become Master of John's old college, Emmanuel, sought John's advice on his plan to launch a Tamesis equivalent for Middle English studies. The result was the publishing house of D. S. Brewer, which in due course merged with The Boydell Press.

as Vice-Principal. In both posts he was effective and far-sighted, but it was difficult for him to continue in college office under a Principal with whom he was increasingly at odds. He had welcomed the Principal's election and that of his predecessor because he had thought that they had the qualities needed to modernise and expand Westfield. In both cases he was rapidly disillusioned, and though one Principal was removed after three years, her successor stayed for seventeen.

John knew that he had something to contribute as an administrator, and from 1970 onwards it was at University level that he made that contribution, notably as Chairman of the Board of Studies in Romance Languages and Literatures 1972–4, member of Senate and Academic Council from 1976, Chairman of the Academic Advisory Board in Language and Literature 1979–83, member of the University Court (the supreme financial committee) 1980–6, Chairman of Academic Council 1980–3, and, in retrospect the most important, Chairman of the Committee of Management of the Warburg Institute from 1978 until 1992. In that post he played a crucial part in the successful defence of the Warburg against attempts to raid its funds and undermine its autonomy. I regretted at the time that he had undertaken so much university work, and I regret it still. His work for the Warburg was supremely worth while, and in some other ways (for instance, as one of the Governors of Birkbeck College) he made a real difference, but in most of the other committee work he could not. The late 1970s and the 1980s were not years in which honest, hard, and skilful work ensured success. A combination of destructive government policies and a changed temper within the university (both in Senate House and in the larger colleges) meant that for much of the time John was swimming against the tide. The endurance that he had developed in his long hours in the Madrid archives, the ability to sit still and withstand boredom—qualities in which he rivalled the late Soviet Foreign Minister, the great Stone-Bottom Molotov (who earned his epithet by outlasting everyone else at meetings)—were later to be invaluable to him in college and university committees, but the number of university meetings drained even his formidable energy to no good purpose.

That was also a time when the smaller colleges, including Westfield, were under constant threat. From 1981 onwards there was growing pressure from the government for what was called rationalisation in universities. Predatory eyes were cast on valuable land in London, and one small college after another vanished into the maw of a larger one. This was bad enough, but what was far worse was the fog of deceit in which the process was enveloped. Those of us who were fighting to retain Westfield's independence knew that the best hope of saving the college lay in John Varey's leadership, and when the Principal decided to take early retirement in 1983, it did not take the electors long to invite John to succeed him. To our immense relief, he accepted, becoming Acting Principal in October 1983 and Principal on 1 January 1984. Sir Norman Lindop, then Chairman of the College Council, described his acceptance as 'an act of great courage, verging on the foolhardy'.[9]

Negotiations for a consortium with Bedford College, only a couple of miles from Westfield, had already foundered before John took office. He tried time after time to reach a solution that would preserve a residential teaching campus in Hampstead: there were successive negotiations with six colleges, but sometimes the other college withdrew, sometimes Westfield found the terms unacceptable. At least twice, John was encouraged by the university to pursue negotiations that were, when they looked like succeeding, vetoed. These betrayals wore down even John's stamina, and when one of them coincided with stress of a different kind, the crisis in the affairs of Tamesis Books (see p. 392, above), the strain proved too much, triggering angina. A heart bypass operation followed, and John was out of action for several months in late 1985 and early 1986 (the college was left in the safe hands of the Senior Vice-Principal, the distinguished medieval historian Henry Loyn, FBA).

By 1987 our options had run out, and the choice was between absorption into King's College and a genuine merger with Queen Mary College. Many colleagues favoured the former, but John knew that only the latter offered the chance of preserving most of what mattered in Westfield and would lead to the creation of a new college that blended the traditions and preserved the strengths of its component parts. With skill and patience, he secured acceptable terms, and persuaded Council to accept them. In the autumn of 1989 the merger took effect, Queen Mary and Westfield College was born, and John retired from the Principalship and returned to full-time research.

In early 1989 the college constituted the History of the Theatre Research Project as an autonomous unit within the Department of Hispanic Studies, appointing John as Director and Charles Davis as Associate Director. This increasingly international enterprise (the Fuentes series expanded rapidly in the last decade of John's life, taking in volumes by Spanish scholars on the theatrical history of their home

---

[9] Foreword to *Golden Age Spanish Literature* (see n. 1, above), p. 9.

towns and cities, and has now reached volume 35) was adopted as a British Academy Research Project in 1995 and recognised by the Union Académique Internationale the following year, and it attracted major grants from the Academy and the Leverhulme Trust. John's collaboration with Norman Shergold was not always easy, despite Shergold's remarkable quality as a researcher (it was his suspension of work on the project while he prepared his *History of the Spanish Stage*, 1967, that led John to begin publishing his work on Galdós: see p. 407, below). The collaboration with Charles Davis, by contrast, was steady, cordial, and increasingly productive. Another aspect of the project was John's leading role in the campaign to restore the seventeenth-century theatre hidden under a cinema in the main square of Alcalá de Henares (an undertaking akin to the restoration of the Globe Theatre—he built links between the two). He and the young Spanish scholars who discovered the theatre had to struggle with entrenched bureaucracy, and even as he went into hospital for the last time he was planning the next steps in the campaign. It aroused in him, at the end of his life, the same passion for the tangible reality of the theatre that had made puppets his schoolboy hobby.

From the late 1970s onwards, honours were heaped on John Varey: President of the Association of Hispanists of Great Britain and Ireland 1979, Ilustre Hijo de Madrid 1980, Cambridge Litt.D. 1981, Corresponding Fellow of the Real Academia Española 1981, Fellow of the British Academy 1985 (he served as Chairman of the Modern Literature section), the first foreign Honorary Member of the Instituto de Estudios Madrileños 1988, and a doctorate *honoris causa* of the University of Valencia 1989. The award of that doctorate was preceded by a three-day international congress held in his honour, and its Proceedings form one of the three Festschriften that marked his retirement.[10] A fourth book is a tribute to his memory (see n. 1, above). A few months after his death, the department of Spanish Literature at the University of Valencia named a new seminar room the Sala John Varey.[11]

---

[10] *Comedias y comediantes: estudios sobre el teatro clásico español: Actas del Congreso Internacional sobre Teatro y Prácticas Escénicas en los siglos XVI y XVII, organizado por el Departamento de Filología Española de la Universitat de València, celebrado en la Facultat de Filologia, los días 9, 10 y 11 de mayo de 1989*, ed. Manuel V. Diago & Teresa Ferrer, Col·lecció Oberta (València: Departament de Filologia Espanyola, Universitat de València, 1991). The other two are *El mundo del teatro español en su Siglo de Oro: ensayos dedicados a John E. Varey*, ed. J. M. Ruano de la Haza, Ottawa Hispanic Studies, 3 (Ottawa: Dovehouse Editions, 1989) and *Golden Age Spanish Literature* (1991; see n. 1, above).

[11] This was the second topographical tribute: several years earlier, one of the new canal-side halls of residence at Queen Mary and Westfield College was named Varey House.

John's nominal retirement lasted nearly ten years. The angina that had struck him in the mid-1980s was under control and did not hinder his work. It was only in the last three of those ten years that ill-health began to be an impediment, as cancer stalked him and finally caught him. But his visits to Spain continued until nearly the end, and his research and the direction of his project went on, under increasing hardship, into the last month of his life. He died on 28 March 1999, ten months after he and Micky had celebrated their golden wedding on a glorious late spring day.

John Varey built for the future. He found able collaborators and encouraged his successors. The institutions that he founded—his department, the History of the Spanish Theatre Research Project and its Fuentes series, Colección Támesis—are set to grow and play their part in twenty-first-century hispanism.

II

It is difficult to overestimate the monumental importance of John Varey's work, not least because the work itself is monumental in size and scope. An academic who much more than pulled his weight in terms of teaching and administration, his prodigious energy and stamina allowed him at the same time to pursue a scholarly vision reminiscent of the vast projects of nineteenth-century gentlemen scholars with little else to do. And a brilliant entrepreneurial streak unusual amongst academics in the past, and unmatched even in today's managerial academic world, enabled him to make that vision a reality. The launching of the Tamesis imprint (see above, pp. 391–2) not only provided international hispanism with a publishing outlet of prime quality, but guaranteed John Varey the vehicle he needed to disseminate the results of both his own and his collaborative researches. As a result he became one of the most prolific and successful academic collaborators there can ever have been in the arts and humanities. Over the years he published in collaboration with seven different colleagues not only sixteen volumes of documents and studies relating to the history of the Spanish theatre, with seven more in preparation at the time of his death, but also a nineteen-volume facsimile edition of the *primera parte* of the plays of Calderón and editions of three plays by other dramatists. In the interstices of these team activities, he published five single-authored books with Tamesis and other presses, and one hundred and twenty-three critical and scholarly articles and essays, very largely on the early theatre (some again in collaboration) but also on the nineteenth-century novelist Benito Pérez Galdós.

If the size of this output is humbling, the significance of the enterprise that dominates it is immeasurable. Whereas critical theories come and go, and the fate of even the most influential criticism is eventually to be relegated to the status of historical curiosity, Varey's contribution to early modern Spanish theatre studies is the rock on which future scholars and critics will have to build. That corpus of indispensable scholarship will always be there, informing the way *comediantes* think and write about the plays. As a commercial, popular theatre the Spanish drama was shaped by the circumstances of its production—the playhouses and their management, performances, audiences, the organisation of the theatrical world, court entertainments, religious festivities. This detailed picture of how the circumstances in which the plays were written influenced what was written and how it was written, is precisely what John Varey, aided by his collaborators, set out to provide with the systematic publication and analysis of the huge cache of documentary sources that lay untapped in Spanish collections. It involved a life-time of archive research, meticulous editing and proofreading, planning on a grand scale, skilful organisation and fund-raising. It also involved, as we have seen, the setting up of a press which he proceeded to turn into a major publisher of Spanish criticism and scholarship, in the activities of which he took a pivotal role. I can vouch for this because, when the typescript of a book of mine that Tamesis was publishing was returned to me for correction three months before John died, when he was already gravely ill, I was astonished and touched to discover that it had been painstakingly edited by John himself. In other words, he was a remarkable man, a scholar equally at home with arcane detail and the large design, an initiator and energiser who anticipated by many years the project scholarship now so much in favour with funding bodies, yet who with apparent enjoyment continued to toil away himself at the coal-face of scholarly endeavour.

To go back to his first major publication is to see all these qualities already in place. The book of his doctoral thesis, *Historia de los títeres en España (desde sus orígenes hasta mediados del siglo XVIII)*, published in 1957, filled a crucial gap in the history of puppetry until the advent of the pseudo-scientific entertainments of modern times (magic lantern, Chinese shadows, optical illusions, and so on). It was a difficult undertaking because, as its author said, 'the births and deaths of puppets are not recorded and they do not sign documents, and puppeteers are even more elusive than their creations', but the work succeeds very well indeed in its declared aim of providing Maese Pedro, the puppeteer who confounds Don Quixote in Part II of Cervantes's novel, with a historical context. It

is rich in range and detail, dealing not only with puppets themselves—
then an adult entertainment—but with allied entertainments as well,
such as mechanical figures and scenes, acrobats and conjurers, carnival
figures, jugglers, and tumblers. It looks at performances in streets, playhouses and palaces, at their repertoire both religious and secular, at their
medieval and classical sources, at their parodic function, and at the way
in which puppet themes introduce into literature the idea of humankind
itself as a puppet. Already evident here is the love of documentary detail,
the pleasure in scholarly archaeology, and the fascination with popular
theatrical forms, with production and performance, which were to lead on
to the major enterprise of recording playhouse, street, and palace theatre
as a whole. Evident, too, in appendices, notes, bibliographies, illustrations, and index is the exhaustive scholarship essential to his subsequent
activities. Clearly present as well, though, are the intellectual ebullience,
the dry wit and the shrewd eye for significant detail which characterise his
writings, and which succeed in making this book, for all its unpromising
title, an entertaining read.

Varey's work on puppets did not end with the *Historia*. In its prologue
he promised to complete his study by publishing the sources for the
period after 1758, the *Historia*'s cut-off point because that year saw the
appearance of the newspaper *Diario de Madrid* and a consequentially
enormous rise in the available information regarding theatrical performances. Varey kept that promise fifteen years later in 1972 with the publication of *Los títeres y otras diversiones populares de Madrid, 1758–1840:
estudios y documentos*. Here he adopted a different approach. The documentation he discovered proved so interesting in its administrative, commercial, and scenographic detail that instead of plucking out the material
that captured his attention as he had done before, he decided to be inclusive, reproducing verbatim the important parts of the documents and
summarising or omitting only routine or formulaic elements. He added an
introduction to provide a general analysis of the material and place the
documents in their social and administrative context, and multiple indices
to help the reader access material in different ways. It was a model he had
already started using in his publication, at this stage with Norman
Shergold, of material relating to the mainstream theatre.

As it turned out, so extensive were the sources for this second stage in
the history of the puppets and other entertainments that the details provided by the *Diario de Madrid* itself had to wait another twenty-three
years until 1995, when they eventually saw the light of day in *Cartelera de
los títeres 1758–1840*. The material Varey extracted is, in the case of each

document entry, structured in the form of impresario, venue, dates, times, admission fees, and programme, and cross-referenced where appropriate both to other document entries and to *Los títeres*. With its analytical introduction, its multiple indices and appendices, its plates of announcements, and its maps of Madrid, it offers a detailed panorama of popular entertainments in Madrid during the second half of the eighteenth century and the first half of the nineteenth, against the background of evolution from the Enlightenment to the rise of liberalism. The seminal work initiated when he was a research student was at last complete.

By the time the first puppet book was published in 1957, Varey had already published ten articles. Some of these were spin-offs from his doctoral work on the puppet theatre itself, but almost immediately this continuing interest began to widen out into other areas of early modern Spanish theatre and festivities. The year of his first article, on the modern Spanish puppet theatre in 1951, also saw the birth, with a joint article on three unedited drawings of the old playhouses in Madrid, of his long and fruitful collaboration with Norman Shergold, who would himself in due course write a magisterial book on the history of the Spanish stage. Together they were to produce seventeen articles, two editions of seventeenth-century plays, and twelve volumes in Tamesis's series of documentary sources, Fuentes para la Historia del Teatro en España, five of these with the collaboration of Charles Davis, who as well as being himself a theatre specialist became Varey's computer guru. Some of their joint articles eventually fed into the documentary sources they published together, but many of them still make their own crucial additions to the sum of our knowledge of the theatre and its world in sixteenth- and seventeenth-century Spain. Varey's other articles—a number of which were written with other collaborators—cover a wide range of subjects: puppets in different places and times, play dates, playhouses, scenography, staging and audience, texts in performance, actors and costume, public spectacle and court ceremonial, memory theatres, the theatre's socio-economic context, *comedia* criticism, interpretative and elucidatory essays on both seventeenth-century plays and the nineteenth-century novels of Galdós, thirty-six articles for the *Oxford Companion to the Theatre*, the revision of 220 articles on Spanish literature and the writing of 35 new ones for *Cassell's Encyclopaedia of World Literature*, and even an article on university entrance requirements.

Most of Varey's work constitutes what is now patronisingly referred to by those of a more theoretical bent as positivist scholarship, but in its implications, reach, and impact it is much more than that. Varey was not just an outstanding theatre historian but a pioneer of the concept of the theatrical identity of drama, of the idea of the play-text as something fashioned to be simultaneously experienced through the eyes and the ears by a present audience, of the theatre itself as part of a rich and varied dramatic life that embraced religious drama in the streets, palace festivities, royal entrances and progresses, and other public celebrations. He realised that every aspect of the text in context and in performance contributed to its identity, to the way in which it communicated and the way in which it was received, and he effectively dedicated his career to providing the peritextual information needed to understand in its every aspect the theatre to which the plays belong. And some of his best criticism, represented by a number of his articles, skilfully exemplifies how the study of such things as the use of space and time, of scenic levels, of connections between imagery and scenography, and between themes and staging, of staging problems, of night scenes, of the relationship between play and audience, of stage directions, of costume, of visual impact generally, illuminates our reading of the plays. The entire way in which we think about the theatre and its individual plays has, almost without our realising it, been irreversibly changed by Varey's work and the example he has set.

In 1987 he published a collection of twenty-two of his articles under the title *Cosmovisión y escenografía: el teatro español en el siglo de oro* (Madrid: Castalia) which epitomises the way in which his research and writing bridge the dramatic and the theatrical. The over-arching themes are ideology and staging and the relationship between the two. Varey took the view that the staging built into a play-text served to emphasise ideas and images contained by the text and therefore to transmit messages and control the audience's response, and twelve of the articles in the collection are devoted to exploring this convergence. The other ten articles employ close textual analysis to expatiate upon the cosmic vision which for him shaped the thinking of the playwrights and their age: 'To a certain extent the *comedia* may be thought of as a ritual act which reinforces the fundamental beliefs of society'.[12] These fundamental beliefs for him were essentially those which constitute Tillyard's once enormously influential Elizabethan world picture of cosmic hierarchy and order, a picture now widely considered to give only a partial insight into the realities of early modern thought and values. While the essays are therefore perhaps less persuasive than they once were, the methodology they use retains its value. The text and its realisation in performance are to be seen not as

---

[12] 'Prefacio', in *Comovisión y escenografía*, p. 12.

separate exercises but as integral to a totalising theatrical identity. Varey's aim in mining texts for performance detail was, by his own claim, not archaeology but re-creation, and he justified his chronological method of examining a text by arguing that, since it was only by meticulously following the plot through that one could hope to recapture the unfolding effect the play had on its audience, description and interpretation were necessarily fused processes. His preferred procedure for textual exegesis might not suit everyone, but the fact that its inspiring principle—the indivisibility of the theatrical experience—can yield interpretations very different from Varey's own is a sign of that principle's strength not its weakness. And a great deal of what he has to say in these essays about seventeenth-century social and ideological issues is as sound, as well-judged and therefore as valuable as it was before we became less convinced by the idea of a monolithic early modern culture where everybody thought the same thoughts and playwrights did nothing but echo them.

Varey's view of a play as a text shaped both by its stage identity and by its social and ideological roots, as a constituent part not only of theatre but of the historical process, is seen in action in two of the play editions on which he collaborated, where text, staging, and ideas are all given their due weight. His edition with Shergold in 1954 of Tirso de Molina's *El burlador de Sevilla* had been a reader's edition for the Cambridge Plain Texts series, and there could not be a greater contrast between it and the edition they published with Jack Sage in 1970 of Juan Vélez de Guevara's two-act *zarzuela, Los celos hacen estrellas,* which was performed before the court in the *salón dorado* of the Alcázar Real on 22 December 1672 in celebration of the birthday of the Queen Mother, Mariana of Austria. This magnificent volume contains the texts, with variants and notes, of the play itself, the *loa* that preceded it, the *entremés* performed between the acts, and the *fin de fiesta* at the end. There is an extensive introduction on the manuscript and first edition, the playwright's life and work, Francisco Herrera el Mozo's water colours for the stage sets, the date of the first performance, the palace where it was held, the mythological text and its accompanying pieces, the composer, Juan Hidalgo, and the dynastic and literary relations between Spain and Austria which formed the play's wider context. Following the texts are a contemporary Spanish version of Vélez's Ovidian source, an essay by Varey on the iconographical portraits of the king's ancestors that looked down upon the scene as the royal family enjoyed the spectacle, another by Jack Sage on the *zarzuela* and Hidalgo's music, and an edition of the score also by Sage. Ample illustrations complete the ambitious enterprise—to recreate as completely as possible the performance of a musical play at court in late-seventeenth-century Spain. No commercial press and few university presses would have touched it, but happily the existence of Tamesis made it possible.

It was Tamesis again, in its series Tamesis Texts, which ten years later published Varey's critical edition, in collaboration with J. M. Ruano, of Lope de Vega's *Peribáñez y el Comendador de Ocaña*. It is the perfect working text for specialists and students alike—rigorously edited, generously annotated, with a beautifully judged introduction, on dating, sources, structure, themes, ideology, imagery, staging, verse forms, and editorial matters, that is neither over-scholarly nor condescendingly reductive. Pepe Ruano's description of the way they worked together is very instructive: 'We divided the work between us. I did the text and end-notes and also wrote the bit entitled "The Present Edition" in the Introduction. He wrote the Introduction. Then, we exchanged our contributions and made comments on each other's work. He was, as always, very generous when commenting on my contribution and graciously accepted the very few comments I dared to make on his. I then travelled to London, stayed in the Principal's residence in Kidderpore for a couple of days and in the evenings went to his house, sat with him in his office and with an open bottle of his best Rioja close at hand we both went painstakingly over every end-note and practically every line in the text, until my eyelids began to close (something that happened much sooner to me than to him) and I took my leave, while he said that he still had a couple more things to do before he retired.' Jack Sage had similarly found Varey 'unfailingly fair, conscientious, humorous, far-seeing and discreetly commanding'.

John Varey's other foray into the arena of *comedia* editions was a very different undertaking. This was the nineteen-volume facsimile edition, prepared by himself and Don Cruickshank and published in 1973, of the first editions of all nine *partes* of Calderón's full-length plays, and, in the case of the first five *partes*, of the reprints which appeared during his lifetime. Our knowledge of the relationship of the editions to one another is due to the work carried out in the field by Edward Wilson and Don Cruickshank, and the first volume of the series, which was edited by Cruickshank, is devoted to textual criticism of Calderón's *comedias* by these two scholars. The last volume, edited by Varey, reprinted thirteen essays by different *comedia* specialists to illustrate the various ways in which Anglo-American scholarship had sought to evaluate the theatre of Calderón over the previous thirty-five years. These book-end volumes are still immensely useful to students and scholars in collecting together significant writings previously scattered in time and place, but the scholarly contribution of the seventeen middle volumes is fundamental. As Varey pointed out, all the original volumes are rare; one is unique. No single library has a complete set and even leading libraries usually have no more than half of the twelve volumes printed before 1681. The facsimile edition therefore made available the material necessary for a textual study of all those works which appeared in the collective volumes of Calderón's plays in the course of the seventeenth century. Copies were selected from libraries in the UK, Italy, the USA, Canada, France, Germany, and Spain, and reprinted in their entirety, with, in the case of any deficiencies, the appropriate pages from another copy printed as an appendix. By Varey's insistence, Cruickshank's name appeared first on the title pages of the series because he did most of the organisational work for the facsimile, but the enterprise was Varey's idea in the first place, he handled all the negotiations with the publisher, took an equal part in discussions about practical details, and double proofread volumes 1 and 19. According to Don Cruickshank, the correspondence between them on the project 'More than anything . . . shows his constant readiness to help and advise and to be informed—as if he had nothing else to worry about but this one project.'

At the time this enterprise was underway Varey certainly had more than enough to occupy him, since it was the early seventies that saw the launch of the Fuentes series. The second two of his own three books on popular entertainments (*Los títeres* and *Cartelera*) would be published in the series in 1972 and 1995 respectively, but the first of the collaborative efforts appeared in 1971. Although the first volume of the series to be published, it was volume 3 in the master publication plan, into which volumes were slotted as and when they appeared. Thereafter volumes appeared in 1972, 1973, 1975, 1979, 1982, 1985, 1986, 1987, 1989, 1991, 1992, 1994, 1995, with three volumes in 1997. Five further numbered volumes are in preparation—numbers 35, 30, 14, 32, and 31—along with two more which have not yet been allocated a number. The first six collaborative volumes were produced with Norman Shergold. In 1961 Shergold and Varey together had published *Los autos sacramentales en Madrid en la época de Calderón* (Madrid: Ediciones de Literatura Española), a collection of documents with accompanying study relating to the Corpus Christi plays performed in Madrid between 1637 and 1681; they had already in two previous articles studied the period down to 1637. Organised as the *autos* were by the Madrid city council, a hoard of documents had survived in the city archives which had been only very partially studied and certainly not reproduced in anything like the quantity and detail to be found here. Their book opened up the world of the seventeenth-century religious theatre as no work had done before, providing information not merely on the development of the *autos* themselves but on every aspect of the festivities—their organisation and administration, the logistics of performance in the streets, the movable carts and the platform that formed the stage, the processions and their progress, the giants and carnival dragons, the audiences from high to low, the actors, the dancing, the costumes, the costs, and payments; nothing is omitted. Plans, illustrations, and analytical indices were provided to help the reader and to bring to life a world that time had largely forgotten. This work published by the two scholars in Spain provided the format, and no doubt to a large extent the inspiration, for the Fuentes series itself. It also provided the format for the way in which the collaborators appeared on the title pages in the series, the order reflecting authorial input (often generously interpreted by Varey), now Varey and Shergold, now Shergold and Varey, later on Varey and Davis or Davis and Varey—a procedure that I know from my own experience induces severe editorial neurosis in those producing references and bibliographies in which these works appear, but scrupulously fair.

Between 1971 and 1979 four volumes of studies and documents entitled *Teatros y comedias* were published (the first three by Varey and Shergold, the fourth by Shergold and Varey), covering the period 1600 to 1699. In 1986 a fifth volume was published, this time by Shergold, Varey, and Davis, covering the years between 1699 and 1719, and in 1994 there appeared a sixth volume by Varey, Shergold, and Davis, taking this particular enterprise down to 1745. As well as providing information about plays, performances, actors and actresses, theatre closures on the occasion of royal deaths, accounts, entry fees, legal wrangles, and so on, over a period of a century and a half, these volumes as they move forward also trace larger patterns: the attempts at social and moral regulation of the theatre and the theatrical world, the policing of performances to maintain law and order, the diminishing role of the charitable brotherhoods, the eventual transfer of administrative responsibliity to the municipal authorities; and the growth of the court theatre. It was entirely appropriate in the light of these later developments that after the first four volumes the next one, *Representaciones palaciegas 1603–1699* (1982), by Shergold and Varey, should be on the palace theatre itself between 1603 and 1699. The documents offer a fascinating insight into the importance of the theatre in the life of the court, how the court influenced theatrical life, and how the court theatre, into which the public was admitted after the court itself had over several days seen the performance, gradually eroded activities in the public playhouses. They also give an instant and vivid picture of a different theatrical world, with their detailed costings, their emphasis on elaborate costumes, scenery, and stage effects, and their constant preoccupation with expenditure on wax—scarcely necessary for afternoon performances in public playhouses open to the air. In 1997, the last volume to be published in the series before John Varey died was a companion volume, albeit with a wider date-spread, on the palace theatre by Margaret Rich Greer and Varey, *El teatro palaciego 1586–1707*. It was planned as the second of a total of four on the court theatre down to the middle of the eighteenth century. The focus in this one is financial and administrative, with costume accounts detailed enough to warrant an appendix on early modern textiles and accessories, and so pressing a concern with protocol, jurisdiction, and precedence that another appendix is provided on official court etiquette. It not only takes us behind the scenes of court life, however, but in the detail it gives us of some of the performances it greatly enhances our understanding of how the court operated, how the play-texts familiar to us translated to the proscenium stage, and how the resulting extravagant display functioned—albeit not without financial strain—as an exercise in self-aggrandisement and self-delusion as Spain's credibility as a powerful and wealthy nation waned.

Whereas the volumes in the Fuentes series mentioned thus far are inclusive in their reproduction of documents relating to theatres and performances over a period of time from 1586 to 1745, others focus more directly on particular aspects of the early modern Spanish theatre. *Comedias en Madrid 1603–1709* (1989) by Varey, Shergold, and Davis, is an alphabetical list (cross-referenced with other Fuentes volumes) of plays, performances, and printings which imposes order on some part of the confusion created by the composition, staging, and publication, often unauthorised, of a vast number of plays many of which have been lost and many of which are referred to in the records by different or adulterated titles. *Genealogía, origen y noticias de los comediantes de España* (1985), by Shergold and Varey, is a compilation of information about hundreds of actors and actresses which makes fascinating and amusing reading. The remaining four volumes published before Varey died—*Los arriendos de los corrales de Madrid, 1587–1719* (1987, Varey, Shergold, and Davis); *Los libros de cuentas de los corrales de comedias de Madrid, 1706–1719* (1992, Varey and Davis); *Los corrales de comedias y los hospitales de Madrid 1574–1615* (1997, Davis and Varey), and its continuation

Los corrales de comedias y los hospitales de Madrid 1615–1849 (1997, Varey and Davis)—all concentrate on financing and administration: the leasing of playhouses, the accounts books, and the changing relationship between the playhouses and the charitable hospitals, whose dependence on the playhouses' proceeds served for many years to protect the theatre from its enemies.

The seven volumes of the Fuentes series in preparation at the time of John Varey's death are a varied group: two volumes on theatrical activity in the Madrid region, a reconstruction of one of the two Madrid playhouses, the Corral de la Cruz, two volumes on the lateral boxes in the Corral de la Cruz and the Corral del Príncipe respectively, an edition of a late eighteenth-century collection of chronological records concerning the origins of the Spanish theatre, and the third volume of the promised four on the court theatre. When completed, the collaborative Fuentes volumes which John Varey masterminded and directed, and in the research, writing, and editing of which he played such a vital part, will number twenty-one. Together with his three works on popular entertainments, his book with Shergold on the *autos sacramentales*, his many articles on theatre and ceremonial, and a collection of document-based essays he co-edited with Luciano García Lorenzo on various aspects of the theatres and theatrical life, *Teatros y vida teatral en el siglo de oro a través de las fuentes documentales* (Tamesis, 1991), the series stands as an enduring memorial to the man, his vision, and his energy. It is a corpus of work based on what García Lorenzo has called in the introduction to that volume (p. 7), 'el ingrato, poco brillante, pero absolutamente necesario trabajo llevado a cabo en archivos [y] bibliotecas', the thankless, unglamorous, but absolutely vital work carried out in archives and libraries that is so essential to our reconstruction and understanding of the past. It has transformed the face of theatre history in Spain. It has added invaluable weight and detail to our knowledge of the workings of the extraordinary theatre that for over a century dominated the cultural life of the nation, creating for its people myths that simultaneously reflected and fashioned its sense of collective identity, and in the process it has provided students of the *comedia* with material and tools they need to pursue their various scholarly and critical goals. What sits there, now so accessible, so ordered, so accurate between the covers of the study-and-documents books—all, with the exception of the book on the *autos sacramentales*, in the Fuentes series—represents a lifetime of arduous work on mountains of documents in the archives of Spain which only John Varey's own rigorous methods made possible. Infinite care was second nature to him, and he and his collaborators copied to one another, scrutinised and deliberated painstakingly over absolutely everything they discovered and wrote. Both initial transcriptions and typed-up documents were checked against the originals, and proofs were in due course checked word for word against the typescript. Varey himself kept the project moving, did the world-wide scanning for relevant material or developments, and with his gift for drawing threads together synthesised the accumulated mass of diverse notes into a comprehensive account. This long-drawn-out process largely accounts for the way in which the preparatory work for the different volumes necessarily overlapped and for the order in which the volumes were published. At the same time it was John Varey's guarantee of the absolute reliability of the end result of a procedure which, certainly in its repeated enactments, would have been too daunting for most of us. Placed within the greater picture of Varey's many other scholarly enterprises and professional responsibilities, it offers persuasive support for Sheldon's theory of human types, with John as the archetypal mesomorph.

While it is clearly on the basis of his huge and multifaceted contribution to Spanish theatre studies that John Varey's reputation stands and will survive, it would be a mistake to underestimate the value of his lasting interest in the nineteenth-century novelist Galdós. He was the editor of an important compilation (*Galdós Studies*, Tamesis, 1970), and the author of a perceptive Critical Guide to one of Galdós's best known novels, *Doña Perfecta* (Grant and Cutler, 1971) and of several articles, the most influential of which, 'Nuestro buen Thiers' (*Anales Galdosianos*, 1, 1966), sparked off examination of the many identifications with real-life political and cultural figures elaborated by Galdós in his fiction. Viewed alongside the weight of his major work, the Galdós publications inevitably take on the appearance of a personal passion indulged from time to time in the interstices of the real business of his research life. But they are an eloquent testimony to a mind of great scholarly range and extraordinary intellectual energy and enthusiasm—which could take unexpected forms. One of the funniest lectures I have had the pleasure of listening to was one John gave at the Association of Hispanists many years ago, when he spoke for an hour on the subject of trains in the nineteenth-century Spanish novel. Alas, he never published it as far as I know.

Reassuring as it might be for lesser mortals to cite this rare example of Varey's scholarship not leading to publication, his legacy is a Herculean record of pioneering published research of enduring value. His work deserves to rank with that of other giants in their different fields—Joseph

Needham's work on Chinese science, Philip Grierson's work on medieval coins, or Tony Wrigley's work on English demography. Like John Varey's their reputations are founded largely on multi-volume works of collaborative scholarship. Like theirs, his pioneering scholarship will be refined and augmented, but it can never be ignored.

Part I   ALAN DEYERMOND
Fellow of the Academy

Part II   MELVEENA McKENDRICK
Fellow of the Academy

Note to Part I.   Most of the information in Part I of this memoir derives from my own observation and from what John Varey and other witnesses told me over the years. Mrs Micky Varey has generously filled gaps in my knowledge and has commented on a first draft.

In parts of this memoir I have drawn on what I wrote in the introductions to the 1991 Festschrift and the 2000 memorial volume. I am grateful to the editor of the latter volume and to the publishers of both for allowing me to do so.   (A.D.D.)

Note to Part II.   I am grateful to Don Cruickshank, Margaret Greer, J. M. Ruano de la Haza, and Jack Sage for the insights they have given me into John Varey's working methods and personal qualities as a collaborator, and to Geoffrey Ribbans for allowing me to draw on his expertise in Galdós studies.   (M. McK.)

GLANVILLE WILLIAMS   *Dona Haycraft*

Glanville Llewelyn Williams
1911–1997

WHEN, IN 1957 at the age of 46, Glanville Williams was elected a Fellow of the Academy his name had long been a byword among both practising and academic lawyers throughout the English-speaking world as that of its sharpest, most radically critical, and most prolific living jurist. He had published three monographs on complex and defective aspects of the common law of obligations whose originality, sophistication, penetration, breadth of reference, historical acuity, and analytical and critical clarity had set new standards for legal writing in this area. He had been the first to demonstrate how the techniques of linguistic analysis could be used to expose the emptiness of much jurisprudential debate and the irrationality of many a legal distinction. And he had capped all this with (what in its second edition was) a nine-hundred page treatise on the general principles underlying the criminal law, which not only marked a fundamental change of direction in his own work but also transformed the study of that subject setting the agenda in it for several decades, and had led to his appointment as the only foreign Special Consultant for the American Law Institute's great project for a Model Penal Code. He had gone on, following paths first trodden by Jeremy Bentham, to appraise and find wanting, many of the sacred cows of the English way of administering criminal justice, equalling his mentor in critical rigour and in the disdain shown for 'Judge & Co.', but writing infinitely more readable prose that re-ignited debates which still continue. He had also made a pioneering and outspoken study of the lengths to which Anglo-American law went to protect human life that would be seen as a seminal text when, nearly two decades later, medical law

Proceedings of the British Academy, **115**, 411–435. © The British Academy 2002.

and ethics began to attract the attention of English Law Faculties. There had, moreover, been very few years in which he had not published half-a-dozen or more papers unravelling doctrinal complexities or critically analysing, often with iconoclastic zeal, judicial decisions and parliamentary legislation. And he had written a best-selling guide for aspiring law students which for half-a-century was for almost all of them to be their first introduction to their chosen profession. On top of all this, he had been active in the cause of law reform as polemicist, committee member, and draftsman.

His election to the Academy could not, therefore, be said to have been premature. He was then a Fellow, and Director of Studies in Law, of Jesus College, Cambridge and Reader in English Law in the university. But he had already held two chairs in the University of London (the first at the London School of Economics, the second—at the age of 39—its senior law chair, that of the Quain Professor of Jurisprudence at University College), and he was to hold two more at Cambridge (initially one of the university's first 'personal' chairs, and then the Rouse Ball Professorship of English Law). On reaching retiring age—he never, of course, really retired—he was rightly acclaimed by another member of the Academy, Sir Rupert Cross, Vinerian Professor at Oxford, as 'without doubt the greatest English criminal lawyer since Stephen'.[1]

I

Born on 15 February 1911, Glanville Williams was the son of Benjamin Elwy Williams of Bridgend, Glamorgan, and his wife Gwladys, daughter of David Llewelyn of Pontypridd. His father, who came from a long line of modest, chapel-going, Carmarthenshire and Cardiganshire farmers, was then a partner in a local firm of tailors. His mother had been a primary school teacher.

The infant was precocious. There was no stage of baby language. On his first visit, aged three, to the dentist, hearing that a milk tooth was to be extracted, he looked up in alarm and asked 'Is it imperative?' An only

---

[1] 'The Reports of the Criminal Law Commissioners (1833–1849) and the Abortive Bills of 1853' in P. R. Glazebrook (ed.) *Reshaping the Criminal Law* (1978), pp. 5, 20. The reference is to Sir James Fitzjames Stephen (1829–94), author of *A General View of the Criminal Law of England* (1863), *A History of the Criminal Law*, 3 vols. (1883) and a *Digest of the Criminal Law* (1877), who drafted a Criminal Code which though it received the blessing of a Royal Commission was not enacted in England, but was adopted elsewhere in the Empire.

child with poor health, sometimes confined to bed, who was uncomfortable in large groups, preferring the companionship of a few close friends, he developed his own interests and games. He built an elaborate model theatre, with performing puppets, and became a sufficiently competent conjuror to perform at school entertainments. Family holidays were often spent on the beautiful Glamorgan coast at Ogmore, where a neighbouring cottage was occupied by the young family of the Reverend William Evans, who (as Wil Ifan) was to be crowned bard at the National Eisteddfod. During the day the children played on the long empty stretches of sand, exploring the rock pools and caves; in the evenings the two families read verse and prose to one another. These holidays left lasting impressions and life-long loves both of the countryside and of the classical poets, novelists and essayists of these islands.

At twelve, he went, with a scholarship, to Cowbridge Grammar School as a boarder. Dogged by a weak chest, he spent almost as much time in the school sanatorium as in the classroom, he nonetheless won a classical scholarship to the University College of Wales at Aberystwyth; to which he went aged 16 in 1927, living (in view of his age and frail health) at the home of his uncle (Sir) William Llewelyn Davis, Librarian of the National Library of Wales, a Celtic scholar, and author of two Welsh grammars. His uncle's efforts to make him a Welsh speaker—his father, as a Carmarthen man, was bilingual but his mother was not—were, however, unavailing. Throughout his life Glanville remained unmoved by the claims of either Welsh nationalism or the Welsh language.

His four years at Aberystwyth were formative ones. (The first, before he turned to Law, was spent on Latin, English, Philosophy, and History.) The Law Department, under the charismatic Professor T. A. Levi, was, in that inter-war period, a remarkable legal nursery. Among the students were a future Lord Chancellor, two Law Lords, a bevy of other judges, and more than half-a-dozen professors of law, while several of the lecturers were also to have distinguished careers elsewhere. A First, and a scholarship, was to take him as an affiliated (i.e., graduate) student to St John's College, Cambridge, where the Law Fellows were Stanley Bailey (who had lectured at Aberystwyth) and (Sir) Percy Winfield. Winfield was to supervise his Ph.D. research—after another First (Division 1), with an outstanding paper in Legal History, in the Law Tripos in 1933—and to secure his election as a Research Fellow of the college in 1936.

While at Aberystwyth the law student had invented an alphabetical shorthand system for taking lecture notes. He patented it (as 'Speedhand')

and compiled a manual,[2] and it was long taught in secretarial schools in Britain and South Africa. He also learnt to play golf on the finely sited course at Harlech and (under the tutelage of members of his uncle's staff) to bind books. Both hobbies were pursued for many years. More significantly, he was active in the university's vibrant pacifist movement, becoming President of the University of Wales branch of the League of Nations Society and representing it at a League conference in the USA in 1931.

II

For all lawyers, whatever their specialism, Glanville's name (and for many, even beyond the circle of friends and colleagues, this was both a sufficient and the customary appellation) is now inseparable from the criminal law, but it was the law of civil obligations, and particularly the law of torts—which governs the payment of compensation for injuries to person, property, business interests, and reputation—on which he cut his scholarly teeth, and established his formidable reputation.[3] Torts lawyers long mourned his desertion of their subject. His Ph.D. dissertation was on 'The History of Tortious Liability for Animals.' It was completed, in little more than two-and-a-half years during which he had also sat the Bar exams. Its examiners (Sir William Holdsworth and Winfield) not only recommended that 'in view of its exceptional merit' the oral examination should be dispensed with, but each also went on to say that if only the dissertation had been in print and its author of sufficient standing, they would have recommended the award of the LL.D. 'The minute study of the authorities, of all periods, printed and manuscript', reported Holdsworth, 'the grasp of principle which he has shown, and his power to criticise the rules and principles which he has expounded, make his thesis an admirable example of the manner in which legal history ought to be studied and applied. It is obvious that it is only a lawyer of very remarkable ability who could turn out a piece of this kind.'[4] The examiners' sole complaint was of the severity of the candidate's criticisms of the illogical reasons offered by judges for decisions that produced practically convenient results. They were, however, mistaken in thinking that increasing age would remedy this trait.

[2] 1st edn. 1952, 8th edn. 1980.
[3] See generally, B. A. Hepple, 'Glanville Williams 1911–1997: Civil Obligations', *Cambridge Law Journal* (1997), 440–5.
[4] Cambridge University Archives.

The dissertation was expanded to become *Liability for Animals. An account of the development and present law of tortious liability for animals, distress damage feasant and the duty to fence in Great Britain, Northern Ireland and the common-law Dominions*, published by the Cambridge University Press in 1939[5] and greeted as 'one of the best legal treatises' to be published 'in England'.[6] The subject is fascinating and complex, presenting problems which go to the heart of notions of legal responsibility and have demanded solutions ever since the human race began to keep animals for its own purposes and to look to tribunals for the settlement of its disputes. For it is the animals, not the humans, who do the damage, and they have wills of their own. Yet taking it out on them, though it has in various societies and in various times been done, affords those whom they have harmed rather limited satisfaction. And the arrival on the scene of motor vehicles had added one more problem: hitherto there had been no reason why animals and humans should not share the highways on more or less equal terms. Although a modern law, the author argued, ought to be based on negligence, penetrating historical analysis[7] explained how and why so much liability without fault had survived.

Someone who could, in his mid twenties, handle such a wide-ranging topic in so masterly a fashion was clearly going to be a jurist to be reckoned with, as a 1938 paper on the 'Foundations of Tortious Liability'[8] had also signalled. Two generations of grand old men (including his own research supervisor) had, he argued, all got it wrong. The law of torts was neither founded on a single general principle that was subject to exceptions, as some of them had concluded, nor was it, as others said, simply a host of single instances. Rather there were several general rules of, and also several general exceptions to, liability, together with stretches of disputed territory. A further sixty years of hard-fought debate, judicial and academic, has confirmed the accuracy of this analysis.

Plans for a year at the Harvard Law School were frustrated by the onset of war in 1939. He registered as a Conscientious Objector and, being (in the event unnecessarily) well-stocked with arguments for his

---

[5] The Syndics, having noted the receipt of several grants in aid of publication (and gravely underestimated sales) magnanimously agreed to bear 'the remaining losses'. At about the same time they agreed to publish David Knowles's *Monastic Order in England* only after his father, a successful businessman, had promised to underwrite the costs.

[6] Dean Cecil Wright of Toronto, *Canadian Bar Review*, 17 (1939), 613, 615.

[7] Which 'represents an important stage in the development of our knowledge' of the emergence of the action on the case: M. J. Prichard, *Scott v. Shepherd (1773) and the Emergence of the Tort of Negligence (Selden Society Lecture)* (1976), p. 35.

[8] *Cambridge Law Journal*, 7 (1939), 111.

interview with the tribunal, was without ado allotted to Civil Defence work and encouraged to continue teaching Law, which he was to do in the company of a handful of the elderly, the medically unfit, and of refugees from Germany. His jurisprudence lectures are remembered by its briefly sojourning students (and those of the evacuated LSE) as a bright spot in a muted Cambridge. He continued, too, to act as a 'Poor Man's Lawyer' (Legal Aid still lay in the future), and to help with the Society of Friends' club for refugees. No new university appointments were being made and when his Research Fellowship and University Assistant Lectureship expired in 1941, he combined practice at the Bar[9]—for the rest of his life he was to marvel at how little law many very successful barristers knew, and even then how often they got that little wrong—with ad hoc law teaching and, during the long vacations, work on a fruit farm.

Among the many legal problems exposed by the outbreak of war was the unsatisfactory state of the law governing contracts whose performance had for that or any other reason become impossible. It remained as the litigation engendered by the First World War had left it. Glanville edited, and added to, a monograph[10] written by one of his contemporaries as a research student who had returned to New Zealand to practise law there. And when the Law Reform (Frustrated Contracts) Act 1943 was enacted he wrote a Commentary on it,[11] which said, elegantly, almost all that has ever needed saying. 'No one who consults this commentary', wrote H. C. Gutteridge, 'can fail to be impressed by the depth of [the author's] learning and by the amazing versatility which he displays. Nothing seems to have escaped his attention. In fact [he] has at times allowed his flair for incisive criticism to get the upper hand of him so that it becomes a little difficult to distinguish between his expository conclusions and his views as to what Parliament ought to have done or the draftsman should have said.'[12]

Having shown his paces as both lawyer and legal historian, Glanville was next to demonstrate his skill as a legal philosopher. A five-part article, 'Language and the Law'[13] and a paper, 'International Law and the

[9] In Walter Raeburn KC's chambers in King's Bench Walk.

[10] R. G. McElroy, *Impossibility of Performance: a treatise on the law of supervening impossibility of performance of contract, failure of consideration and frustration*, ed. with additional chapters by G. L. W. (Cambridge, 1941).

[11] *The Law Reform (Frustrated Contracts) Act 1943* (1944) and *Modern Law Review*, 7 (1943), 66.

[12] *Law Quarterly Review*, 61 (1945), 97.

[13] *Law Quarterly Review*, 61 (1945), 71–86, 179–95, 293–303, 384–406; Ibid. 62 (1946), 387–406; supplemented by '*A lawyer's Alice*', *Cambridge Law Journal*, 9 (1946), 171–84.

Controversy concerning the word "Law"',[14] which, but for war-time publishing difficulties, might well have appeared together as a monograph, were the first serious attempt to apply the philosophical technique of linguistic analysis to law and jurisprudence. In the paper on international law, he sharply attacked the many jurists and international lawyers who had debated whether international law was 'really' law. They had been wasting everyone's time, for the question was not a factual one, the many differences between municipal and international law being undeniable, but was simply one of conventional verbal usage, about which individual theorists could please themselves, but had no right to dictate to others. This approach was to be refined and developed by H. L. A. Hart in the last chapter of *The Concept of Law* (1961) which showed how the use in respect of different social phenomena of an abstract word like 'law' reflected the fact that these phenomena each shared, without necessarily all possessing in common, some distinctive features. Glanville had himself said as much when editing a student text on jurisprudence[15] and he had adopted essentially the same approach to 'The Definition of Crime'.[16]

In 'Language and the Law', he ranged more widely, taking as his starting point C. K. Ogden's and I. A. Richards's *The Meaning of Meaning* (1923). He showed, with examples from a vast variety of legal rules and decisions, and references to a host of juristic debates, that the resolution of legal and jurisprudential questions called for careful attention not just to the different meanings and uncertainties attaching to almost all words, but to (at least six) different sorts of meaning, behind which value judgements almost always lie concealed. It was with these, rather than verbal distinctions and semantic issues, that the jurist should be primarily concerned. The mistakes of supposing, for instance, that abstract concepts could usefully be discussed otherwise than in regard to 'concrete referents', that law had an existence other than as a 'collection of symbols capable of evoking ideas and emotions, together with the ideas and emotions so evoked', that uncertainties in the meaning of words could be eliminated by technical legal definitions, that there were any 'single' facts to which single terms could be applied, and that distinguishing between the 'substance' and the 'quality' of a thing, or between a person's 'identity' and 'attributes' could resolve legal problems,[17] were all ruthlessly

---

[14] *British Yearbook of International Law*, 22 (1945), 146–63.

[15] Sir John Salmond, *Jurisprudence*, 10th edn. (1947), p. 33.

[16] *Current Legal Problems* (1955), 107–30.

[17] Elaborated on in a classic article: 'Mistake as to Party in the Law of Contract', *Canadian Bar Review*, 23 (1945), 271–92; 380–416. Later examples of this genre are 'Forgery and Falsity',

exposed, as was the claim of the extreme logical positivists that ethical, and therefore legal, statements were meaningless. As Hart said, 'these articles not only sweep away much rubbish, but also contribute much to the understanding of legal reasoning'.[18]

Many of their arguments were incorporated and developed in an edition of Sir John Salmond's classic student text-book on *Jurisprudence*,[19] many pages of which were extensively revised or rewritten, marking out ground which others were later to till. A key theme (sections IV–VI) of Hart's influential lecture, *Definition and Theory in Jurisprudence* (1953) was foreshadowed in the treatment of the juristic controversy as to whether legal corporations were to be regarded as 'real' or 'fictitious' persons.[20] Glanville's concentration on legal rules and rulings did, however, lead him to exaggerate the arbitrariness of ordinary linguistic usage, and so to underestimate the connections which underlie it, with the result that these writings had more influence among lawyers than philosophers.[21]

In 1945 his war-time connection with the LSE solidified with his appointment as Reader in English Law there. He became Professor of Public Law the following year. He did his duty by the title of his chair[22] with (among several other papers) a scathing denunciation of the shabby reasoning offered by the Law Lords for holding that William Joyce ('Lord Haw-Haw'), a United States citizen of Irish birth, owed allegiance to the British Crown, and so had committed treason when he broadcast for the Germans during the war.[23] And he wrote another elegant commentary on another reforming statute, the Crown Proceedings Act 1947,[24] in which Parliament had at last recognised both that the immunity of the Crown (i.e., government departments) from civil suit could no longer be justified, and that legal fictions were not the right way to the outcomes which justice required. His principal interest still

---

Criminal Law Review (1974), 71 (demonstrating the fatuity of a general offence of forgery) and 'The Logic of "Exceptions"' *Cambridge Law Journal* (1988), 261 (discussed at page 428 below).

[18] 'Philosophy of Law and Jurisprudence in Britain (1945–52)' *American Journal of Comparative Law*, 2 (1953), 354, 361.

[19] See above n. 15. The editor's alterations and rewritings are listed in Appendix V.

[20] Ibid. p. 330.

[21] Cf. J. Wisdom *Philosophy, Metaphysics and Psycho-Analysis* (Oxford, 1953), pp. 249–54, which show that Wisdom had not read the papers of which he was so critical with any care.

[22] S. A. de Smith's classic *Judicial Review of Administrative Action* (1st edn., 1959; 5th edn., 1999) began as a Ph.D. dissertation under his supervision.

[23] 'The Correlation of Allegiance and Protection', *Cambridge Law Journal*, 10 (1948), 54–76.

[24] (1948).

lay, however, in the darkest areas of private law. The immensely obscure and (as he demonstrated) gravely defective rules governing cases where a legal obligation is owed, or harm has been caused, by more than one person, were made the subject of two complementary treatises,[25] totalling over 700 pages, which half-a-century later had not been replaced. The 'great analytical and dialectical ability'[26] displayed in them was admired by judge[27] and jurist alike.[28]

It was not until the early 1960s that Glanville decided to devote himself single-mindedly to the criminal law. But it is in what Professor B. A. Hepple has described as his 'astounding' Inaugural Lecture as Quain Professor in 1951 on 'The Aims of the Law of Tort'[29] that his work in private law may be seen to culminate.

> This has never been bettered as an account of the social function or *raison d'être* of the law of tort, in particular the action for damages. . . . He concluded that there was a lack of coherence with the law . . . trying to serve a multiplicity of purposes but succeeding in none. . . .[30] The future student of the intellectual history of this branch of the law may place him at the end of one period of legal scholarship and the beginning of another. He brought the 'scientific' positivism of early twentieth century scholars, such as Salmond and Winfield, to its apotheosis, but his utilitarian concerns with the wider purposes and policies of the law were a harbinger of the socio-legal revolution in legal scholarship which began in the late 1960s.[31]

III

Criminal Law: The General Part, first published in 1953, second edition 1963, stands high in the list of great books written about English law in the twentieth century.[32] It was another astonishing achievement, transforming scholarly and (rather more slowly) professional attitudes to its subject. The mapping of the territory was so comprehensive, the analysis

---

[25] *Joint Obligations. A treatise on joint and joint and several liability in contract, quasi-contract and trusts* (1949) and *Joint Torts and Contributory Negligence. A Study of Concurrent Fault in Great Britain, Ireland and the Common Law Dominions* (1951).

[26] Lord Wright, *Law Quarterly Review*, 6 (1951), 528.

[27] Lord Justice Denning, ibid., 66 (1950), 253.

[28] L. C. B. Gower, *Modern Law Review*, 13 (1950), 400.

[29] *Current Legal Problems*, 4 (1951), 137.

[30] *Cambridge Law Journal* (1997), 444–5.

[31] Ibid. 441.

[32] It was awarded the Ames Prize by Harvard University.

so penetrating, the critique so trenchant, and the prose, enriched with echoes of the Bible and the English classics, so lucid and so elegant. In over (in its second edition) 900 pages there is not a sentence that is obscure or ambiguous or superfluous. It has provided a programme for debate and further research which only now is beginning to be travelled beyond. Much of his own subsequent writing on the criminal law—including the innovatory *Textbook* (first edition 1978)—was devoted to developing, elaborating, and defending the principles propounded in *The General Part*, to which he adhered with remarkable consistency and, in almost all instances, well-warranted tenacity.

It is, first and foremost, its creativity and vision, its breaking out of the straitjacket of traditional legal categories, that makes *The General Part* such a great book. The masterly survey and description of the case and statute law, for which the rest of the common law world was scoured to supplement the rather sparse English material, was there to serve a higher purpose. For 'unfortunately, as has appeared only too plainly from these pages, there is no unanimity about anything in criminal law; scarcely a single important principle but has been denied by some judicial decision or by some legislation.'[33] Nor was the author much concerned to predict how future courts would respond to particular issues, for he took a dim view of the rough and unthinking ways in which 'the charmed circle of the judiciary' frequently resolved questions of criminal liability. Placing few bets he felt no need to hedge them. Rather, he set out to persuade his readers not that England had, but that it was possible for a common law jurisdiction like it to have, a criminal law that was fair and just because principled, internally consistent and rational (the criteria were professedly utilitarian which was why he thought a general 'lesser of two evils'—he called it a necessity—defence so important).[34] The discretions conceded to judges and juries (he profoundly distrusted both) had, therefore, to be kept to the minimum. The cases and statutes that stand in the way are identified, and the arguments for and against them deployed for the benefit of counsel, judges, and Parliament. The statutory reforms that are

---

[33] *Criminal Law: The General Part* (1953), p. 435; cf. also p. 130. All further page references are, unless otherwise indicated, to this (first) edition. For a fuller discussion see P. R. Glazebrook, 'Glanville Williams 1911–1997: Criminal Law', *Cambridge Law Journal* (1997), 445–55.

[34] pp. 567–87; 'The Defence of Necessity', *Current Legal Problems* (1953), 216; *Sanctity of Life*, pp. 286–7; 'A Commentary on *R v. Dudley and Stephens*', *Cambrian Law Review* (1977), 94; 'Necessity', *Criminal Law Review* (1978), 128. Its introduction, at his urging, into the Model Penal Code (Art. 3) has been said to represent 'a revolution in [legal] thinking': G. P. Fletcher, *Basic Concepts of Criminal Law* (New York, 1998), 142.

needed are then clearly indicated. The Benthamite Criminal Law Commissioners of 1833 and 1845, with their master himself (whose fondness for neologisms he shared) are, it is evident,[35] men after the author's own mind and heart.

Heart as well as mind. The aim was not intellectual tidiness for its own sake—though intellectual untidiness and the logical fallacy was always very shocking but a criminal law that would operate less heavy-handedly, less discriminatorily, and be less susceptible to the gales of vindictive passion and emotion.[36] Legal argument was, of course, relished. But what lay behind the missionary zeal evident in all his writing about English criminal justice was his belief (for which *The Sanctity of Life and the Criminal Law* (1956) provides further extensive evidence) that, being entangled with the 'mystical' concept of retribution,[37] it was quite unnecessarily punitive. Far too often its enforcement did more harm—caused more avoidable human suffering—than it prevented, and to this the form of the substantive criminal law significantly contributed.

Judges were distrusted not just because they were frequently guilty of 'astonishing assumptions of legislative power'[38] but because they appeared 'convinced of the efficacy of punishment as medicine for all social divergences'[39] and adopted 'a crude retaliation theory, where the degree of punishment is linked rather to the amount of damage done than to the intention of the actor.'[40] So he always opposed the extension of the criminal law, either analogically or legislatively, to omissions to prevent harm.[41] The courts and the prisons were already overburdened with those who cause it; the need for them to deal also with those who failed to prevent it had never been demonstrated. And juries, those fig-leaves for which judges reach when embarrassed by the nakedness of their own reasoning, were not to be trusted to determine the limits of criminal liability since 'to entrust the defendant's liberty to a jury on these terms is not democracy; it is certainly not aristocracy; it is the despotism of small,

---

[35] e.g., pp. 28, 54, 65–6, 77, 108, 230, 242.

[36] p. 463.

[37] p. 458.

[38] p. 125; 'Statute Interpretation, Prostitution and the Rule of Law', in C. F. H. Tapper (ed.), *Crime, Proof and Punishment* (1981), p. 71.

[39] p. 90.

[40] p. 109.

[41] e.g. pp. 3–7, 477, 'What Should the Code do about Omissions?', *Legal Studies*, 7 (1987), 92; 'Letting Offences Happen', *Criminal Law Review* (1990), 780; 'Criminal Omissions—the Conventional View', *Law Quarterly Review*, 107 (1991), 86.

nameless, untrained, ephemeral groups, responsible to no one and not even giving reasons for their opinion'.[42]

The aim, therefore, was law that was as clear and certain as the best lawyers could make it, with the minimum of offences and these narrowly, rather than broadly, defined. And among *The General Part*'s many strengths, and an important factor in its persuasiveness, is its repeated demonstration, as the author confronts one question after another, that adherence to a few simple principles and to a consistent terminology reflecting them, would do a great deal to reduce the criminal law's unfairness, harshness, uncertainty, and irrationality.

The principles he found (and recommended) are these. The description of the prohibited occurrence must be seen as including all the legal rules relating to the offence save those concerning the defendant's fault.[43] For all offences that merit the name of crimes, including those where Parliament had been silent on the point, proof that the defendant intended or knew that he was or, at the very least might be, bringing about that occurrence so described should be required.[44] That an ordinary—a reasonable—person in the defendant's position would have realised that he was or might well be doing so supports an inference, but no more than an inference, that the defendant himself realised that. Such inferences are rebuttable by the defendant.[45] For those offences where there are good reasons for departing from the last two principles there should be liability only where the defendant was proved to be negligent.[46] Further, it is rarely, if ever, practicable for the criminal law to distinguish between the defendant who intended the occurrence that was prohibited and the defendant who knew that it was virtually certain that he would bring it about.[47] It is, on the other hand, often desirable to distinguish between such a defendant and one whose fault lies in knowingly taking an unreasonable risk of doing so, this (advertent recklessness) being a form of negligence.[48] The prosecution must prove both the occurrence and the

---

[42] 'Conspiring to Corrupt', in R. E. Megarry (ed.), *Law in Action* (1965), pp. 71, 76; 'Law and Fact', *Criminal Law Review* (1976), 472, 532; 'The Standard of Honesty', *New Law Journal* (1983), 636.

[43] pp. 15–16, 19.

[44] pp. 21, 59, 138.

[45] pp. 49–51, 77–81.

[46] pp. 29, 87–8; *The Mental Element in Crime* (Jerusalem, 1965) (hereafter *M.E.C.*), p. 59.

[47] pp. 35–9; *Sanctity of Life*, p. 286; *M.E.C.*, pp. 15, 24 and 'Oblique Intention', *Cambridge Law Journal* (1987), 417.

[48] pp. 59–62, *M.E.C.*, pp. 27, 29, 32 and 'Intention and Recklessness Again', *Legal Studies*, 2 (1982), 189.

required degree of fault beyond reasonable doubt.[49] The only significance to be attached, therefore, to the description of a matter as one of defence is that a defendant who invokes it may fail if he does not introduce some credible supporting evidence.[50]

It was not suggested that the courts always adhered to these principles—many a statement is carefully qualified by the phrase 'on the view advanced in this book' or by the word 'generally'—nor that adherence to them would produce fully nuanced moral judgements. All that was contended for was that these were the fairest and most practicable principles for law courts—human tribunals—to follow when what was at stake was liability to state-inflicted punishment. So judges should not pick and choose between the various elements of the prohibited occurrence because, once they started doing that, there was no point at which the slide to liability without fault could be halted.[51] It was, likewise, essential that advertent recklessness should be recognised as a distinct form of fault, for then there would be little reason for law enforcers to strive after any stricter liability.[52] Each principle had its place and its purpose in this carefully constructed scheme.

Much, if not all, of the scheme now sounds boringly orthodox. And as is the fate of all orthodoxies, its principles are now being attacked by retributivist critics who, as they hanker after those that satisfied eighteenth- and early nineteenth-century lawyers, sometimes appear to forget that what the argument is all about is not only blame but liability to state-inflicted punishment, and the amount of it that should be ladled out. Deterrence and prevention being, in Glanville's view, the only moral justifications for punishing its citizens that were open to a state, the principles (and rules) of criminal liability should reflect that. This might mean an extension of the criminal law (for instance, to catch intending criminals at an earlier stage,[53] and even those who had made a big mistake,[54] or those who dealt in the proceeds of any sort of crime, and not just in stolen goods[55]). Or it might mean the widening of a defence (in favour, for

[49] pp. 77–81, 355, 691–719.
[50] pp. 173–4, 719; 'Offences and Defences', *Legal Studies*, 2 (1982), 189, and 'The Logic of "Exceptions"', *Cambridge Law Journal* (1988), 261.
[51] p. 159.
[52] Chap. 7, passim.
[53] p. 486; 'A Fresh Start with the Law of Attempt', *Cambridge Law Journal* (1980), 225; 'The government's Proposals on Criminal Attempts', *New Law Journal*, 80 (1981), 104, 128.
[54] pp. 487–503; 'Criminal Attempts—A Reply', *Criminal Law Review* (1962), 300, 'Attempting the Impossible—A Reply', *Criminal Law Quarterly*, 22 (1980), 49.
[55] p. 183.

example, of those who unwittingly furthered the enforcement of the criminal law[56]). But either way he was ready to argue for the changes that consistency with his view of the moral justifications for criminal liability and punishment seemed to him to require.

In 1953 the principles of liability for which he was contending were by no means orthodox, as *The General Part* itself, and a decade later, *The Mental Element in Crime* (1965) recognised. Other doctrines had not only historical but contemporary support: the latter coming from such powerful judicial figures as Lords Reid, Denning and, most pervasively, Diplock. They rejected a unitary view of the criminal occurrence, did not distinguish between intending and knowingly taking the risk of harm, saw no objection to convicting of serious crimes defendants who were not shown to have been anything worse than negligent, and allowed, where a statute said nothing about fault, no more than that a blameless defendant might go free if he proved that he had not been negligent.[57]

This debate about what Glanville justifiably described as 'the kindergarten part of the criminal law'[58] is not yet at an end. There are even those who question the validity and desirability of the very attempt to generalise.[59] The weakest points in his scheme were the failure to deal sufficiently with (though he touched upon), first, the problem presented when elements of a prohibited occurrence are described adverbially or adjectivally and, second, with applying uniform principles to statutes regulating so many different human activities—from being helpful to the King's enemies to misleading the public about one's medical qualifications—many of these statutes having been drafted without any regard to, or in ignorance of, those principles. And he was perhaps, just a little too ready to extract a 'common law principle' out of a decision interpreting and applying a particular statute.

Remarkably few of the issues of principle that have since come before appellate courts are not touched upon in *The General Part*, and very much more often than not these courts have sooner or later gone the way to which it pointed—albeit more quickly and readily in Canada, Australia, and New Zealand than in England, though even here there are some indications of a new and more liberal judicial generation, working in and

---

[56] p. 25.
[57] Lord Denning: *Responsibility Before The Law* (Jerusalem, 1961), passim; Lord Diplock: *Gould* [1968] 2 QB 65; *Sweet v. Parsley* [1970] AC 132, 163; *Hyam* [1975] AC 66; *Caldwell* [1982] AC 341.
[58] *M.E.C.*, preface.
[59] e.g., N. Lacey, 'Contingency, Coherence and Conceptualism', in A. Duff (ed.), *Philosophy and The Criminal Law: Principle and Critique* (Cambridge, 1998), pp. 9, 29–36.

stimulated by the bracing climate of the Human Rights Act 1998, being increasingly receptive of the principles for which the book contended.[60]

For the next forty years Glanville was to defend, reaffirm and exemplify the themes of *The General Part* in an unceasing stream of articles, as well as in its enlarged (by more than 200 pages) second edition and in the thousand page *Textbook of Criminal Law* (1st edition 1978; 2nd edition 1983), designed, in the first place, for undergraduate readers. Those themes were combined there with a highly critical survey of the law governing individual offences of personal violence and fraud. Such, however, was his continuing and overriding preoccupation with the fault needed for criminal liability that, somewhat oddly, he discussed it at length before considering the different sorts of occurrence for which that liability might be imposed. And reviewers pointed out (as they had forty years earlier[61]) that 'the line between description and prescription is not always as clear as one might expect from an author who takes Williams' evidently positivist line'.[62] But this is, of course, one of the reasons why his writings have proved to be so enormously influential.

The articles were frequently hard-hitting and a degree of irritation crept into some of the later ones. Most spectacular of all was the attack[63] on the House of Lords' decision[64] that someone who thought, mistakenly, that he was doing something which, if he had in fact been doing it, would have been a crime, did not commit an offence (of 'attempt'). It led the bruised Law Lords, as they sorrowfully acknowledged, to change their minds within a year and hold that such a criminally intentioned, but mistaken, person should indeed be convicted.[65] This was all the more remarkable since the issue is a difficult one, for though such a person is wickedly intentioned, nothing that is legally proscribed will have been either done or risked. Much, therefore, can be, and has been, written on both sides of the question, and courts around the world have reached different conclusions.[66] What carried the day was

---

[60] Notably in a remarkable trio of House of Lords' decisions: *R v. D.P.P.* [2000] 1 All ER 561; *K* [2001] 3 All ER 897; *Lambert* [2001] 3 All ER 577.

[61] Text at n. 12 above.

[62] N. Lacey, 'The Territory of the Criminal Law', *Oxford Journal of Legal Studies*, 5 (1985), 453, 454.

[63] 'The Lords and Impossible Attempts or *Quis Custodiet Ipsos Custodes?*', *Cambridge Law Journal* (1986), 33.

[64] *Anderton v. Ryan* [1985] AC 567.

[65] *Shivpuri* [1987] AC 1.

[66] The legislative history had been lengthy and contentious. The Law Commission had been in favour of liability, the Home Office's lawyers against it. Glanville's evidence to the House of

Glanville's exhaustive demonstration that distinguishing between a defendant who was trying to do what was factually impossible of achievement (whom nearly everyone agreed ought to be convicted) and one who was mistaken in other ways was forensically impracticable. This was but the latest occasion on which his critical analysis had deprived a decision of the House of Lords of all real authority.[67] Indeed, the abandonment of the quaint convention forbidding explicit reliance in argument or judgment on the writings of the living to which English courts were still adhering in the 1960s was due in some considerable measure to him. His writings were at the head of those that were just too formidable to be left unacknowledged.

Almost as much attention was devoted to the law governing the powers of the police, to the procedure followed at criminal trials, and to the admissibility (and exclusion) of evidence at them, as to the substantive criminal law, but his work here was never built into a grand treatise. Instead there is a shorter book, 'profound and thought-provoking',[68] *The Proof of Guilt* (1st edition 1955, 3rd edition 1963) based on his Hamlyn Lectures, together with over two dozen articles. These writings show him as keen to have laws which would ensure the conviction of the guilty as the acquittal of the innocent. For if the substantive law took the lean, utilitarian shape he believed it should, it would be absurd not to remove all obstacles to its effective and accurate enforcement.[69] This coolly rational approach to highly emotive issues was to bring the liberal-minded scholar some strange allies, and even stranger opponents. For here, too, he was, in the comprehensiveness and comparative sweep of his scrutiny of the rules, procedures, and institutions of the English criminal justice system, a pioneer, providing a stimulus for other scholars,[70] whose work in its turn generated much public debate which still continues, and to which he was himself, until well into his eighties, a prominent contributor.

Commons' Special Standing Committee persuaded it in favour of the Law Commission's (and his own long-maintained) view, but the draftsman of the Criminal Attempts Act 1981, though then instructed to do so, had still failed to deal adequately with the point. See P. S. Atiyah, *Pragmatism and Theory in English Law* (1987), 180–183.

[67] Earlier instances are *Joyce v. DPP* [1946] AC 347 (see n. 23 above); *DPP v. Smith* [1961] AC 290 after a turn over article in *The Times*, 12 Oct. 1960 and *Modern Law Review*, 23, 605; and *Shaw v. DPP* [1962] AC 220 after *The Listener*, 66, 275, 280.

[68] J. R. Spencer, *Cambridge Law Journal* (1997), 456.

[69] See Spencer's persuasive interpretation, ibid. 456–63.

[70] Notably Professor W. R. Cornish, *The Jury* (1968) and Professor Michael Zander (who was an undergraduate pupil), who has written extensively on the provision of legal services and on trial procedures.

There were—and are—many areas of concern. Professor J. R. Spencer has picked out[71] half-a-dozen of the most salient to which Glanville drew attention. First among them was the need for the police to be given power to detain suspects for questioning. This happened, of course—people were always 'helping the police with their inquiries'—but the practice could only be regulated if it was first legalised. These interviews should, however, he said, always be tape-recorded. Eventually the police came to see that this would be a protection not only for suspects against being manipulated, but also for the police themselves against defence allegations that a confession had been fabricated or obtained by improper means. A quarter of a century later the detentions were authorised, and the tape-recording required, by the Police and Criminal Evidence Act 1984. The requirement has transformed the nature of criminal trials.

Also attacked were the rules that during a trial forbade reference to, and comment on, a defendant's failure to offer any exculpatory explanation of the conduct for which he was being tried either when he was first arrested and charged or at the trial itself. These rules, like others which excluded relevant and credible evidence and were subjected to similar criticisms, flew in the face of human experience, were a bizarre shackle on the prosecution, and could be a trap for the innocent. Here it took even longer to overcome long-standing professional shibboleths, as the Criminal Justice and Public Order Act 1994 to a large extent eventually did.

There was, too, the inherent unreliability of an eye-witness's identification of a suspect, and therefore the need, here and elsewhere, for an effective system of appeal against a jury's findings. Parliament had long since been ready to grant this,[72] but the judges had dragged their feet, for fear of undermining the jury system. For if appellate judges move from overruling the decisions of other judges to overturning jurors' verdicts, who would take those verdicts seriously—why, indeed, should jurors take themselves seriously? It remains to be seen whether the Criminal Cases Review Commission established by the Criminal Appeal Act 1995 will enable this dilemma to be resolved.

Being more alert than most lawyers to technological developments,[73] Glanville also saw that many of the problems that arose when it was necessary to rely on the evidence of children could be met by video-recording it at the first opportunity, when the child's recollection would

---

[71] See above, n. 68.

[72] Criminal Appeal Act 1907.

[73] *The Textbook of Criminal Law* (1978) is believed to be the first law book printed in the United Kingdom directly from the author's disks.

be fresher and the surroundings less harrowing and intimidating than a court room many months later. A long campaign, which Spencer was to join,[74] led to the establishment of a government committee,[75] and the enactment in the Criminal Justice Act 1997 of some, though not all, of their proposals.

Excoriated, too, were the frequent departures made by Parliament, aided and abetted by the judges, from the principle that proof beyond reasonable doubt by the prosecution of the case it adduced required disproof beyond reasonable doubt of defences raised by a defendant. This, however, was a case that made no progress at all (except with the Criminal Law Revision Committee in its Eleventh Report (1982)) until the Human Rights Act came along. The Law Lords were then to find, and to acknowledge that they had found, in Glanville's oft-repeated view[76] that a statute requiring a defendant to prove some exculpatory matter should be read as requiring only that he should adduce credible evidence of it (which the prosecution would then have to disprove), the way to square the intransigence of the Home Office and other government departments, which Parliament had so constantly endorsed, with the protection given to the presumption of innocence by the European Convention.[77] Lord Cooke thought, indeed, that 'one could hardly ask for more than the opinion of Professor Glanville Williams' that such a reading was possible.[78] The argument, as deployed in 'The Logic of "Exceptions"',[79] is, characteristically, as bold as it is elegant and simple. The courts read the word 'prove' in a statute, even when occurring within the same section, as meaning 'prove beyond reasonable doubt' when it is the prosecution which is doing the proving, and as 'prove on a balance of probabilities' when it is the defendant. 'Having swallowed this camel, why strain at the remaining gnat', when 'the fate of individual human beings' is at issue, of reading it, as the presumption of innocence demands, as meaning 'adduce sufficient evidence to raise a reasonable doubt'?[80] For, as he exhaustively

---

[74] 'Child Witnesses', in Peter Smith (ed.) *Essays in Honour of J. C. Smith* (1987), p. 188; 'Video-taping Children's Evidence', *New Law Journal*, 137 (1987), 108; 'The Corroboration Question', ibid. 131; 'More About Videotaping Children', ibid. 369. 'Child Witnesses and Video-technology: Thoughts for the Home Office', *Journal of Criminal Law*, 51 (1987), 444, though published under Spencer's name, was really, he says, a joint effort.

[75] *Report of the Advisory Group on Video Evidence* (Home Office, December 1989).

[76] See above, n 50.

[77] *Lambert* [2001] 3 All ER 577.

[78] *R v. DPP ex parte Kebilene* [2000] 2 AC 326.

[79] See above, n. 17.

[80] p. 265.

demonstrated, there was no logic at all in the distinction, so often relied on by the courts, between a rule and the exceptions to it. It was merely a matter of the draftsman's (linguistic) convenience. 'Looking for the line between a rule and an exception is . . . like looking in a dark room for a black cat that isn't there'.[81] There is, in this judicial turn-about, an element of irony. For, as a Benthamite who like the master considered human rights to be 'nonsense upon stilts', and ever distrustful of the judiciary, Glanville had always been opposed to investing it with the power to overrule or rewrite Parliament's enactments. The judges, it has to be said, continue to express a higher regard for him, than he did for them.

IV

It will be apparent that Glanville's legal scholarship was not scholarship done just for scholarship's sake. As Hepple has said, 'he was an accomplished master of the precedents, he could dazzle with his powers of rational analysis, he could be irritatingly logical, but ultimately it was the social justification in modern society for any legal rule which mattered most to him.'[82] His scholarly work was, therefore, seen and almost invariably undertaken as a necessary preliminary to the improvement and reform of especially unsatisfactory or underdeveloped areas of the law, and for this reason it was zealously pursued. And when, as President of the Society of Public (i.e., University) Teachers of Law (1974) he set about transforming it from an (ineffective) pressure group and social organisation into a learned society, law reform was the theme he proposed for every subject section at the annual meeting. While writing *The General Part* he both served (inevitably) on the [Goddard] Committee on the Law of Civil Liability for Damage Done by Animals (which reported in 1953) and edited *The Reform of the Law* (1951) for the Haldane Society. The book advocated a 'Ministry of Justice' to 'keep the law under review' (which became the Law Commission's terms of reference). By far the longest chapter was devoted to the criminal law, and much of the agenda, it is reassuring to find, has been accomplished. The need for reform is, as has been said, a constant refrain of *The General Part*, and there is scarcely a reform proposal that has not been endorsed by some official body, often at his own prompting, either from within or without.

---

[81] p. 278.
[82] See above, n. 3 (445).

He lobbied vigorously for the establishment of the Criminal Law Revision Committee,[83] and for twenty-three years (almost all its effective life) was its mainstay and the source of many of its ideas.[84] About half the working papers that the Committee considered came from him. They were often very lengthy and closely detailed, and this, at least at first, irritated its judicial and practitioner members, but increasingly he gained their respect and attention, and persuaded them that they should meet all day, and not just after the courts rose, if they were to do the Committee's business adequately. He did not, however, always get his own way, though he was usually right. The Theft Act 1968 would have been a much less unsatisfactory measure if his advice had been followed. In the years 1971–5 he was also serving on the [Butler] Committee on Mentally Abnormal Offenders and on the Law Commission's working party on the Codification of the Criminal Law, a cause to which he was passionately devoted, and in which he, like Stephen,[85] was to be most grievously disappointed. When in 1967 the Commission, encouraged by an exceptional Home Secretary (Roy Jenkins), first espoused it, Glanville proceeded to draft a large part of a code to show how he thought it ought to be done. The Commission quailed before it. For the draft was lengthy, detailed and highly systematised, reflecting his belief that if the draftsman could foresee an eventuality—and he, of course, could think of a great many— then a rule should be provided to govern it. Thirty-five years, and more than a score of reports, consultation documents and working papers later very little has, for want of a directing mind with comparable vision, been achieved. One example of his drafting did, however, reach a statute book: Ireland's Civil Liability Act of 1961 in substance enacts the 'Suggested Codifying and Amending Measure' in chapter 22 of *Joint Torts and Contributory Negligence*.[86]

It was, perhaps, his many letters to *The Times*[87] in support of one legal reform after another which, like his *Third Programme* broadcasts, best displayed his consummate ability to go directly to the point and expound it to non-lawyers with great succinctness and total clarity. They were matched by 'the closely typed and closely reasoned memoranda which,

---

[83] *The Times*, 10 June 1952; 'Reform of the Criminal Law and its Administration', *Journal of the Society of Public Teachers of Law*, 4 (1958), 217.

[84] Sir John Smith, 'The Sad Fate of the Theft Act 1968' in W. Swadling and G. Jones (eds.), *The Search for Principle: Essays in Honour of Lord Goff of Chieveley* (Oxford, 2000), pp. 97, 98.

[85] See above, n. 1.

[86] See above, n. 25.

[87] A selection are printed in *Cambridge Law Journal* (1991), 1.

deaf to every rebuff, he regularly sent to every Minister, civil servant or M.P. who he thought might listen to his views.'[88] But his persistence and patience in law reform causes were nowhere more fully displayed than in the unremitting support he gave to the campaigns for the modification of the criminal law of abortion, and the legalisation of voluntary euthanasia.

He drafted all four parliamentary Bills (1952, 1961, 1965, and 1966) that preceded the one successfully promoted by David Steel in 1967, and he was a member of the widely based committee which Steel formed to advise him. Glanville disapproved, however, of many of the compromises which Steel made to secure the support needed for its enactment— notably, the dropping of the clause which referred expressly to the mother's incapacity to care for her child, and the requirements for a second medical opinion and notification to the Department of Health.[89] It was natural enough that the author of *The Sanctity of Life and the Criminal Law* should in 1962 have been elected President of the Abortion Law Reform Association, and he thereafter worked closely with its chairman, Vera Houghton, and the parliamentary sponsors of the unsuccessful Bills. But 'his views were always far ahead of those of the [Association's] other members' and he seemed 'indifferent and indeed almost unaware of the outrage some' of them caused.[90] As he had made clear at the 1963 AGM he favoured a law which would, quite simply, permit a registered medical practitioner to perform an abortion during the first trimester, and at any time in order to preserve the mother's life. A third of a century later even the most fervent pro-life campaigner would probably consider this preferable to the irrational and vague provisions of Steel's (now amended) Abortion Act and the wide-spread humbug and deceit to which they give rise. Glanville's own satisfaction at the 1967 Act's success in driving abortionists from the back streets was mixed with sadness that the medical profession had betrayed the trust placed in it by Parliament.

He wrote and spoke equally tirelessly for the amelioration of the law governing voluntary euthanasia and mercy-killing. His position here was similarly uncomplicated, if over-simple. If it was not unlawful to kill oneself there was, he thought, no good reason for it to be a crime to help someone who wanted to die to do so, and absurd that if he happened no longer to be able to put an end to his own life it should be murder

[88] Spencer, see above, n. 68.
[89] Hindell, Keith and Simms, Madeleine, *Abortion Law Reformed* (1971), pp. 133–41, 158, 175–8.
[90] Ibid., p. 119.

actually to kill him. (His wife, Lorna (née Lawfield), whom he had first met through a common friend from Bridgend when she was an undergraduate at Newnham College, and who made with him a true, and immensely supportive marriage of like minds that lasted for more than fifty-seven years, wishing to spare him the unceasing correspondence and the desperate—and despairing—telephone calls she had good reason to expect would ensue, did, however, persuade him to decline an invitation to become President of the Voluntary Euthanasia Society, which as one of its Vice-Presidents he long supported.) A deep interest in medical developments and a willingness to meet doctors in debate on their own ground was supported by wide reading in the current literature. Week by week *The Lancet* and *The Justice of the Peace* were scrutinised with equal care.

V

For lawyers who knew him only in his published writings, their image of Glanville was, no doubt, that of the unrelenting controversialist wielding the scalpel and sometimes the sabre. He certainly found it difficult to resist the temptation to put right a judge, or a fellow academic incautiously venturing into print. Pupils, colleagues and friends encountered a very different person who may also be glimpsed in *Learning the Law*. Written in less than a month in 1944 to meet the needs of students, many of whom were soon to return to their books after the interruptions of war, it combines penetrating insights and astringent comments on legal institutions with astute awareness of what bemuses the student and what he needs to know first, and it offers a host of practical tips on how to set about the whole business, conveyed with a sense of enthusiasm and a slightly conspiratorial air—the author was most definitely on the students' side—in language of marvellous lucidity. '"Rather unconventional" [the author] calls it, and the epithet is justified', commented Lord Macmillan. 'Nothing quite like this has been attempted hitherto.'[91] It was no wonder that it was on every reading list and that its publishers paid their highest royalties ever on it.[92]

Much time and thought was given to how law could be best taught and law students examined, considerable inventiveness was displayed in devising new ways of doing so—the potential here, as in the police sta-

---

[91] *Law Quarterly Review*, 61 (1945), 305.
[92] 11th edn., 1982 (this edition reprinted eleven times); 12th edn. (by A. T. H. Smith), 2002.

tion and the court room, of tape and video recorders was quickly grasped and utilised—and the methods of American Law Schools admiringly observed during periods as a Visiting Professor at several of them. He met, it must be said, with rather limited success in persuading his Cambridge colleagues to experiment, and with even less from an inveterately conservative student body. But he was never discouraged and he had, when Chairman of the Faculty, one lasting success: the introduction into the formal structures of the Law Tripos of undergraduate dissertations, seminars and short, examined, lecture courses on new and developing areas of the law. The *Textbook of Criminal Law* published in the year he retired from his Cambridge chair (1978), which marked a further advance in the scholarly treatment of the criminal law nearly as great as that made by *The General Part*, is constantly interspersed with the questions and comments of a critical and/or incredulous student, with its text divided in the manner of *Les Guides Bleu* between large ('what you mustn't miss') and small ('worth seeing if you have a bit more time') print, which shows him as concerned as ever with the learning problems of the law student.

Few of the Cambridge undergraduates whose studies he for a decade (1956–1966) directed at his Cambridge college then realised quite how great a scholar he was.[93] What struck them was his modest manner, the absence of any trace of condescension, the clarity of his exposition, and the simplicity and purity of his Socratic way of teaching. Intellectual idleness (among either dons or students) was the only failing that he found difficult to forgive. The undergraduates later discovered the trouble he had taken to see that the less as well as the more able among them were placed in suitable solicitors' firms and barristers' chambers. In the Faculty at large he was, as he had been in London, alert to identify, encourage and support those wishing to embark on an academic career—as several present members of the Academy have testified. He did not hesitate to back his own judgements against those of boards of examiners. For his colleagues there was an old world courtesy, thoughtful kindly consideration,

---

[93] His initial connection with the college was as its external assessor in the search for a Law Fellow to succeed Professor (Sir) Robert Jennings on the latter's appointment to the Whewell Chair of International Law. None of the three short-listed candidates, all of whom subsequently enjoyed careers of great distinction, succeeded however, in commanding the majority necessary for election. Faced with this impasse, Glanville, who had continued to live in Cambridge, hesitantly inquired of Jennings whether he thought it would be improper of him to say that if an invitation were extended he would himself be delighted to become a Fellow of Jesus. The candidates whom he had interviewed were, naturally, more than a little surprised at this outcome.

the notably patient hearing of them out, and only then the gentle criticism of their ideas. Uncompromising as he was on many ethical issues—in particular on abortion, euthanasia, population growth and sexual behaviour—and in his pacifism (which was held against him in Cambridge where the Law Faculty's most influential figures had served in one or both World Wars and also strongly disliked the extreme utilitarian views expounded in *The Sanctity of Life and the Criminal Law*), there was no hint of self-righteousness. He constantly inquired about the safety of a colleague's son sent to the Gulf War.

A total dedication to the life of the mind—the dinner table was an occasion for exploring a new idea or testing the arguments in a new book, not for gossip or idle chatter—the moral seriousness with which he approached every task, and a capacity to work tirelessly and seemingly effortlessly from morn to night, and to abstract himself from his immediate surroundings—he would read while walking in the country and he composed on his portable typewriter while commuting on the train from Cambridge to London—help to explain how a prodigious scholarly output was combined with so much committee work and public activity, without his ever giving the appearance of being busy or pressed for time. And as he approached his eightieth birthday he published articles that were as fresh, forceful, and compelling as anything he had written in the previous fifty years.[94]

His tastes and recreations were simple ones: the countryside[95]—and especially (earlier) sailing on the Broads and (later) canoeing down rivers (camping or B&B rather than a hotel). Second-hand Jaguar cars were driven sedately. Gadgets of all sorts fascinated. New card and parlour games—some with legal themes—were invented. The classical English poets and novelists were read aloud in the evenings with his wife.

He could be persuaded, just, to accept honours that came after the name. In his fifties, the Middle Temple made him a Bencher, and he was given Silk. There was an Honorary Fellowship from his college, and honorary degrees from half-a-dozen universities—including the special

---

[94] e.g., '*Finis for Novus Actus?*', *Cambridge Law Journal* (1989), 391; 'The Mens Rea for Murder: Leave it alone', *Law Quarterly Review*, 104 (1989), 387 (preferred by the House of Lords Select Committee on Murder to one by Lord Goff) and 'Criminal Omissions—the Conventional View', ibid., 107 (1991), 86.

[95] The reader of the *Textbook* is warned that although picking wild flowers is not theft she may nonetheless commit an offence under the Conservation of Wild Creatures and Wild Plants Act 1975, s.4 (as amended) by 'plucking a posy consisting of such listed plants as ghost orchid, alpine cow-thistle and oblong woodsia' (2nd edn. (1983), p. 735).

tribute for one of its own teachers of a Litt.D. from Cambridge in 1995—
together with election as a Foreign Honorary member of the American
Academy of Arts and Sciences (1985). But the knighthood offered on the
recommendation of the Lord Chancellor and the Law Lords when he
retired from his Cambridge chair was declined. Although Glanville was
not, as his wife is, a member of the Society of Friends, he practised the
Quaker virtues, and respected their values and customs. Deeply modest, he
'thought it incongruous that a man who had refused to wield a bayonet
should theoretically bear a sword'.[96]

He died peacefully at home on 10 April 1997 at the age of 86.

P. R. GLAZEBROOK
Jesus College, Cambridge

Note. The writer is most grateful to Glanville Williams's widow, Lorna Williams, and
their son, Dr Rendel Williams of the University of Sussex, and also to Sir Roger
Toulson, and Professors Kurt Lipstein, S. F. C. Milsom, and Sir John Smith for information and advice, as well as to Professors B. A. Hepple and J. R. Spencer with whom
he joined in the tributes printed in *Cambridge Law Journal* (1997), 427–65. There have
been heavily drawn on for this Memoir, as has the obituary he wrote for *The Society of
Public Teachers of Law's Reporter* (Autumn 1997), 23–5. There is a (nearly) complete
and indexed list of the published writings to 1977 in P. R. Glazebrook (ed.),
Reshaping the Criminal Law: Essays in Honour of Glanville Williams (1978), pp.
449–68. A supplement to 1997 is available from the writer.

[96] Spencer, *Cambridge Law Journal* (1997), 439.

VINCENT WRIGHT

Vincent Wright
1937–1999

> I am happy to live with my intellectual schizophrenia—to preach the need for comparative method, to practice timid comparison, to close my door on occasion in Nuffield and write history, and to profit from the networks of colleagues and friends created and consolidated by both politics and history.[1]

HERE WAS VINCENT WRIGHT almost perfectly summed up by himself: cheerful over and above everything (we all remember his laughter, his infectious sense of humour, and his indomitable optimism); acutely self-aware, and sober in his assessment of the intellectual demons which assailed him; modest, and without a trace of pompousness; gregariously sociable, and enjoying life to the full, while at the same time making the most of the opportunities which it afforded him. There was also a whiff of the religious—hence the reference to preaching. He had stopped believing a long time ago, and described himself as rabidly anticlerical; but he also readily confessed that his moral and philosophical outlook was forever steeped in a Catholic culture.

Born in 1937, in Whitehaven, in the then county of Cumberland, Vincent Wright's interest in the European Continent stemmed in part from his miner father Walter Wright's strong support for the Popular Front in France and of the Republicans in the Spanish Civil War. He also inherited from his father a favourable view of the 1945 Labour Government and a prejudice against the Tories. It was his mother, Mary Wright, who imparted a fervent Catholicism that was initially nurtured by

---

[1] 'The path to hesitant comparison', p. 176, in H. Daalder (ed.), *Comparative European Politics. The Story of a Profession* (1997).

Proceedings of the British Academy, **115**, 439–463. © The British Academy 2002.

a Catholic primary school. He did not have a high opinion of the traditional Whitehaven Grammar School, which he considered was too devoted to preparing its pupils for examination success by instruction rather than education. He thought that Clemenceau's comment on the *Polytechniciens*—'they know everything there is to know—but nothing more'—fitted his own school experience all too well. He refused to join the Whitehaven Old Grammarians and had no regrets when the school was transformed into a comprehensive school.

Before going to the LSE to study Government for the B.Sc. (Econ.), he did his National Service in the Royal Navy, spending most of his time on the aircraft carrier HMS *Bulwark*. As well as affording him plenty of spare time to read the many history books in the ship's library, his experience in the navy taught him how important institutions are in attracting loyalty, as well as the vulnerability of authority, lessons that were to stand him in good stead in his subsequent research and publications. At the LSE his natural inclination to scepticism was reinforced by the dominant influence in the Government Department of Michael Oakeshott. He acquired a good grounding in history there but no inculcation of the capacity to undertake comparative studies, which was to come later.

His doctoral research for the LSE started at the Paris *Institut d'Etudes Politiques*, where he came under the influence of René Rémond, whose approach to politics had a predominantly historical bent. He was persuaded to abandon his initial inclination to work on the history of ideas in favour of a detailed study of the electoral history and geography of Basses-Pyrénées. He spent two blissful years in the local archives in Pau, in the process acquiring a profound and enduring love of provincial France, as well as the ability to overcome the intimidating obstacles placed in the way of the seeker after knowledge by French officialdom. From that initiation, he acquired an incomparable grasp of the interaction between central and local politics and administration, as well as the complex relations between state prefects and local notables that was to permeate so much of his subsequent work.

Throughout his career Wright was pulled in conflicting directions by the contrasting concerns and methodological demands of history and politics. Politics was about generalisation, comparison, and theoretical parsimony, while historical enquiry was the domain of particularism, scepticism, and complexity. And yet he found fruitful ways of building bridges between the two spheres—notably by inviting each discipline to draw sustenance from the strengths of the other, and by fiercely resisting attempts to confine each of these academic endeavours within artificially closed boundaries. He was one of the least sectarian and most open-minded scholars one could ever hope to meet—immensely knowledgeable but insatiably curious; supremely gifted and at the same time immensely generous; very English but also a genuine cosmopolitan. All forms of parochialism were anathema to him, and he was, in this sense, a real *intellectuel républicain*.

These qualities very much shaped the way in which his historical work unfolded. After completing his doctorate on the politics of the Basses-Pyrénées in the nineteenth century, Wright began his academic career first at the University of Newcastle and then at the London School of Economics as an historian of French public administration. His two key works, *Le Conseil d'Etat sous le Second Empire* (1972) and *Les Préfets du Second Empire* (1973, with Bernard le Clèrc) established his reputation as one of the leading figures in the field. After moving to Oxford to an Official Fellowship at Nuffield College in 1977, Wright increasingly devoted himself to comparative politics. But he nonetheless continued to carry out and publish research on various aspects of French political and administrative history throughout the 1980s and 1990s. He made time for this research—most notably on the Freemasonry and on the prefects of the 1870–1 republican Government of National Defence—through his extraordinary capacity for work, and his tireless ability to sift through large quantities of archival sources. Even the briefest of visits to Paris would rarely be allowed to pass by without spending a few hours at the Bibliothèque Nationale, the Archives Nationales, or the military archives at Vincennes; and his ability to charm (or if necessary bully) his way past suspicious and wary departmental archivists was remarkable.

Wright was proud of his archival Stakhanovism. Many a friend, colleague, or student will no doubt remember arriving at a French public archive shortly after opening hours to find him already seated at his desk, with an expression of mock disapproval on his face and a dramatically over-elaborate glance at his watch.

Wright's synthesis between politics and history found its substantive expression in his constant preoccupation with political and administrative power in modern France—where it was exercised, through which institutions, and by which individuals and groups; in his later years he became especially concerned in the fate of these institutions and elites in the critical circumstances of war. In the final months of his life he worked with Karma Nabulsi on two articles exploring the tensions and rivalries among different branches of the French state during the Franco-Prussian war of 1870–1. Throughout his life Wright remained a self-defined

Jacobin; he defended the principle of the general interest, was instinct-ively suspicious of 'groups' (whether functionally or territorially based), and believed in the fundamental importance of state institutions in upholding legal, administrative, territorial, and cultural unity.[2] This cul-tural Jacobinism, which he upheld in vigorous discussions with all his colleagues in France and in the Anglo-American world, largely defined the focus of Wright's historical research.[3]

France's administration remained close to Wright's heart throughout his career. His early major works focused on two *Grands Corps*, the Prefectorate and the Conseil d'Etat (with whose members he retained very close personal ties). He frequently attended meetings and confer-ences at both institutions. At the same time his substantive interests were much broader. Among his distinctive historical contributions were stud-ies on the abortive Ecole Nationale d'Administration of the Second Republic;[4] the prefects of police of the Second Empire;[5] Gambetta's *cab-inet* at Tours during the Franco-Prussian war;[6] the role of secretaries-general and directors of central administrations;[7] and the bureaux of the Ministry of War.[8] Both the central and local branches of the Ministries of the Interior, Justice, Finance, Public Instruction, and War also fea-tured prominently in his writings, partly in their own right, and partly because he did not believe that the history of individual administrations could be written in isolation.

In substantive terms, the themes which dominated Wright's approach to administrative history were 'fragmentation' and 'institutional con-straint'. The nineteenth-century French state, according to him, was conceptually based on a Jacobin–Napoleonic blueprint which was 'statist, powerful, centralized, hierarchically-structured, ubiquitous, uniform,

---

[2] For a flavour of Wright's sense of Jacobinism, see his article 'Question du'un Jacobin anglais aux régionalistes français', *Pouvoirs*, 19 (1981), pp. 119–30.

[3] The theme of Wright's Jacobinism will be explored in a forthcoming collection of historical tributes to his work, to be published by Oxford University Press: *The Jacobin Legacy in Modern France* (edited by Sudhir Hazareesingh).

[4] 'L'Ecole Nationale d'Administration de 1848–1849: un échec révélateur', *Revue Historique*, CCLV/1 (1976).

[5] 'Les préfets de police 1851–1880: problèmes et personnalités', in *Les préfets en France 1800–1940* (Geneva, 1978).

[6] 'L'administration du Ministère de l'Intérieur en temps de crise: le cabinet de Gambetta à Tours en 1870', *Administration*, LII (Autumn 1976).

[7] 'Les secrétaries généraux et les directeurs des administrations centrales: pouvoirs et pouvoir', in *Les directeurs de Ministère en France* (Geneva, 1976).

[8] 'Les bureaux du ministère de la Guerre', *Revue Historique des Armées*, III (1993).

depoliticized, instrumental, expert and tightly controlled'.[9] However, despite the general adherence of most nineteenth-century French regimes to its broad outlines, this Jacobin model never matched what he was fond of calling the 'untidy reality'. France was in this sense a perfect object of study for his quest to overcome the dualism between the historian's desire to particularise and the political scientist's search for parsimonious explanatory models. Wright saw that in France, statism was repeatedly challenged and subverted from within as the various administrations' functional powers seeped away; centralisation was often mythical; hierarchies crumbled in the face of bureaucratic rivalries; the rhetoric of omnipresence masked insufficiencies in staffing at the local levels; 'depoliticized' agents of the state often assumed blatantly political functions; and 'expertise' was sometimes a cover for incompetence, or worse still an excuse for partiality and partisanship. The narrative of the nineteenth-century French state was thus neither epic nor linear; its development was marked rather by discontinuities and constraints. This, for example, is how Wright typically ended his contribution on the prefects of police under the Second Empire: 'ici comme ailleurs dans le domaine de l'administration, les généralisations sont dangereuses et les hypothèses normalement trompeuses'.[10]

Bureaucratic power was also frittered away as a result of vertical conflicts and functional inconsistencies within the same institution. Second Empire prefects were asked by their political masters to maintain a strictly depoliticised local order, but also to intervene in all elections to secure the victory of 'official' candidates—thus making themselves the principal agents of politicisation. But the real difficulty was that the French state lacked a fundamental sense of unity, and its different bodies tended to see themselves as rivals (and indeed adversaries) rather than partners. Often the product of conflicting and long-standing institutional 'myths', such rivalries sometimes had a sound basis in reality. The Ecole Nationale d'Administration of 1848 succumbed to a large part because of the undisguised hostility of the University and the traditional administrative elites.[11] Under the Second Empire, the Conseil d'Etat's role as the final court of appeal against administrative dysfunctions could often lead

---

[9] Vincent Wright, 'The administrative machine: old problems and new dilemmas', in Peter Hall, Jack Hayward, and Howard Machin (eds.), *Developments in French Politics* (1990), p. 116.
[10] Vincent Wright, 'Les préfets de police pendant le Second Empire: personnalités et problèmes', in Jacques Aubert *et al.*, *L'Etat et sa police en France (1789–1914)* (Geneva: Droz, 1979), p. 102.
[11] Vincent Wright, 'L'Ecole Nationale d'Administration de 1848–49: un échec révélateur, *Revue Historique*, CCLV/1 (1976).

to the quashing of prefectoral decisions and even the annulment of municipal elections—rulings which exasperated and frequently infuriated the Ministry of the Interior.[12] In times of crisis, when resources were scarce and pressures on the administration intensified, these centrifugal tendencies were exacerbated even further. During the Franco-Prussian war of 1870–1, there were systematic clashes between military authorities and their civilian counterparts (prefects and municipal agents). Under the Vichy regime, the prefects saw their authority undermined by the growing reluctance of most parallel local state agencies to co-operate with them.[13]

Through Wright's portrayal of the French administration, we see that paradoxically (a word he loved using) the state was not as powerful as its critics believed, or even as its Jacobin apologists hoped; its political masters were generally able to maintain overall control over the institution. However this instrumental control (and the fragmentation which accompanied it) had its limits. 'Heroic' attempts to transform state institutions often ended in failure or at the very least in diluted outcomes; and state elites showed considerable capacities of adaptability, flexibility, and even opportunism. There were thus strong elements of institutional continuity—especially at the 'cultural' level—alongside the rifts and schisms which marked the development of the French state. Finally Wright did little to conceal his general sympathy, respect, and even admiration for the state elites he evoked. He often stated that the overall quality of the French administration was much higher in the nineteenth century than that of the British bureaucracy. He recognised that the French state often enacted condemnable policies, and Wright never wavered in his censoriousness when it came to denouncing administrative evil as a general concept— whether the arbitrary brutality of the *Commissions Mixtes* of 1852, the infamous *loi de sureté générale* of 1858, the 'bigotry, narrow mindedness and intolerance'[14] of the early Third Republic, or the deportations organised by Vichy agents. But there was for him always a silver lining—repressive French regimes contained 'liberal' institutions; repressive intentions (and actions) were counteracted by political considerations, social imperatives, and conjunctural factors; local despots such as the Bonapartist prefect Janvier de la Motte were involved in quaint sexual rituals;[15] and if all

---

[12] *Préfets du Second Empire*, pp. 128–30.
[13] Sonia Mazey and Vincent Wright, 'Les Préfets', in Jean-Pierre Azéma and François Bédarida (eds.), *Vichy et les Français* (Paris, Fayard, 1992).
[14] Vincent Wright, 'The coup d'état of December 1851: repression and the limits to repression', in Roger Price (ed.), *Revolution and Reaction: 1848 and the Second French Republic* (1975), p. 328.
[15] *Préfets du Second Empire*, p. 260.

else failed he would point out that repressive institutions contained sensitive souls—like the Bonapartist prefect of police Boitelle, a 'discreet and tolerant' man who tried to forget his dastardly deeds by painting his own water colours and smoking exquisite cigars.[16]

Wright's French historical writings also consistently dwelled on the local sphere—a world which he discovered with his doctoral research on the Basses-Pyrénées in the early 1960s, and which instilled in him a love of provincial France which remained with him throughout his life.[17] All the visitors to his country house in the Lot will remember the hospitality which he and his partner Basil Smith lavished upon his guests, and his indomitable attachment to the Quercy *terroir* (and particularly its wonderful culinary delights). Wright's French provincial world was deeply and indeed almost inescapably politicised, but often in ways which did not immediately meet the eye. And for him the real craft of the historian lay in unearthing conflicts which lurked below the tranquil surface of provincial life: family feuds which were in fact expressions of long-standing ideological differences; conflicts about burial rights which were in reality battles between secular and religious systems of values; and administrative measures—such as the closure of an inn—which were underhand attempts to clamp down on a republican *aubergiste*.

But politics in this localised sense was not just a story of a Jacobin state imposing its will on hapless communities: the moral of the tale was indeed often the reverse. Focusing on the local arena was for Wright an important means of bringing out the limits of state power. The pages of the *Préfets du Second Empire* provide countless examples of how the idiosyncracies of a particular locality could fatally undermine the authority of a prefect vested with the most awesome formal powers. 'Thicker' subcultural variables could prove equally frustrating for the potentates of the state: a Bonapartist prefect could do little in a territory dominated by the republican party, and even the most anti-clerical republican prefect had to tread warily if he happened to find himself *en terre Catholique*. Power thins out in space: Wright found that this physical law also applied just as clearly to the political realm.

Wright's emphasis on the sub-national level was also driven by the belief that France's 'collective' experience of politics could not be deduced merely by examining what was occurring at its Parisian epicentre.

---

[16] *L'Etat et sa police* (op. cit.), p. 92.
[17] The Basses-Pyrénées from 1848 to 1870, a study in departmental politics. (unpublished Ph.D., University of London, 1965).

Although culturally a Jacobin, Wright rejected the Jacobin view of nineteenth-century French history, which depicted the construction of a modern nation-state in terms of the imposition of 'central' social and political values on a passive and backward 'periphery'. For Wright such accounts represented a huge oversimplification (as well as an unacceptable reliance on teleology). The republicans won because their local organisations—especially at municipal level—had already begun to establish the political and ideological basis for republican hegemony in the cities and many of the provincial towns of France during the 1860s. Looking at politics 'from the bottom up' was not a self-indulgent exercise in political archaeology, but an indispensable instrument for making sense of the complex interactions between the national and local spheres.[18]

The study of elites constituted the third, more sociological, aspect of Wright's study of power, alongside and in conjunction with its territorial and institutional aspects. As an historian he showed relatively little interest in the peasantry—a lack of concern which perhaps stemmed from his early immersion in the Basses-Pyrénées, where he found villagers to be relatively 'indifferent' to politics.[19] What fascinated him as a political sociologist was the dialectic between the rulers and the ruled—how each group influenced the other and learned to live with each other. But although he was concerned mostly with elites, he was not exclusively attached to the strong and powerful. He wrote sensitively about the humble victims (mostly from the republican rank-and-file) of the 1851 coup d'état—about the cruelty and suffering endured by those who resisted, the callous lack of social solidarity at local level, the devastatingly brutal impact on their families, and the irreversibly broken lives.[20]

One of Wright's major contributions as an administrative historian was his sociological treatment of bureaucratic elites, which was anchored in a deep-seated belief that the functional powers of the French state (and the limitations upon these powers) could not be explained by formalistic and juridical principles alone. Political and administrative power also stemmed from existing social hierarchies. As his analysis of both the Prefectorate and the Conseil d'Etat showed, a significant proportion of

---

[18] This theme is developed in Sudhir Hazareesingh and Vincent Wright, 'Le Second Empire: enjeu politique de la commune et la commune comme enjeu politique', in F. Monnier and J-P. Machelon (eds.), *Histoire des communes de France* (Paris: Editions du Seuil, 2001).
[19] Vincent Wright, 'Députés et conseillers-généraux des Basses-Pyrénées de 1848 à 1870', *Bulletin de la Société des Sciences Lettres et Arts de Pau*, 5 (1970), p. 155.
[20] Guy Thuillier and Vincent Wright, 'Les dossiers des pensionnés du 2 Décembre 1851', *Le Mouvement Social*, 94 (Jan.–March 1976).

recruits from both corps under the Second Empire came from the aristocracy and the *haute bourgeoisie*; conversely only a very small section of the administrative elite came from humble backgrounds. The first general conclusion was thus that there was little evidence of mobility; there were indeed natural sociological limits to the application of the Bonapartist myth of the French state. In Wright's terse formula: 'la conception de l'administration française comme une "carrière ouverte à tous les talents" restait un idéal prêché par beaucoup, chéri par certains, mais mis en pratique seulement par un très petit nombre'.[21] Another important factor limiting the broadening of the social base of the administration was the economic cost of certain offices. For all the *préfets de première classe*, for example, the possession of large personal fortunes was not only desirable but necessary, because of the exorbitant costs of holding office.[22] Closure of another kind was achieved through the maintenance of family networks within and across the higher institutions of the French state. In the Conseil d'Etat there were veritable dynasties, and members of the Council enjoyed close links with families in the Army, the diplomatic corps, the magistracy, and the prefectoral corps.[23] Family networks typically 'reached out into all branches of public life',[24] and thus created an invisible but highly effective method of ensuring continuity of access to high offices for the well-heeled.

Wright's French state was thus *corporatiste* in some senses of the term: institutions possessed distinct and non overlapping identities, which they fought to maintain (generally successfully); social elites enjoyed privileged access, and in the cases of some families the higher civil service was regarded as a *chasse gardée*. But there were significant factors which also cut across these corporatisms—most notably the purges, which allowed regimes with distinct social bases (such as the republicans in the 1870s and 1880s) to distribute the spoils of office to their clientèle.[25] Wright also found little evidence in the early days of the Third Republic to support the proposition that the French state was covertly penetrated by minority groups and secret corporations. There was thus no 'république protestante'

---

[21] Howard Machin and Vincent Wright, 'Les élèves de l'E.N.A. de 1848–1849', *Revue d'Histoire Moderne et Contemporaine*, XXXVI (1989), p. 637.

[22] 'Les préfets Emile Ollivier', *Revue Historique*, CCCCLXXXVI (July–Sept. 1968), p. 124.

[23] *Conseil d'Etat*, p. 61.

[24] 'The reorganization of the Conseil d'État', *International Review of Social History*, XIV (1969), p. 188.

[25] 'Les épurations administratives de 1848 à 1885', in Paul Gerbod *et al.* (eds.), *Les épurations administratives XIXe et XXe siècles* (Geneva: Droz, 1977).

in the substantive sense of the term. There were of course protestants who occupied positions of power in the new administrative (and indeed political) order after 1870, but they were internally divided, and whatever little group affinities they possessed were countermanded by political, administrative, and psychological imperatives.[26] Despite the views to the contrary of leading historians of the subject, Wright similarly believed that in broad terms the same phenomenon applied to the French Jews, who could not really be identified as a self-conscious collectivity in the republican bureaucratic elite.[27] He also came to the same 'anti-corporatist' conclusion with regard to Freemasonry, often regarded as the principal occult influence on French republicanism in the 1860s and 1870s. The Government of National Defence of 1870–1 was notoriously viewed as the product of a masonic conspiracy, because several of its leading members (notably Gambetta) were masons, as were many of its appointees to high administrative positions. A closer look, however, suggested that these conjunctions were largely fortuitous, and that there was little personal or ideological solidarity among the fragmented and fissiparous collectivity of Freemasons during these years.[28]

Wright's interpretation of power was strikingly Weberian, in the sense that what emerges from his reading of the French nineteenth century is the extraordinary fluidity of administrative and political rule. Power was not the same as authority, and indeed the formal instruments of governance (institutional rules and principles, laws, coercive instruments) were often not the real sites where power was exercised. Informal networks could be extremely powerful, both at national level (through the penetration of elite administrative institutions) and local level (through the holding of *pouvoir notabilier*).[29] This emphasis on informality also explained Wright's avoidance of the grand theoretical frameworks for explaining power. His reluctance in this respect was a product not only of his inherent scepticism of 'theory' (where the influence of his mentor Oakeshott was very powerful)[30] but also of his consistent commitment to his own brand of methodological individualism. Here again Wright could be seen

---

[26] Vincent Wright, 'Les protestants dans la haute administration 1870–1885', in *Actes du Colloque Les Protestants dans les débuts de la Troisième République* (Paris, 1979), p. 245.

[27] Vincent Wright, 'La réserve du corps préfectoral', in P. Birnbaum (ed.), *La France de l'Affaire Dreyfus* (Paris, 1993).

[28] Vincent Wright, 'Francs-maçons, Administration et République: les préfets du gouvernement de la Défense Nationale 1870–1871', *Revue Administrative*, CCXXXX–I (Nov.–Dec. 1987 and Jan.–Feb. 1988).

[29] 'Députés et conseillers-généraux des Basses-Pyrénées de 1848 à 1870' (op. cit.), pp. 160–1.

[30] 'The path to hesitant comparison' (op. cit.), pp. 164–5.

as a disciple of Weber; in his social and political explanations he constantly strove to make sense of social and political phenomena in terms of individual actors and their motivations.

Wright's commitment to the complementarity of historical and political enquiry appears forcefully in his scholarly work on the French Freemasonry, which yielded several articles and a posthumously-published book (jointly-authored with Sudhir Hazareesingh), *Francs-Maçons sous le Second Empire*.[31] The French Freemasonry of this period shared many characteristics with Wright's own persona: a fondness for international travel, and for attending conferences; a *penchant* for creating and consolidating networks; a natural tendency towards sociability; a love of *la bonne chère*; and—last but not least—a virulent anticlericalism.

This book also brings together all of Wright's intellectual passions as an historian: the social and political history of provincial France in the nineteenth century; the relationship between the state and local associations; the interface between political and social elites at the local level (and especially the roles played by the ever-present *notables*); and the territorial dissemination of the influence of the republican party. *Francs-Maçons sous le Second Empire* is based on an exhaustive trawl of administrative and Masonic archives in Paris and in the provinces. The interface with Masonic officialdom gave rise to some comical encounters, most notably when Wright succeeded in convincing the archivist of the Grande Loge Nationale in Paris that 'Nuffield' was the name of a British Masonic lodge. The book challenges the principal myths concerning the Masonry—namely that it was merely a united and disinterested philanthropic organisation (the 'internal' myth); that it was a perpetual conspiracy against all forms of established order (the Catholic myth, first propounded by Abbé Barruel in 1797); and finally that the Masonry of the 1860s and 1870s was merely a recruitment centre for the republican party (the republican historiographical myth).

The archival evidence reveals a far more complex picture. The provincial Masonry was unevenly represented across France, and the Lodges themselves took on a variety of forms in different localities—here purely philanthropic and apolitical, there proto-republican, but elsewhere strongly penetrated by liberal or Bonapartist *notables*. The Masonry was also deeply divided, and the provincial brothers often fought bitter battles

---

[31] Sudhir Hazareesingh and Vincent Wright, *Francs-Maçons sous le Second Empire: les loges provinciales du Grand-Orient à la veille de la Troisième République* (Collection Carnot) (Rennes: Presses Universitaires de Rennes, 2001).

with each other over personal, social, ideological, and religious issues. In overall terms *Francs-Maçons sous le Second Empire* underscores the sheer plasticity of the nineteenth-century French masonry—a useful quality which enabled the institution to survive through a period of great political and ideological turmoil in French national politics.

Both implicitly and explicitly, the book makes a powerful statement of the complementarity of historical and political-science research. The Freemasonry of the Second Empire and early Third Republic offers a privileged object of study for some of the core questions which Wright believed should interest political scientists: how institutions shape behaviour and mediate conflict, and how they may retain loyalty under conditions of stress. *Francs-Maçons sous le Second Empire* also returns repeatedly to one of Wright's favourite themes both as an administrative historian and political scientist: the limits of positivism. The formal rules governing membership of the Masonry were extremely rigid and centralised during this period, and the Parisian authorities of the Grand Orient de France made repeated attempts to bring their provincial brethren under hierarchical control. But the rules they codified often had limited application in the different corners of the French *hexagone*. Indeed the 'operational code' of the Masonry was an entirely unreliable guide to the manner in which power was really exercised within the institution. This again brings out the importance of the Weberian conclusions about power, namely that its formal and juridical character is often its least significant dimension, and that its reality often lies in its less tangible aspects. In the Masonry as elsewhere, the formal instruments of governance were often not the real means through which political and intellectual power was exercised. Informal networks—such as those based on family traditions, cultural affinities, or social authority—could be extremely powerful, bypassing and overriding the powers of established cadres.

Francs-Maçons sous le Second Empire ultimately provides an ideal testing ground for the limits of theoretical models in explaining social and political realities—another favourite theme in Wright's scholarly work both in history and in political science. The French Freemasonry during this period offers little comfort to the advocates of rational choice explanations of individual and collective strategies. Rather than an all-knowing rational maximising self-interest, the archival evidence finds masonic behaviour to be grounded in a complex admixture of reason, interest, emotion, tribalism, and affective memories. Wright's legendary scepticism about macro-theoretical explanations (and rational choice models in particular), which permeated his work in political science, was thus reinforced by the conclusions he reached in his historical explorations across nineteenth-century France.

Bertrand Russell described the happy man as he who is neither pitted against himself nor divided against the world. Such was Vincent Wright: although he was pulled in different directions he was always able to channel these intellectual conflicts and tensions into creatively successful outcomes. He thus left us with a vivid, humane, and highly individual account of nineteenth-century France. His knowledge of the French terrain was extraordinary, and it was a delight to accompany him on a trip to any part of the country, whether rural or urban. He was always eager to make new discoveries, to track down local monuments and archives, and get to the heart of whatever issues were confronting a locality. Like all good historians he genuinely empathised with the objects of his research; indeed he sometimes said that if he could have had a different life he would have loved to have been a (republican) Prefect. But with Wright one often felt that there was something more—that he could reach into their souls, and bring out into the open the wonderful complexities (and sometimes absurdities) of their existence.

One of the most attractive features of his personality was his free spirit, and his absolute refusal to be bound by social, institutional, or academic convention. 'I would rather clean windows than be Warden of Nuffield' he once remarked at a dinner he hosted in Paris, among whose guests was the then head of his college. There was also a serious aspect to his independence of temperament. What made Wright a superb historian was that he was doubly an outsider, constrained neither by disciplinary shackles within France (or for that matter anywhere else) nor by the tacit accommodations often necessitated by physical propinquity. He also wasted no time with all the fads which have seized the historical confraternity in recent decades, such as 'cultural' history ('the history of shitting' was the savage description he once gave of some aspects of this endeavour).

As a political scientist in Oxford, he was completely free to follow his historical inclinations, and in particular to give a free rein to his natural instincts towards intellectual heterodoxy. He revelled in the subversion of orthodoxy, at times indeed stretching this trait to the point of provocation. But his bold revisionism helped to revolutionise our understanding of the French state in the nineteenth century, and his studies of the Prefects and the Conseil d'Etat under the Second Empire will long retain their classic status among French historians. Wright thus belongs to that extremely small group of distinguished non-native historians—Richard Cobb, Theodore Zeldin, Robert Paxton are others who spring to mind—

who successfully established themselves in France during their lifetime as authoritative figures in their particular historical fields. There can perhaps be no more fitting tribute to his extraordinary talents than to remember that Wright achieved this feat while effectively holding down a job in an altogether different discipline, in which his achievements were equally remarkable.

The Comparative Categorisation of Untidy Reality

Resolutely shunning synthetic generalisations based upon spurious over-simplifications, Wright was not content simply to fall back upon the re-assuring singularities of historical description. While the subject matter was complex, explanation necessitated recourse to analytic conceptual categories. Although he retained a historically-sensitive allergy to models and a reluctance to let methodological concerns dictate the problems to be investigated, as a social scientist he accepted the challenge that model building and methodological rigour posed. So, while conceding that 'comparison and history are intrinsically ill-suited partners', he did not allow the historian's 'ingrained scepticism' and eye for detail to paralyse his concurrent work on comparative politics.[32] In fact, the two sides of his research were interdependent. His historical work protected him from the universalising fallacies which some political scientists have sought to import from economics—which Richard Rose calls 'landless theory'—while his comparative politics protected him from the historian's tendency to assume uniqueness.[33] Vincent Wright's systematic analyses combined the respect for national and sub-national diversity with the circumspect use of generic concepts capable of crossing national borders. He adopted what Richard Rose has dubbed a 'bounded variability' that avoided accumulating 'empirical data that will sink under its own weight'.[34]

Stylistically, Wright's splitter's predilection for stressing diversity means that his writings are replete with words such as complexity and cleavage, tension and dissension, variety and fluidity, diffuseness and

[32] Vincent Wright, 'The Path to Hesitant Comparison', in H. Daalder (ed.), p. 176. One may consider that Vincent Wright was too ready to concede the incapacity of political scientists to do creative work in comparative political history. The names of Sammy Finer, Stein Rokkan and Charles Tilly, among others, come to mind.

[33] Rose, R., 'Comparing Forms of Comparative Analysis', *Political Studies*, XXXIX/3 (1991), p. 452.

[34] Ibid., pp. 447, 448.

chaos, incrementalism and fragmentation, precariousness and fragility, contradiction, competition and confrontation. It is also reflected in the enumeration of impressively long checklists that are a distinctive feature of his attempts to avoid glib generalisations. However, while he was insistent on the need to particularise, Wright showed, first in the case of France and then in his more explicitly comparative work, that a superficial knowledge might rigidly separate what a more profound awareness could reunite. Paradoxically, Wright ultimately minimised the peculiarity all too frequently attributed and self-attributed to French politics by showing that when one descends to the detailed cases of what actually happens, French practice is not so different from that of other countries as French principles would lead one to believe. As such, it is a salutary corrective to a culturalist emphasis on what is irreducibly special and reunites the study of politics after appearing to dismember it. Thus, the impulse towards systematic comparison existed implicitly in his single country work, becoming capable of incorporation as a case study because it was intrinsically comparable. As we shall see, it was only in his later work that Wright accepted that the systematic comparison of a limited number of West European countries meant starting, as Rose puts it, from 'the logic of a matrix'.

Wright preferred to initiate and edit most of his comparative work in collaboration. Given the need to mobilise a vast amount of information from a range of countries and his concern that only a specialist could be relied upon to have access to the detailed data and the understanding of how to evaluate it, there was a great temptation to recruit a team rather than undertake the work himself. However, it was also consistent with his inductive type of analysis, with the capacity to generalise coming at the end rather than at a beginning. To pull the various contributions together, not merely the conclusion but the introduction to the edited book or special issue of a journal had to await the findings of the others. Wright preferred to run the risk of a loss of overall coherence. To avoid the whole becoming less than the sum of the parts, Wright's own contribution would seek to compensate for the divergences between authors by incorporating as much as possible of their diversity into his comprehensive comparative analysis. The resulting complexity underlined the fact that the truth is seldom simple once it is subjected to close investigation.

Vincent Wright described the LSE Government Department (he was always keener on 'government' rather than politics as a focus) as his 'intellectual home'.[35] Rather than William Robson (who commissioned his *The*

---

[35] Vincent Wright in Daalder (ed.), p. 164.

Government and Politics of France) it was Michael Oakeshott who was acknowledged by Wright as the sceptical intellectual influence upon him, first as a student and later as a colleague. France was taught by William Pickles (he delivered the lectures and Dorothy wrote the textbooks) and it was he who aroused Vincent Wright's lifelong preoccupation with France and encouraged him to engage in postgraduate studies in France. It was by his personal example that Bill Pickles reinforced Wright's 'instinctive dislike for the pompous and pretentious . . . intellectual scepticism' and 'pugnacious and argumentative style'.[36] It was to Dorothy and William Pickles that he gratefully dedicated *The Government and Politics of France*.

Macro-politics from above: the view from Paris

Before publishing his general book on France in 1978, Wright—who in 1969 had returned to LSE—showed himself ready to generalise about the contemporary French politico-administrative system. With a self-assurance born of close contact with thoughtful state officials, as well as his solid grounding in administrative history, Wright successfully challenged in a highly influential article the view that senior civil servants occupied a hegemonic position in the French Fifth Republic. He forcefully made six points, of which three can be picked out. First, the Gaullist Republic had no consistent theory of administration because its proponents 'could not decide whether the basic aim of their measures was to make the administration more autonomous, more efficient, more subordinate or more democratic'.[37] Second, 'the French civil service is particularly prone to internal tensions and dissensions', between and within fragmented ministries.[38] Third, the politicisation of the senior civil service was not new and had been both exaggerated and oversimplified.

Wright used the insight into the workings of the French state provided by his historical perspective to show that 'the political and administrative traditions accumulate and survive in unhappy and precarious balance'.[39] Combining *Ancien Régime*, Napoleonic and post-Napoleonic, parlia-

---

[36] Howard Machin and Vincent Wright (eds.), *Economic Policy and Policy Making under the Mitterrand Presidency, 1981–84* (1985), p. ix.

[37] Vincent Wright, 'Politics and Administration in the Fifth French Republic', *Political Studies*, XXII/1 (1974), p. 50; cf. 51–2.

[38] Ibid., p. 52; cf. 53–5.

[39] Ibid., p. 63.

mentary and post-parliamentary sedimentations, 'it is a world composed of entrenched traditions, half-remembered rules and conveniently forgotten stipulations, of complicity and conflict, ideological clashes and masonic collusions, political chicanery and petty administrative corruption, personal rivalries and political alliances, unabashed self-interest and embarrassing idealism, compromising commitments and watchful opportunism, unforgivable cowardice and praiseworthy courage, naked ambition and calculated disinterest. It is a highly *personalized*, complex and confused world, rendered difficult to analyse and defiant of comparison by the unceasing interplay of irritating human imponderables.'[40] Wright ends by ridiculing the 'adepts of overarching theories of comparative administration, those unrepentant builders of models' whose ranks he was still refusing to join in 1974.[41]

The Government and Politics of France generalised this analysis by a Jacobin fearful of the fissiparous tendencies that were persistently turning the myth of a 'One and Indivisible Republic' into the reality of a dissensual and divided one. Wright's self-proclaimed 'Jacobinism' was exacerbated precisely by the fear that, despite its arrogant pretensions, the centre might not hold. Having demythologised the claims of the French state to omnipotence and omnicompetance, he proceeded to hand out lessons in modesty which prompted in his informed French audience an unsuspected masochism as this verbally sadistic foreigner held up for their contemplation a mirror in which they recognised familiar features which they refused to make explicit. 'Power is diffused' with the government resembling 'a huge Byzantine court riddled with feuding factions', interacting or mutually avoiding each other at the centre of 'a chaos of decision-makers', 'enmeshed in a concatenation of competing and contradictory forces . . . and if they are not always the helpless spectators of the fate of their country . . . their freedom of action is often singularly limited' by history and the outside world.[42]

While Wright was at this stage more inclined to Franco-French comparison, indeed suggesting—in words that mock the habitual examination question—that there was 'more to compare than to contrast'

---

[40] Vincent Wright, 'Politics and Administration in the Fifth French Republic', *Political Studies*, XXII/1 (1974), p. 65.

[41] Ibid., p. 65. By 1990, in a chapter on 'The Administrative Machine: Old Problems and New Dilemmas', Wright would structure his argument around 'The Napoleonic Model of Administration' and 'The Distortion of the Napoleonic Model', chap. 6, in Peter Hall, Jack Hayward, and Howard Machin (eds.), *Developments in French Politics* (Basingstoke, 1990).

[42] Vincent Wright, *The Government and Politics of France*, 1st edn. (1978), pp. 231–2.

between the Fourth and Fifth Republics' in their susceptibility to 'fitful and supine incrementalism',[43] he was prepared to extrapolate his comparison much further. His visceral scepticism led him to assert that in a world of perpetual flux (with much of it remaining in darkness, while most of the rest is impenetrably complex) the political analyst was hard put to locate where and by whom decisions were being taken.[44] One could be forgiven for despairing to the point of being deterred from engaging in so hazardous an investigation but Vincent Wright regarded the difficulties as a challenge to intellectual ingenuity rather than an alibi for defeatism.

At a time when it was customary to stress the omnipotence of the President of the Fifth Republic, Wright characteristically emphasised that 'he is enmeshed in a complex web of personal, historical, constitutional and political restrictions'.[45] Even before the 1986 advent of 'cohabitation' between an adversarial President and Prime Minister—a situation that Wright later called 'cohabitension'—he stressed that presidential power 'rests on precarious constitutional and political foundations . . . which may not last'.[46] Even when the Prime Minister and most ministers were selected by the President 'there has emerged around the President a system of institutionalised tension, not only between them[47] but also between his staff and theirs, between Prime Minister and the other ministers as well as among them and with their junior ministers'. Wright pointed out that while such tension damaged policy co-ordination and could result in vacillation or paralysis, it avoided the 'stultifying search for consensus' that he detected in pre-Thatcherite Britain.[48]

Wright catalogued the fragmentation, not only of the political and administrative executive but also the parties and parliament, rejecting the claims of the latter's Fourth Republic omnipotence and its Fifth Republic impotence. In the case of French pressure groups, he was not content with a simple dichotomy but presented four models . . . only to argue that 'all are inadequate and somewhat simplistic in their explanations'; saying of one of them that 'like most models, it raises more questions than it answers, and it is too neat and too selective in its choice of facts to con-

---

[43] Vincent Wright, *The Government and Politics of France*, 1st ed. (1978), p. 230, 232; cf. 106.
[44] Ibid., p. 231.
[45] Ibid., p. 227; cf. 228–9.
[46] Ibid., p. 57; cf. Vincent Wright, 'The President and the Prime Minister: Subordination, Conflict, Symbiosis and Reciprocal Parasitism?', in J. Hayward (ed.), *De Gaulle to Mitterrand. Presidential Power in France* (1993), chap. 4.
[47] *The Government and Politics of France*, p. 80; cf. 81–2.
[48] Ibid., p. 83.

vey the full complexity of the situation'.[49] Going on to describe 'the untidy reality' in all its complexity with delectation, Wright concluded: 'In short, the relationship between the state and the groups during the Fifth Republic is like the rest of government—infinitely complex and intrinsically untidy.'[50]

Wright was unduly dismissive of his 'textbook' (not all of which are born free and equal), which he only reluctantly updated,[51] preferring to concentrate upon first-hand research that did not force him to make generalisations and even implicit cross-national comparisons that still made him feel uncomfortable. Believing as he did that reality was always shifting, he did not relish the unending pursuit of a description and analysis that reduced a dynamic process to a misleadingly static picture. He preferred instead to reiterate that 'the biggest decision-maker in any political system is the past'[52] and was later to look with favour on the approach theorised as 'historical institutionalism' which he had been unconsciously practising for many years. However, further staging posts in his successive approximations to explicit reconciliation with comparison were necessary before a reluctant and minimalist theorist would be willing to accept some sacrifice of his intellectual scruples and enduring reservations.

Bilateral and circumscribed comparison

Vincent Wright explained his concurrent 1970s ventures into comparison in part by 'the constant stream of invitations to lecture in French universities on British politics, which forced me into constant, if largely implicit, Franco-British comparison. These invitations extended my contact to that tiny band of French academics who were beginning to be interested in explicit comparison.'[53] This led him to co-edit a book on *Local Government in Britain and France*, which did not attempt to conceal 'the revealing fact that different approaches to apparently similar subjects betray the differing preoccupations and priorities of France and Britain'.[54]

---

[49] *The Government and Politics of France*, pp. 174, 176.
[50] Ibid., p. 198; cf. 185–7.
[51] Vincent Wright in Daalder (ed.), p. 168.
[52] *The Government and Politics of France*, pp. 229–30.
[53] Vincent Wright in Daalder (ed.), p. 168.
[54] Jacques Lagroye and Vincent Wright, (eds.), *Local Government in Britain and France: Problems and Prospects* (1979).

More ambitiously, in February 1978 appeared the first issue of *West European Politics*, the brainchild of Vincent Wright and Gordon Smith, his LSE colleague in the Government Department. Mutual empathy led them first to create a Master's degree in West European Politics and then the journal. 'It reflected Vincent's approach to comparative politics via the best inductive route: an initial comprehensive grounding in the study of a single country, from bottom to top and then from top to bottom.'[55] Smith's German specialism and Wright's French specialism were extended and expanded pragmatically in latitudinarian fashion. In retrospect, Wright was fully entitled to confess: '*West European Politics* remains an object of some pride: its breadth, eclecticism and accessibility, its openness to young academics (and even to research students), convey, however unwittingly, a plea for pluralism and tolerance within the European comparative politics community.'[56]

The year 1984 saw the publication of an edited book (to which he contributed a third of the content): *Continuity and Change in France*, in which continuity of the Mitterrand presidency was emphasised institutionally, in its personnel and in its policies. 'The Socialists may claim that they are inaugurating a new régime but, in truth, they are merely strengthening the existing one.'[57] While his heart was not in electoral analysis, he demonstrated that he could undertake it with both the comprehensive clarity and mastery of detail that he showed with more enthusiasm in his studies of administration and public policy. He also attached great importance to the personality of political leaders as a contingent factor that discouraged attaching undue weight to the forces of anonymous determinism. His ability to sum up an important politician in a lapidary pen portrait is flamboyantly evident in the extended introduction to this volume. On the Right, Prime Minister Barre was described as 'a pragmatic liberal with a dogmatic style',[58] while Giscard's 'attenuated liberalism' masked 'the progressive transformation of President Giscard d'Estaing from an enlightened reformer into an apprehensive conservative'.[59] On the Left, Prime Minister Mauroy was 'conciliatory, jovial, extrovert, overtly political and avuncular',[60] while President Mitterrand

---

[55] Jack Hayward, 'Incomparable Comparatist. Vincent Wright, 1937–1999', *West European Politics*, 22/4 (1999), p. i.

[56] Vincent Wright in Daalder (ed.), p. 169.

[57] Vincent Wright (ed.), *Continuity and Change in France* (1984), p. 67; cf. 64–74.

[58] Ibid., p. 18; cf. 35–6.

[59] Ibid., p. 18; cf. 14–17.

[60] Ibid., p. 53.

was 'better as a manoeuvrer than as a manager'.[61] He concluded his 1984 review of the 1981 change of president: 'François Mitterrand inherited from his predecessor a long list of problems, broken promises and unsolved contradictions. The early evidence suggests that he may bequeath his successor with a similar record.'[62] Events were to show that Vincent Wright's scepticism was well directed.

A year later, *Economic Policy and Policy Making under the Mitterrand Presidency*, subjected a pivotal u-turn to searching criticism and heralded an increasing concern with political economy that would take a more comparative turn after nationalisation gave way to privatisation, following the Socialist new love affair with big firms. Owing to an 'overestimation of the potential of the public sector as an instrument of *dirigisme*' further nationalisation did not provide the leverage over industry anticipated, partly because government control was often ineffective and the firms were financially weak: frequently 'vast, fragile and incoherent holding companies'.[63] 'This post-1981 complex Hapsburgian industrial mosaic of some 4,300 firms, employing 2,400,000 people in France (or 22 per cent of the industrial workforce) and 24,000 abroad' exacerbated problems.[64] As a result, 'the processes of decision making accentuated the disjointed, reactive, confused, piecemeal, contradictory and often irrational nature of the decisions'.[65] Although none of this was new, the Left's ambitions made matters worse. 'In 1982, there were no fewer than 300 industrial policy mechanisms, 150 different procedures for aid to industry (including sixteen different categories of help for exports, eleven for boosting employment and eight for energy and saving)' so that piecemeal intervention frustrated the claims to planning.[66] Wright was to return to these problems in a comparative context when first privatisation and then core executive co-ordination were subjected to searching analysis.

The subject of 'The Politics of Privatisation in Western Europe' was chosen for a conference that led to the publication of a tenth anniversary special issue of *West European Politics*.[67] Edited by Vincent Wright with his Nuffield colleague, John Vickers, it was the political scientist rather

---

[61] Vincent Wright (ed.), *Continuity and Change in France* (1984), p. 42; cf. 43.
[62] Ibid, p.75.
[63] Howard Machin and Vincent Wright, pp. 17, 21; cf. 23.
[64] Ibid., p. 20.
[65] Ibid., p. 17.
[66] Ibid., p. 11; cf. 10–16.
[67] John Vickers and Vincent Wright (eds.), 'The Politics of Privatisation in Western Europe', *West European Politics*, 11/4 (1988).

than the economist who played the leading role. As Wright subsequently explained the choice:

> privatization is a gold mine for political scientists, for it raises profound philosophical and moral questions about property rights, about the concept of the state and of the nature of public goods, and about the balance between state, market and society. For public policy specialists, it provides valuable material for analysing well-known phenomena, ranging from policy diffusion and policy reversal to policy slippage and policy fiasco, as well as enabling the testing of rational choice theory, theories of regulation, interest group theory, and approaches based on policy networks and policy communities. My own interest in privatization is twofold. Firstly, as with public-sector reform generally, I am interested in the unintended and paradoxical nature of the reform programmes. Secondly, as a comparatist, I am interested in explaining the differences in the privatization programmes.[68]

The 1988 anniversary issue is concerned with the shift towards the policy preferences of profit-seeking entrepreneurs from the budget-maximising bureaucrats and vote-maximising politicians that had been the preoccupation of political scientists, and signposted a research focus that remained active until Vincent Wright's death.

Against the marketising mania that had taken hold in the 1990s, Wright suggested that 'we may be witnessing less the process of state retreat than of state reshaping'.[69] This became the subject of a special issue of *West European Politics*, co-edited with Wolfgang Müller. American political scientists belatedly decided from the mid-1980s to bring back the state they had unceremoniously expelled from the behavioural analysis of politics, while from the mid-1970s, European political scientists were empirically downgrading the role of the state, victim simultaneously of domestic overload and European integration. In their generalising introduction to 'The State in Western Europe: Retreat or Redefinition?' Müller and Wright identified five major interconnected pressures combining to reduce the role of states. They were ideological, political (including public opinion), international, European Union and technological. More specifically in a characteristic Wright enumeration,

> state retreat may be seen in the adoption of a wide range of policies: budgetary squeeze; privatization (a multi-dimensional phenomenon); deregulation (which ranges from the removal of controls to the reduction in administrative formalities); marketisation (the introduction of competitive market forces to some sectors to replace bureaucratic systems of allocation); devolution of state authority

---

[68] Vincent Wright in Daalder (ed.), p. 173.
[69] Vincent Wright (ed.), *Privatization in Western Europe* (1994), p. 40; cf. 1–43.

to non-elected state officials at the territorial level, in public sector industries or in semi-autonomous administrative agencies, or to private agents charged with the implementation of public policy; territorial decentralisation to sub-national 'governments'.[70]

In his personal contribution on 'Reshaping the State: the implications for public administration', Wright insisted that 'each West European country has a unique blend of factors which explains persistent divergences in spite of clear evidence of convergence. In short, national contexts matter'.[71] Specificities could not simply be submerged under generalities.

Vincent Wright returned to this theme in his 1997 introduction to the special issue of *Modern and Contemporary France*. Asking whether we were witnessing the end of *dirigisme*, he 'emphasised that, *in comparative terms* [his emphasis], extensive *dirigisme* was a distinctive feature of the French system'.[72] However, he pointed out that '*dirigisme* was probably always more powerful as a rhetorical mobilising device and as a pervasive myth—hence the persistent nostalgia for a politically constructed golden age—than as a strategy or coherent set of matching policies. In truth, the French model masked a messy reality in which public and private intertwined in which private interests were often more powerful than public actors, in which the latter were fragmented and divided, in which macro and micro-economic objectives were frequently in conflict, and in which "industrial policy" was inconsistent and sometimes incoherent, reactive and defensive rather than proactive and strategic. . . .'[73] However, 'the state has retained its role as travelling *salesman* (and is especially active in France's important arms trade), as *advocate* (in trade negotiations and in the EU generally), as *regulator*, and as *cushion* for its companies (through tax relief, subsidies, grants, research contracts, export aid, and public procurement and various ill-concealed protectionist devices) . . . In short, *dirigisme* has been transformed, but this had entailed neither the end of the state nor of French exceptionalism.'[74] What Wright described as his 'instinctive and intellectual Jacobinism (which survived the years of mindless centralisation in my own country)',[75] achieved a more landless, theoretical and comparative formulation in the 'new institutionalism',

---

[70] Wolfgang Müller and Vincent Wright (eds.), 'The State in Western Europe: Retreat or Redefinition?', *West European Politics*, 17/3 (1994), p. 8.
[71] 'The State in Western Europe', p. 122.
[72] Vincent Wright 'La fin du dirigisme', *Modern and Contemporary France*, V/2 (May 1997), p. 151.
[73] Ibid., p. 151.
[74] Ibid., pp. 152–3.
[75] Vincent Wright in Daalder (ed.), p. 194.

particularly in its historical institutionalist variant, which became the final resting place for this tireless champion of the resurgent state.

The Historical Institutionalist Reconciliation:
the empirical analysis of
inertial reality

In his last, posthumously published contribution to *West European Politics* (a special issue on 'The Changing French Political System', a project that he supported from its inception) Vincent Wright expressed his pleasure that 'Political scientists have once again become more interested in institutions, and even at last, in the law. It is now generally accepted that individual and group preferences are embedded in and shaped by institutions, an historically-forged amalgam of bodies, rules, procedures, norms, customs, rites, which generates its own conventions, path dependencies and notions of appropriateness.'[76] While common to all West European countries, this was especially true of France, as he had shown in his work on bureaucratic reform. However, when it came to explaining cross-national differences in privatisation programmes, 'Historical institutionalism is without doubt a good explanatory starting point, but my research suggests two caveats. The first is that in an area such as privatization institutionalism needs to be extended beyond the already broad category of political and governmental institutions, conventions, rules, customs, prejudices, instincts and culture, in order to embrace economic and financial institutions ... The second caveat relates to the growing impact of the cumulative and intense pressures of an economic, ideological, political, financial and technological nature—some international or European Union in character, others purely domestic—that are sweeping aside some of the impediments rooted in historically-embedded institutionalism.'[77] The 'indispensable bedmates' of history and political science[78] were proving to be turbulently inclined to tumble each other out of bed.

Vincent Wright was persuaded, partly as a result of his increasing encounters with American political science in its non-rational choice manifestations, to countenance the use of theoretical frameworks, but

[76] Vincent Wright, 'The Fifth Republic: From the *Droit de l'Etat* to the *Etat de Droit*', in R. Elgie (ed.), *The Changing French Political System* (2000), p. 92.
[77] Vincent Wright in Daalder (ed.), p. 174.
[78] Ibid., p. 172.

being allergic to abstraction, he did so in a highly circumspect manner. He acknowledged in particular the influence of Peter Hall, James March, Johan Olsen, and Guy Peters in the final approximation to a theorised cross-national comparison. It was the ultimate stage in an ongoing dialectic between the 'intellectual indolence' of confinement to historical singularity and the intellectual exertions of generic conceptual frameworks providing guidelines to bounded variability.[79] Thus, of one of several unfinished ambitious pieces of research, 'Governing from the Centre: Core Executive Policy Co-ordination', a six country comparative project that adopted the comparative 'logic of the matrix' referred to earlier, Wright could not refrain from declaring: 'As with all comparative work, an apparently straightforward project, based on a relatively simple matrix, quickly ran into a methodological and definitional quagmire . . .'[80] from which it has, fortunately been possible to re-emerge, if not unscathed.

Vincent Wright was a towering figure in the study of comparative politics, where one's personal contribution is more especially a function of a capacity to collaborate and learn with others. He had an exceptional ability to bring out the best in others by provocative intellectual interaction. His unselfish singularity was to find its full embodiment in the multiplier of collective effort. Bridging as he did the humanities and the social sciences, he found a natural home in the British Academy, to which he was elected in 1995, serving in its Overseas Policy Committee.

An insatiable intellectual curiosity in exploring differences comparatively provided the motivating impetus to Vincent Wright's many sided activities as a committed political scientist. To the end, Vincent Wright remained willing to pay the price in complexity of exerting a grip on political reality. In the tireless task of tidying up reality, he was finally prepared to work with matrices and models, at least as points of departure. His typologies clarified without simplifying because tidiness came second to authenticity. The dialectical clash of interpretative thesis and antithesis of strategic interaction in shaping political outcomes was more important than building an ephemeral synthesis.

JACK HAYWARD
Fellow of the Academy
SUDHIR HAZAREESINGH
Balliol College, Oxford

[79] Vincent Wright in Daalder (ed.), pp. 173, 176.
[80] Ibid., p. 175. See Jack Hayward and Vincent Wright, *Governing from the Centre. Core Executive Coordination in France* (Oxford, 2002).

PROCEEDINGS OF THE BRITISH ACADEMY

Since 1905 this series has provided a unique record of British scholarship in the humanities and social sciences, by publishing the highly regarded Academy lectures, and through its memoirs of the lives and scholarly achievements of recently deceased Fellows of the Academy.

The series includes thematic volumes that stem from symposia specially convened to address particular subjects.

Volumes published in 2001 and 2002

106. *The Speciation of Modern* Homo sapiens, ed. T. J. Crow (2002) 0-19-726246-5

107. *Two Capitals: London and Dublin 1500–1840*, ed. P. Clark & R. Gillespie (2001) 0-19-726247-3

108. *Provincial Towns in Early Modern England and Ireland: Change, Convergence and Divergence*, ed. P. Borsay & L. Proudfoot (2002) 0-19-726248-1

109. *Henry Sidgwick*, ed. R. Harrison (2001) 0-19-726249-X

110. *The Origin of Human Social Institutions*, ed. W. G. Runciman (2001) 0-19-726250-3

111. *2000 Lectures and Memoirs* (2001) 0-19-726259-7

112. *The Evolution of Cultural Entities*, ed. M. Wheeler, J. Ziman & M. A. Boden (2002) 0-19-726262-7

113. *Bayes's Theorem*, ed. R. Swinburne (2002) 0-19-726267-8

114. *Representations of Empire: Rome and the Mediterranean World*, ed. A. K. Bowman, H. M. Cotton, M. Goodman & S. Price (2002) 0-19-726276-7

115. *Biographical Memoirs of Fellows, I* (2002) 0-19-726278-3

116. *Indo-Iranian Languages and Peoples*, ed. N. Sims-Williams (2002) 0-19-726285-6

117. *2001 Lectures* (2002) 0-19-726279-1